EUROPE AFTER THE VERSAILLES TREATY

Ceded by Germany

Demilitarized zone (Rhineland)

Ruhr Basin

Germans

———————— Boundaries of new, independent nations

------------- Brest-Litovsk Treaty line, 1918

NORWAY

Oslo

NORTH
SEA

DENMARK

IRELAND

ENGLAND

London

Amsterdam

NETH.

Berlin

Elbe R.

Oder

GERMANY

RUHR

ATLANTIC

OCEAN

CHANNEL
ISLANDS

Brussels
BELG.

LUX.

Paris

SAAR

THURINGIA

SUDETENLAND

Prague

Vie

Loire R.

Danube R.

FRANCE

Berne

Vichy

SWITZ.

Rhône R.

Locarno

Innsbruck

SO. TYROL

Branau
am Inn

AUSTRIA

Bad

PORTUGAL

Trieste

Po R.

Fiume

Lisbon

Tagus R.

Madrid

ITALY

Ebro R.

SPAIN

CORSICA

Rome

SARDINIA

Tangier

Strait of Gibraltar

Casablanca

SPAN. MOROCCO

Algiers

MEDITERRANEAN

Palermo

SICILY

MOROCCO

ALGERIA

Tunis

TUNISIA

LIBY

0   500 miles

HITLER'S WAR AIMS

IDEOLOGY, THE NAZI STATE,
AND THE COURSE OF EXPANSION

By the same author

Hitler's War Aims (Vol. II): The
Establishment of the New Order

The Age of Nationalism and Reform, 1850–1890
Friedrich Von Holstein: Politics and Diplomacy
in the Era of Bismarck and Wilhelm II
The Holstein Papers (edited with M. H. Fisher)

HITLER'S WAR AIMS

IDEOLOGY, THE NAZI STATE, AND THE COURSE OF EXPANSION

by Norman Rich

I

W · W · NORTON & COMPANY · INC ·

NEW YORK

Copyright © 1973 by W. W. Norton & Company, Inc.

Library of Congress Cataloging in Publication Data
Rich, Norman.
  Hitler's war aims.
  CONTENTS: v. 1.   Ideology, the Nazi State, and the
course of expansion.
  Includes bibliographical references.
  1. Hitler, Adolf, 1889–1945. 2. Germany—Foreign
relations—1933–1945. 3. World War, 1939–1945—
Occupied territories. 4. National socialism.
5. World War, 1939–1945—Germany. I. Title.
DD256.5.R473   943.086′092′4   78–116108
ISBN 0–393–05454–3

PRINTED IN THE UNITED STATES OF AMERICA

2 3 4 5 6 7 8 9 0

For Ning

"Der Mensch kann sich aber auf eine doppelte Weise entgegengesetzt sein: entweder als Wilder, wenn seine Gefühle über seine Grundsätze herrschen; oder als Barbar, wenn seine Grundsätze seine Gefühle zerstören" (A human being may deny his humanity in a twofold manner: either as a savage, when his feelings rule over his principles; or as a barbarian, when his principles destroy his feelings.) Schiller, *Ueber die ästhetische Erziehung des Menschen. Vierter Brief.*

Contents

CONTENTS

List of Photographs

List of Maps

Preface

On the walls of the Roman Forum Mussolini hung a series of maps contrasting the growth of the ancient Roman Empire with Italy's contemporary position. No comparable maps hung in Berlin. Hitler, far from basing an expansionist program on the example of any ancient German empire, scornfully repudiated the heritage of Germany's most successful imperial dynasties, the Hohenstaufen and the Habsburg, and with it the perennial German drive to the south and west. Not that Nazi Germany was without its maps. Ethnic maps, linguistic maps, geopolitical maps, maps embodying every variety of claim and speculation decorated Nazi party offices, government buildings and schoolrooms. But most of these maps had the quality of an academic exercise, and their very profusion diluted their effect and gave them an air of unreality. In *Mein Kampf*, to be sure, Hitler had set forth a very clear and very specific program for expansion into Eastern Europe at the expense of Russia; but few of Hitler's contemporaries, especially foreigners, had bothered to read this ponderous volume carefully, if at all, and fewer still could believe that the extreme views set down by Hitler, the frustrated political adventurer, would continue to be taken seriously by Hitler, the responsible statesman.[1]

Hitler himself, especially during his first years in power, vigorously disavowed all expansionist ambitions, and many of his contemporaries, at home and abroad, believed him. Even those who did not, however, were confused by the contradictions and inconsistencies in Nazi policies and statements. In *Mein Kampf* Hitler had called for German expansion at the expense of Russia, yet one of the first moves of Nazi foreign policy had been the conclusion of a nonaggression pact with Poland, the very state that lay across Germany's path to Russia. He had denounced a colonial policy, yet the Nazis embodied a demand for colonies in their party platform. He called for the union of all Germanic peoples and the eventual destruction of non-Aryan races, yet he concluded alliances with the Italians and the Japanese.

xi

How were such conflicting programs and policies to be interpreted? Contemporary observers, Germans and foreigners alike, were badly confused. There were those who dismissed the entire racial business as a farce, convinced that Hitler was nothing more than a political opportunist for whom pan-Germanism and anti-Semitism were merely exploitable slogans. Others feared that Nazi racial theories posed a threat to Germanic countries such as Switzerland and the Netherlands. Still others believed that Hitler was doing no more than giving voice to legitimate German grievances, and that once these were met the Nazi dictatorship would become a bastion of stability in a thoroughly unstable Europe and the continent's most reliable bulwark against Bolshevism.

To conceal or obscure whatever his real intentions may have been, Hitler dedicated no small part of his diplomatic and propagandistic skill. In his public speeches and diplomatic conversations he monotonously intoned his desire for peace, he signed friendship treaties and nonaggression pacts, he was lavish with assurances of good will. In his conduct of both domestic and foreign affairs he tried to give his actions the appearance of legality, of seeming to conform to standards of German or international law; or, if this were impossible, to explain them on the basis of generally accepted principles that would at least give them the appearance of legitimacy. Upon coming to office he announced that he wanted no more than justice for Germany, a principle that soon developed into a demand for equality in the community of nations and the re-establishment of full German sovereignty. When this goal was achieved with German rearmament and the remilitarization of the Rhineland, he based a new set of demands on the right of all Germans to self-determination. In each case he appealed to principles the Western world had come to accept as almost sacred.[2]

Not until the German armies marched into a Czechoslovakia deprived of its strategic frontiers and military fortresses by the Munich agreement did Hitler make it perfectly clear that his policy was not based on the principles of national sovereignty and self-determination. Shortly afterward he seemed to make it equally clear that his policy was not based on any principles whatever. For in August 1939 the self-proclaimed defender of European civilization against Bolshevism concluded a nonaggression pact with the Bolshevik government and proceeded to surrender half of Poland and other large areas of Eastern Europe to Soviet dominion. The champion of the Nordic race then turned his armies against Denmark and Norway, the Netherlands and Britain. He conquered Western Europe and the Balkans. He launched a campaign in North Africa. And when he finally did attack Russia, it was again in defiance of all principles he had laid down regarding the disastrous nature of a two-front war. On the basis of this record it is easy to conclude that Hitler, far from being guided by ideological considerations or having any definite expansionist goals, was simply a political adventurer who took advantage of the opportunities that fate and the follies of his opponents had thrust upon him.

But there was another side to the Hitler record. The systematic extermination of the Jews, the ruthless implementation of racial policies in Germany and the German-occupied territories, the massive population transfers to alter the racial configuration of Europe—programs such as these, carried out with almost total disregard for political, military, or economic consequences, cannot be dismissed as the policies of a political opportunist. They can only be explained as the policies of a fanatic ideologue, an explanation all the more cogent because in the years before coming to power Hitler had described the essential features of these policies with absolute frankness in *Mein Kampf,* a book he had written, as he stated in his preface, to explain the objectives of his movement to his followers and to set down the basic elements of his doctrine in permanent form. And in fact *Mein Kampf,* with all its turgid redundancies, contains a clear and frighteningly logical exposition of Hitler's political and racial principles, the goals he intended to pursue in both domestic and foreign affairs, and the means he proposed to employ in the realization of those goals. Far more important, Hitler remained true to those principles, which constituted fundamental guidelines for his political conduct from the time he emerged from his prison in Landsberg am Lech in 1924 to his death in the rubble of Berlin.[3]

Naturally there were deviations, major ones, from Hitler's ideological program. Besides being a fanatic ideologue, Hitler was a pathological egotist whose lust for power and dominion expanded with the prospects that opened before him, often in defiance of all rules he himself had laid down for the conduct of policy. His lack of restraint and, indeed, of all sense of proportion are reflected in his plans for architectural monuments which were to commemorate his rule— mammoth structures designed to impress and overawe, devoid of all respect for humanity, of all consideration for human needs and human capacities; concrete expressions, in the most literal sense, of the Führer's megalomania.[4]

There were, however, other and even more compelling reasons for Hitler's ideological deviationism. Like all rulers, even the most absolute and authoritarian, Hitler was dependent on the physical and human resources at his disposal for the execution of his policies, a dependence which inevitably restricted his freedom of action.[5] More restrictive still was the fact that he was constantly obliged to take into account the forces ranged against him, and to respond to the moves, or suspected moves, of his opponents. There was the further problem that Hitler himself was frequently uncertain about the tactics he should pursue; so great were his hesitations and vacillations at many critical moments in his career that his closest associates had doubts about his firmness of purpose. Far from being in control of events or pursuing a systematic plan of diplomatic and military conquest, as he liked his followers to believe, he was constantly obliged to adapt his policies to unexpected contingencies. He appears to have had his hand forced by events in Austria in 1938, to have been taken by surprise by the outcome of the Munich crisis and by Britain's declaration of war in 1939. Throughout the war itself the majority of his actions were largely determined by military considerations. His ideology did not call for the invasion of Scandinavia or the Balkans, for the campaign in North Africa, or for war with the United States. Nor, to push the point to its logical extreme, did it call for Germany's ultimate defeat. So frequently, and finally so completely, was Hitler diverted from his ideological course that the question may again be raised whether ideology was not, after all, a negligible factor, and whether it made the slightest difference if Hitler's primary territorial objective was Russia or Rangoon.

As a problem of logic this difference may indeed seem inconsequential, but it was certainly not inconsequential to the millions of Slavs and Jews exterminated as a direct result of Hitler's racial theories; nor was it inconsequential to the millions of Germans who were driven far beyond their capacities and to ultimate disaster on the strength of Hitler's belief in their racial superiority. Any work dealing with Hitler's war aims must, therefore, come to grips with the ideological factor and constantly take into account the impact of his ideology on his policies.

There remain, however, the problems raised by Hitler's opportunism and the exigencies of expediency. As a result of political and military necessities, real or imagined, he conquered territories which played little or no part in his ideological program, or which he had specifically rejected as suitable areas for Germanic expansion. Hitler's ideology provides almost no clue to his ultimate intentions in the Balkans; he was uncertain about the racial status and hence about the political future of the French and the Walloons; he did not even have any specific program for dealing with conquered Nordic peoples such as the Danes and the Dutch. Further, as it became clear that the majority of conquered peoples, Nordic and non-Nordic alike, were far from enthusiastic about Hitler's New Order and were engaging in wide varieties of passive and active resistance, Hitler resorted to exceptional measures to hold the conquered peoples in line and keep up their economic contributions to the German war effort.

PREFACE

Because opportunism and expediency played so great a role not only in determining Hitler's political and military actions but in the policies he pursued in the occupied territories, these factors necessarily exercised a powerful influence on his conception of his war aims. It follows that these aims cannot be regarded as fixed or immutable, but that they must be studied as something in the process of constant change and development. To arrive at a realistic and comprehensive understanding of Hitler's aims, it is therefore necessary to look beyond the plans he formulated in his political writings or in the memoranda he prepared as guidelines for political or military action. In other words, while it is essential to pay due regard to what Hitler *said* he was going to do, it is even more important to examine what Hitler actually *did* do, or what he ordered done in his name.

To describe the interaction of Hitler's words and deeds and record the development of his war aims on the basis of the policies he actually pursued in Germany and the German-occupied countries is the purpose of this book. An introduction, which attempts to place Hitler and Nazi Germany in historical and moral perspective, is followed by a brief description of Hitler's racial ideology and of the expansionist program based on his ideological conceptions. The succeeding chapters are devoted to an analysis of the political system Hitler imposed on Germany, of the men and institutions that carried out his orders and put his policies into practice—an analysis, in short, of the machinery of expansion, which was at the same time the prototype of the New Order. The focus then shifts to the actual course of Nazi expansion: to Hitler's diplomatic and military conquests, the timing of his expansionist moves, and his motives for occupying or attacking various states which had not originally figured in his expansionist plans.

A second volume will be devoted to an examination of the policies Hitler actually pursued in dealing with all the peoples and territories which came under his dominion, his treatment of Jews and Slavs, of Nordics and Latins, as well as his plans for the future of these peoples and the lands they inhabited.

The subject of war aims, even more than most historical topics, admits an almost unlimited extension of coverage and variety of interpretation. It may therefore be in order to explain at the outset that several problems which might be considered important or even crucial to an understanding of Hitler's purposes have not been treated as fully as they perhaps deserve. There is, for example, no detailed examination of Hitler's military strategy or description of his military campaigns. Very little is said about Hitler's opponents, or about resistance movements either in Germany or the German-occupied territories. There is almost no discussion of the historiography and the differing interpretations of the Nazi era and the Second World War. And, perhaps the most serious omission of all, there is no substantial analysis of the socioeconomic framework of Nazi Germany and the countries under German occupation. To have covered these topics adequately would have meant writing a different book, or adding immeasurably to the length of this one. They have therefore been touched upon only when they seemed to have a direct bearing on the main themes selected for investigation.

In preparing the present work, I have endeavored to base my account on contemporary documents, while bearing in mind the purposes for which such documents may have been prepared and collected, in the belief that contemporary directives and memoranda are more accurate reflections of intentions and policies than explanations prepared after the event. Consequently I have made sparing use of trial testimonies, affidavits, memoirs, and interviews, especially when such sources contained information for which there was no corroborating contemporary evidence. In quoting from English translations of books or documents, which are generally more accessible to English-speaking readers, I have occasionally deviated from the translation to bring it closer to my interpretation of the original. All emphases in quoted passages are in the original unless otherwise indicated.

For the opportunity to do research in European archives, I am indebted to the Warden and Fellows of Saint Antony's College, Oxford, and to that most splendid institution, the John Simon Guggenheim Memorial Foundation, for fellowships which made it possible for me and my family to enjoy two delightful years in Europe, by no means all of which were spent in communion with the Nazis. Grants from Michigan State and Brown universities, and from the American Philosophical Society, enabled me to check sources in America and have paid for much microfilm and typing.

My good friend and former editor in chief of the captured German Foreign Office documents, Dr. Paul Sweet, has given me the benefit of his comments and criticism based on his rare combination of erudition and judgment. My thanks, too, to Professor Hans-Adolf Jacobsen, for sending me a number of documents; to Professors Thomas J. Knight, Edgar E. Knoebel, and Johannes Postma, who allowed me to use their unpublished manuscripts on the German occupation of Belgium and the Netherlands; to Mrs. Anne Thomas Stevens and Mrs. Mary M. Shuford for valuable editorial assistance; to Mr. James Mairs for his help with pictures and maps; and to Mr. Donald Lamm of W. W. Norton and Co., the ideal editor and publisher.

A special debt of gratitude is owed to Dr. Hans-Günther Seraphim of the Staatliches Archivlager, Göttingen, who placed at my disposal the valuable indexes of the postwar trials and other documents of the Nazi era compiled by himself and his wife, the late Frau Elsa Seraphim, together with microfilms and transcripts of the documents themselves.

Above all I am indebted to my wife for critical advice and professional assistance. To her this book is dedicated as a small token of gratitude for contributions that go far beyond the realm of scholarship.

Introduction:
The Historical Background

Among the many problems involved in the study of war aims, some of the most complex and controversial are immediately posed by the title of this book, with its implication that Germany's aims in the Second World War were essentially the aims of Hitler. Yet how much, in fact, can German policies during the Nazi era be attributed to Hitler, and how much were they an expression of the will of the German people, or at least of dominant elements in German society? To what extent was the Nazi era not a nightmarish interlude in German history, as some writers have attempted to demonstrate, but the logical or even the inevitable product of German historical development, of German intellectual and social traditions, of profound and indelible forces in the German national character?

No final and perhaps not even a generally satisfactory answer can be given to these questions. To ascribe to the Germans, or to a Germanic race, a uniquely large portion of original sin is to succumb to Hitler's own concepts of race and racism. Yet the fact is undeniable that a group of people living together in a particular geographic area, speaking the same language, sharing similar experiences and traditions, do develop certain habits of thought and conduct which differentiate them from other groups of people. This was certainly true of the Germans, although German history is so lacking in continuity and German traditions are so fragmented that Germans frequently differ from each other as much as from members of other European national groups.

The most obvious feature which lends a distinctive quality to the German experience is the geography of the territory inhabited by the German-speaking peoples. Without natural barriers of any kind to

INTRODUCTION

separate them from other nationalities or to delimit their territories, they have invaded neighboring lands and, in turn, have been the victims of invasion ever since Germanic tribes first settled in Central Europe.

There were notable periods of Germanic expansion during the Middle Ages. Such expansion, however, did not have the character of a "national" movement. German secular rulers for the most part attempted to extend their dominion to the south and west, into Italy or France, countries which were generally more prosperous and enjoyed better climates than the Germanic lands. The most tenacious and successful protagonists of the Germans' famous *Drang nach Osten* were not German secular rulers but the monastic and chivalric orders of the Church, which carried on a policy of expansion toward the east not in the cause of Germanization but to convert the heathen peoples of Eastern Europe to Christianity, or at any rate the Roman Catholic form of it. In the later Middle Ages, German merchants and traders also played a prominent part in the *Drang nach Osten,* again not for national reasons but for the sake of economic gain.

The fact is that, until the nineteenth century, Germans by and large did not think in terms of national loyalties or a national mission. This was one reason why even the most powerful German rulers failed to unite the German-speaking peoples or bring them under any kind of effective control. Until the formation of the German Empire in 1871 there was no such thing as a German national state; Germany was not even, like Italy, a geographic expression.

There is a saying attributed to Voltaire that the ancient Holy Roman Empire was neither holy nor Roman nor an empire; but, although German states formed the core of the empire and by the fourteenth century, with the loss of some of its most important non-German possessions, it came to be called the Holy Roman Empire of the German Nation, neither was it German. Its emperors sought to rule over Germans and non-Germans alike; their ideal was universality, in the medieval sense, not nationalality. The individual German states, on the other hand, whether secular or ecclesiastic, jealously guarded their regional rights and privileges with no concern for the interests of "Germany."

The Protestant Revolution, which in the beginning appeared to be something of a German national movement, won over scarcely more than half of the German population and served to make religion yet another (and major) force contributing to the divisions among Germans, divisions which multiplied further with the breakup of the Protestant movement into rival sects. The efforts of the Habsburg emperors to impose political as well as religious unity on the empire during the Thirty Years' War were frustrated as much by the forces of German particularism as by the intervention of foreign powers.

THE HISTORICAL BACKGROUND

The Peace of Westphalia of 1648 which ended the Thirty Years' War recognized the sovereignty and independence of some three hundred German states, most of them too weak to maintain themselves unaided but too jealous of their sovereign rights (and too unconcerned about "national" interests) to rally to the old empire or enter into some other kind of effective German union. The individual German princes sought to defend or extend their dynastic territories, as they had done for centuries, while the weaker states were constantly exposed to the depridations of neighboring powers, German as well as non-German.

After 1648 the Austrian Habsburgs, who by this time had virtually become hereditary Holy Roman emperors and who had territorial holdings in every part of Europe, managed to maintain the position of the empire as a great power (though at times only barely); only one other German dynasty managed to attain great power status. This was the Hohenzollern house of Brandenburg-Prussia, which produced a number of talented rulers in the seventeenth and eighteenth centuries. By fostering the development of a loyal government bureaucracy and devoting a major share of the revenues of their state to the maintenance of a strong army, the Hohenzollerns succeeded in crushing particularist forces, consolidating their authority over their scattered holdings, and extending their territories at the expense of their neighbors, including the Austrian Habsburgs.

The role of able leadership and of military power in the development of Brandenburg-Prussia, a development seemingly crowned by Prussia's unification of Germany in 1871, helps explain the emphasis many Germans have placed on the desirability of a strong executive authority and a strong army. The bitter experience of the smaller German states during and after the Thirty Years' War, and of Austria and Prussia as well in the time of Napoleon, seemed to demonstrate that the only effective protection of a continental people without natural frontiers was membership in a militarily powerful state.

With the general growth of national self-consciousness in Europe in the nineteenth century, German nationalists, dismayed by the victimization of German territories during the centuries of German weakness, began to clamor for the creation of a unified German national state on the French model which would have the power to mobilize German resources effectively and put an end to the encroachments of foreign powers.

Throughout the first half of the nineteenth century the chances for German unification seemed dim. Napoleon, to be sure, had abolished the ancient Holy Roman Empire with its universalist traditions and had consolidated the majority of petty German states into larger political units for the sake of administrative efficiency. After Napoleon's defeat much of his reorganization of Germany was allowed to stand, with the result that by 1815 the three-hundred-odd German states had been reduced to thirty. These were linked together in a newly created Germanic Confederation under the chairmanship of Austria; but, although this confederation encompassed almost all German-speaking territories, it was anything but an effective German national union. On the contrary, it seemed to regularize and perpetuate German particularism; for within the confederation there existed a de facto balance of power between the two strongest German states, Austria and Prussia, while the smaller states, jealous as ever of their sovereign rights and in a better position to defend them, acted as a balance between Austria and Prussia, swinging their weight from one to the other to prevent either from gaining the ascendancy. Meanwhile outside the confederation the two strongest continental states, France and Russia, held the ring of the German balance of power, for it lay in the interests of both to prevent the formation of an effective German union which would inevitably pose a threat to their security.

The stalemate in Germany was broken by Prussia under the leadership of Bismarck. In three short wars the military forces of the smaller German states were crushed; the multinational Austrian Empire was excluded from German affairs; and France, the most serious foreign obstacle to German unification, was defeated. Prussia's success was due in large measure to Bismarck's painstaking and skillful diplomacy, above all to his ability to localize all three conflicts and prevent the intervention of Russia. But no German, and no foreigner either for that matter, could ignore the fact that Bismarck's diplomacy had been based on strength, and that final success had come as a result of victories on the battlefield. Foreign powers hastened to emulate Prussia's system of compulsory military service and other features of the Prussian military organization. Among Germans, on the other hand, the success of Prussia seemed to confirm the argument for a strong army and aroused admiration for Bismarck's policy of iron and blood.

It was a misfortune for Germany and the world that Bismarck's iron and blood policy proved to be his most memorable legacy. For, with the apparent triumph of that policy, many of his compatriots overlooked or failed to understand altogether the far more fundamental qualities of his statecraft, above all his recognition that politics is the art of the possible in which it is essential to bear in mind the limitation of one's own strength and the strength of one's opponents. No one was more aware than Bismarck that a policy of iron and blood, in other words war, was a dangerous gamble which should be adopted only as a last resort, and then only after the most careful preparations had been made to secure all possible political, military —and moral—advantages. This was the essence of Bismarck's famous *Realpolitik*, an essence few of his successors seemed to comprehend.

The prayers of German nationalists appeared to be answered with the creation of the German Empire in 1871; but with the unification of Germany under Prussia the German problem took on a new and critical aspect. Germany, so often the victim of foreign invasion in recent centuries, now emerged on the European political scene as the strongest single military power on the continent, fully capable of doing some invading of its own. France, the first victim of the new Germany, was invaded during the war of 1870–71, and at the close of that war lost the provinces of Alsace and Lorraine.

Once the German Empire had been formed, however, Bismarck appears to have been primarily concerned with consolidating the new state and reassuring its neighbors about Germany's peaceful intentions. The chancellor was justifiably apprehensive about the centuries-old forces of German particularism; but above all he feared the formation of a coalition of foreign powers whose interests had been violated and whose very existence seemed threatened by the new German union.

Although Bismarck's methods of dealing with the problem of national security often seemed complicated, they were based on simple principles. His first concern was to make Germany itself strong. Hence the constitution he drew up for the new empire provided for a strong executive, and his government adhered to the Prussian tradition of maintaining a strong army. Bismarck was also aware that Germany alone could never be strong enough to defend itself against a coalition of powers. To prevent the formation of such a coalition and to strengthen Germany's own position, he sought to build up a network of alliances on the principle that in a Europe dominated by five great powers, Germany should seek to be one of three.

So far as Germany's territorial position was concerned, Bismarck regarded the new empire as a satiated state which could not benefit from further territorial expansion in proportion to the risks involved. Paradoxically, although he opposed a colonial policy, he acquired a modest colonial empire for Germany in the 1880s; but in doing so he appears to have been motivated primarily by broader considerations of foreign and domestic policy. Certainly he had no illusion that overseas colonies could contribute in any significant way to Germany's national security so long as Britain ruled the waves and Germany had to contend with the rival powers of Russia and France on the continent. In response to the arguments of a German colonial enthusiast who pointed out further desirable territorial acquisitions on the map of Africa, Bismarck is supposed to have said, "Your map of Africa is very handsome, but my map of Africa lies in Europe. Here lies Russia and here lies France, and we are in between: that is my map of Africa."

Throughout the period of Bismarck's chancellorship, but especially during his last years in office, there were many Germans who questioned his conception of Germany as a satiated state. In a world increasingly obsessed with doctrines of imperialism and the belief that the status of a great power was in direct proportion to the amount of territory it controlled, these Germans could not help but compare Germany's position with that of Britain and France, with their immense colonial empires, or of Russia and the United States, whose territories straddled entire continents. For the time being, these Germans reasoned, Germany might maintain its great power status on the strength of its army, backed up by German science and industry. But over the years Germany could never hope to keep up with powers able to draw on the populations and productive capacities of great territorial empires; in time Germany would inevitably sink back into the ranks of the second- or even third-rate powers from which the states of Germany had so recently emerged with their unification. Thoughtful observers might well ask why Germans should find great-power status so necessary or desirable, and point to Sweden or Switzerland as examples of minor powers which were doing very well for themselves. German advocates of power, however, could draw on the less happy example of Poland, whose weakness had led to its complete obliteration as a state, and to Germany's own experience during and after the Thirty Years' War, when so many German states had fallen victim to predatory neighbors. They could argue further that even Sweden and Switzerland had so far maintained their sovereignty and independence only because they had been lucky enough to occupy a favorable position within the European balance of power. Should that balance ever be overthrown, these states would have no more control over their fate than Poland—or the peoples of Asia and Africa.

After his fall in 1890, Bismarck's conception of Germany as a satiated state was not immediately abandoned by his successors. Caprivi, the new chancellor, and Holstein, his principal adviser on foreign affairs, were not expansionists. They did, however, object to Bismarck's alliance system, in particular to his alliance with Russia, which they regarded as incompatible with Germany's alliance with Austria. What they proposed instead was an alliance of states dedicated to the preservation of European stability, which in their view was threatened primarily by France and Russia. To take the place of the Russian alliance they wanted an alliance with Britain, and at the beginning of Caprivi's chancellorship they made substantial colonial concessions to Britain as evidence of their desire for a closer political partnership. They reasoned that with the British navy controlling the sea lanes of the world, Germany and Austria could keep France and Russia in check and thus maintain international stability on the continent—which meant that, for all intents and purposes, the continent would be controlled by Germany. What these men forgot was that the British, who for some three hundred years had steadfastly opposed the efforts of any single power to control the continent militarily, were not likely to lend their support to German efforts to accomplish this purpose by diplomacy. And, indeed, the British resisted all proposals for the kind of alliance the Germans desired. Frustrated and uncomprehending, the Germans turned back to Russia, which meanwhile had formed an alliance with France, then back to Britain again—an inconsistent and somewhat undignified diplomacy which came to be known as the policy of the zigzag course.

This was not at all the policy desired by Emperor William II, who had dismissed Bismarck in 1890 and who soon became the advocate of a vigorous German expansionist policy. But now the question arose: Where was Germany to expand? To this question William had no carefully considered answer, and in his quest for colonies he, too, pursued an inconsistent and contradictory course. In the Near and Far East, in Africa and the Pacific, he put forward claims and initiated policies which brought him into conflict with all the great powers of the world and had much to do with his country's diplomatic and moral isolation in 1914.

Emperor William was not the only German with territorial ambitions. Indeed there was hardly a German leader or interest group, at least among the upper and middle classes, who did not advocate large-scale annexations in the name of national self-interest or national security, and during the First World War hopes ran high in Germany that many of these ambitions were about to be fulfilled. If the Germans had won a decisive victory in that war, they had proposed to annex or establish their influence over territories in both Eastern and Western Europe which would give them political, military, and economic hegemony over the continent, and to acquire overseas colonies which would ensure Germany's status as a world power.[1] That these territorial ambitions were not mere theoretical exercises was demonstrated by the peace treaty of Brest-Litovsk, which the Germans concluded with the Bolshevik government of Russia in March 1918. By the terms of this treaty Russia gave up most of its non-Russian territories in Eastern Europe, including Finland, Lithuania, Russian Poland, the Ukraine, and Transcaucasia. The future status of these territories was to be determined "in agreement with their populations," but all were clearly destined to come under German dominion either directly or as German satellites.[2]

The Germans, however, were not alone in their desire for territorial annexations. The leaders of Allied powers shared the fears of their German counterparts that their rule would be discredited if they could not produce substantial gains for their people in return for the costs and sacrifices of the war. For the Allies there was the further problem of having to bolster mutual confidence among themselves and provide incentives for remaining in the war, which they did by promising one another large-scale territorial gains at the expense of their enemies. Beyond that they found it necessary to outbid the Germans in making territorial offers to neutral powers such as Italy to lure these countries into the war on their side. The territorial aims of the Allies were necessarily more limited than those of Germany because the greater powers among them (Britain, France, Russia, Italy, and the United States) and even the minor powers (such as Belgium and Portugal) already controlled a substantial part of the world's territory. Even so, Allied war aims were far from modest.[3] France was to regain the provinces of Alsace and Lorraine, lost to Germany in 1871. This was an understandable ambition, and the French never made any secret of it. What was secret, however, was the large number of agreements and understandings arranged among the Allied powers in the course of the war providing for extensions of territory or spheres of influence in other parts of the world. The French, for example, secured Russia's consent to extend their control over a substantial part of western Germany. France and Britain arranged to divide Germany's African colonies as well as what remained of the Ottoman Empire in North Africa and the Near East, most of which they controlled already. The Italians, in addition to receiving Austrian territory south of the Brenner Pass which they had long claimed because of the large Italian-speaking population inhabiting this area, were to receive a large strip of the Dalmatian coast, numerous islands in the Adriatic and the eastern Mediterranean, and a share of the spoils in Africa and the Near East.

So far as Europe was concerned, however, by far the most important concessions were made to Russia, which was promised Constantinople and the Straits and a substantial extension of territory at the expense of Germany and Austria. Had the war ended in an early victory for the Allies, Russia in effect would have fallen heir to both the Habsburg and Ottoman empires in East-Central Europe, and Russian dominion would have extended from Finland and the Baltic, through Central Europe and the Balkans, to the Mediterranean—an even greater sphere of influence than was conceded to the Soviet government in the Second World War.

Not to be outdone by the European powers, Japan laid claim to Germany's Far Eastern colonies north of the equator, and compelled the Chinese government to submit to demands which were intended to reduce the immense territory of China to the status of a Japanese protectorate—and this despite the fact that China was technically an ally of Japan in the war against Germany.

That the lands and peoples of East-Central Europe did not fall under Russian dominion after the First World War was due to the failure of the Allies to win a quick victory, and to the Bolshevik Revolution in Russia. When the Bolshevik government withdrew from the war, it denounced the secret treaties concluded by the Tsarist regime with the Western powers. Russia was not represented at the Paris Peace Conference, and Woodrow Wilson, the American president, refused to recognize the existence of the secret treaties concluded among the Allies before the United States entered the war. Inspired by an idealistic desire to arrange a just and lasting peace, he insisted that in Europe, at least, the various nationalities should be given self-government on the basis of the principle of self-determination.

Wilson was obliged to compromise on many points, but his principles were applied with considerable consistency in Europe, especially in the territories of the defeated powers. The Habsburg and Ottoman empires, and part of the German and Russian empires as well, were partitioned and replaced by a mosaic of small states. Although the boundaries of these states were theoretically drawn up according to the principle of self-determination, the jumble of nationalities in East-Central Europe was such that each of these states inevitably included national minorities which resented their subjugation to the dominant national group. Rent by national strife, for the most part militarily weak and economically unstable, the states of East-Central Europe were to fall easy prey to Germany and Russia once these powers had recovered their strength.

If the Germans were not alone in having extensive territorial ambitions, neither were they alone in fostering an exaggerated patriotism, militarism, or anti-Semitism. These and similar phenomena could be found in all European states in 1914 in one form or another. But differences in degree are often far more important than similarities, and many students of German history, with the evidence of the German record in the twentieth century before them, see reason to believe that in Germany the various manifestations of these phenomena assumed a particularly vicious and virulent form.

A multitude of explanations have been offered to account for the peculiar nature of the German problem, which is generally regarded as having its roots deep in the German past: in the failure of Germanic tribes to share in the civilizing experience of Romanization; in the Lutheran conception of subservience to the state; in the brutalizing effects of the Thirty Years' War; in the role of the Prussian army in German politics and society; in the amoral politics of Frederick the

Great and Bismarck; in Hegel's apotheosis of the state; in the nationalist teachings of Fichte and Treitschke; in Nietzsche's philosophy of the superman; in the racial doctrines of Wagner and Stöcker—it is a list which could be extended indefinitely.

Yet this Germany of militarism and racism was also the Germany of Bach and Goethe, of Kant and Lessing. As late as 1914 there were few unprejudiced observers who discerned qualities in the German people which set them apart from their more humane and civilized neighbors. On the contrary, in comparison with many European states of that time, for example the Russian and Habsburg empires, or even Britain with its Irish and labor problems, Germany seemed unusually orderly and well administered. Its bureaucracy was efficient and more honest than most, its citizenry industrious and law-abiding. If the German government was more authoritarian than that of Britain or France, it was considerably less so than that of Russia. The rights of German citizens and their property were protected by laws which were on the whole honestly and effectively enforced. German workers were protected by the most comprehensive social welfare legislation in the world. Despite the undeniably strong current of anti-Semitism in German society, Jews enjoyed full legal equality and on the whole fared well in Germany, so much so that thousands of Jews migrated to Germany from Eastern Europe to improve their status and to escape pogroms and other more violent forms of anti-Semitism. Germans continued to make outstanding contributions to European culture. German universities, technical schools, and conservatories of music attracted students from every part of the world. In sum, Germany in 1914, far from being a pariah among nations, was a leading member of the European civilized community.

What did set Germany apart in 1914 was the quality of its leadership. Political philosophers throughout the centuries have mused about the lack of wisdom with which the world is governed, but in history's ship of political fools Emperor William II still stands out as something exceptional. For over a quarter of a century his adolescent posturings, bombastic pronouncements, ill-considered statements and policies, kept European politics in a turmoil and aroused alarm and consternation among political observers throughout the world. Moreover, like most vain and inept rulers, he selected sycophants and toadies to aid him in running his government, officials who upon occasion succeeded in outdoing the political stupidities of their master.

The point is still hotly debated as to whether German policy in the years before the First World War was more wicked and immoral than that of other powers, but there can be no question that in the eyes of much of the world it appeared to be so. Under the rule of William II, Germany gained the reputation of being a saber-rattling disturber of the peace, and the fear and mistrust of the German Empire, which had subsided somewhat in the Bismarck era, grew steadily until the climax of 1914, when, in the view of Germany's enemies, their worst fears about Germany seemed confirmed.

The government of William II, however, cannot be held solely or even primarily responsible for the brutalization of German life and the breakdown of standards of common decency that took place during the Nazi era. This breakdown can be ascribed in part to conditions common to all modern industrialized societies. The industrialization of Western Europe produced a mass migration from rural areas to the cities involving approximately 90 per cent of the population. This mass migration, which reached its peak in Germany in the final decades of the nineteenth century, inevitably meant a severance of ancient ties with parish and manor, with familiar modes of life and conduct, and a corresponding loss of emotional and psychological security. During this same period, with advances in medical knowledge and a general rise in material prosperity, there occurred an unprecedented increase in the size of the German population, most of which was also absorbed in the cities. By the twentieth century Germany had been transformed from a predominantly rural into a predominantly urban society.

Urban societies, always more susceptible to mass stimulation than more scattered rural populations, were now more exposed than ever before to intellectual and emotional pressures with the development of new methods of mass communication, especially the popular press, and the general adoption of systems of compulsory (and for the most part state-controlled) elementary education. Never before had governments possessed such powers to influence and control public opinion, but at the same time, never before had ideologists and propagandists of every stripe, whether revivalists, revolutionaries, or merchants, possessed such effective means for bringing their ideas and goods to the attention of the public.

There was a ready market for both ideas and goods. With the loss of many traditional values and loyalties, there began a frantic search for new values. Men turned to new religions, to faith in science, to new political and social doctrines. But the cult that claimed the largest number of adherents was nationalism, a belief that the natural social and political unit of human society is composed of a group of people who conceive of themselves, no matter how artificially, as belonging to the same racial or national community. Nationalism evidently provides men with something essential to the human spirit: a sense of identity, of membership in a community which is somehow different from—and superior to—other national or racial communities.

INTRODUCTION

The cult of nationalism was sedulously fostered by the governments of national states such as France, and it provided the only ideological common denominator for new national states such as Germany and Italy. But nationalism proved a threat to the very existence of multinational states such as the Habsburg and Ottoman empires; even in Britain, that most stable of European states in the nineteenth century, Irish nationalism developed into a festering sore undermining the foundations of the British political system—as nationalism was later to undermine the entire British Empire.

Closely allied with nationalism was the so-called new imperialism which, as a more intensive search for markets and raw materials, was another concomitant of industrialization. Imperialism, however, had the enthusiastic support of broad segments of the population with little or no economic stake in imperial expansion, a popularity that can be explained in part as an extension of the self-esteem of members of national communities capable of engaging in imperialistic enterprises.

National rivalries and tensions, which grew steadily more strident and vicious during the early years of the twentieth century, finally erupted in the First World War. This war, like others before it, brought out some of the finest qualities of the human spirit—man's capacity for sacrifice, his tenacity and heroism—but to a far greater extent it nourished some of the worst qualities of the human character. For four years men were systematically trained in the use of violence, for four years hatred and slaughter were extolled as the highest human virtues, for four years men were exposed to suffering and death, their sensibilities blunted to the pain and suffering of others. The brutalizing effect of war was a common experience to the population of all belligerent powers, and it left its mark on them all. But in Germany the terrible torment of war ended in defeat and national humiliation, in political and economic collapse, a shock all the greater because until the last days of the war the German government had encouraged its people to believe in ultimate victory or at worst an honorable stalemate.[4]

An armistice concluded on the basis of Wilson's Fourteen Points [5] was followed by the Treaty of Versailles, which violated many of these points and which was imposed on Germany without benefit of negotiation. By the terms of the treaty the Germans lost far less territory than the French and Russians had at one time claimed, and certainly far less than they themselves would have taken from their opponents had they won the war. But their territorial losses, especially in Eastern Europe, were nevertheless substantial. The Germans and their allies were obliged to assume full responsibility for causing the war and consequently the obligation to pay for the cost of the war, a reparations bill so large that the total sum was not even named at the time of the treaty's signature.[6] To the vast majority of Germans the Treaty of Versailles appeared to be a dictated and unjust peace, a treaty designed to keep Germany in permanent political and economic subjugation to the victor powers. Further, they regarded it as a violation of both the spirit and letter of the armistice agreement which eliminated all moral obligation on their part to live up to its terms.

A more immediate source of bitterness for the Germans was the failure of the Allies to lift their economic blockade during the seven months after the armistice while a final peace treaty was being drawn up and until it was signed by the German government.[7] As a result the Germans suffered more hunger and outright starvation during the first winter of peace than at any time during the war, and an influenza epidemic ravaged the weakened German population. During this same period Allied troops occupied certain sectors of Germany in accordance with the terms of the armistice agreement. Occupation forces are never popular, but in this case the Germans were convinced that the Allied troops, particularly the French and the Belgians, were deliberately doing everything in their power to make them feel the full extent of their defeat and national humiliation.

Thus the Weimar Republic, a democratic German government which the Allies had demanded as a condition for making peace, was born in an atmosphere of disillusionment and hate. Worse still, it was this government which was compelled to sign the Treaty of Versailles and thereby became associated in the public mind with the onus of defeat and Germany's subsequent misfortunes.

In January 1923 French and Belgian troops occupied the Ruhr, the heartland of German industrial strength, on the grounds of a default in German reparations payments. The Germans responded with a campaign of passive resistance, which the German government supported by printing paper currency which in a few months was literally worth less than the paper it was printed on. The German inflation brought about the economic ruin of the most stable elements in German society, the people who worked hard and saved their money, and who in general supported the existing social order.

A short period of prosperity was followed by another and far more serious economic depression. By 1932 there were over six million unemployed in Germany, one out of every three members of the regular German labor force, a situation which directly affected one out of every two German families. In Berlin, government succeeded government, each seemingly more impotent that its predecessor to stem the tide of economic chaos. Hunger and disease once again stalked the land, gangs of unemployed roamed the streets, and the armed forces of militant political groups carried violence and disorder to every city and town. It was not to the Germany of Bach and Goethe that Hitler brought his simplistic message of national salvation, but to a Germany under the sign of the Horsemen of the Apocalypse—war, famine, pestilence, and despair. Far more than the Germanic tribes or Luther, than Bismarck or William II, than industrialization and imperialism, it was the First World War and its aftermath that created the seedbed of Nazism.

The record of German misfortune during and after the First World War, however, is not enough to explain the triumph of Nazism. Other countries had suffered through war, revolution, and economic chaos without producing a Hitler—although they did produce a Lenin and a Stalin, a Mussolini, and other more or less sinister varieties of dictators and demagogues. The big difference in Germany, and the biggest single factor in the triumph of Hitler was—Hitler. With his Chaplinesque moustache, his hysterical manner and patently absurd racial theories, his humble background and record of professional and political failure, he was dismissed by many Germans as a nonentity, a vulgar rabble-rouser disgorged from the gutter in a period of turmoil who would sink back into the sewers from which he came as soon as more settled conditions had been restored. It was some time before these Germans, and with them the entire world, recognized that Hitler was not only a force to be reckoned with but possessed political and diplomatic talents of the highest order. Yet throughout most of his career Hitler was to benefit from his opponents' underestimation of his abilities, an underestimation that persists in many chronicles of the Nazi era whose authors are understandably reluctant to ascribe political genius to a man responsible for some of the greatest and most repulsive crimes in history.

Adolf Hitler was born in April 20, 1889, in the Austrian border town of Braunau am Inn, the fourth child of the third marriage of an Austrian customs official named Alois Hitler.[8] There is a grim irony in the fact that the man who was later to make proof of an Aryan background a life and death matter for millions of Europeans was himself without such proof, and that to the present day the identity of one of his grandparents is unknown.

Hitler's father Alois was born in 1837, the illegitimate son of a domestic servant named Maria Anna Schicklgruber. Five years after giving birth to Alois, Maria Anna married a journeyman miller named Johann Georg Hiedler. Alois continued to use the name Schicklgruber, but in 1877, thirty years after the death of his mother and twenty years after that of his stepfather, he had his birth legitimatized with the aid of a gullible village priest by having Hiedler recognized as his real father. This action may have been nothing more than a gesture of gratitude to the Hiedler family which had brought him up, for Alois's illegitimacy does not appear to have injured his career or to have troubled him much otherwise. For some reason, however, he did not adopt the name Hiedler but one of the many variations of that name, Hitler.[9]

By dint of industry and ability, Alois Hitler rose to the highest grade in the Austro-Hungarian customs service open to a man of his social background and educational qualifications. He had a reasonably good income, and his children appear to have been raised in an atmosphere of domestic stability.

In 1894 Alois Hitler, after a brief assignment in Passau (Germany), was transferred to the Danubian city of Linz, where Adolf Hitler completed his elementary (*Volksschule*) education and then attended the secondary school which stressed modern as opposed to classical subjects (the *Realschule*). His secondary school record was uneven and undistinguished, marked by a lack of discipline and perseverance. So poor was his work that he was not allowed to return to the Realschule in Linz in 1904 and had to be sent to a comparable school in Steyr, some forty kilometers to the southwest. In 1905 he dropped out of school altogether, allegedly for reasons of health, but in any case there was almost no chance that he would have been admitted to an *Oberrealschule*, the next rung in the Austrian educational ladder. After the death of his mother in December 1907 (his father Alois had already died in 1903) Hitler moved to Vienna, where he remained despite the blow to his ambition to become an artist caused by his failure to gain admission to the Vienna Academy of Art.

It was in Vienna that Hitler appears to have imbibed most of his theories about race and nationality.[10] The Austrian capital was inhabited primarily by Germans at the beginning of the nineteenth century; but in the course of its industrialization there was an influx of non-German laborers from every part of the heterogeneous Habsburg Empire, with the result that the social and class tensions common to all industrialized societies were exacerbated by ethnic rivalries. Vienna, far from serving as a national melting pot, was transformed instead into a national cockpit where hatreds flared high and the most extreme theories on the subject of race and nationality found ready acceptance from members of all ethnic groups. At the beginning of the twentieth century the Germans remained in the majority, but they felt themselves to be under constant political and economic pressure from other nationalities. Time and again in the years before the First World War they elected as their mayor Karl Lueger, an effective sponsor of social welfare legislation, whose socialism was inextricably combined with German nationalism, Roman Catholicism, and anti-Semitism. Vienna, the city of music and gaity of popular romance, was at the same time a city infected by national, social, and economic

paranoia. It was hardly a coincidence that one of the most famous
methods for the treatment of mental illness was developed in Vienna
—by a Jewish doctor.

Among the many racial theories to which Hitler was exposed in Vienna, some of the most influential appear to have been those of a certain Adolf Lanz, who had assumed the pen name of Jörg Lanz von Liebenfels. Lanz's theories were based on a belief in the existence of an
Aryan master race and a crude form of social Darwinism. Applying
the theory of the survival of the fittest to racial questions, Lanz
taught that the Aryans, like all living creatures, were engaged in a
struggle for survival. Being inherently superior to all other races, the
Aryans were destined to triumph in this struggle and eventually ex-
terminate all lesser races; but they would only be certain of victory if
they remained pure and avoided mixing with lesser breeds, especially
Jews. Not without reason has Lanz been called the man who gave
Hitler his ideas.[11]

But there was no dearth of racial theorists in Vienna, or anywhere
else in Europe for that matter, for Hitler to draw upon. Besides Lanz
he appears to have been much influenced by the racial theories of the
Frenchman, Count Gobineau, and by the Englishman, Houston Stew-
art Chamberlain; and there must have been hundreds of lesser racial
theorists who affected his thinking. In a revealing passage in *Mein
Kampf* about his years in Vienna, Hitler stated that the reading he
had done during this period supplied him with the basic knowledge
on which he still fed. "During this time I formed a picture of the
world and an ideology which has become the granite foundation of
my deeds. I only had to add a little more knowledge to what I acquired at that time; I did not have to revise anything." [12] In fact Hitler was to absorb numerous other ideas in later years, notably the
geopolitical theories of Karl Haushofer which shaped his views about
the need for a territorial land mass *(Lebensraum)* as a basis for national security, but there can be little doubt that a firm ideological
foundation was laid in Vienna.

During the first year of his stay in Vienna, Hitler appears to have
lived on his patrimony and a modest orphan's pension, but already in
1909 he was in serious economic difficulty. In December of that year
he sought refuge in a hostel for the homeless *(Obdachlosenheim)*, and
in February 1910 he moved to a men's hostel *(Männerheim)* where he
remained until he left Vienna for good in the spring of 1913. All this
time he did no regular work, but earned a precarious living from the
sale of his sketches and paintings. While leading the life of a social
derelict in Vienna, Hitler failed to register for military service as required by Austrian law when he first became eligible for the draft in
1909, a requirement he continued to ignore in the three following
years. It is possible that already at this time he had come to feel con-

tempt for the polyglot Habsburg Empire and that he consequently had no desire to fight for its preservation.

In June 1913, having reached the age of twenty-four and apparently believing that he was now safe from the Austrian draft, Hitler left Vienna for Munich, where he hoped his talents as an artist would win greater recognition. Here he was arrested at the request of the Austrian government and extradited to Austria. His various maneuvers to avoid the draft now proved to have been unnecessary, however, for he was found physically unfit for military service.

Hitler soon demonstrated that he had no objection to military service as such and that his physical disabilities were not serious. He greeted the outbreak of war in 1914 enthusiastically and immediately enlisted—but in the German, not the Austrian, army. Throughout much of the war he served as a staff courier assigned to the hazardous task of conveying messages to front-line positions. He was wounded twice, and awarded the iron cross of the first and second class—rare distinctions for a private soldier at that time. But although he consistently demonstrated his bravery, he was never promoted beyond the rank of corporal because his superior officers believed he could never command respect from men of lower ranks. In the army as in civilian life he remained a loner, he neither drank nor smoked, and was seemingly wholly dedicated to the tasks of war.

Stunned and infuriated by Germany's defeat, Hitler enrolled after the war in a Bavarian army unit responsible for the nationalistic education and surveillance of other soldiers. In carrying out his duties in connection with this job, he came as an observer in September 1919 to a meeting of a recently formed political group called the German Workers party. This party was allegedly dedicated to the ennoblement of the German worker and his welfare, but its brand of socialism was similar to that of Mayor Karl Lueger of Vienna in that it was closely linked with German nationalism and anti-Semitism. Like several other German nationalist groups of that time, it had adopted the swastika as its symbol. Shortly after attending that first meeting, Hitler joined the German Workers party as its fifty-fifth member and was immediately appointed to its leadership committee.

As his army job was soon to be abolished, Hitler began to devote all his time to politics. From the beginning he demonstrated unusual talent as an orator and political organizer, and he soon maneuvered himself into the de facto leadership of his party. In 1920 the name of the party was changed to correspond with its nationalist emphasis and was thereafter called the National Socialist German Workers party (*Nationalsozialistische Deutsche Arbeiterpartei*, or NSDAP). In the following year Hitler made himself uncontested leader of the party and assumed the title of Führer.

Although the party remained small, it attracted the support of a number of prominent nationalist extremists, among them General Erich Ludendorff, one of Germany's most famous wartime commanders. With such seemingly powerful backing and inspired by the success of the Bolshevik revolution in Russia, Hitler attempted to take advantage of the disintegrating political and economic situation in Germany following the French occupation of the Ruhr to overthrow the Bavarian government in Munich. But Hitler's so-called Beer Hall Putsch of November 1923 was badly mismanaged and easily suppressed. Hitler was arrested, sentenced to five years in prison, but released after serving less than one year.

After leaving prison Hitler once again took over the leadership of the National Socialist party, and from that time he devoted all his time and energy to party work: organization, speechmaking, fund raising, and planning party tactics and strategy. Fourteen years after first entering politics as a member of the German Workers party, Hitler was appointed chancellor of the German Reich.

Hitler's success, and the authority he exercised over his followers, can be attributed first of all to his own physical and intellectual qualities. He possessed an immense store of energy and stamina, which sustained him through grueling election campaigns, public ceremonies and private conferences, yet left him with sufficient resources to carry on the personal direction of party (and later of state) affairs. He had unusual powers of concentration, an excellent memory for facts and figures. His was not a great mind, much less a generous or cultivated mind, but it was a mind capable of assimilating rapidly a large amount of information that he considered relevant or that fit into his self-contained and simplistic ideological framework. All other information was either overlooked or consciously thrust aside, a mental facility that prevented distraction from the single-minded pursuit of his objectives.

Like all successful politicians, Hitler had a strongly developed craving for power, together with an instinct for how to attain and hold it. It would be an error, however, to believe that craving for power was his sole or even his most important political motivation. Perhaps the greatest source of Hitler's strength derived from his sense of mission, a fanatic belief that he had been selected by destiny to lead the German people out of the wilderness to a permanent status of security and greatness. He was absolutely certain of what he wanted and where he was going, even if he might occasionally be in doubt as to how to get there. Supporters and opponents alike were constantly astounded by the daring of the man, by his willingness to disregard all conventions in politics, economics, or war. He was a gambler, who time and again staked his own and his country's fortunes on diplomatic or military moves that were hazardous in the extreme, confident that destiny would not, could not, allow him to fail. No obstacle was so great that it could not be overcome by a supreme effort of will, no problem so complex that it could not be solved by direct, determined action.[13] It was this belief in his destiny, this sense of mission and purpose, that gave Hitler such a hold over his followers—and such faith in himself.

As a speaker he was unsurpassed in modern times in his ability to win over mass audiences. Part of his success lay in the crude but compelling logic of his arguments about Germany's need for national and social security, and how this security might be achieved. He made frequent use of the technique of turning away criticism of his own policies by pointing to the sins of others. But Hitler was above all a demagogue. He preferred to give important speeches late at night, when the minds of his listeners were dulled, against a dramatic backdrop of torchlights, banners, and massed ranks of uniformed men. Modulating his voice from tones of quiet exhortation to strident hysteria, he played on popular fears and prejudices, whipping his listeners into a state of frenzied enthusiasm, drowning doubts and scruples in a wave of emotion.

Hitler was equally effective in smaller conferences or personal confrontations. Here, too, he generally tried to overwhelm his audiences with a combination of logic and passion, alternating threats with promises, dire warnings with expressions of pious sincerity. Through all the rhetoric, however, there was a strand of cynical calculation. Hitler was convinced that every man had his price, and he had a flair for sensing what that price might be, whether it was peace, power, status, money, or simply personal security. By telling his listeners what they wanted to hear, and offering them what they wanted to get, he succeeded with remarkable frequency in gaining his point or at least causing potential adversaries to lower their guard.

Rarely has a political leader offered so much to so many. To the unemployed and workers of every kind he offered jobs and economic security; to the peasants he offered the prospect of more land and greater national prestige; to the middle classes he offered jobs suitable to their station and an end to the threat of proletarianization; to big business he offered the prospect of lush government contracts and a free hand for private enterprise in the name of "creative individuality"; to the military leadership he offered rearmament and power; to German nationalists he offered the restoration of national self-respect, a renaissance of traditional German values, and the uprooting of foreign, particularly Jewish, influences; to youth he offered action and involvement, an opportunity for sacrifice and commitment; and to all Germans he offered strong and purposeful leadership, economic recovery, and the re-establishment of law and order.

Yet for all the varieties of Hitler's appeal, despite economic depression and political chaos, and despite the feverish activity of Nazi party members and their leader, Hitler and his party never succeeded in winning more than 37 per cent of the votes of the German people in a free election. Even in March 1933, after Hitler's appointment to the chancellorship, with the machinery and funds of central and local government at their disposal, the Nazis won only 44 per cent of the votes, their Nationalist allies a bare 8 per cent.

Once the Nazi government had consolidated its power, however, and the instruments of control and propaganda had been perfected, the Nazi regime appeared to gain in popularity until it seemed to enjoy the enthusiastic support of the vast majority of the German people. Even discounting the claims of Nazi publicists on the subject and the fact that Nazi popular demonstrations were brilliantly stage-managed, there is good reason to believe that much of this popular enthusiasm was genuine. Not only was Nazi propaganda conducted with rare skill, but the government lived up to many of its promises: Germany was given strong leadership, the economy did recover, the unemployed were given jobs, big business received its lush contracts, Germany was rearmed, German national prestige was restored, and German foreign policy moved from triumph to triumph in a manner that was nothing short of miraculous. The Führer seemed indeed the national savior he had proclaimed himself to be.

Even so, it is difficult to gauge the true popular support enjoyed by any government, and in the case of an authoritarian regime which prohibits all expressions of dissent it is almost impossible. Nazi instruments of repression and control were not altogether efficient or foolproof. Far from it. But the men who operated them were tough and ruthless, and they adopted methods that had already proved their worth in other authoritarian states, particularly the Soviet Union. The more innocuous opponents of the regime received warnings to cease all political activity, they were threatened with personal violence and imprisonment, or, what often proved to be even more effective, with the loss of their jobs and consequently of their economic and social status. People considered to be a genuine danger, on the other hand, generally simply disappeared, hustled off in the dead of night to prisons or concentration camps where they might face torture or death. People with families were particularly vulnerable to pressure, for they could be confronted not only with threats to their own persons but to those of wives, children, or parents. For them it required not only great personal courage and moral dedication to oppose the regime, but a willingness to sacrifice their families as well—a sacrifice few men or women find themselves able to make. Thousands of opponents of the regime fled abroad, and with that their ability to exercise any immediate influence in Germany ceased. But far more remained in Germany out of love of country, for family or economic reasons, or because they believed that they could only fight the regime effectively at home. Still others clung to positions of influence, including positions in the Nazi government, in the belief that they could ameliorate conditions from within or at the very least prevent worse things from happening.

The large majority of Germans, however, unquestionably accepted the Nazi regime, some with enthusiasm, some in the fatalistic belief that it was the only alternative to Communism. But, whether they supported or opposed the regime, most Germans, in the manner of people everywhere, apparently went about their daily affairs without giving much thought to problems of government and high-level policy. Among those who did, there were many who appear to have believed sincerely in Hitler's professions about his peaceful intentions —and with far more justification than the foreign statesmen who were similarly gulled by Hitler's propaganda. When war came in 1939, Nazi leaders were seriously worried about the lack of popular enthusiasm for the conflict, and even the great victories over France in 1940 never seemed to stir up the degree of popular support for war that had existed in 1914.

Stories of Nazi atrocities circulated, and circulated very freely, in the Third Reich, but many patriotic Germans were able to recall how false had been the atrocity stories circulated during the First World War and, having grown wise with experience, simply refused to believe what they heard about Nazi prisons and concentration camps. These stories were foreign or Jewish propaganda, they would say, and in any case they could not be true "because we Germans don't behave that way." Even the most gullible German, of course, could not be blind to the persecution of Jews and the repression of opponents of the regime, but such abuses were accepted by Nazi apologists as the unfortunate concomitants of the political and social revolution which the Nazi movement represented. Nazis even took some pride in the fact that their revolution had been carried out with far less violence and bloodshed than comparable revolutions in France and Russia.

Withal, however, most Germans showed a curious lack of understanding for Hitler's real intentions. "*Wenn das der Führer wüsste*" (if only the Führer knew about *that*) was one of the most commonly heard remarks in the Germany of the Third Reich, meaning that if only Hitler knew of the abuses perpetrated by his officials he would quickly put a stop to such behavior. Göring, Goebbels, Ley, the average *Gau* or *Blockleiter* might be reviled or held in contempt for their ostentation, corruption, immorality, and arrogant posturing—but the

Führer, that was something else again. In his simple uniform jacket, adorned only with the iron cross won on the field of battle, celibate, vegetarian, accepting no pay but the royalties from his writings, dedicating himself totally and unreservedly to the service of his people— the Führer was *untastbar*, beyond reproach. It was a job of image making on the part of Nazi propagandists almost unparalled in its success, and it was, as we now know, a totally false picture. Hitler's personal habits were simple because he was not interested in good food and drink. To preserve the myth of Hitler's celibacy, his mistress Eva Braun had to spend most of her life hidden from public view. The public heard nothing of the billions of marks actually spent or earmarked to be spent on private dwellings and public palaces for the Führer and his lieutenants. But the greatest illusion of all was that Hitler was not aware of the atrocities carried out under his regime. The evidence now available is as clear as it is irrefutable that Hitler not only knew about them, but that the grimmest and most massive of these atrocities were carried out as a result of his personal orders.

Hitler himself, although as Führer he theoretically embodied the will of the German people, certainly had no confidence that the Germans understood *his* will or the radical nature of his program; one of his chief concerns throughout his career was that his successors would fail to carry through what he had begun. For this reason Hitler was convinced that his New Order not only had to be established in his lifetime, but established in so solid a manner that it could survive any amount of future German sentimentality and political stupidity. History had shown him how great had been the follies of previous German rulers, and he himself had observed the quality of German leadership in his own time. The politicians, the businessmen, the generals, and most contemptible of all, the old aristocracy—he had taken the measure of them all and outdone them all with what, in retrospect, must have seemed quite ridiculous ease. The Krupps, the Moltkes, the Hohenzollerns—these were not the people to whom you could safely entrust the future of Germany. Nor were Nazi leaders much better, for, so far as Hitler could see, even the most ruthless and powerful among them could be transformed with a word or look into groveling yes men.

As for the German people in general, how admirable they were with their narrow concepts of honor and legality, their blond and blue-eyed innocence; and yet—the undercurrent in Hitler's attitude is unmistakable—how contemptible: the perennial dupes of Gauls and Anglo-Saxons, the gullible victims of every Jewish peddler. These were not the people who would understand the need for radical solutions to geopolitical and racial problems, much less have the iron will to carry them out. Himmler expressed the despair Hitler must have felt when he lamented, "And there they go, all eighty million Germans, and each one knows a decent Jew." [14]

And in fact Hitler did not entrust the real leadership of Nazi Germany to the Germans. The major policies and decisions of the Nazi era were not the policies and decisions of his Nazi lieutenants, much less those of the German generals, the big industrialists, the Junker landowners, the bureaucrats, or any other individuals or groups who in the past might have been considered to speak for Germany. Open rearmament, the remilitarization of the Rhineland, the annexation of Austria, the rape of Czechoslovakia, the attack on Poland and Russia, the declaration of war against the United States, the destruction of the Jews, the racial reconstruction of Europe—these were all the policies and decisions of Hitler, and the war aims which are the subject of this book were predominantly, if by no means exclusively, the aims of Hitler.

This does not mean to suggest that many of the aims of Hitler were not approved or supported by large numbers of Germans, or that other German leaders and interest groups did not have substantial war aims of their own. There is ample evidence that they did, and an important book could be written on this subject. Nor does it mean to suggest that Hitler was some kind of cruel accident in German history whose regime cannot be considered part of the main course of Germany's historical development. Not only was it part of that course by the fact of its very existence, but no German regime had ever governed so large a proportion of the German-speaking population or appeared to enjoy such widespread support, at least during its years of success.

But if the Nazi era cannot be considered apart from the main course of German history, neither can it be considered apart from the history of Europe or indeed of mankind as a whole. For surely the most significant lesson of the Nazi experience would be overlooked if the Hitler movement were to be regarded as an exclusive product of German history or of German moral deficiencies.

Hitler, far from deriving his inspiration from exclusively German sources, was above all a prophet of the cult of nationalism, which was unquestionably the most powerful spiritual force in pre-1914 Europe and which has since swept over the peoples of the Americas, Asia, and Africa to become one of the most powerful spiritual forces throughout the modern world. Hitler's phenomenal success in Germany was due in large measure to his ability to tap this uncanny reservoir of popular emotion, to offer simple and clear-cut solutions to man's eternal search for security—political, economic, and psychological. The most frightening aspect of the Hitler legacy is not the exclusivity of his appeal to the sentiment of nationalism, but its universality.

There were, however, two fundamental differences between Hitler's nationalism and nationalism as it was conceived by the majority of nineteenth-century national political leaders, including those of Germany. The first of these was Hitler's identification of nation with race. The concept of nation as a racial phenomenon had already been widely disseminated in the nineteenth century and had been given considerable emphasis in Germany, but no German national government had ever used the concept of racial nationalism as a basis of national legislation or as a guideline for national policy. On the contrary, the Prussian-German government had done its best to Germanize the Poles, French, and other non-German inhabitants of the empire, and it had placed no legal obstacles in the way of the assimilation of Jews into the German national community. Hitler, on the other hand, believed it was impossible to Germanize peoples of another race. In his view a man was born into a certain race, and there was nothing he or anyone else could do afterward to change his racial status. Thus non-German races could never be truly Germanized, and all efforts to do so could only lead to the bastardization and degredation of the Germanic race.

A second fundamental difference which distinguished Hitler from his nineteenth-century predecessors was that he pushed his ideas to their ultimate—one hesitates to use the word *logical* in this connection—conclusion. As Hitler viewed the problem, the German population was too small and its territorial base too limited to guarantee the survival of the racially superior Germans in the world arena of racial competition; if the German race was to survive, both its population and territorial base would have to be extended—at once and on a vast scale: This was the essence of the Hitler idea. Bismarck had rejected proposals for further German expansion after 1871 on the ground that the absorption of more non-German nationalities would weaken rather than contribute to the strength of the German Empire. Hitler's nationalism went far beyond such narrow conceptions. His expansion called not for the absorption but the enslavement and eventual annihilation of rival races in territories conquered by the Germans. His model was not that of his former Habsburg rulers, with their indiscriminate annexation of peoples of different races and religions, but that of the Nordics of North America, who had ruthlessly swept aside lesser races to ensure their own ethnic survival.

In recent years Americans and Englishmen have begun to, or been obliged to, take stock of their own racist record; but there is no need for Anglo-Saxons to indulge in an orgy of self-accusation and guilt. The human yearning for power, glory, security, territory, and all other motives that turn man against his fellow did not originate with the Anglo-Saxons, nor did they end with the death of Hitler. Throughout the period of recorded history Slavs and Latins, Asiatics and Africans, Aztecs and Incas have all indulged in conquest and the annihilation of groups who stood in their way, often on a massive and brutal scale. In the process these peoples were not necessarily organized along racial, much less national, lines—feelings of racial or national identity are, after all, artificial products of human society and not immutably fixed by natural law—but as tribes, clans, city states, kingdoms, empires. It is the nation state, however, which seems to claim the loyalty of the vast majority of the world's population in contemporary society, and in most nation states the search for security has become the cardinal principle of national policy. Since the end of the Second World War this search has frequently been accompanied by the defense of national interests (or, depending on the point of view, their extension) in areas far beyond a particular state's national boundaries, whether in Central Europe, Latin America, the Middle East, or Southeast Asia. More sinister still, a growing number of these national states now have resources and weaponry at their disposal which may soon make Hitler seem like little more than a primitive pioneer in the deadly game of ethnic imperialism.

PART ONE

Ideology and the Nazi State

CHAPTER 1

The Ideology of Expansion[1]

Not the least of Hitler's crimes against the German people was his exploitation and perversion of some of Germany's most cherished values, notably the German veneration for a broadly conceived (and generally somewhat vague) ideal of humanist culture. Yet it was with undoubted sincerity that Hitler, the frustrated artist, paid homage to the German ideal of *Kultur* and made it the foundation of his entire ideological system. It was his conviction that only through culture was the beauty and dignity of a higher humanity, the only justification for the existence of mankind, to be attained. To clear away the obstructions to true culture was the aim of the Nazi revolution; to build on the healthy foundations of the past the goal of the Nazi renaissance.[2]

But if Hitler was sincere about his admiration for culture (however perverse his own conception of culture may have been) [3], there is also no doubt that he self-consciously exploited the cultural ideal to provide his followers with a moral impulse more edifying than a mere drive for political power, and a value to reinforce the emotional qualities of nationalism. In culture Hitler thought he had found a spiritual counterpoise to supernatural religions; and, even more important, an ideal he believed could overtrump the crass materialism of Marxism.[4]

Indeed, the ideal of culture might have been even more effective than that of a classless society in transcending the narrow ideological boundaries of nationalism had not Hitler strait-jacketed his own principle the moment he advanced it. For in a concomitant proposition he maintained that only members of the Aryan race were endowed with the creative ability to produce great culture.[5] The preposterous nature of this claim, instead of rendering the entire Nazi movement ridiculous, actually contributed to its strength, for it made Nazism something more than a political movement; it made the acceptance of

3

National Socialism an act of faith—but a faith open only to Germans.[6] For this reason, although the Nazi faith might concentrate tremendous moral energy in one group of people, the racial bomb would never explode with a chain reaction. By limiting the cultural ideal to the Aryans, Hitler had merely loosed upon the world another German particularist religion.

The assumption that the past and future of human civilization depended exclusively on the Aryans, that therefore they alone among the peoples of the earth deserved to live and prosper—this was the basis on which rested the entire superstructure of Hitler's ideological program, his concept of the role of party and state, his plans for the future of the German people. Race, far from being a mere propagandistic slogan, was the very rock on which the Nazi church was built.

Hitler never appears to have had any doubts about the literal truth of his racial theories, nor did his more fanatic followers. With greater objectivity Alfred Rosenberg, the self-appointed high priest of the Nazi movement, saw the difficulty educated people might have in accepting the racial doctrine, and he attempted to give it intellectual plausibility by calling it a myth—*the* myth of the twentieth century. But the racial myth, he hastened to add, embodied the essence of truth, and in an excess of analogical zeal he declared that the mysteries of the blood had overwhelmed and supplanted the old sacraments. Rosenberg actually acclaimed the particularist character of National Socialism and rejected universality as the intellectual concept of a decadent society.[7] This can hardly have been Hitler's intention. There can be no doubt that for him the Germanic race, supporting as it did the entire complex of his values, was, from a spiritual standpoint, in itself universal. Herein exactly lay the implication of his ideas. Because the Germans were the only true creators of culture, because they were universal in a cultural sense, it followed that they had the moral right to be universal in a territorial sense as well; in other words, that they had a moral right to world territorial dominion.

Hitler did not dwell at length on the morality of German territorial expansion. After his many years of patriotic brooding on the subject, this was something he by now took for granted. What concerned him most at the time he wrote *Mein Kampf,* and in all his subsequent analyses of the problem, was the desperate immediacy of the Germans' territorial requirements.

As Hitler surveyed the international scene, the position of the Germans seemed grim. Across the channel lay England, jealous of any potential rival on the continent and perennial opponent of any effort on the part of the Germans to improve their position.[8] But if England desired no increase in German power, France desired no German power at all. The French attitude toward Germany was founded on the motive of self-preservation. Only through the obliteration of Ger-

4

many could France maintain its world importance. French policy would always be one of waiting to engage in the final destruction of the Germans.[9]

Great as was the danger from France, however, Hitler believed that the truly vital threat to the existence of the Germans lay in the east, where a vast expanse of territory provided the breeding grounds for an inexhaustible supply of a particularly brutal species of humanity. These lesser breeds, separated from Europe by no natural barriers, had been held at bay over the centuries only by the bravery of the Germans, whose racial qualities had enabled them so far to withstand a numerically superior foe. But the peoples of the east, although inferior racially and lacking creative ability, could and did imitate German technology and organization. With their unlimited numbers, equipped with German-invented weapons and using German military techniques, it was only a question of time before these eastern masses would overrun the insignificant area to which the Germans were restricted.[10] The exigencies of Germanic security could only be met by the possession of more land. Hitler examined the alternatives to territorial expansion and rejected each as he considered it.

The Germans could, Hitler reasoned, follow the French example and restrict the percentage of population increase by a wider use of birth control. But once propagation was limited, the natural struggle for existence which selected those who were most worthy to survive would give way to an effort to keep alive every human being that was born. The number of people would certainly be restricted, but the value of each individidual would also be lowered. A people that defied nature in this way would some day be forced to give up its place to a stronger generation. To restrict the natural growth of the German population would mean nothing less than to rob the German people of their future.[11]

Hitler next disposed of the possibility of solving the problem by the intensification of domestic production. Through industry and trade food could be purchased to support a growing population, but the First World War had proven to Hitler that an imported food supply was hardly a source of security to a nation. Real economic security could only be achieved by ensuring a people its daily bread within the sphere of its domestic economy. There was, however, a limit to the possibility of increasing agricultural productivity. In Germany higher living standards had already consumed the increased yield resulting from better farming methods, and the constant use of artificial fertilizers was beginning to burn out the soil. A further growth of German agricultural production, therefore, seemed out of the question.[12]

Hitler was a thoroughgoing Malthusian in his fear of the time when it would no longer be possible to adapt the fertility of the soil to the increasing population. In the distant future, nature would have to solve this problem in her own way, but Hitler believed that in his own era only those nations would be in distress which lacked the will to secure for themselves the soil they required of the world. Should the Germans out of mistaken humanitarianism restrict their own expansion and thereby be forced to limit their population, they would be overwhelmed in the future by the sheer weight of numbers of inferior races who had space to reproduce without limit.[13]

Hitler's decisive argument in favor of territorial expansion, however, was the disastrous effect of territorial deficiency on the German military position. It was not only a question of inadequate manpower. Hitler's study of military history had convinced him that a nation's strategic security was in direct proportion to its territorial dimensions. Military victories over nations restricted to narrow boundaries were always more easily achieved and more complete than over nations inhabiting a large land mass. As Germany was situated at the time Hitler wrote *Mein Kampf*, a coalition of hostile powers could not only defeat Germany. They could destroy it for good.

What was involved here, Hitler said, was not the fate of some insignificant Negro tribe; the German mother of all life was in danger. The threat embraced not simply a people, but world civilization. Greater territory alone could give the Germans adequate security for the present; only more land could guarantee their future. Since the rest of the world could not become German, the Germans would have to spread more widely over the rest of the world. This was not simply a moral right; it was a moral duty.[14]

Hitler next addressed himself to the question of where the most practicable territorial acquisitions could be made at the lowest possible cost. Although a demand for colonies was embodied in the official Nazi party program, Hitler himself was convinced that overseas colonies could meet but few of Germany's requirements. The problem was not one of conquering and exploiting people, but of acquiring agriculturally useful space. The majority of so-called colonial territories were hardly fit for large-scale European settlement. Nor would overseas colonies provide the national security Hitler demanded of an expansionist policy. The Netherlands and Portugal were cases in point, and even Britain was no longer proof to the contrary. In admiring the strength of the British Empire, Hitler said, one was prone to forget its dependence on the Anglo-Saxon world as such. Not Britain's colonial empire but its fortunate linguistic and cultural communion with the United States was the real strength of its position. So for Britain, too, security ultimately resided in the resources of a continental power. Germany, which could not depend on American support, must seek its security elsewhere. Overseas colonies were for Hitler no more than a diplomatic and propagandistic weapon. He definitely rejected them as a solution to German needs. The struggle that would in any case be involved in the acquisition of territory could be carried out most suitably, not in faraway lands across the sea, but in the home continent itself. Through the conquest of contiguous territory the natural reproduction of the race, its bread, and its strategic security would all be assured.[15]

Hitler then specifically named his intended victim. If one wanted land and soil on the European continent, the conquests of real value for the future could be achieved by and large only at Russia's expense. There was no question but that there had to be a final reckoning with France, but the defeat of France would be a hollow victory if German policy were restricted thereto. The elimination of the French threat would have and would retain significance only if it provided the rear cover for an enlargement of the German domain in Eastern Europe. National Socialism, therefore, consciously abandoned the foreign policy of the Second Reich. Germany was to cease its fruitless pursuit of a colonial policy and, above all, its drive to the south and west. The Third Reich intended to resume the Germanic expansionist program where it had stopped six hundred years ago, and to press once again over the routes of the medieval crusading orders into the lands of the east.[16]

Hitler believed that fate itself had given the Germans an advantage at this point. In the surrender of Russia to Bolshevism, the Russian people had been robbed of that intelligentsia which heretofore had produced and guaranteed Russia's stability as a state. The Russian Empire was not an achievement of the Slavs, but rather a wonderful example of the state-building capacity of the Germans as leaders of an inferior race. According to the precepts of Hitler's theology, inferior nations with German organizers had more than once expanded into powerful state structures and endured as long as the nucleus of the constructive race maintained itself. As a result of the Bolshevik Revolution, however, the Germanic governing stratum of Russia had been destroyed and replaced by that ferment of decomposition, the Jews. Russia was ripe for Germany's plucking.[17]

Hitler envisioned a German future based primarily on independent German landowners. The lands which in the past had been profitably Germanized were those which the ancient Germans had acquired by the sword and settled with German peasants. The mission of the National Socialist movement was to give the German nation such political insight as to see its future goal fulfilled, not in the intoxicating impressions of a new Alexandrian campaign, but in the consolidation of military victories by the industrious labor of the German peasant.

7

The Germans would thereby gain not only national security but social security. A nation in communion with the soil would no longer be subject to the restlessness that besets industrial societies and would automatically be freed from many of the social evils of the industrial age. Industry and trade would be forced out of their unwholesome positions of leadership in the national economy into the framework of a more balanced national life. Cities were to be decentralized and made the servants rather than the focal points of society. A people living close to nature and the real fountains of life, a people divorced from the artificial cultural flowering of city pavements, would form a stable society, rich in its appreciation of the real values of life, a sound foundation for true cultural creativity. Never should Germany feel itself secure until it was able to give each citizen his own bit of earth. To possess his own land and to till his own soil was the most sacred right of man.[18]

Hitler had no intention of repeating the mistakes of the ancient Germans whose conquests of land had included conquests of people. The incorporation of non-Germans had in the past resulted in the cleavage in the soul as well as in the body politic of the nation which had been so disastrous in German history, and which had so long prevented the Germans from assuming their natural position of leadership in the world. To establish a sound foundation for German security, the acquisition of soil would have to be accompanied by the purification, by which Hitler meant the Germanization, of the population.[19] In the many areas where Germanization would be impossible, the indigenous population was to be made useful, or removed. In this way alone could expansion be effected without diluting and thereby defeating the conquerors. It was only necessary to recall the suicidal example of the Spaniards, whose intermarriage with inferior native peoples had resulted in racial degradation and national decay. The British, although largely avoiding the error of intermarriage, were also pursuing a mistaken policy, for ultimately they would find it impossible to hold together an empire of three hundred million with a population of forty-five million.

Neither Spain nor Britain should be the models of German expansion, but the Nordics of North America, who had ruthlessly pushed aside an inferior race to win for themselves soil and territory for the future. To undertake this essential task, sometimes difficult, always cruel—this was Hitler's version of the White Man's Burden.[20]

Hitler warned that the fulfillment of his program would require work and sacrifice on an unprecedented scale. The needs of the German race could only be met by pouring into their fulfillment the undivided devotion and entire energy of the German people. The entire authority of the state, too, would have to be dedicated to this end. All

8

policies would have to be based on the consideration of the future security of the German race. To guarantee this security, and with it the future of world civilization, any and all means were justified. One had to make clear to oneself that this goal could only be achieved through fighting, and quietly to face the passage at arms.[21]

There would be war. The attacker would have to overcome the proprietor. Professors and other intellectuals might talk of peaceful economic conquest, but such folly could emanate only from the wishful thinking of those unacquainted with life. Only naïve idealists could believe that through friendly and civilized behavior a people might gather the fruits of its ability and endeavor in peaceful competition. Where had economic interests not clashed as brutally as political interests? There were those who pointed to Britain as an example of the success of peaceful economic penetration, but it was precisely in Britain that this theory was most strikingly refuted. No nation had more savagely prepared its economic conquests with the sword, and none had defended those conquests more ruthlessly.[22]

Although Hitler looked to the east as the land of the German future, he realized that in all probability he would not be allowed a free hand there. The moment Germany was deeply involved in campaigns in the east, France would almost certainly seize the opportunity to fall on Germany's flank. The result would be a two-front war, which would be all the more dangerous because the French, by penetrating German land or air defenses in the Ruhr, could deal a mortal blow to the German war economy. To enable Germany to neutralize or eliminate the French threat, Hitler advocated alliances with Italy and Britain. For this purpose he was prepared to concede Italy hegemony in the Mediterranean and give up all German claims to the South Tyrol, and to abandon or drastically curtail Germany's colonial, naval, and economic rivalry with Britain. Hitler actually concluded an alliance with Italy and, as late as his attack on Russia in 1941, he clung to the hope that the British, recognizing how much to their own advantage was the destruction of Russia and international Bolshevism, might yet be persuaded to concede Germany supremacy on the continent in return for a German guarantee of the British Empire and other favors.[23]

By the later 1930s, however, Hitler had begun to take into account the possibility that his efforts to woo Britain might fail, and that a major drive to extend German dominion in the east would be opposed by Britain as well as France. In that event the danger to the Ruhr would be even greater and it would be all the more necessary to knock out the threat in the west before launching his drive in the east.[24]

Hitler foresaw the possibility of a near future totally consecrated to the needs of war. During that period the abnormal demands of military necessity might exclude cultural tasks altogether, but the sacrifice would be justified. The cultural opportunities of a nation were almost always linked to its political freedom and independence. After the concentration of all endeavor in military affairs had won the required freedom, there would follow a period of compensation in which the hitherto neglected fountains of culture would flow as never before. Out of the Persian Wars had emerged the Golden Age of Pericles, and out of the tortured era of the Punic Wars the Roman state, too, began to dedicate itself to the service of a higher culture. So it would be with Germany.[25]

The conquest of Russia was to be the first step. What would be required by Germans at a later date would have to be left to subsequent generations. The development of great world-wide national bodies was naturally a slow process. But of one thing Hitler was certain, and he concluded *Mein Kampf* with the thought: "A state which, in the epoch of race poisoning, dedicates itself to the cherishing of its best racial elements, must some day be master of the world." [26]

When the Aryan race should at last have spread over the entire world, one might then think of an era of peace as an ideal. But it would be a peace supported not by the palm branches of tearful pacifists, but founded on the victorious sword of a people of overlords who had put the world into the service of a higher culture.[27]

CHAPTER 2

Hitler, the Party, and the State

The Rule of Hitler

One of the most remarkable features of the history of Germany under National Socialism was the extent to which Hitler imposed his personal authority on the German people and state. The point cannot be stressed too strongly: Hitler was master in the Third Reich. In the political cockpit of postwar Germany he had triumphed over experienced politicians, many of them with strong military and financial backing, and over the power-hungry adventurers who made up the leadership corps of his own and other upstart political parties. After coming to power he subjected business and labor, the army and the police, and indeed every significant group and organization to his control. In the vicious conflicts for authority among the officials of the Third Reich, there was never any question of challenging the authority of Hitler himself. On the contrary, these conflicts were submitted to Hitler for arbitration, and his decision, although it might be resented, was nevertheless unquestioningly accepted. Deviationists among his supporters there might be, opponents might occasionally sidetrack or sabotage his programs, but in all essential respects it was Hitler who determined German policy during the Nazi era.

With all his idealization of the German people, Hitler handled Germans and foreigners alike with the same cynical calculation. In dealing with subordinates he frankly acknowledged his principles of collaboration: No official should be informed of any policy in which he was not immediately concerned; none should be told more about a policy than was absolutely necessary; and none should learn about a policy earlier than its effective execution demanded.[1] What Hitler told his associates depended entirely on what he wished them to know; and, perhaps to an even greater extent, on what he wished

11

them to think. Every speech, every statement, was consciously geared to the audience involved. Herein lies the explanation for the apparent contradictions in many of the plans Hitler spun into the political atmosphere of prewar and wartime Europe. His intention was clearly to retain absolute control of policy making and to keep the reins of authority in his own hands.[2]

Despite the immense power wielded by Hitler and his concentration of authority in his own person, the rule he imposed on Germany and subsequently on the greater part of Europe bore little resemblance to the centralized and logical administration introduced during the period of the French Revolution and Napoleon. Hitler and his henchmen talked much of German order and efficiency, but neither their party nor state administrations were characterized by these qualities.

The administrative confusion already existing in Germany due to the overlapping institutions of the central government of the Reich, the state government of Prussia, and the governments of the smaller German states was compounded after the Nazis came to power by the juxtaposition of the Nazi party administration and the various state administrations.[3] The appointment of the heads of the party offices to similar offices in the state made for a certain co-ordination of leadership, yet the offices themselves were deliberately kept separate to preserve both as instruments of control. Because of the existence of this dual administration, it was often impossible to determine through which channels an official was operating and where the authority in a particular field actually lay.[4] This system was favored by Hitler for it left him in the role of supreme arbitrator, but it did not contribute to administrative efficiency.

Neither did other Hitlerian rulership techniques. To enable his officials to carry out their assignments most effectively he gave them broad authority and considerable freedom of action, thereby taking advantage of their drive and initiative while at least partially satisfying their craving for power. At the same time he developed a complex system of checks and balances among party and state offices by actively sponsoring competition among his subordinates, assigning high-ranking officials to strategic positions within the spheres of competence of their rivals, and creating new offices to supervise or co-ordinate the activities of the old. The majority of high-ranking officials were directly responsible to Hitler, but even those who were not were encouraged to appeal to him over the heads of their nominal superiors.

Hitler's deliberate encouragement of initiative and rivalry among his followers brought to the fore the most power hungry and ruthless among them, a group of leaders who undeniably succeeded in getting things done, but who in the end generally added to the administrative confusion. For once in a position of power these men sought to build up their own administrative empires and to provide jobs for their personal supporters, a procedure that led to the establishment of new agencies and offices to add to those regularly being created by Hitler.

The result was a veritable administrative maze, a crisscross of competences and overlapping of powers and responsibilities that further exacerbated the rivalries among Nazi leaders. It was a system fully in line with Hitler's conception of the organic growth of German political institutions; [5] for the various offices of party and state, their functions, and the power relationships among them were in a process of constant flux. Administrative redundancy and bureaucratic infighting, were, in fact, the predominant characteristics of Nazi rule in Germany and the German-occupied territories.

Because of the nature of this rule, diagrams or simple descriptions of the Nazi administrative organization are virtually meaningless, especially if they are meant to apply to an extended period of time. At best the Nazi government can be understood by examining some of the theories behind it, and by following the process of its development.

The Role of the State and Party in Nazi Political Theory

In National Socialist political theory the state was conceived as a means to an end, which was defined by Hitler as *"the care for the preservation of those racial primal elements which, supplying culture, create the beauty and dignity of a higher humanity."* But that was not all. In his next sentence Hitler went on to say: *"We, as Aryans, are therefore able to imagine a state only to be the living organism of a nationality which not only safeguards the preservation of that nationality, but which, by a further training of its spiritual and ideal abilities, leads it to the highest freedom."* With these words Hitler stated as succinctly as he ever stated anything his conception of the triple position of the state: as the living organism of a nationality, as the preserver of the nationality, and as the molding force of the nationality. The state was, therefore, not solely a functional apparatus that could be used or laid aside at will. The state was an emanation of the *Volk*, and the form in which the *Volk* attained to historical reality and spiritual stature.[6]

Had Nazi theorists rigidly held to Hitler's conception of the state as an outgrowth of the *Volk*, they would have been compelled to acknowledge the legitimacy of every governmental structure in German history, including the one they overthrew. They circumvented this difficulty by absolving the Germans from all responsibility for those state systems which failed to harmonize with National Socialist political philosophy. The Weimar Republic, for instance, far from being a Germanic creation, was an excrescence of Jewish-capitalist influences. Even Bismarck's Second Reich was not totally free from foreign corruptions and could not be regarded as the perfect prototype of a Germanic state structure.

Not surprisingly, the Nazis had trouble finding examples of their version of an ideal German state; eventually they were compelled to turn to an era almost totally lacking in written or archaeological records. The ancient Germans, Nazi historians said, had developed a high culture in all fields, be it in dress, artistic creativity, or communal organization. "The point of view based on Latin sources, and especially on Tacitus, that the ancient Germans were barbarians who led the most primitive sort of existence had to be thoroughly revised." Without the inconvenience of sources, the Nazis proceeded to create the ideal Germanic past in their own image, and demonstrated, at least to their own satisfaction, that their movement was a renewal of the purest form of Germanic social organization.[7]

The conception of the state as an organism of the people made possible a justification of the state's interference in every phase of the people's existence. There could be no private sphere of individual rights beyond the authority of the state. The basic component of the state was not the isolated individual, but the *Volksgenosse*,[8] who was an organic part of the community. The state had been born out of the necessity of regulating the community according to certain laws. The state therefore had the right to demand that every *Volksgenosse* live according to those laws, which were in themselves an organic product of the people.[9]

While seeming to grant absolute authority to the state, Nazi theorists took care not to accord the state and its laws a position of inviolability. "The state is no longer an independent idol before which all else must bow down," said Rosenberg.[10] The absolute value was not the state, but the *Volk*. The *Volk*, however, was no stagnant organism; it throbbed with dynamic energies striving toward higher and more perfect forms. The progress of the nation demanded that the leaders "create for the Germanic community forms which are ever new and suited to its vital development." [11] With this interpretation of the relationship between *Volk* and state, the Nazi political philosophers subjected the people to the authority of the state, while giving their own leaders the right to change it as they thought fit.

The National Socialist emphasis on the *Volk* was not simply a casuistic rationalization of their leaders' position above the law. Hitler recognized what so many administrators neglect—that it was not so much the structure of the organization that mattered as the spirit of the men who filled it. "We must distinguish sharply between the state as a vessel and the race as the content," he said. One might draft a model constitution or plan the most perfect military campaign, yet both would be worthless unless the people for whom the constitution was intended were imbued with a desire to maintain the spirit of its laws, or the men who made up the army had the will to fight. Hitler believed that the basic weakness of all rival German parties except the Communist was their failure to provide their followers with a militant faith. In describing the difficulties of earlier German nationalist movements he wrote: "The question involved was not that of a new party, but that of a new life. The latter alone was able to summon the internal strength to fight out this gigantic struggle." The problem was not, "How can we manufacture arms?" but, "How can we produce that spirit which enables a people to bear arms?" [12]

With all his emphasis on the importance of the spirit to fill an organization, Hitler was even more aware of the need for an organization to channel the spirit. The effectiveness of Marxism, he believed, was due in large measure to its embodiment in a powerful and highly efficient political organization, which had heretofore been opposed in Germany by a hodgepodge of political sentiments lacking all form and definition. "Victories are not won by such weak weapons!" Hitler said. "Not until the international view of life—politically led by organized Marxism—is opposed by the *völkisch* view of life, just as uniformly organized and led with equal fighting energy, will success take the side of eternal truth." [13]

Hitler conceived of the National Socialist party as an instrument to embody and fight for the *völkisch* view of life; and the spirit he thought to have evoked for the movement was nothing less than the *Weltanschauung* [14] of the German people. The party was to crystallize around itself the feelings of the people, which seemed buried, and the strength of the people, which seemed lost.[15] Nazi leaders looked upon their movement as a revolution in the deepest sense because it was meant to overturn and banish all non-German values. "National Socialism," said Goebbels, "has simplified the thinking of the German people and led it back to its original primitive formulas." [16]

Hitler intended the National Socialist party to fulfill two decisive tasks. The first of these was to bring the German people back into harmony with their own conceptions, by which Hitler meant winning them over to National Socialism. This was primarily a matter of education. The second task, inseparable from the first, was "to join the

15

people and the state into the unity of the nation." This meant getting control of the state.[17]

National Socialist education, according to Hitler, was to be no weak emphasis on so-called objective viewpoints, but "a ruthless and fanatically one-sided orientation as to the goal to be aimed at." He had described the nature of this goal in *Mein Kampf*, which Nazi youth was to learn by heart "to answer the questions of doubtful and deliberating critics." In the place of objectivity National Socialist education was to inculcate faith, because faith was more difficult to undermine than knowledge. The decisive changes effected by men in world history had not been brought about by leaders able to convince their followers through reason, but by those capable of winning their unquestioning loyalty and inspiring them with fanatic enthusiasm.[18]

The emphasis of party educators was to be on youth. Young people were less likely to be contaminated by factual knowledge than their elders, and were generally more susceptible to appeals to idealism and emotion. The entire work of education was to find its culmination in branding indelibly, through instinct and reason, the race sense and the race feeling into the hearts and minds of the next generation of Germans. "The *völkisch* state will have to see to it," Hitler said, "that by a suitable education of youth, a mature generation is produced for the ultimate and greatest decisions of this globe." [19]

CHAPTER 3

The Attainment and Consolidation of Power[1]

Effective control of *völkisch* education of course could only be achieved after the fulfillment of the party's second decisive task, namely gaining control of the state. Hitler had many theories and plans about how such control might be effected, but they were never so clearly formulated as his views on diplomatic tactics or the ultimate goals of Nazi policy.

During the turbulent period of the Ruhr occupation and the inflation, Hitler evidently hoped to emulate the success of the minority Bolshevik party in Russia, but, after the failure of his Munich Putsch in 1923, he did not again attempt a violent overthrow of the government. Instead he concentrated on establishing his personal control over the party and building up its national and regional organization with the primary object of scoring successes at the polls. While still in prison following the 1923 uprising, he told a visiting party member,

> When I resume active work it will be necessary to pursue a new policy. Instead of working to achieve power by an armed *coup*, we shall have to hold our noses and enter the Reichstag against the Catholic and Marxist deputies. If out-voting them takes longer than out-shooting them, at least the results will be guaranteed by their own Constitution! Any lawful process is slow. But already, as you know, we have thirty-two Reichstag deputies under this new program, and are the second largest party in the Bavarian parliament. Sooner or later we shall have a majority—and after that, Germany. I am convinced this is our best line of action, now that conditions in the country have changed so radically.[2]

17

Nazi leaders were absolutely candid about the ultimate purpose of their parliamentary tactics. "We enter the Reichstag," Goebbels wrote in an article of 1928, "in order to supply ourselves in the very arsenal of democracy with its own weapons. We become members of the Reichstag in order to paralyze the Weimar sentiment with its own institutions. If democracy is so stupid as to give us free travel privileges and per diem allowances for this destructive service, that is its affair." [3]

Hitler spoke in much the same way ten days after the great Nazi election victories in September 1930.

> If today our action employs among its different weapons that of parliament, that is not to say that parliamentary parties exist only for parliamentary ends. For us parliament is not an end in itself, but merely a means to an end. . . . We are not on principle a parliamentary party—that would be a contradiction of our whole outlook—we are a parliamentary party by compulsion, under constraint, and that compulsion is the constitution. The constitution compels us to use this means. . . . And so this victory that we have just won is nothing else than the winning of a new weapon for our fight. . . . It is not for seats in parliament that we fight, but we win seats in parliament in order that one day we will be able to liberate the German people. [4]

A prominent Nazi political theorist was equally explicit and rather more succinct: "The parliamentary battle of the NSDAP had the single purpose of destroying the parliamentary system from within through its own methods. It was necessary above all to make formal use of the possibilities of the party-state system but to refuse real co-operation and thereby render the parliamentary system, which by its nature is dependent upon the responsible co-operation of the opposition, incapable of action." [5]

Hitler had not renounced the use of force in seizing power; he simply feared he did not have enough force to do so successfully. "My decision to obtain power constitutionally," he told his associates later, "was influenced primarily by my knowledge of the attitude of the Wehrmacht *vis à vis* the Chancellorship. If I had seized power illegally, the Wehrmacht would have constituted a dangerous breeding place for a *coup d'état* . . . ; by acting constitutionally, on the other hand, I was in a position to restrict the activities of the Wehrmacht to its legal and strictly limited military function." [6]

During the years of prosperity in Germany following the introduction of a stable currency, Hitler's parliamentary campaign was a failure. In the Reichstag elections of December 1924, just after he came out of prison, the Nazis lost over 1,000,000 votes and over half the seats they and their allies had won in the previous May, their total vote being reduced to 907,300, their seats in the Reichstag to 14. In 1928 their vote fell still further and their representation in the Reichstag was reduced to 12. During the same period they failed to gain control of a single state parliament. They did, however, succeed in enlarging their party membership from 27,000 to over 100,000 and in extending their party organization to every part of Germany.[7]

Not until the coming of the great depression did the Nazis make any significant headway in the German parliamentary system, but then their rise was spectacular. After registering small gains in regional elections in 1929, they established themselves as a major national party in the Reichstag election of September 1930 by winning 107 seats and 6,410,000 votes (18.3 per cent of the total votes cast) as compared to their 1928 showing of 12 seats and 810,000 votes (2.6 per cent of the total). In July 1932 they more than doubled their strength in winning 230 seats and 13,746,000 votes (37.3 per cent of the total).

Nazi electoral gains in 1929 were achieved in part through their exploitation of general hostility to the German government's acceptance of the Young Plan, which provided for the payment of war reparations until 1988, and through their alliance with the German Nationalist party, which gave them greater social respectability and access to new sources of funds and influence. Growing unemployment, however, had already set in during 1928, and the New York stock market crash of October 1929 added to the economic, and even more to the psychological, effects of this development.

After 1929 Nazi electoral gains appear to be directly related to the rise in German unemployment. According to official figures, which did not include unregistered unemployed and part-time workers, 1,300,000 employable workers were unemployed in September 1929; one year later this figure had risen to 3,000,000; a year after that to 4,350,000; and in 1932 to 5,100,000. In the winter months of 1931–32 and 1932–33 unemployment exceeded 6,000,000, which meant that one out of every two families was affected.

To register a protest against the existing governmental system, which seemed incapable of dealing with the catastrophic economic situation, and in their desperate search for some kind of remedy, no matter how extreme, the middle classes and peasants turned in large numbers to the Nazi movement, which promised all things to all people, while the urban laborers tended to look to the Communists, whose vote rose from 3,265,000 in 1928, to 5,283,000 in July 1932, and to almost 6,000,000 in November 1932.

Despite the impressive showing of his party at the polls, Hitler's goal of an absolute electoral majority eluded him. His gains had been achieved largely at the expense of the small parties of the middle and the right; but having swallowed these he found himself unable to go further. In the various national and local elections during the spring and summer of 1932 the percentage of the Nazi vote increased very little, and in the Reichstag elections of November of that year they suffered a serious defeat, losing 2,000,000 votes and 34 seats. In December they suffered a further setback in Thuringia, previously a Nazi stronghold. These Nazi electoral defeats may have been the result of a slight improvement in the economic situation in the autumn of 1932, but it is more probable that the Nazi movement had reached its peak in July and that opportunistic supporters were beginning to lose faith in the party. In contrast to Nazi losses in the November elections, the Communists gained over 700,000 votes. Serious rifts began to appear within the Nazi party, financial support was drying up, the party was deeply in debt.[8] "The year 1932 has brought us eternal ill-luck," Goebbels wrote in his diary toward the end of December. "The past was sad, and the future looks dark and gloomy; all chances and hopes have quite disappeared." [9]

Had the opposition to Hitler within the Nazi party found able or determined leadership, had the parties of the center and left closed ranks against him, the history of Germany might have been very different. But in his domestic policy in the early 1930s as in his foreign policy later in the decade, Hitler was fortunate in the quality of his opponents. His principal adversary in the Nazi party, Gregor Strasser, who stood for a more radically socialist version of National Socialism, lost stomach for a showdown fight and, instead of leading a revolt against Hitler, he resigned from the party and fled abroad. Meanwhile the effectiveness of rival political organizations continued to be hampered by inner-party feuds. The leaders of the parties of the middle and the right, instead of closing ranks against Hitler, sought to make a deal with him in order to enlist him as an ally against the left and in their own factional struggles, confident that they could control Hitler and get rid of him when they no longer found him useful.

Hitler was willing enough to make a deal. Having failed to secure a popular majority in his own right he realized he needed to secure support from other quarters; but for a time all negotiations with other parties foundered because Hitler's price was too high. In January 1933, however, Hitler reached agreement with the conservative ex-chancellor Franz von Papen. Papen did not have decisive Reichstag votes to offer. The strength of his bargaining position lay in his close association with President Hindenburg, whose emergency powers under the Weimar constitution included the right to appoint a chancellor without a parliamentary majority and to promulgate legislation without parliamentary sanction. Papen had a good deal of difficulty persuading the conservative and aristocratic Hindenburg to accept Hitler; he eventually succeeded only by demonstrating to the president's satisfaction that the conditions he had imposed on Hitler would make him a "chancellor in chains."

Papen's terms indeed seemed stringent. Hitler agreed to respect the Weimar constitution, to maintain law and order, and to leave reliable experts at the head of all important government departments. Papen was to be vice-chancellor with the right to be present at all official interviews between the president and chancellor, a right no minister had heretofore possessed. In addition Papen was to be head of the government (*Reichskommissar*) of Prussia, a position which gave him authority over the administration—and the police—of the largest of the German states. Appointments to the key cabinet posts of foreign affairs and defense (with authority over the armed forces) were reserved for the president, and almost all other positions in the cabinet were to be filled by well-known and politically trustworthy conservatives. The new chancellor was to have only two cabinet appointments: the Ministry of the Interior (without control of the police), and a Ministry without Portfolio. This composition of the cabinet seemed to guarantee a decisive voice for conservative interests; for, according to the Weimar constitution, questions of policy were to be determined by the entire cabinet and differences of opinion were to be settled by majority vote. As conservatives also controlled the German army and exercised a preponderant influence in business and financial circles, they would, in effect, govern the country. Hitler himself would be safely under their control, and his mass movement would provide desirable popular support for their administration.[10]

Although the Nazis liked to refer to the events of January 1933 as their seizure of power, no seizure of any kind was involved. Hitler was appointed chancellor by the president on January 30, 1933, in full accordance with the letter of the law. The National Socialist revolution that took place after that date was not a seizure but a consolidation of power, a gradual extension of control over the instruments of power, and the use of those instruments to impose Hitler's political and ideological program on Germany. In the process of carrying out this revolution Hitler insisted on maintaining the fiction of legality, fearing that any flagrant violation of the law might serve as an excuse for the conservative leaders to call upon their allies, the German generals, to overthrow him.[11]

Hitler evaded cabinet control by circumventing or simply ignoring it. His first step in the legal consolidation of power was to ask President Hindenburg to dissolve the Reichstag and call for new elections. He made this request with the obvious calculation that by the time new elections were held his followers would have exerted sufficient pressure on the German voters to give him the two-thirds majority in the Reichstag needed to pass constitutional amendments, and therewith the power to secure legal passage of any legislation he desired. The president and his advisers saw through Hitler's game, which was transparent enough, but Hindenburg himself had long insisted on having a chancellor with a working majority in the Reichstag. As Hitler had foreseen, neither the president nor his advisers dared oppose him on this issue. Accordingly the Reichstag was dissolved and new elections were set for March 5.[12] "The struggle is an easy one now," Goebbels wrote in his diary on February 3, "since we are able to employ all means of the state. Radio and press are at our disposal. We shall achieve a masterpiece of propaganda. Even money is not lacking this time." [13]

To leave as little as possible to chance, Hitler persuaded the president on February 4 to issue a decree "For the Protection of the German People," which was ostensibly intended to help the government preserve law and order.[14] It conferred on government officials the right to prohibit public meetings and the wearing of a uniform. All political meetings had to be announced to the police forty-eight hours in advance, and they could be forbidden "if public security would be endangered." Newspapers could be suppressed for similar reasons. As the enforcement of the decree was shortly to be almost entirely in the hands of the Nazis, it soon became apparent which German people it was designed to protect.

In Prussia it was Papen who once again unwittingly opened the door to Nazi influence. On the grounds that the Prussian government was in a state of confusion, he persuaded the president to issue a decree on February 6, 1933, transferring all powers of the Prussian Ministry of State to himself as Reich governor.[15] Papen undoubtedly expected this decree to strengthen his own position, but he had not reckoned on Nazi ruthlessness or the person of Hermann Göring, whom he had been obliged to accept as Prussian minister of the interior.

Göring was one of the few Nazi leaders who had won national renown before the Nazis came to power, or who, apart from Hitler himself, enjoyed any widespread personal popularity.[16] He was also one of the few Nazi leaders to come from a Prussian, or at least a semi-Prussian, background. A number of his paternal ancestors had been high-ranking Prussian civil servants, and his father, Heinrich Göring, had been selected by Bismarck to be the first governor of German Southwest Africa. Göring's mother, however, was Austrian, and Hermann himself was born in a sanatorium in Bavaria in January 1893 while his father was consul-general in Haiti. As a child Göring spent a great deal of time in Austria and Bavaria, and he became deeply attached to both countries. It was as a member of the Bavarian Group of the Nazi party that he first rose to prominence in the party's affairs.

During the First World War, Göring achieved fame as a flying ace. He was awarded the *Pour le Mérite,* Germany's most distinguished military decoration; at the close of the war he was commander of the celebrated Richthofen squadron. Embittered by defeat and the terms of the Versailles treaty, he joined the Nazi party in 1922, and was severely wounded in the Munich Putsch in November of the following year. After being amnestied in 1925 for his part in that affair, he became Hitler's chief negotiator with military, business, and conservative leaders. In contrast to the shy and awkward Hitler, Göring was a genial extrovert who got along well with people and gave the Nazi party a front of respectability.

But beneath Göring's jovial, easy-going manner, and his seemingly innocent enjoyment of medals and uniforms—the butt of so many jokes at home and abroad—lay the characteristics of the typical Nazi leader: driving ambition, tempered by neither conscience nor scruple, with the added qualities in his case of guile and political resourcefulness. Sir David Maxwell-Fyfe, Britain's deputy chief prosecutor at the Nuremberg trials, characterized him: "He had a quick brain, an excellent memory, a complete mastery of political approach to mass German opinion, courage, and power to get himself liked by the great majority of people that he met. When these qualities are coupled with complete ruthlessness, vanity, and greed, you have a figure that could not be laughed off." [17]

In 1933 Göring came to the fore as a principal instrument in Hitler's consolidation of power. As Prussian minister of the interior, he was nominally under the authority of Papen, the head of the Prussian government. Göring, however, simply ignored Papen and proceeded to carry out a systematic purge of the Prussian civil service, including the police. With Göring appointees in all key positions, there was nothing Papen could do to assert his authority for there was no one to carry out his orders. Not Papen, therefore, but Göring profited from the transfer of power to the Reich governor.

While extending Nazi power in Prussia, Göring used every means at his disposal to influence the outcome of the forthcoming elections. On February 17 he ordered the Prussian police actively to support the Nazi party militia, the *Sturm Abteilung* (SA), and its ally, the nationalist *Stahlhelm* veterans' organization, in combatting "enemies of the state" and suppressing Communist acts of terrorism. "Police officials who make use of firearms in the execution of this duty can count on my support regardless of the consequences of their action," his order said. On February 22 Göring went so far as to reinforce the regular police force with "special constables," which meant the outright enrollment of the Nazi militia in the regular Prussian police.[18]

On February 27 the Reichstag was set on fire, an act apparently perpetrated by a deranged Dutch arsonist named Marinus van der Lubbe as a demonstration of protest against the Nazi regime, but one so convenient for Nazi purposes that Göring later boasted of having engineered the whole incident himself.[19] The Nazis charged that the fire was part of a world-wide Communist conspiracy, the signal for a Jewish-Bolshevik attempt to seize control of the German government. To defend the German people from further acts of Communist violence, they now demanded new and far more extensive emergency powers. In response to Nazi pressure, the president on February 28 issued a decree "For the Protection of the German People and State," which suspended all rights of the individual previously guaranteed by the Weimar constitution.[20] Far more significantly, it provided that if any German state government such as Bavaria or Baden failed to take adequate measures to preserve public security and order, the central Reich government should have the right to intervene and establish its own authority. This decree, in effect, broke whatever resistance German state and local government might have offered to Nazi control, for it empowered Hitler to install his henchmen in all state governments with powers similar to those Göring was already exercising in Prussia.[21]

With the promulgation of the presidential decrees of February 4 and 28, the Nazis had a free hand to deal, legally, with their opponents, and they made full use of their opportunities. Thousands of leftist leaders, including all Communist deputies and officials, were arrested, as were other prominent opponents of the regime. Those not jailed were subjected to physical violence and intimidation. Goebbels's propaganda machine had all the facilities of the state at its disposal, and the Nazi militia roamed the streets with complete freedom to employ any kind of brutality. Yet with all the cards seemingly in their hands, and despite their frenetic activity, the Nazis still polled only 43.9 per cent of the total vote in the Reichstag elections of March 5, their Nationalist allies a bare 8 per cent. Together these parties still lacked the two-thirds majority needed to pass constitutional amendments.

Hitler did not pause to interpret the election results, but set to work to create his two-thirds majority. The Nazis had allowed Communist candidates to stand for election on March 5, perhaps to preserve the appearance of legality but more likely to flush out and identify Communist sympathizers. They now declared the Communist party to be illegal on the basis of the president's decree of February

28, and the eighty-one elected Communist deputies were not invited to take their seats in the Reichstag. This cut down the opposition significantly, but by now all Reichstag deputies were under the severest kind of physical and psychological pressure. With the Kroll Opera House, where the Reichstag was now meeting, surrounded by Nazi storm troopers, every deputy was aware that voting against the Nazis might result in physical violence, imprisonment, or death. With considerable heroism the Socialist deputies resisted Nazi pressure, but all other parties succumbed, and on March 23 the Reichstag passed the so-called Enabling Act. With some justification the Nazis called this law the First Organic Statute of the Third Reich, for it conferred the power to issue decrees, heretofore the prerogative of the Reichstag or, in emergency situations, of the president, on the Reich government and therewith gave Hitler supreme legislative as well as executive power.[22]

After March 23 the Reichstag was without power of any kind and was significant only as an indication of Nazi intentions in occupied territories. For those areas which Hitler proposed to incorporate in his Greater German Reich were distinguished by having the right to be represented in the Reichstag, if only by representatives chosen by himself.[23]

With the Reichstag reduced to nullity, Hitler proceeded against rival political parties. The Communists had already been outlawed. On May 10, 1933, all socialist parties were prohibited. On June 21 the Stahlhelm was incorporated into the Nazi party (it was dissolved altogether on November 11, 1935). On June 27 the Nationalist party dissolved itself, and on July 5 all Catholic political organizations were obliged to disband. Since the Nazis claimed that they alone represented the true will of the German people, they published a law on July 14, 1933, making the reconstruction of old parties or the formation of new ones an act of treason.[24]

Upon the death of President Hindenburg on August 2, 1934, Hitler eliminated the last office to rival his supreme authority in the central government. Using the powers vested in him by the Enabling Act, he issued a decree merging the offices of Reich president and Reich chancellor and transferring the powers heretofore exercised by the president to himself.[25] This was a move of great significance, for the president was supreme commander of Germany's armed forces (article 47 of the Weimar constitution). The title of Reich president with its republican connotations was almost never used by Hitler thereafter. His title remained the same as before: Führer and Reich chancellor.

Nazi control over the individual German state (*Länder*) and municipal governments went forward with their extension of control over the central government. The president's decree of February 28, 1933, which allowed the Reich government to take over a state government whenever public security and order appeared to be in danger, opened the way for the installation of Nazi regimes in each state government in Germany.

By a Co-ordination Act (*Gleichschaltungsgesetz*) [26] of March 31, 1933, the parliaments of the *Länder* were deprived of all authority. A second Co-ordination Act of April 7, 1933, provided that each state government was henceforth to be administered by a Reich governor (*Reichsstatthalter*), who was to be appointed by the Reich president at the advice of the Reich chancellor. The Reichsstatthalter was to see to it that his state was ruled according to the political guidelines laid down by the chancellor, and for this purpose he was given almost unlimited local authority, including the right to promulgate laws for his particular state.[27]

Under the Reichsstatthalter law, Papen was ousted from his position as Reichskommissar of Prussia, an office that was now abolished. Hitler himself assumed the new post of Reichsstatthalter of Prussia, but on April 10 he delegated his authority to the newly appointed minister-president of Prussia, Hermann Göring. In the other German states Hitler's nominee for the position of Reichsstatthalter was generally the local party Gauleiter.[28] In this way party and state leadership were united, but party and state offices were deliberately kept separate to preserve both as instruments of control.[29]

A Reconstruction Act (*Gesetz über den Neuaufbau des Reichs*), published on the first anniversary of Hitler's appointment, provided for the dissolution of all state parliaments and the transfer of all remaining sovereign rights of the Länder to the government of the Reich. Henceforth all state governments were to be no more than administrative subdivisions of the Reich government, and their Reichsstatthalters were to be under the direct authority of the Reich minister of the interior.[30]

Fearful lest he had conceded too much power to the minister of the interior, Hitler issued a decree on the second anniversary of his appointment placing the Reichsstatthalters more directly under his personal control and giving himself the exclusive right to appoint and dismiss them as well as members of their governments. At the same time the individual Reich ministers were given the power to issue instructions in their various fields directly to the Reichsstatthalters without going through the Ministry of the Interior. This law, which was described as the keystone in establishing the unshakable unity of the Reich, actually did no more than concentrate further authority in the person of Hitler while allowing greater freedom of action to the individual Reich ministers and the Reichsstatthalters.[31]

ATTAINMENT AND CONSOLIDATION OF POWER

Municipal governments, too, were placed more firmly under Reich and party authority. By a law of January 30, 1935, all burgomasters were to come under the supervision of party and state officials, who were to ensure that their policies were in harmony with those of the Reich government. All important measures contemplated by a municipal government required the approval of party and state supervisory officials.[32]

CHAPTER 4

The Instruments of Control:
The National Socialist Party

In the course of Hitler's struggle for power, the National Socialist party had been built into a formidable political organization. After he became chancellor, the party was assigned the tasks he originally had envisaged for it, namely to channel the folk spirit and educate the nation; but the party as such retained importance primarily as an instrument of control within the state.

At the head of the party was Adolf Hitler, whose status was clearly defined in party doctrine:

> The National Socialist party is Hitler, and Hitler is the party. The National Socialists believe in Hitler, who embodies their will. Therefore our conscience is clearly and exactly defined. Only what Adolf Hitler, our Führer, commands, allows, or does not allow is our conscience. *We have no understanding for him who hides behind an anonymous conscience, behind God, whom everyone conceives according to his wishes.*[1]

Party discipline was defined in similar terms. The National Socialist commandments stated, "The Führer is always right!" "Never go against discipline!" "That which promotes the movement, Germany, and your people, is right!" All party members were obliged to swear eternal allegiance to Hitler, and to promise unconditional obedience to him and to all subordinate Führers appointed by him.

"The basis of the party organization is the Führer idea," the party handbook stated. "The general public [*Allgemeinheit*] is unable to rule itself either directly or indirectly." All authority flowed from the supreme Führer to subordinate Führers, who were invested with

28

Führerlike authority within the fields of competence delegated to them, and who in turn could confer similar powers on their subordinates. The flow of authority from the highest to the lowest party functionary was known as the *Führerprinzip*, the fundamental principle of rulership in the Third Reich. Just as absolute authority flowed from the top to the bottom of the party hierarchy, so absolute loyalty and obedience was owed from the bottom to the top, with each party member ultimately responsible to the person of the supreme Führer, Adolf Hitler.[2]

The Party Administration

To implement and channel this theoretical authority was the task of the party organization. As head of the party Hitler was served by a Führer Chancellery, which took care of his routine household arrangements, and by the far more important Central Party Office (later the Party Chancellery), which supervised the entire party organization.[3]

Operating beside the party's Central Office were a number of senior party officials called *Reichsleiter,* each in charge of a major branch of the party organization such as the party treasury, judiciary, or militia. A few Reichsleiters, for example Goebbels and Darré, later occupied positions in the Reich government comparable to their positions in party government. Thus Goebbels was party propaganda leader and Reich minister of propaganda, Darré the head of the party office for peasant affairs and Reich minister of food and agriculture. Each Reichsleiter had a sizable central office in Berlin, with subordinate offices throughout the party's regional organization to carry out directives on the local level. In December 1934 the Reichsleiters of the party were given a rank equivalent to the highest offices in the state.

For purposes of the party's regional administration, Germany was divided into Gaus, which were supposed to represent old Germanic administrative units but which corresponded far more closely to recent state administrative divisions than to any ancient domain of Saxony or Thuringia. There were thirty-two such party districts within the Old Reich, each Gau being headed by a Gauleiter appointed by the Führer.[4] The Gau was subdivided into *Kreise*[5] headed by a *Kreisleiter* appointed by the Führer at the suggestion of the Gauleiter, and *Ortsgruppen*[6] headed by an *Ortsgruppenleiter* appointed by the Gauleiter at the suggestion of the Kreisleiter. Finally there was the *Zell* led by the *Zellenleiter,* and the *Block* under a *Blockleiter.*[7]

The Gauleiter and his staff were responsible for establishing the authority of the party within their district, and ensuring that all local activities were being conducted according to National Socialist principles. In the course of the war the party Gauleiters were made Reich defense commissars for their respective districts, and their powers were extended until they controlled almost every aspect of the civilian war effort.

The authority of the Gauleiter flowed through the hierarchy of the party's territorial organization in accordance with the *Führerprinzip*. The Blockleiter at the bottom supervised some forty to sixty households and was regarded by the party leadership as the key instrument of local control. It was his duty to win over all persons in his Block to National Socialism, and to report all disaffection to the proper authorities. Each Blockleiter was required to keep a card index file on all his constituents with a complete record of their activities and attitudes.

In addition to its territorial organization, the party maintained a multitude of functional organizations: the party militia, the Hitler Youth, the National Socialist Woman's League, labor, educational, cultural, and athletic societies, which increased enormously in number and scope after the Nazis came to power. After 1933 there was scarcely any activity that was not organized by the party in some fashion. Through these organizations the party was able to control almost every aspect of German life and society.

"There is no institution in this state which is not National Socialist," Hitler boasted in 1938; "the greatest guarantee of the National Socialist revolution lies in the complete domination of the Reich and all its institutions and organizations, internally and externally, by the National Socialist party." [8]

Supervising this immense organizational complex was the party's Central Office, which played a major role in state as well as party affairs. This office went through many changes in the course of its development. Originally set up by Gregor Strasser as the party's Political Organization Department, it was dismantled when Strasser resigned from the party and re-established as the Central Party Committee under Rudolf Hess. In April 1933 Hess was named Hitler's deputy in the party, and his committee was subsequently known as the Office of the Deputy of the Führer.

The Hess office was divided into departments to deal with every aspect of the party's many activities and to serve as a liaison between party and state offices. In December 1933 Hess was brought into the Reich cabinet as minister without portfolio, and soon afterward he was authorized to participate in the drafting of all Reich legislation to represent the party's point of view. In 1938 this authorization was extended to include the legislation of all Länder governments, which meant that all state legislation had to be cleared through his office before it could come into effect. Hess, for his part, had the right to initiate legislation on behalf of the party. His office also played a strategic role in the selection of personnel, for the credentials of all candidates for appointments to state and party offices reserved for the decision of the Führer had to be examined first by the Führer's deputy.

Besides these functions it was the task of the Führer's deputy to assert the will of the party in the organization of the state, to settle differences between state and party offices, to investigate complaints, and to ensure that all state activities were in line with the policies and ideology of the party.[9]

When Hess flew to Scotland in May 1941 in a vain effort to persuade the British to make peace with Germany and was interned for the duration of the war, his office was restored to the immediate control of Hitler, who renamed it the Party Chancellery and appointed Hess's former deputy, Martin Bormann, as its director.[10]

Bormann was the least public of the major wielders of power in the Nazi hierarchy, and even after the war he retained the reputation of a man of mystery—Hitler's evil genius, the brown eminence of the Nazi organization.[11] In fact there was little that was mysterious about Bormann. He was an efficient but unimaginative bureaucrat, distinguished only by an insatiable lust for power, fanatic faith in the Führer, and complete dedication to the cause of National Socialism.

Born in Saxony in 1900, the son of a postal clerk, he was too young to serve in the First World War. After the war he joined the illegal Rossbach free corps, but in 1923 was arrested and later condemned to a year's imprisonment for the murder of a member of this organization who was suspected of being a spy. Upon his release from prison in 1925 he joined the Nazi party, attached himself to Hitler, and through his talents as an administrator and willingness to act as a factotum he gradually made himself indispensable. Although happily married and evidently deeply attached to his wife and many children, his primary loyalty was to Hitler, whom he served with dogged devotion and whose views he accepted with unquestioning faith.

Although Bormann was not given Hess's title of deputy Führer when he succeeded to the directorship of the party bureaucracy, he exercised the same powers as Hess and gradually extended them to make his office one of the major power centers of the Third Reich. The entire party organization and all party officials were subjected far more firmly than heretofore to the control of the Central Office, and every opportunity was used to assert its influence in state affairs as well. A Hitler decree of January 1942 reaffirmed the right of the head of the Party Chancellery to be associated from the beginning

31

with the drafting of all state legislation, it expressly forbade state and party offices to communicate with each other directly or through any channel other than the Party Chancellery, and it required that the Party Chancellery review all nominations for critical appointments before submitting them to the Führer.

In the months that followed Bormann used his influence to broaden the powers of the party officials through Germany, for every increase in the authority of the party functionaries under his control meant a corresponding extension of his own.

Great as were the powers exercised by Bormann through his party office, his greatest source of strength lay in his personal relationship with Hitler to whom he had constant access. In April 1943 he was officially named Hitler's personal secretary. In that capacity he was able to decide what persons Hitler should or should not see, what documents he should read, and how problems should be presented to him. He attended Hitler's official conferences, he was his regular companion at mealtime and during moments of relaxation; it was Bormann who generally drafted the documents recording Hitler's decisions which were sent out as instructions to state and party officials.[12]

The Party Militia

Among the party's many functional organizations none was more important during the early years of the movement than the party militia, the *Sturm Abteilung* (SA),[13] which was later to be overshadowed by its subsidiary formation the *Schutz Staffel* (SS),[14] the praetorian guard of the Führer. SA and SS men were the chief organizers of party rallies, the defenders of party meetings and disrupters of rival meetings, the door-to-door canvassers during election campaigns, the loungers about the polls to intimidate the opposition and apply last-minute pressure on the fainthearted or undecided.[15]

Many members of the SA were former soldiers trained in the techniques of violence and not averse to its use. With the coming of the great depression, however, the principal recruits of the SA were unemployed workers attracted by the prospect of pay, food, and the chance of something to do. These men took seriously the socialist and labor emphasis of their party's name, with the result that the SA became the center of political radicalism as well as the fighting arm of the party. As the SA grew in size it grew in militancy, so much so that Hitler had trouble controlling it. To restore discipline in the SA he appointed as its chief of staff Ernst Röhm, a tough professional soldier who had taken a job in South America as an organizer and trainer of the Bolivian army. Röhm returned to Germany in 1930, and in two years had built the SA into a well-organized force of four hundred thousand men.

Although highly successful as an organizer, Röhm did little to curb the radical militancy of the SA. On the contrary, he made himself the spokesman of the party's left, and after Hitler came to power he expressed the dissatisfaction of many of his men with their share of the new jobs and plunder. With the numbers of the SA swelled to over two million by the end of 1933, he put pressure on Hitler to implement more rapidly the socialist portion of the National Socialist program. Seeing in the conservative leadership of the German army a major obstacle to socialization, he advocated the incorporation of entire units of the SA into the regular army to convert it into a genuine people's army—or, at any rate, a genuine Röhm army.

Hitler resented Röhm's pressure and thought his policies dangerous. For the time being he remained dependent on the support of industrial and financial magnates, and on the sufferance of the regular army. He therefore tried to rein in the bumptious Röhm, and in December 1933 he made him a member of the Reich cabinet. Röhm was not repressed or appeased. In February 1934 he proposed the creation of a new Reich Ministry of Defense which should control both the regular army and the party's paramilitary formations, a clear indication that he had not abandoned his plan to unite these forces, presumably under his own direction.

The army was seriously alarmed, but so was Hitler—and so were Röhm's rivals in the Nazi party. As Röhm's power and influence grew, a curious alliance appears to have been formed between two of these rivals, Hermann Göring and Heinrich Himmler, head of the SS and chief of the police forces in every major German state with the exception of Prussia.[16]

Unlike Göring, Himmler had not played a critical role in Hitler's rise to power; but after 1933 no Nazi leader contributed more to the party's consolidation of power or did more to put Nazi racial theories into practice in Germany and the German-occupied territories.[17] Himmler was comparable to Bormann in his dedication to the principles of National Socialism; but, in contrast to Bormann, whose role was largely restricted to interpreting and transmitting Hitler's orders, Himmler developed organizations and recruited the personnel for carrying out those orders.

Himmler's family and educational background could hardly have been more conventional or respectable. His father, a Bavarian schoolmaster and tutor to a prince of the Bavarian royal house, named his son after Prince Heinrich of Bavaria and persuaded the prince to act as the boy's godfather. Heinrich Himmler was brought up a devout Roman Catholic, his school record was fair but in no way outstanding. Too young to see active service in the First World War, he became a student of agriculture after the war and in 1922 earned a degree in that subject. But his only practical experience in agriculture, on which he was later to place so much political and social emphasis, was as manager of an unsuccessful chicken farm.

In the same year that he took his degree in agriculture, Himmler joined the Nazi party and became a member of the fledgling SS, at that time a small subdivision of the SA that acted as Hitler's personal bodyguard. He took part in the Munich Putsch of 1923, but otherwise failed to distinguish himself. Thus it evoked considerable surprise in party ranks when in 1929 Hitler appointed him head of the SS.

Neither in appearance or temperament did Himmler seem suitable for this position. He was a flabby little man, with narrow shoulders and a prominent stomach. The pince-nez glasses he habitually wore gave him the look of a sadistic school master. He was given to worry, and suffered from frequent nervous headaches and stomach cramps of such severity that they often contorted his body in agony.[18] Himmler, however, soon showed that he had talents to compensate for these unfortunate personal qualities. He proved to be a skillful organizer with an uncanny instinct for the realities of power, and in the next years he was to demonstrate an ability amounting to genius for maneuvering himself into positions through which he might exercise that power.

The Göring-Himmler alliance grew out of the power relationships within the party and state as they existed in 1934. Both men were inordinately ambitious, both saw in Röhm a major obstacle to their ambitions: Göring because he himself aspired to the control of Germany's armed forces; Himmler because, as head of the SS, he resented his subordination to Röhm within the SA and Röhm's refusal to allow the SS to play a greater role in party and state affairs. On April 20, 1934, Göring put the seal on his alliance with Himmler by making him chief of the Prussian police, including the newly formed *Geheime Staatspolizei* (Gestapo), an appointment that climaxed a year-long Himmler campaign to control the state police forces throughout Germany.[19] Göring and Himmler now appear to have gone to Hitler with evidence that Röhm was planning a coup d'état, and to persuade him to take action against the SA leader.

Hitler needed little persuading. Röhm and his two million SA men had become a dangerous menace. To minimize the danger involved in a blow against so large a force, he ordered Röhm and the entire SA to take a month's leave. With the regular SA formations disbanded, troops of the regular army were ordered to stand by to deal with possible emergencies, while Himmler carefully positioned his SS men and police. On June 30, 1934, while Röhm was vacationing at

Bad Wiessee, Hitler struck. Röhm and other prominent SA leaders were arrested and shot, as was Gregor Strasser, Hitler's former rival for leadership in the party and its foremost radical theorist. At the same time Hitler struck down potential rivals on the right, including General von Schleicher, former chancellor and perennial schemer, and several leaders of the Catholic Center party. To the German people Hitler explained that Röhm and his lieutenants in the SA had joined with the right in a plot to overthrow the government. The result of the June 30 blood purge was the elimination of the SA as a power factor in the Nazi government.[20]

Out of the shambles of the SA, the SS under the leadership of Himmler took its place as the most influential private army of the Nazis. On July 30, 1934, the SS was made an independent organization within the Nazi party; its leader, previously subordinate to the chief of staff of the SA, was made directly responsible to Hitler.[21]

The SS remained connected with the SA, but instead of being subordinate it now formed a supervisory body within the larger organization—as it did within the whole of Germany. "From this center of information all political life in all its details and all its manifestations is watched and judged according to the principles of National Socialism," an official party spokesman stated in defining the role of the SS. "The SS had erected this organization against all those who were hostile to the Führer and the nation." [22]

Himmler had been preparing the SS for this role for some time, and with Hitler's full approval he built it up into an elite force within the party and the state. Members were selected with great care for their physical fitness, but above all for their fanatic devotion to the person of Hitler and the principles of the National Socialist movement. On the belt of each SS man was inscribed the motto *"Meine Ehre ist Treue,"* which in this case meant absolute loyalty to Hitler and his faithful paladin, Reichsführer SS Heinrich Himmler.

Hitler was full of admiration for Himmler's achievement. Since the origin of the SS in 1922, Hitler said, its members had always been the "tough ones" of the party. "But it was with Himmler that the SS became that extraordinary body of men, devoted to an idea, loyal unto death. I see in Himmler our Ignatius de Loyola. With intelligence and obstinacy, against wind and tide, he forged this instrument." [23]

At the beginning of the war Himmler succeeded in accomplishing what Röhm had tried in vain to do. He introduced entire units of the SS into the regular army, the so-called *Waffen-SS.* In actual military operations these troops were under the orders of the Wehrmacht, but in all other respects they remained under the authority of Himmler, who used them to implement Nazi ideological programs—and to extend his own power—in the occupied areas.

At first a 10 per cent limit on the proportion of SS men in the army was imposed, but the number of SS divisions grew steadily in the course of the war. Toward the end they even lost their character of specially trained elite troops as the quality of the recruits and the time available for their training declined. Moreover Himmler secured exclusive rights to recruit Nordic manpower in the German-occupied territories, not necessarily the elite in their particular countries, and set up entire SS divisions composed of such troops. His object was to have under SS control the most important armed force of each occupied country at the end of the war.[24]

The Party and the State

With the National Socialist assumption of power in 1933, there began a general penetration of party members into government offices. From the beginning, therefore, there could be no clear-cut dichotomy between party and state. In a law to ensure the unity of party and state of December 1, 1933, Hitler declared that the party as bearer of the German idea of state was inextricably connected with the state. In that same law, however, he withdrew party and SA members from state law and placed them under special party law for all matters affecting their duty to the Führer, *Volk,* and state.[25]

Hitler's ideal seems to have been the eventual total union of party and state. With the fulfillment of its mission to educate the people and control the state, the party would eventually bring the nation into perfect harmony with itself. When this condition should have been achieved, the need for the party as such would have ceased to exist.[26]

Party members in general failed to recognize the withering away of their organization as an ideal. Through their status in the party, they tried to ensure themselves a superior position within the Germanic community.[27] As the party gradually embraced an ever-increasing portion of the German people, various units within the party set themselves up as self-conscious representatives of higher ideals of Germandom. Most conspicuous among these was the SS, with its rigid racial qualifications, its physical standards, its breeding requirements, and its stated purpose to form a Germanic elite for all time.

The party as such never lost its identity, however, and continued to play a role separate from the state. Since party leaders were also leaders of many state institutions, their dual status was constantly a factor. The Gauleiters, for example, were party officials controlled through the Party Chancellery. But as a rule the Gauleiters were also heads of the local state government as well, and in that capacity came under the Reich Ministry of the Interior. They were thus subject to the control of both party and state officials. In exercising their own authority, however, they could operate through either party or state channels and appeal to party or state officials against the authority of each other, a situation that allowed them considerable freedom of maneuver. Ultimately, of course, they could always appeal to Hitler, to whom they were directly responsible, although whether in Hitler's capacity as state or party leader was never determined.[28]

Hitler's own dual position produced the following decision in a district court of Berlin: "The Führer of the party is at the same time the Führer of the state. It is up to him to decide whether he is acting in the one capacity or in the other. To us it is sufficient that the name of Adolf Hitler is affixed to the order." [29]

CHAPTER 5

The Instruments of Control: The State

In the state as in the party Adolf Hitler was the Führer, and after the Nazis came to power the government of the state, like that of the party, was based on the *Führerprinzip*. According to official party doctrine, the authority of the state as such had ceased to exist. "We must speak not of the state's authority but of the Führer's authority if we wish to designate the character of the political authority within the Reich correctly. The state does not hold political authority as an impersonal unit but receives it from the Führer as the executor of the national will."

As the Führer possessed all authority, so he possessed all responsibility. "The political direction of the Reich is the task of the Führer. The Führer selects, in all fields of political development, the goals to be attained, he determines the methods to be used, and makes all fundamental decisions when necessary." [1]

By August 1934 Hitler had acquired powers in the state to match his pretensions. As chancellor he had supreme executive authority, after the passage of the Enabling Act he had supreme legislative authority, and with the merger of the offices of president and chancellor after the death of Hindenburg he acquired supreme command of the armed forces.

Administration

As president and chancellor, Hitler was served by a Presidential Chancellery and a Reich Chancellery. The former was headed by Dr. Otto Meissner, who had held this position under both Ebert and Hindenburg. This office dealt primarily with problems of protocol and ceremony—state visits, the bestowal of decorations, and the like.[2]

Far more important was the Reich Chancellery under Dr. Hans Heinrich Lammers, one of Hitler's first appointees to a state office. Trained in law and constitutional history, Lammers, since 1921, had been senior government counselor (*Oberregierungsrat*) in the Reich Ministry of the Interior. Here he was director of the division of constitutional and administrative law, a position that involved interpreting the Weimar constitution, although Lammers was an avowed monarchist and a member of the Nationalist party and the Stahlhelm. In February 1932 he joined the Nazi party. According to his own testimony, he had never met Hitler when he was summoned to the Hotel Kaiserhof on January 29, 1933, and asked whether he would accept the position of state secretary in the Reich Chancellery. Hitler told him he needed an expert in constitutional and administrative law. As Lammers recalled the conversation later, Hitler said, "I am not familiar with administrative red tape nor do I want to bother with it; but I do not want to make a fool of myself. I need an official who is familiar with this ground."

After Lammers accepted the post, Hitler's instructions were brief. He did not want any red tape or to have routine documents thrust under his nose. "I only want to have to sign when it is absolutely necessary, namely laws, directives, decrees, documents of appointments, letters to foreign chiefs of state or foreign ambassadors, etc." [3]

Lammers proved an ideal man for the job. Over fifty at the time of his appointment, he was an experienced and mature bureaucrat, meticulous, attentive to detail, thoroughly familiar with administrative routine. He was a master at condensing and summarizing the enormous volume of official business submitted to Hitler, much of it technical and complicated, and at drawing up documents recording his decision. It was to Lammers that the frequent conflicts of authority among officials of the Third Reich were submitted for arbitration, and it was Lammers who determined when and in what form they should be presented to Hitler. He retained this strategic position in the government until the 1940s, when he was gradually frozen out by Bormann, head of the Führer's Party Chancellery.

Under Hitler the Reich Chancellery played a far more significant role in the German government than under previous chancellors. After the passage of the Enabling Act Hitler largely dispensed with cabinet meetings, and he disliked receiving individual cabinet ministers about routine affairs. As a result the Reich Chancellery became a principal channel of communication between government ministers and the chancellor, and between ministers with each other.

All Hitler's decrees were drawn up in the Reich Chancellery, all draft legislation of the Reich ministries or other offices invested with legislative powers were submitted to the Reich Chancellery, circulated to other government departments concerned (including the party Central Office), and reviewed before being sent to Hitler for final approval and signature. It was Lammers's responsibility to ensure that all Reich legislation was in accordance with Hitler's intentions and that all necessary legal procedures had been observed. After 1939 Lammers as a rule was required to cosign decrees, thus indicating his acceptance of this responsibility.

By the nature of his postition Lammers, like Bormann, was one of the few governmental officials who had regular access to Hitler; but, unlike Bormann, he did not exploit his many opportunities to gain personal power. By his defense counsel at Nuremberg, he was described as conspicuously lacking in dynamism. The course of his career bears out this characterization. Almost to the end of the Nazi era he remained the perfect bureaucrat: hard-working, a master of routine, an effective executor of the orders and policies of others, but without policies of his own and with no apparent desire to influence policy.[4]

By no means all correspondence of the supreme Reich leadership went through the Reich Chancellery. This office was primarily concerned with legislative procedures, not with policy making, nor was it the only clearing house of communications with Hitler. Questions of personnel and all state-party relations went through the Party Chancellery; military affairs went through the *Oberkommando der Wehrmacht* (OKW), organized in 1938 as a sort of military chancellery;[5] foreign affairs went through the Foreign Office—the list could be extended almost indefinitely—but all of these offices operated under the direct authority of Hitler.

Hitler's treatment of the cabinet, which was not officially under his direct authority and which might have acted as a counterweight to that authority, is illustrative of his methods of consolidating his power. When he was elevated to the chancellorship, he was bound by preappointment promises to select a cabinet dominated by conservative ministers through whom the conservative leaders who had arranged his appointment thought to control him. Hitler, in fact, kept his promise with regard to the cabinet, but he paid scant attention to the provision in the Weimar constitution, which he had agreed to respect, requiring that questions of policy be determined by the entire cabinet. He rarely bothered to consult the cabinet as a body but dealt instead with the individual ministers about their respective fields, either directly or through the Reich Chancellery. The last time the cabinet met for purposes of discussion was in November 1937 over the draft of a penal code. In February 1938 it met again, but only to be

40

informed by Hitler of changes involving Neurath and Blomberg, the ministers of foreign affairs and war.[6]

As the role of the cabinet changed, so did its membership. Alfred Hugenberg, the leader of the Nationalist party who had been head of two ministries, Economics and Food and Agriculture, was forced out as early as June 27, 1933, and was replaced in both capacities by sound Nazis.[7] Hugenberg's fate was ultimately shared by all conservative members of Hitler's cabinet. Papen was forced out in July 1934. No new vice-chancellor was appointed. In February 1938 Baron Constantin von Neurath gave way to the Nazi Joachim von Ribbentrop at the Foreign Office, and General Werner von Blomberg resigned as minister of war.

To add to the confusion, or dilution, of the powers of the Reich cabinet and its ministers, several heads of noncabinet organizations were given the rank of Reich minister. The chiefs of the army, navy, and OKW, for example, as well as the heads of the Presidential and Reich chancelleries, were accorded this rank, while others, usually the heads of Nazi party organizations, were allowed to take part in cabinet meetings whenever problems involving their spheres of activity were discussed. This was the case with Himmler as chief of the German police; Ernst Bohle, head of the party's office dealing with Germans abroad; Baldur von Schirach, the Reich youth leader; Konstantin Hierl, the party labor leader; and Otto Dietrich, the party press chief. As the cabinet never met after most of these men were allowed to attend its meetings, the right of participation was an empty honor. It is worthy of note, however, that Hitler nevertheless took the trouble to pack the cabinet with Nazis.[8]

Under Hitler the various Reich ministers were no longer responsible to the cabinet as a whole, to the Reichstag, or to any other individual or corporate body, but solely and directly to Hitler. Their actual power varied widely according to their personal drive and ability; but it was ultimately dependent on their personal relationship with Hitler. Ministers were empowered to draft legislation and sign decrees, but only after their drafts had been reviewed in the Reich and Party chancelleries, circulated to all other departments concerned, and approved by Hitler. Ministers were allowed considerable freedom of operation in carrying out their tasks, an application of the *Führerprinzip* which required that all subordinate Führers exercise maximum initiative in their respective fields. Hitler, however, could alter those fields at will, co-ordinate them under new offices with broad emergency powers, and issue decrees affecting them without consulting a minister or obtaining his cosignature. In effect, Reich ministers were reduced to the role of heads of departments, and departments of very uncertain status at that.

41

Besides the offices headed by Reich ministers, there were a number of other state and party offices that Hitler had made directly responsible to himself. All such offices were known as Supreme Reich Authorities (*Oberste Reichsbehörden*). These included, in addition to the Reich ministries and the various chancelleries of the Führer, the highest Reich law courts, the highest Reich financial institutions, including the Reichsbank, major co-ordinating or planning agencies such as the Office of the Four-Year Plan, the Office for Territorial Planning (*Reichsstelle für Raumordnung*), the Reich Housing Office, the Ministerial Council for the Defense of the Reich, and others. During the war many more such offices were created with emergency powers to deal with specific problems such as transportation, public health, public utilities, and racial questions. Finally, there were the heads of all German occupation governments, who were also directly responsible to Hitler, and were therefore also Supreme Reich Authorities.[9]

All heads of German government departments were dependent for the execution of their orders and the proper functioning of their organizations on the officials who staffed those departments, the majority of them members of the professional civil service. A purge of the civil service began immediately after Hitler's appointment. On April 7, 1933, this purge was codified in a decree "For the Restoration of the Professional Civil Service," which provided that civil servants could be dismissed if they had been active in the Communist cause, if they were non-Aryan, or if their "previous political activities did not guarantee they would at all times be unreservedly committed to the national state."[10]

Nazi meddling with the civil service did not mean an automatic decline in the quality of the German bureaucracy. Nazi officials were often endowed with considerable skill, and their forceful, direct methods were frequently effective in cutting through bureaucratic red tape to a solution of a problem. Moreover the rank and file bureaucrats in the majority of departments were not greatly affected by the law of April 7, for most of them were neither Communists, non-Aryan, or active politically. Thus, even the crudest Nazi party hack, if placed in charge of a state office, would generally have beneath him an experienced staff that could tidy up his orders and keep the office operating in a reasonably effective way.

A civil service law of January 25, 1937, introduced new requirements for membership in the bureaucracy.[11] Henceforth all public officials were not only expected to be members of the party, but assiduous exponents of National Socialist ideology; unconditional support of political aims of the regime was to be considered a more important qualification than objective administrative competence. State offi-

42

cials were required to take the same oath as party officials by pledging allegiance and absolute obedience to the person of the Führer instead of to an abstract conception of state. Appointments to all higher posts in the civil service were reserved for the Führer, who was to make these appointments personally or through the deputy Führer of the party. Thus all senior appointments were placed under party control and, in effect, the entire state civil service was subjected to party supervision.

Among the Supreme Reich Authorities, none appeared to possess broader powers for exercising control within the state than the Reich Ministry of the Interior, which since January 30, 1933, had been under the direction of Wilhelm Frick, a participant in the 1923 Munich Putsch and the most experienced bureaucrat among the Nazi leaders.[12]

Before the Nazis took over, responsibility for carrying out the laws of the central (Reich) government had been left to the ministries of the interior of the individual German states (Länder); but under the Nazi administration this responsibility was centralized in the Reich Ministry of the Interior. On November 1, 1934, the Ministry of the Interior of Prussia was merged with that of the Reich; and, although other German states retained departments that were still called ministries of the interior, they were little more than regional departments of the Reich ministry.[13]

Among the eight principal divisions of the Reich Ministry of the Interior, the most important was Department 1, which had jurisdiction over all matters concerning the internal structure of the Reich. Its responsibilities included the drafting of all legislation affecting the Supreme Reich Authorities, the supervision of Reich, Länder, and local administrations, the supervision of relations between party and state, and the regulation of questions of citizenship and nationality. In 1935 this department came under the direction of Wilhelm Stuckart, an energetic and ardent Nazi official who held the rank of state secretary in the ministry.

With so many aspects of the administration under its authority, Department 1 would seem to have been a major power center of the Reich. That it was not was due to the fact that many of its powers were also delegated to other departments, some of which were in a position to exercise them far more effectively. This was true, for example, of both the Reich and Party chancelleries, whose heads had regular access to Hitler and consequently constant opportunity to influence his decisions. Under Bormann, the Party Chancellery all but eliminated Stuckart's influence, as it eventually also eliminated the influence of Lammers and the Reich Chancellery.

Even more illusory was the authority of Department 2, which was supposed to be in charge of personnel and administration for the entire civil service, including all German police forces after their removal from the control of the Länder. Control over personnel, however, was actually exercised by Hitler personally or by the party's Central Office, which also claimed supervisory authority over all operations of the civil service. Thus Department 2 was left with little more than routine administrative functions. In the field of police administration its powers were undercut by Himmler, who by 1934 became de facto head of all German police forces. Although specifically designated chief of the German police in the Reich Ministry of the Interior, Himmler escaped the ministry's control by making all higher-ranking police officers members of the SS, and whenever necessary issuing his orders to them in his capacity as head of the SS.

The Ministry of the Interior appeared to be given fresh opportunities for establishing its influence when the period of Nazi territorial expansion began, for it was assigned the task of co-ordinating the policies and legislation of all Reich and party offices in the occupied territories. Under the direction of Stuckart, central offices were set up within the ministry for each occupation government. In areas to be annexed to the Reich, they were to supervise the integration of Reich and local administration; elsewhere they were to work for maximum uniformity between Reich and occupation administrations.

The powers of these central offices, like those of departments 1 and 2, were never so great as they appeared. The various agencies involved in occupation government regarded the supervision of the central offices as disagreeable curbs on their authority, and their persistent efforts to escape effective supervision were generally successful. On the whole the role of the Ministry of the Interior in the occupied territories was restricted to supplying occupation governments with experienced administrative personnel. There was some hope in the ministry that bureaucrats trained in its ranks would help to assert its authority in occupation governments, but its hold on the loyalty of these men was rarely sufficient to fulfill such expectations.

Despite his failure to give effective support to the Ministry of the Interior, Hitler persisted in assigning it co-ordinating functions in Germany as well as the occupied territories. In September 1938 he appointed Wilhelm Frick plenipotentiary-general for the administration of the Reich, with Himmler as his deputy and Stuckart as head of the plenipotentiary's office. In this capacity he was to co-ordinate the ministries of the Interior, Justice, Education, Religion, and the Reich Office for Regional Planning for Purposes of Reich Defense. As plenipotentiary-general for administration, Frick was appointed to a Ministerial Council for the Defense of the Reich under the chairmanship of Göring at the beginning of the war. In none of these positions, however, did he play a significant part in determining or even greatly influencing government policy. Very much like Lammers he remained above all a bureaucrat, and in struggles for the actual control of power he proved no match for Göring, Himmler, or Bormann.[14]

The Police

A crucial task in taking over the government of a state is securing control of its arsenals. Hitler had been careful to see to it that the most powerful force within Germany, the army, should not oppose him. It was to take several years before this important weapon could be subordinated to the role of a Nazi instrument. In the meantime the Nazis made sure of a more accessible source of power, the German police.[15] Göring, in particular, moved swiftly to lay his hands on this touchstone of authority. Immediately upon his appointment as Prussian minister of the interior on January 30, 1933, he began a purge of the Prussian police force and the replacement of unreliable elements with men he thought he could trust. Once his control over the Prussian police had been established, he did not scruple to use it for political purposes or to augment its numbers by enrolling entire units of the party militia in the police as special constables. "To begin with," Göring wrote a year later in describing his activities, "it seemed to me of the first importance to get the weapon of the criminal and political police firmly in my own hands. Here it was that I made my first sweeping changes of personnel. Out of thirty-two police chiefs I removed twenty-two. Hundreds of instructors and thousands of police sergeants followed in the course of the next months." [16]

Elsewhere in Germany the route to Nazi control of the police was opened by the presidential decree of February 28, 1933,[17] which allowed the Reich government to intervene in state and local governments in the interest of law and order. By the March 5 elections, Nazis were established in key positions in police forces all over Germany. After the elections, the Nazification of German police forces was carried out systematically under the supervision of the Reich Ministry of the Interior. Control of the German police more than anything else permitted the Nazi revolution to retain its sham appearance of legality.[18]

In Prussia, Göring published a decree on April 26, 1933, reorganizing the political police to make it a more effective instrument in combatting enemies of the state. This was the origin of the notorious Gestapo, which in the first instance was confined to Prussia alone and was directly responsible to Göring in his capacity as Prussian minister of the interior. In subsequent decrees the Gestapo was made independent of other Prussian state authorities, which were required to obey all orders of Gestapo officials and to co-operate with them in carrying out their tasks.[19]

Apart from Göring, the Nazi leader most zealous in establishing control over the German police was Reichsführer SS Heinrich Himmler. Despite his record as an early member of the party and as commander of the Führer's praetorian guard, Himmler was by-passed when Hitler installed a Nazi government in Bavaria under General von Epp on March 9, 1933; his only reward in the Nazi take over of the second largest German state was the appointment as acting chief of police in the city of Munich. Himmler, however, succeeded rapidly in extending his authority. On April 1, 1933, he was appointed chief of police for the entire state of Bavaria, and by the end of January 1934 he had managed to gain command of the police forces of every German state with the exception of Prussia and Schaumburg-Lippe.

Paralleling the work of Göring in Prussia, Himmler began setting up secret sections in the police forces under his own command. Then on April 20, 1934, presumably as a reward for his co-operation with Göring against Röhm, he was given command of the Prussian police, including the Gestapo. With his appointment as head of the police in Schaumburg-Lippe on June 2, 1934, Himmler found himself in control of all police forces in Germany. As police chief of Prussia he was under the nominal authority of Göring, the Prussian minister of the interior; in other states, under that of the Reich Ministry of the Interior. With the merger of the Prussian and Reich interior ministries in November 1934, the Prussian police, too, came under the Reich Ministry of the Interior.[20]

On June 17, 1936, Hitler officially sanctioned the unification of the German police under Himmler and conferred on him the title of Reichsführer SS and chief of the German police in the Reich Ministry of the Interior. With this appointment he was given the right to participate in meetings of the Reich cabinet when problems affecting his sphere of operations were discussed. A year later Hitler ordered that Himmler's decrees as chief of the German police should have the same validity as the decrees of Reich ministers and become part of the law of the land.[21]

After the union of the German police under Himmler, the German police system can no longer be considered apart from the SS. To strengthen his hold on the police, Himmler appointed SS men to key positions throughout all German police organizations, or appointed police officers to equivalent ranks in the SS. At the same time he took care not to integrate his dual sources of power entirely. Like many other Nazi leaders, he found it convenient to operate in various capacities. As police chief he was directly and personally responsible to the Reich minister of the interior, but as Reichsführer SS he was responsible only to Hitler and could by-pass the Ministry of the Interior altogether. Frick complained to Hitler, but Hitler replied through Lammers, "Tell Herr Frick that he should not restrict Himmler as chief of the German police too much; with him the police is in good hands. We should allow him as much free rein as possible." [22]

The exact nature of the process by which Himmler acquired control over all German police organizations may never be known—the records of political bargaining, infighting, and intrigue are not generally preserved—but informed contemporary observers assigned a great share of the credit to the head of Himmler's intelligence department in the SS, Reinhard Heydrich. [23]

Heydrich was one of the few Nazi leaders who looked like the Nazi ideal of Germandom. He was tall, blond, blue-eyed, coldly handsome, and well proportioned. He was also intelligent and gifted. A member of a musical family—his father was director of the Conservatory of Music in Halle an der Saale, his grandfather director of the Royal Conservatory in Dresden—he had received a fine musical education and played the violin with professional skill. He was an accomplished athlete, a fine swimmer and tennis player, an outstanding fencer. At school he was consistently first in his class.

Presumably for reasons of patriotism he joined the German navy after leaving school, and as a naval cadet served under Captain (later Admiral) Canaris, the future chief of the German counterintelligence. In 1930 he was cashiered from the navy, allegedly for refusing to marry a girl he had made pregnant who was the daughter of a friend of the commander in chief of the navy, Admiral Raeder.

A year later Heydrich, now jobless, was recommended to Himmler. Although Heydrich was still only twenty-seven, Himmler was so impressed by his qualities and qualifications that he brought him into the SS and almost immediately put him in charge of organizing a new intelligence department he had set up within his elite guard. As the Security Service of the Reichsführer SS (*Sicherheitsdienst*, or SD), this department was to become the principal intelligence agency of the Nazi party; on June 9, 1934, it was given a monopoly status as the sole intelligence and counterespionage agency of the party, its organizations, and affiliated formations. [24] In his new position Heydrich quickly demonstrated a keen appreciation of the power that comes with the possession of information; in his files he accumulated data on prominent figures in every walk of life and every political party.

The man who appears to have profited most from this information was Himmler, who is supposed to have used it for purposes of bargaining and blackmail to secure appointment to the offices he coveted either for himself or his lieutenants. It may be that this was how Himmler worked his way into the control of the police in the various states of Germany.

There is a theory, supported by a good deal of credible evidence, that Himmler meanwhile had Heydrich under his own control by possessing information that the racial credentials of this paragon of Teutonism were blemished by a Jewish grandmother, the wife of the director of the Dresden Conservatory. Instead of dismissing Heydrich, Himmler is said to have exploited the situation knowing that Heydrich was at his mercy and that he could be compelled to go to any lengths to prove his loyalty and the superiority of his German over his Jewish blood.[25]

This theory admits a degree of cynicism in Himmler's attitude toward race that was not at all characteristic. Whatever the truth of the matter, Heydrich served Himmler loyally and Himmler recognized his worth. In 1932 Heydrich was formally named chief of the SD, and thereafter he was rapidly promoted through the ranks of the SS. When Himmler became head of the police forces in all Bavaria, Heydrich was given his former post as chief of police in Munich, and when Himmler moved his headquarters to Berlin in 1934, Heydrich accompanied him as his principal aide.

On June 26, 1936, after his appointment by Hitler as chief of the German police, Himmler created a new branch of the German police from sections of the Gestapo and the Criminal Police (*Kriminalpolizei*, or Kripo) which he called the Security Police (*Sicherheitspolizei*, or Sipo). This office was also placed under the command of Heydrich, whose SD was still part of the SS and thus a party, not a state organization. The main task of the Sipo, according to the official decree setting it up, was to ensure co-operation between central and local government, between party and state offices, and, above all, between the party and the Wehrmacht, which the Nazi leadership was still treating with respectful caution.[26] What it amounted to was a state police supervisory organization to parallel the party's SD, and thus a second channel of authority for Heydrich and Heydrich's superior officer, Heinrich Himmler.

Shortly after he had set up the Sipo, Himmler unified the secret political police throughout Germany by requiring that the term *Gestapo*, heretofore the name of the Prussian secret police, be used for the secret police of all German states, and that the organizational structure and administrative procedure of the Gestapo be adopted by all German police forces.[27] A law of February 10, 1936, had authorized the Gestapo to combat subversive movements in every part of Prussia.[28] It was now recognized nationally as a superior office, independent of legal restrictions and the authority of other Reich offices, but empowered to give orders to those offices and to use their facilities in carrying out its tasks.[29] In subsequent orders from Hitler, the Reichs-führer SS and chief of police in the Reich Ministry of the Interior was authorized to take all necessary measures for the maintenance of security and public order, even if these transgressed the legal limits hitherto laid down for this purpose.[30]

Soon after the outbreak of war, the various branches of the German police were reorganized and centralized in a Central Office for Reich Security (*Reichssicherheitshauptamt*, or RSHA), which included the Gestapo, the Kripo, the Sipo, and the SD, which now became a state as well as a party organization. The decree establishing the new organization, dated September 27, 1939, was to go into effect October 1.[31]

The formation of the RSHA provides an interesting example of Himmler's method of working through a variety of organizations to extend his authority and by-pass that of other state or party offices. An order of September 26, 1939, concerning the use of letterheads laid down the rule that the RSHA was to be used for internal correspondence, and chief of the Security Police (Sipo) and SD for correspondence with outside authorities, but that in certain cases the letterhead Reichsführer SS or even Reich minister of the interior might be desirable. The Secret State Police Office (*Geheimes Staatspolizeiamt*) and the Reich Criminal Police Office (*Reichskriminalpolizeiamt*), being executive offices within the RSHA, were authorized to use their own letterheads. As head of the RSHA, Himmler continued to use the title Reichsführer SS and chief of the German police, while his deputy director, Heydrich, used the title chief of the Sipo and SD.[32]

Heydrich remained deputy director of the RSHA after his appointment as acting Reich protector of Bohemia and Moravia in September 1941. After Heydrich's assassination in June 1942, Himmler took over the leadership of the RSHA personally, but in January 1943 he again delegated the office to another, this time to Ernst Kaltenbrunner, who held the position to the end.[33]

When the period of Nazi territorial expansion began, Himmler and Heydrich organized special task forces, *Einsatzgruppen* or *Kommandos,* to accompany troops of the regular army into occupied territories to deal with problems of political security and to carry out "special tasks," which generally meant the implementation of Nazi ideological programs such as the roundup of Jews. After the RSHA was formed these special task forces came under its jurisdiction, and with the rapid extension of German conquests a separate department was set up in the RSHA to supervise operations throughout the German sphere of influence. This department was divided along territorial lines, with special sections for the various countries or areas within Germany's power orbit.[34]

In the course of the Polish campaign a new rank of police officer came into being in accordance with a decree of November 13, 1937, which provided that, in the event of mobilization, a senior SS and police officer (*Höherer SS-und Polizeiführer,* or HSSPF), nominated by the Reichsführer SS, would be appointed for every military district to take command of all forces belonging to the Reichsführer SS and chief of the German police (meaning all regular SS, Waffen-SS, police, and special task forces.) After September 1, 1939, HSSPFs were appointed for all military districts in Germany, but it was primarily outside Germany, where the lines of power and authority were not yet fixed, that they became key figures in the administrative system. Responsible for all questions of security and race, terms that admitted infinite elasticity of interpretation, they were nominally subordinate to the military or civilian heads of the local German occupation governments; but, in fact, they owed their primary allegiance to Himmler and, on all matters of importance, they took their orders from him. This situation was made very clear by a decree of November 2, 1939, which stated that SS and police officials were subject to the orders of the heads of the local German government "in so far as these did not conflict with the orders of the Gestapo or higher authorities." To make the situation even more plain, a directive of December 18, 1939, stipulated that "the HSSPF is the representative of the Reichsführer SS and chief of the German police for all matters which are the latter's responsibility." [35]

As for the authority of the police in general, an RSHA decree of April 15, 1940, stated that

> the legal validity of state police regulations does not rest on the Reich President's decree of February 28, 1933, 'For the Protection of People and State'; the powers required by the Gestapo for the execution of all measures necessary to their task stem *not from specific laws and ordinances but from the overall mission allotted to the German police in general and the Gestapo in particular in connection with the reconstruction of the National Socialist state.*[36]

The Army

The greatest single obstacle to the plenitude of National Socialist power within the German state was the army.[37] Not only did the army constitute a significant power factor in its own right, but it was still one of the most respected institutions in Germany with traditions that represented a serious counterpoise to the philosophy of Hitlerism. The army, however, failed to move against Hitler during his first years in office.[38] Those years gave Hitler time to instill his own spirit into a new generation and to win over or remove the older members of the officers' corps.

Through his merger of the offices of chancellor and president upon the death of Hindenburg in August 1934, Hitler made himself supreme commander of the Wehrmacht. Immediately afterward he required that all members of the armed services take a new oath of loyalty, an oath no longer to the chief of state, the constitution, and the fatherland, but to the person of Adolf Hitler, Führer of the German Reich and nation, to whom they were obliged to swear unconditional loyalty and obedience.[39] Thereafter the members of the armed forces could oppose Hitler only at the cost of breaking this oath.

That the loyalty oath was not such an insuperable barrier to action against Hitler as some German generals tried to make it appear in postwar apologias is demonstrated, according to the generals' own testimony, by the involvement of many of them in plots against the Nazi regime.[40] Nor did Hitler propose to rely on a mere oath to control the regular army.

A far more significant step in the establishment of this control was the reintroduction of universal military conscription on March 16, 1935,[41] which most German generals welcomed because it represented an important stage in the restoration of Germany's military strength. The more farsighted realized that the old army was about to be overwhelmed by a youth vibrant with Nazi ideas, but they, too, did nothing to oppose the measure. When the army leaders were later to plan their moves against the Hitler regime, they faced the possibility that their conscript soldiers could not be trusted to carry out their orders.

Hitler, for his part, remained uncertain about the loyalty of the generals, who alone in Germany possessed the power to impose an effective check on his policies. At a critical conference on November 5, 1937, when he first broached the possibility of war against Austria and Czechoslovakia to a select group of senior military and civilian officials, he found his views challenged by Blomberg, the minister of war, Fritsch, the commander in chief of the army, and Neurath, the foreign minister.[42] All three expressed reservations about Hitler's analysis of the military and diplomatic situation, in particular his belief that the threat of Italy would keep France neutral in such a conflict, and that Britain would not intervene. Fritsch and Neurath subsequently re-emphasized their disagreement in personal conferences with Hitler.[43] Three months later Blomberg, Fritsch, and Neurath had been removed from their positions, the military command structure had been reorganized, and the Foreign Office had been placed under a reliable Nazi.

It is impossible to know whether the expressions of disagreement with the policies advocated by Hitler during the November 5 conference had anything to do with the personal and organizational changes that took place so soon afterward, or whether Hitler was personally responsible for the particularly sordid methods employed in getting rid of Blomberg and Fritsch. As chancellor and supreme military commander he could have dismissed them without scandal, just as he dismissed Neurath. Nor had he any compelling reason to drop Blomberg, who had become an enthusiastic Nazi and could probably have been persuaded to go along with any policy Hitler proposed. Neurath, however, was the head of an office without intrinsic power, whereas Blomberg and Fritsch were members of a social-military caste with a highly developed esprit de corps and leaders of the most powerful organization in Germany. Against them Hitler may have hesitated to move without strong justification. Moreover, it is difficult to believe that even the highest Nazi officials would have dared to employ such gross tactics without their Führer's knowledge and approval. His subsequent displays of shock and anger at the revelations and his professed desire to retain Blomberg and Fritsch mean nothing. Hitler was a good actor as well as an unscrupulous liar.[44]

Whatever Hitler's involvement may have been behind the scenes, the actual campaign against the German generals was conducted primarily by Göring and Himmler, whose interests and ambitions once again coincided, as at the time of the Röhm Putsch. Göring aspired to Blomberg's position as head of all three branches of the armed forces, while Himmler, like Röhm before him, wanted to break the army leadership as a stronghold of resistance to National Socialism.

Göring and Himmler were aided by rifts in the ranks of the generals. Blomberg had been Hindenburg's selection as minister of war in Hitler's original cabinet, but his subsequent enthusiastic acceptance of Nazism disgusted many of his colleagues who nicknamed him the Rubber Lion (*Gummilöwe*). Blomberg, therefore, could not count on the solid support of the German officers' corps.

The campaign against Blomberg turned on his infatuation with a girl of humble origin. Ordinarily a German general would not have been allowed to marry beneath his social station, but Hitler gave his consent in this case and both he and Göring were present as the only witnesses at Blomberg's wedding on January 12, 1938. Almost immediately afterward the Berlin police discovered documents showing that Blomberg's wife had been a prostitute with a police record. After the war a German police official confessed that he had forged these documents, at whose orders he did not know. Forged or not, the documents ruined Blomberg. Göring informed him that his marriage had so disgraced the honor of the German army that the generals demanded his resignation, and even a divorce would no longer save him. Hitler did not intervene on Blomberg's behalf, nor did he recall him to active duty during the war, despite his shortage of experienced commanders.

Hardly had the police exposed the seamy past of Blomberg's wife than they produced a dossier purporting to show that Werner von Fritsch, the commander in chief of the German army, was a homosexual. When Fritsch protested his innocence, he was confronted with a witness who swore to having had unnatural relations with him. In the case of Fritsch there is no doubt that the charges against him were false. The chief witness against him later broke down under cross-examination and admitted that he had been bribed by Himmler and Heydrich, an admission that was to cost him his life. Fritsch's innocence was subsequently established by a military court of honor.[45] Meanwhile, however, he had been obliged to resign until his name could be cleared. By the time this had been done his case was overshadowed by Hitler's annexation of Austria, a foreign policy triumph that made an army coup against Hitler unthinkable. Fritsch was never restored to his old position, but merely named honorary commander of his former regiment, the twelfth artillery. In the first month of the Polish campaign he was killed at the front.[46]

Whether or not Hitler was ultimately responsible for the campaign against Blomberg and Fritsch, he took advantage of their removal to reorganize the command structure of Germany's armed forces.[47] Any expectations Göring may have had to succeed Blomberg were quickly shattered. The position of minister of war was abolished, or rather it was absorbed by Hitler himself, whose status as supreme commander of the Wehrmacht was given renewed emphasis. Under his direct command he established the office of the High Command of the Armed Forces (*Oberkommando der Wehrmacht,* or OKW), which was to serve as his personal military staff, a sort of Wehrmacht chancellery, and carry out tasks previously performed by the Ministry of War.

As head of the OKW Hitler appointed General Wilhelm Keitel, an obsequious military bureaucrat. Although he was Blomberg's son-in-law and indebted to him for his previous high position in the Ministry of War, Keitel did not make a gesture to save him, nor did he subsequently ever oppose Hitler on a major—or even minor—issue.[48] To succeed Fritsch as commander in chief of the army, Hitler named General Walther von Brauchitsch, an appointment made only after Brauchitsch had assured Keitel that he was prepared to lead the army closer to the regime and its philosophy, to choose a more suitable chief of the army general staff if this should seem desirable (the present holder of that position, General Ludwig Beck, was an outspoken opponent of the Nazi regime), and to recognize the new organization of the high command. Raeder remained commander in chief of the navy, Göring head of the Luftwaffe. Göring's only personal compensation for his part in the intrigues against Blomberg and Fritsch was promotion to general field marshal, which made him the highest ranking officer in the Wehrmacht although not its overall commander.

Hitler's elimination of the Ministry of War removed the one office capable of co-ordinating all three branches of the armed forces, for the OKW was not a supreme military office but a channel for the orders of Hitler. He remained the immediate commander of each of the three branches of the Wehrmacht, to which he could—and frequently did—issue orders directly without going through the OKW. In the course of the reorganization of the army sixteen high-ranking generals were relieved of their commands, and forty-four others, together with a large number of senior officers, were transferred to other duties.[49]

On the same day the resignations of Blomberg and Fritsch and the reorganization of the army were announced, Neurath was replaced as foreign minister by Hitler's minion Joachim von Ribbentrop. As compensation Neurath was appointed head of a Secret Cabinet Council to advise the Führer on foreign affairs, a body that never met.[50]

Army indignation against these arbitrary measures and vile methods might have crystallized into actual revolt had Hitler suffered a foreign political setback or some similar loss of prestige, but quite the opposite occurred: In March came the annexation of Austria; in September the Munich triumph. Meanwhile Nazi officials were steadily building up their authority at the expense of the army, in particular Heinrich Himmler, Reichsführer SS and chief of the German police.

CHAPTER 6

The Instruments of Control: Racial Offices

When the period of Nazi territorial expansion began, the number of offices held by Himmler and the power he exercised through them was formidable. Although some afforded him vastly greater power than others, he demonstrated remarkable ingenuity in making use of them all to insert his influence in every part of the Reich administrative system and later in the German occupation governments. As head of the police he could claim authority over the entire field of security; as head of the SS he claimed authority over the entire field of race, since it was the responsibility of the SS to ensure the breeding and selection of the highest racial types.

Through a combination of claims and pressure tactics, he succeeded by 1939 in bringing the majority of existing agencies and all new agencies dealing with racial questions under his leadership. These included the Central Office for Race and Resettlement (*Rasseund Siedlungshauptamt,* or RuSHA); [1] the Ancestral Heritage Office (*Ahnenerbe*), to investigate the racial credentials of Germans who were to be resettled; the Well-of-Life (*Lebensborn*) orphanages for racially valuable children; [2] and the Liaison Office for Ethnic Germans (*Volksdeutsche Mittelstelle,* or VoMi), which dealt with ethnic Germans abroad, either to use them to further Nazi purposes in foreign countries, or to bring them back to the bosom of the Reich. [3]

Control of these scattered racial offices did not satisfy Himmler. In September 1939 he had united all German police services under the Central Office for Reich Security (the RSHA). [4] In the following month, with Germany's victory over Poland assured, he persuaded Hitler to allow him to set up a supreme supervisory office for racial questions. This was the Reich Commission for the Consolidation of

55

the German People (*Reichskommission für die Festigung des deutschen Volkstums,* or RKFDV), to which Hitler assigned primary responsibility for carrying out the Nazi racial programs.

In his (unpublished) decree of October 7, 1939, establishing the new office, Hitler stated that the Greater German Reich now had the opportunity to provide land for all Germans who formerly had been forced to emigrate. To the Reichsführer SS he was assigning the tasks of repatriating all Germans living outside the Reich, of resettling them in the Reich (including the newly annexed territories), and of eliminating all foreign elements within the Reich which represented a danger to the German state and people. For this purpose the Reichsführer SS was given authority over all Reich offices and all administrators in the newly occupied territories. [5]

To implement his new authority, Himmler set up an executive office for his consolidation commission under SS Oberführer Ulrich Greifelt, the head of the Office for Immigrants and Repatriates (*Leitstelle für Ein-und Rückwanderung*) which Himmler had established in June 1939 to deal with the resettlement of Germans from the South Tyrol. This executive office originally consisted of no more than twenty persons, its main job being to act as a sort of clearing house for Himmler's orders as head of the consolidation commission to other Reich offices, which had the staff and equipment necessary for putting them into effect.[6] "The main burden for carrying out these great duties on the spot," Himmler wrote in one of his first directives, "rests on the shoulders of the Reich governors and chiefs of provincial administration in the new territories. I have at the same time made the senior SS and police officers attached to them my representatives in my capacity as Reichskommissar for the consolidation of the German people." [7]

The chief significance of Himmler's appointment as RKFDV was that this position gave him yet another channel of authority, and one almost ideally suited for by-passing the authority of other state and party officials. Further, his new position reinforced his control over racial matters and over the multifarious problems this question involved. Speaking on behalf of Himmler, Greifelt claimed that the duties of the RFKDV required "absolute plenary powers" if they were to be satisfactorily carried out, and that "in the new eastern territories every aspect of life must be considered from the point of view of the RKFDV." [8]

To deal with the problems of German racial consolidation, Himmler not only used existing Reich offices but regularly found it necessary or desirable to create new ones. In October 1939 he reorganized an existing office as a Central Land Office (*Zentralbodenamt,* or ZBA) to compile an ethnic register of all agricultural property in the new provinces and to plan future evacuations and resettle-ments. This office was eventually to become responsible for the actual sequestration of Polish and Jewish agricultural property.[9] In the same month he set up the Central Immigration Office (*Einwandererzentral-stelle,* or EWZ) composed of representatives from the ministries of the Interior, Health, and Labor, and his own Office for Race and Resettlement, whose job it was to process the repatriation of ethnic Germans (primarily those evacuated from the territories con-ceded to Russia) and decide who was eligible for Germanization.[10] The German Resettlement Trusteeship Corporation (*Deutsche Umsiedlungs-Treuhandgesellschaft,* or DUT) was founded early in November to manage the accounts of persons who were obliged to leave property behind upon being resettled and who were to be given the equivalent in newly annexed lands. Eventually it was used by Himmler to claim jurisdiction over all agricultural property in the occupied territories.[11] The founding of the Central Office for Evacuation (*Umwandererzentralstelle,* or UWZ) for the deportation of Poles and Jews,[12] was followed by the establishment of a special department in the RSHA under Adolf Eichmann to give priority to the evacuation of Jews.[13]

There followed the formation of the East German Agricultural Cor-poration (*Ostdeutsche Landbewirtschaftung GmbH,* or *Ostland Ge-sellschaft*) to manage the agricultural property confiscated from Poles and Jews; [14] the Resettlement Staff (*Ansiedlungsstab*) to co-ordinate the resettlement of ethnic Germans in the Old Reich and Austria; [15] the Guidance Office for Germanic Peoples (*Germanische Leitstelle*) to deal with the resettlement of persons from the Germanic countries of Western Europe.[16]

The construction of this immense and complicated bureaucratic ap-paratus was not meant to serve Himmler's personal ambition and lust for power alone. Like Hitler, he was passionately and fanatically ded-icated to the realization of National Socialist aims. This fanaticism explains in part the secret of his strength. But it also explains how, when the war was at its height in Russia, he could be less concerned with getting men and supplies to the front than with the mass shifting of peasants, their livestock, equipment, and household goods from one end of Europe to another in carrying out his massive racial resettle-ment programs; how he could allow those same peasants, whose pro-duction was so desperately needed in wartime Europe, to languish for months and years in relocation centers; how he could employ thou-sands of able-bodied men throughout the war in determining the racial backgrounds of conquered peoples, compiling heredity charts and ethnic surveys, and implementing gigantic resettlement programs in wartime; or how he could order the mass execution of Jews in concentration camps, unconcerned by the fact that they were manufacturing arms and clothing for the Wehrmacht—all this in the interests of realizing the great National Socialist idea.

The Nazi use of economic assets was never characterized by efficiency, however, for almost all Nazi leaders, if not to the same extreme extent as Himmler, regarded the economy primarily as a means to an end. It was therefore hardly surprising that the Nazi operation of the economy was almost exclusively determined by political and ideological considerations.

CHAPTER 7

The Instruments of Control:
The Economy[1]

The Nazis' repudiation of Marxist theory did not prevent them from recognizing in the economy the basic source of their strength. Their stress in economics, as in all other fields, was on the spirit with which problems were approached. If the individual citizen were properly imbued with the principles of National Socialism, he would produce for the common good of the *Volk* to the utmost of his ability and in whatever capacity the *Volk* deemed most beneficial.[2] At the same time, as in all other fields, the Nazis maintained a bewildering number of organizations to channel the spirit and ensure that the people remained in harmony with themselves. The situation in the economy was if anything more confused than elsewhere, for there were no economic experts among the top-ranking Nazi leaders. Their economic administration was characterized by the constant creation of new offices to co-ordinate or reorganize the activities of the old, as though by the mere proliferation of offices they could stimulate production or make good Germany's economic deficiencies.

During the first years of the Nazi regime the emphasis was on control, above all on the control of the people involved in the economic process, and in this period organizations were formed to embrace each major group of German producers: business, labor, agriculture, and the professions.

Production and the Producers

In dealing with business enterprises, the Nazis at first restricted themselves to working through existing management bodies on the theory

59

that by controlling the leadership of such enterprises they could control the enterprises themselves. This system had the added advantage of giving business leaders the temporary illusion that they were being left in charge of their own affairs. Not only were the great cartels left intact, but a compulsory cartelization law of July 1933 empowered the Reich minister of economics to integrate independent enterprises into the cartel system and thus bring them under cartel control.[3]

German business leaders were not left long with an illusion of independence, however. A law of February 27, 1934, authorized the Reich minister of economics to establish certain business associations as the sole representatives of their branch of the economy, and for this purpose to reconstitute or dissolve existing associations, create new ones, appoint new leaders, and provide them with new charters. According to the official explanation of this law, it was designed "to give the minister of economics the opportunity to introduce order in the multiplicity of economic associations, and eventually to ensure state control over all associations and their members." To carry out this task he was empowered to issue decrees and to take all measures he considered necessary, even if they conflicted with existing legislation.[4]

Following the promulgation of this decree, German business was reorganized along territorial and functional lines under a newly formed Reich Economic Chamber within the Reich Ministry of Economics. Many local chambers of commerce and functional associations were already in existence in one form or another when the Nazis came to power. The big change effected by the Nazis was to bring them all together into a tightly knit national organization, and to make membership compulsory. Every entrepreneur was required to belong to his local economic chamber and to the appropriate functional group for his business. Leadership was according to the *Führerprinzip*. The leaders of the main economic chambers and associations were appointed by the minister of economics, and these leaders in turn selected their subleaders. The charter of each chamber and association was drawn up by its leader, who had the task of guiding his organization according to National Socialist principles.[5]

The broad powers given the Reich minister of economics over the German business world were extended in May 1935 when Hjalmar Schacht, acting minister of economics and president of the Reichsbank, was appointed by Hitler to a new post as plenipotentiary-general for military economy (*Wehrwirtschaft*).[6] Schacht's policies, however, were not sufficiently radical to suit Hitler, who in October 1936 delegated emergency economic powers to Göring as plenipotentiary of a new Four-Year Plan. After Schacht's resignation in the following year, Göring co-ordinated the Ministry of Economics into the Four-

Year Plan—taking care to preserve its controls over German business.[7]

On May 2, 1933, the Nazis dissolved all trade and labor unions. To take the place of the disbanded unions, and incidentally to take over their property as well, they established the German Labor Front (*Deutsche Arbeitsfront,* or DAF) as an association (*Gliederung*) of the Nazi party. In its official charter of October 24, 1934, the DAF was described as the organization of all producing Germans, intellectual and manual, which was to include, in particular, the members of all former labor and management organizations. Its principal task was to ensure that every individual should take his place in the economic life of the nation wherever he might be of greatest value to the community, and if necessary to provide special professional training for that purpose. In addition it was to guarantee labor peace, arbitrate disputes between workers and employers, and take care of its members whenever they should be in need. As head of the DAF Hitler appointed Dr. Robert Ley, a high-ranking party official, who was to select his subordinate leaders and determine the membership of the DAF under the general supervision of the party.[8]

Embracing as it did both management and labor, the DAF constituted an important instrument of control over a large segment of German manpower. Labor, however, was to be controlled on many different levels and through many different agencies. In addition to the DAF there were organizations for peasants, craftsmen, and professional people, and special labor-control legislation.

A law of January 30, 1934, "For the Regulation of National Labor" gave factory owners or managers a Führer status in their organizations, with complete authority over their workers as well as complete responsibility for their output and welfare. By delegating Führer powers to factory owners the Nazis seemed to be delivering labor into the hands of management, but their law also provided for the supervision of all economic enterprises by party officials, a provision that may not always have benefited the workers but that gave party officials legal authority over all entrepreneurs—and, through them, over their staffs.[9]

A law of February 28, 1935, supplemented by later decrees, required that each workman possess a labor book containing his entire job record as well as his racial background. He was also obliged to register with official employment agencies so that whenever necessary he could be assigned to jobs where he would be of greatest benefit to the community.[10]

Compulsory labor for all men between the ages of eighteen and twenty-five was introduced with the establishment on June 26, 1935, of the Reich Labor Service (*Reichsarbeitsdienst,* or RAD). This compulsory labor service, which was later extended to women, was to last for six months.[11]

The RAD was a paramilitary organization which drafted men for limited periods and used them for special projects requiring mass manpower. A more permanent form of compulsory labor was introduced by Göring as head of the Four-Year Plan with a law of June 22, 1938, which made all German citizens liable for service in any job and in any area where they might be needed, and for a program of retraining for such a job if this were necessary.[12] Within the Four-Year Plan, a plenipotentiary-general for labor was appointed with authority to supervise the recruitment and allocation of labor throughout the Reich, and later throughout the German-occupied territories.

For the control of persons engaged in any kind of cultural activity, the Nazis set up a Reich Cultural Chamber (*Reichskulturkammer*) under Goebbels's Ministry of Propaganda, with subsidiary chambers for writers, the press, radio, the theater, music, the creative arts (*bildende Künste*), and the film. No one was permitted to engage in any of these activities professionally unless a member of one of these groups, and membership might be forfeited by "professional misconduct," meaning failure to conform to the dictates of Goebbels and the party leadership.[13]

Similar organizations were created for civil servants, teachers, students, the legal, medical and other professions, and even the Protestant clergy.[14] The concordat with the Holy See of July 20, 1933, although recognizing the right of the Catholic Church in Germany to manage its own affairs, contained a provision that placed its clergy under the protection of the state "in the same manner as civil servants." Catholic bishops before taking office were obliged to take an oath of loyalty to the German Reich and the local German state (*Land*), and to swear to refrain from all activity likely to be harmful to the state.[15]

Control over German agriculture was inaugurated in September 1933 with the creation of the Reich Food Estate (*Reichsnährstand*), which was supposed to embrace all persons engaged in or deriving their income from agriculture, including all manufacturers, processors, and distributors of agricultural products. Forestry and horticulture, hunting and fishing, bakeries and breweries, beet-sugar manufacture and beekeeping, were all classified as agricultural enterprises. The Reich Food Estate was to promote all aspects of German agriculture, and ensure a uniform agricultural policy for the country. Like the Reich Economic Chamber it was organized along territorial and functional lines, with a network of territorial and functional subdivisions. The head of the Food Estate was the Reich peasant leader, who was empowered to issue decrees, regulate production and distribution, fix wages and prices, and take all measures he considered necessary in carrying out his tasks. He was also to incorporate all organizations in any way associated with agriculture into the agricultural estate in any manner he thought desirable. R. Walther Darré, Reich minister of food and agriculture, was appointed Reich peasant leader on January 12, 1934. He thus became the supreme authority in the field of German agriculture until the creation of Göring's Four-Year Plan.[16]

Fundamental to the agricultural policies of the Third Reich was the welfare and security of the German peasant, who according to National Socialist ideology represented the ultimate guarantee for the preservation of the German people. The sword might conquer the soil required by the Germans in the future, but only the plow could hold it.

The most important piece of Nazi legislation in this connection was the Reich Hereditary Farm Law (*Reichserbhofgesetz*) of September 29, 1933, which stated in its introduction:

> The Reich government wants to maintain the peasantry as a blood source of the German people. The peasant farms [*Bauernhöfe*] shall be protected against excessive indebtedness and parcelling through inheritance so as to remain forever in the possession of free peasants as a heritage of the community [*Sippe*]. The goal will be a healthy distribution of agricultural property, for a large number of self-sustaining small and medium-sized peasant farms, distributed as evenly as possible throughout the entire country, constitutes the best guarantee for the healthy preservation of people and state.

The law provided that farms large enough to be self-sustaining, as a rule not over 125 hectares, were to become hereditary estates if they were the property of a person legally entitled to be a peasant (*Bauer*). To establish legal status as a *Bauer*, German citizenship, proof of German or German-related blood (back to January 1, 1800), and an honorable character were required. Large estates could be registered as hereditary (*Erbhöfe*) upon special application if there was a public interest involved (a provision that avoided stirring up the large landowners, including the Junkers, against the regime). The hereditary estate could not be sold, mortgaged, or, in case of previous mortgage, foreclosed. It was to pass undivided to the heir, who according to German "customary" law would be either the eldest or the youngest son. The will of the deceased could not change the rank of the heirs. No person could own more than one hereditary farm. Descendants of peasants who were not heirs were entitled to monetary remuneration, and education according to the social standards of the estate. In case of extraordinary need, they were granted the right of *Heimatszuflucht,* that is, they might come back to the family farm if they could not gain a living elsewhere. Local courts were set up to handle the legal aspects of the system, which was to be under the supreme authority of the Reich minister of justice and the Reich minister of food and agriculture.[17]

What was to happen to the many peasant sons whose place in the family succession deprived them of all land? In the past they had drifted to the cities or emigrated abroad, but the Nazis had other solutions in mind. These peasants, the nonheirs whose propagation was constantly encouraged by the National Socialist movement, formed Germany's famous *Volk ohne Raum.* These were the men for whom it would be necessary to conquer land and soil in the east, the sturdy peasants who would eventually extend the broad base of Germanism until the German *Volk* had been established, indestructibly, upon this earth.[18]

The Four-Year Plan

The reorganization and control of German economic life that took place during the first years of Nazi rule did not satisfy Hitler. Bad harvests in 1934 and 1935 necessitated a large-scale import of food and drained off Germany's reserves of foreign currency, which Hitler insisted should be used primarily to purchase scarce raw materials essential for armament production. In April 1936 he instructed Göring to study means of improving the raw materials and foreign exchange situations. In the following month, Göring set up a special staff under Colonel Fritz Loeb whose studies formed the basis of the subsequent Four-Year Plan.[19]

Hitler was concerned with far more than bad harvests. His ideological program demanded that the German economy be prepared for war in the near future, and recent experience evidently convinced him that none of his present economic officials or business leaders understood the problem or was capable of acting with the necessary energy and ruthlessness. Hitler seems to have concluded that only a sound Nazi of proven capacity could deal with the economic situation, and in the summer of 1936 he addressed a long memorandum to Göring explaining the desperate immediacy of Germany's economic requirements and the need for a massive emergency economic program, a policy statement that amounted to a review of the ideas set forth in *Mein Kampf.*[20]

Since the outbreak of the French Revolution [Hitler said], "the world has been driving at a constantly accelerating pace toward a new conflict, the extreme solution of which is Bolshevism, whose essence and goal is the elimination and displacement of the hitherto leading social classes of humanity by international Jewry. No nation will be able to avoid this historical conflict. *Ever since Marxism, as the result of its victory in Russia, has established one of the greatest empires of the world as a base of operations this question has become a threatening one. An ideologically divided democratic world faces a determined will to attack based on unified authoritarian ideology.*

The military strength of this will to attack, Hitler continued, was growing with ever-increasing speed from year to year, as statistics on the growth of the Red Army showed. Germany, because of its unfortunate geographic position, would inevitably be the focal point of Bolshevik aggression. This was an unpleasant fact, but one that German leaders could not escape. Hitler did not intend to prophesy when the attack would take place, but only expressed the certainty that it was inevitable. A victory of Bolshevism over Germany would not lead to a new Versailles treaty, but to the final annihilation and extermination of the German nation and, with it, of Western European civilization. To confront successfully and eventually to eliminate this danger was the crux of the task of the German political leadership, to which all other considerations had to be subordinated.

It was time, Hitler declared, that the economic leadership, too, should recognize the nature of this task. The nation did not live for the economy, but the economy for the nation. German economic policy could have only one goal and one purpose: the preservation of the nation's existence.

The only definitive solution of Germany's economic problems was an extension of its living space. This was the principal future task of the political leadership. Meanwhile the economic leadership would have to work with the resources at hand. For this purpose a number of basic principles should be observed: The German economy was to be placed on a war footing immediately; there should be no stock piling of raw materials if this meant a limitation in the present manufacture of arms—the essential thing was to have a maximum supply of weapons for immediate use in war, not stock piles that could be later converted into weapons; no attention should be paid to gold reserves or balance of payments deficits as such, but rather all means should be used to purchase essential resources unavailable in Germany; whenever possible essential materials should be produced at home, no matter how uneconomical such production might be, in order to save foreign exchange for raw materials Germany could not produce under any circumstances; all available oil and ore resources should be tapped, the manufacture of synthetic rubber, aluminum, and other essential materials should be undertaken at once on the largest possible scale. In conclusion Hitler set Germany's economic leadership a single clear-cut task: "The German economy must be mobilized for war within four years."

Taking the four year limit set by Hitler as his guide, Göring responded to Hitler's memorandum with a Four-Year Plan for the German economy which relied heavily on the recommendations of the economic staff he had set up in the previous May. This plan was accepted by Hitler, who announced it publicly at the Nuremberg party rally of September 9, 1936. His official decree of October 18 on the subject stated that Germany's national interests required the unified management of all the resources of the German people, and that the Four-Year Plan was intended to ensure the rigorous co-ordination of all party and state offices for this purpose. Göring, as plenipotentiary for the Four-Year Plan, was authorized to take all measures he considered necessary, to issue decrees, and to give orders to all state and party offices and their affiliated organizations.[21]

In his first decree after his appointment, Göring announced that he intended to work as much as possible through existing economic agencies, and that new offices would be set up only when absolutely necessary. To secure advice before making fundamental decisions, he set up a consultative council, under his chairmanship, which included the heads of all important Reich offices.[22]

To administer his own organization, Göring set up a Central Office of the Four-Year Plan, which he conceived as a sort of Reich chancellery of economics to supervise and co-ordinate the activities of the various Reich economic departments and any new offices that might be established. As head (state secretary) of this Central Office and his deputy in affairs concerning the Four-Year Plan, Göring appointed Paul Körner, his former personal secretary and a senior official in the government of Prussia.

Under the Central Office Göring set up subordinate offices to deal with the most critical sectors of the German economy: the production and distribution of raw and synthetic materials, agricultural production, labor, price administration, and foreign exchange. Each of these offices within the Four-Year Plan was to direct the activities of existing offices in their various fields.[23]

Under the auspices of the Four-Year Plan there began the drive toward economic self-sufficiency that was to characterize German economic policy during the last years of peace under the Nazi regime. Great new industrial complexes, the Hermann Göring Werke, were built for the speedy and often extravangantly costly production of iron and steel, aluminum, artificial rubber, oil, and other materials essential to the German war economy.[24] But primarily the Four-Year Plan was concerned with the direction of existing economic agencies; not surprisingly, therefore, it was involved from the beginning in altercations with other economic offices and officials.

Rivalries for Economic Authority

Foremost among Göring's early opponents was Hjalmar Schacht, acting minister of economics, president of the Reichsbank, and plenipotentiary-general for military economy. In assigning extraordinary powers to Göring, many of them identical with powers previously delegated to Schacht, Hitler had not bothered to inform Schacht or to alter his assignment in any way. Schacht, therefore, decided to ignore Göring's claims to authority over his various departments and in December 1936 instructed his officials that they might supply information to the offices of the Four-Year Plan but that they were to continue to take their orders exclusively from himself. Blomberg tried to heal the breach between Schacht and Göring by explaining that their spheres of operations in no way impinged on each other, the Four-Year Plan being responsible for eliminating bottlenecks in the German war economy, whereas the plenipotentiary-general had the task of mobilizing existing economic resources for war. His formula failed to settle anthing. After a year of futile struggle, Schacht resigned as acting minister of economics in December 1937, a move Hitler assumed to mean his resignation as plenipoteniary-general for military economy as well. Schacht stayed on as president of the Reichsbank until January 1939.[25]

Göring himself now took over the Ministry of Economics for a short time with the object of making it "a strictly organized and effective instrument controlled by the plenipotentiary for the Four-Year Plan." Having placed the Ministry of Economics firmly under his own authority, Göring transferred to it some of the most important departments of the Four-Year Plan, including the offices for the production and distribution of raw materials and new offices for research and development.[26]

In February 1938 Göring turned the Ministry of Economics over to Walter Funk, Reich press chief and under state secretary in the Reich Ministry of Propaganda and Public Enlightenment. Schacht's former position as plenipotentiary-general for military economy was also given to Funk at this time, and in January 1939 he succeeded Schacht at the Reichsbank. Göring evidently expected Funk to be a completely subservient instrument, but Funk disappointed him by trying to use his position as plenipoteniary-general to build up his own

authority. In December 1939 Göring put an end to these pretensions by ordering that henceforth the functions of the plenipotentiary-general should be restricted to matters concerning the Ministry
of Economics and the Reichsbank, and that the actual office of the
plenipotentiary-general be dissolved.[27]

After Göring's reorganization of the Ministry of Economics in January and February of 1938, his deputy in the Four-Year Plan wrote:
"In the course of these weeks the structure and organization of the
state control of the economy has been laid down once and for all." [28]
The new economic controls, however, were to be no more permanent
or final than the old ones had been. Further controls of the economic
administration followed with the appointment of special plenipotentiaries within the Four-Year Plan to co-ordinate production and distribution in still more fields of critical importance. There had been a
plenipotentiary for iron and steel production and allocation since
1937. Subsequently plenipotentiaries were appointed for chemical
production, construction, motor transport, public utilities, mineral oil
extraction and production, communications, mining, machinery, and
labor. These plenipotentiaries were empowered to take whatever
measures they considered necessary in their respective fields, and to
issue orders to all Reich offices. "The plenipotentiaries-general act on
my direct orders," Göring stated in his decree on the subject of July
16, 1938, "and are therefore covered by the full power I have been
given by the Führer." [29]

The bewildering proliferation and reorganization of German economic offices did not cease after the outbreak of war, and the large
number of economic offices set up in the various occupied areas
added to the confusion. Within this administrative maze, Göring was
undoubtedly the most powerful figure in German economic life during the initial stages of Nazi territorial expansion, a power that was
to be extended into the occupied areas. For to preserve unity in the
administration of the economy, Hitler authorized Göring to issue orders directly to all German occupation governments. In October 1940
Hitler renewed the Four-Year Plan for another four years.[30]

Economic unity, however, was not to be established or maintained
by decree. Göring lacked a large and reliable economic bureaucracy
to carry out his orders. Even after his reorganization of the Ministry
of Economics, his Four-Year Plan remained primarily a co-ordinating
agency dependent on other offices for the implementation of its policies. The heads of these offices were not necessarily loyal to Göring,
the more ambitious among them being intent on building up their
own administrative empires, while all were subject to pressure from
rival Reich or party leaders. In the course of the war, economic offi-

cials in occupied areas, far from Berlin and constantly faced with emergency situations, made themselves increasingly independent of the Four-Year Plan or found it more expedient to co-operate with other Supreme Reich Authorities.

But the greatest blow to Göring's efforts to maintain unified control of the economy was his gradual loss of Hitler's confidence. During the Polish campaign the army encountered serious armament shortages which were blamed on Göring. To remedy this situation, Hitler set up a new economic co-ordinating office in March 1940 independent of Göring—the Ministry of Armaments and Munitions—which he placed under the direction of Dr. Fritz Todt.[31] Göring's prestige slipped further with the failure of his Luftwaffe to establish German air supremacy during the Battle of Britain in the summer of 1940. By autumn of that year other agencies had begun to exercise more effective authority than Göring over several sectors of the economy.[32]

Prominent among Göring's economic rivals during the early stages of the war were the economic offices of the army, which were under the general direction of the Military Economy and Armaments Office (*Wehrwirtschaft-und Rüstungsamt,* or Wi-Rü Amt). Originally established in 1927 as the Army Ordnance Office (*Heereswaffenamt*), it became in November 1934 the army's principal armaments office under Colonel (later General) Georg Thomas.[33] In direct competition with the Thomas organization was the armaments office of Göring's Luftwaffe, which refused to co-operate with the army's office and which benefited greatly from its commander's influential positions in party and state, especially after he became head of the Four-Year Plan. Thomas for his part was obliged to co-operate closely with the Four-Year Plan to secure allocations for the army.

The Wi-Rü Amt had one major advantage over Göring. It was part of a large and powerful organization, with ample personnel and a network of regional economic offices (armament inspectorates and commands) under its direct control. When the war began, special military economic staffs were attached to army units with orders to secure all economic assets likely to be valuable to the German war economy, particularly items in short supply. These economic task forces were specifically instructed to take their orders only from the army economic offices, or from the heads of the local military government. The replacement of military by civilian administrations, which usually took place a few weeks after the conquest of an area, brought Göring back into the picture; but by this time the army had taken over the most obvious economic assets and established its regional inspectorates and commands throughout the conquered territory. Lacking a large staff of his own, Göring was obliged to work through these regional army economic offices or to transfer their personnel to his own regional offices, where they generally continued to co-operate more closely with the army than with him.

The troubles of the Wi-Rü Amt were not confined to its rivalry with Göring, but involved almost every other German economic agency, including the Reich Ministry of Armaments and Munitions, which Hitler set up in March 1940 specifically to relieve the army's armament shortages. In May 1942 the armaments section of the army's Military Economy and Armaments Office, by far its most important division, was detached from the army office and incorporated into the armaments ministry, since February 1942 under the direction of Albert Speer. With the armaments section went control of the army's network of regional armament inspectorates and commands, which now also came under Speer. General Thomas, while remaining head of the truncated army economic office, was also left as head of the armaments section under its new management; but conflicts with Speer led to his removal from the armaments ministry in November 1942. Early in the following year, embittered and weary of constant infighting, Thomas asked to be relieved of his duties as head of the army economic office as well, which henceforth played a minor role in the overall economic picture.[34]

A more formidable personal rival to Göring than Thomas was Dr. Fritz Todt, builder of the autobahn and Göring's plenipotentiary-general for construction in the Office of the Four-Year Plan. In 1938 Hitler entrusted Todt with the building of the West Wall (the Siegfried line), and during the war, with the building of the Atlantic Wall and an East Wall as well. In addition, Todt was charged with the construction and repair of all installations needed by the Wehrmacht, including roads, bridges, railroads, barracks, and bunkers. The *Organisation Todt* (OT) which he set up to cope with these formidable tasks required immense economic resources, and Todt was given the powers necessary to secure them in Germany and the occupied territories.[35]

In March 1940, after Göring's lapses in the armament field had become apparent, Todt was named Reich minister for armaments and munitions (*Reichsminister für Bewaffnung und Munition*).[36] This new ministry, which was not subject to the control of the Four-Year Plan, was to co-ordinate the activities of all government and private enterprise engaged in the manufacture of armaments and to improve production from a technical point of view. As plenipotentiary-general for construction, Todt remained under the jurisdiction of Göring and his Four-Year Plan; but as Reich minister, entrusted with many of the same tasks as Göring's office, he was directly responsible only to Hitler, a situation that did not contribute to the clarification of Germany's economic administration or to smoother relations among its various economic departments.

On February 8, 1942, Todt was killed in an airplane accident. Bypassing Göring altogether, Hitler appointed Albert Speer, an architect he had chosen to direct the planning and reconstruction of German cities after the war, to take over Todt's various offices.[37] Göring made a futile attempt to bring Speer under his control by appointing him plenipotentiary-general for armament tasks in the Four-Year Plan, but Speer ignored Göring as Todt had done. Operating directly under Hitler as minister of armaments and munitions, he rapidly extended his power and influence. A little over a month after his appointment, the chief of the army economic office reported to his staff after a conference with Speer, "The Führer regards Speer as his principal organ, his confidential agent for the entire economic area. Speer alone has authority today. He may interfere in the affairs of all other departments. Already he has placed himself above all departments. . . . We will have to infiltrate the Speer organization and co-operate with it, otherwise Speer will go his own way." [38]

Co-operation with the Speer ministry did the army economic leaders little good. As has been seen, in May 1942 the armaments section of the Military Economic and Armaments Office was transferred to the Speer ministry, and with it control over the regional armaments inspectorates and commands. A little over a year later Hitler transferred the most important functions of the Reich Ministry of Economics, which in February 1938 Göring had made an instrument of the Four-Year Plan, to the Speer ministry. These included control of the entire field of raw materials and industrial production. In view of his enlarged sphere of operations, Speer's title was changed to Reich minister for armaments and war production.[39]

In the field of labor allocation, too, Göring's powers were drastically curtailed. On March 21, 1942, Hitler named Fritz Sauckel, his Gauleiter in Thuringia, plenipotentiary-general for labor in the Four-Year Plan under the direct authority of Göring. As noted earlier, there had been a plenipotentiary-general for labor in the Four-Year Plan since 1938, but Sauckel was given new and, eventually, almost unlimited power in this field.

> To guarantee the necessary labor force for the entire war economy, especially for armaments [Hitler's order of appointment read], requires the uniform direction of the utilization of all available labor corresponding to the needs of the war economy, including workers recruited abroad, prisoners of war, as well as the mobilization of all as yet unused labor in the Greater German Reich, including the Protectorate, the Government General, and the occupied territories.[40]

Göring attempted to retain authority over Sauckel by emphasizing that he was an official of the Four-Year Plan and demanding that he seek Göring's approval for all important measures in the labor field.[41] Hitler, however, issued his orders directly to Sauckel without bothering to consult Göring, and Sauckel himself behaved as though he were responsible only to Hitler. To circumvent Göring altogether he worked through the old Reich Ministry of Labor, which still commanded a large staff of labor experts, and never appeared in the offices made available to him through the Four-Year Plan.[42]

For the recruitment and allocation of labor, Hitler authorized Sauckel to appoint plenipotentiaries responsible to him in all civil and military offices, with the power to issue orders to all officials in the execution of their tasks. As his plenipotentiaries in the Reich, Sauckel appointed the local Gauleiters; in the occupied areas he appointed the heads of the occupation governments or high-ranking members of those governments. "The raw materials and productive capacity of the conquered territories and also their human labor force shall be totally and conscientiously exploited through the recruitment and allocation of labor for the benefit of Germany and its allies," Sauckel declared in his first major public pronouncement.[43]

Within the next months Sauckel proceeded to ever-harsher measures in his recruitment of labor, finally instituting compulsory labor service for men and women throughout almost all the German-controlled territories. As German demands for labor increased, so did efforts to evade them, until at last Sauckel was compelled to resort to mass roundups of workers. The labor force recruited in this manner was hardly the most efficient or reliable, while the repercussions of such methods of recruitment were catastrophic for the German occupation governments,[44]

CHAPTER 8

The Control of Power

Despite the Nazis' efforts to centralize and co-ordinate their administrative institutions, the proliferation of agencies and the competition between them was such that the German government was in many ways more decentralized and certainly less efficient than in pre-Nazi times. As a result, for all his dictatorial powers, Hitler's immediate control over many government departments may have been less effective than that of some of his predecessors. But if he himself was no longer able to exercise such control, he had made it quite impossible for anyone else to do so. At no time during the era of Nazi expansion was he confronted with effective opposition; throughout this period he successfully maintained ultimate authority and decision-making powers.

Many Nazi leaders whose influence loomed large in particular fields played a comparatively minor role in the formulation of expansionist policies because of the nature of their offices. This was the case, for example, with Goebbels, whose propaganda ministry was nevertheless to be an important instrument of control in the occupied territories.

Ribbentrop, who posed as a prime formulator of German foreign policy before the war, was never much more than a spokesman for Hitler, if anything more prolix. He may have encouraged Hitler's hopes about the possibility of friendship with Britain—certainly his 1935 naval agreement with that country was a major foreign policy coup—but his influence was at no time decisive, and by the time the war broke out it was negligible. During the war he tried to claim that occupied territories not actually annexed to the Reich were still foreign countries and hence the administrative concern of the Foreign Office, a claim he advanced with considerable tenacity but usually in vain.

The organization that should have played a major role in determining German expansionist policies was the German army. Not only was the army the prime executor of expansionism; it was also first on the scene in all conquered territories and set up the first occupation governments. By insisting on the priority of military security requirements, army leaders might have retained predominant influence or, at least, an important voice in determining occupation policies.

But Hitler, through his various purges and administrative reorganizations, had done his work well. Army leaders raised no effective objections to his expansionist program; they permitted the incorporation of entire SS divisions into their organization; they condoned (even though they might deplore) the activity of Himmler's task forces immediately behind the front lines; and they meekly surrendered their administrative powers in occupied territories to Nazi "civilian" governments when called upon to do so. Although regional military commanders subsequently possessed the right to assume supreme command in an area whenever military security was at stake, in no significant instance did they make use of this prerogative to assert or extend their influence, as Himmler regularly did in the name of political security or racial purification.

This does not mean that army leaders were spineless or otherwise tacit or overt supporters of the Nazi regime. Many suffered martyrdom in opposing Nazi policies, many more refused to co-operate with Nazi officials. The terrible dilemma of German officers, and indeed of all government officials who opposed the regime, was that any consistent effort on their part to block the implementation of Nazi policies would mean transfer, dismissal, or the concentration camp. Some accepted the risk of these alternatives; they were dismissed from their positions, and no more was heard from them. Others, believing that by remaining in office they could still exercise some influence on policy, found themselves caught in the vicious cycle of accepting and then gradually being obliged to participate more and more in the inexorable stepping up of Nazification programs, until they too at last resigned or became irretrievably implicated. Army leaders, with so much actual power under their command, might have engaged in active rebellion, but mutiny is a distasteful alternative for soldiers, especially in wartime; and German officers, conscious of their own qualms, were justifiably doubtful whether, if they did raise the standard of rebellion, their troops would carry out their orders. What a real leadership personality might have done under these circumstances is another matter, but Hitler had taken care to remove all potential opposition leaders from offices of power, and his multifarious supervisory organizations successfully prevented the development of new ones. In fine, army leaders, despite all their apparent opportunities, never exercised a decisive role in occupation policies except in a few peripheral areas which were never firmly under German control and consequently remained under military government.

All real influence in occupation policies, certainly in long-range policies, was reserved for Nazi leaders; and among these only three, Göring, Bormann, and Himmler, stand out as major figures involved at the center of the policy-making process. In the early stages of Nazi expansion, the most influential member of this trio was Göring. Commander of the Luftwaffe, supreme authority over the economy of Germany and all German-controlled territories, he was appointed at the beginning of the war chairman of a Ministerial Council for the Defense of the Reich, a body that was supposed to co-ordinate Germany's administrative and economic leadership.[1] At the same time he was officially designated Hitler's successor.

Göring differed from Nazi leaders like Bormann and Himmler, and from Hitler himself, in not being obsessed with ideological questions. With some justification he has been compared to an Italian Renaissance despot. He loved power for its own sake, and he frankly exulted in the pomp and luxury that power could bring. Although a firm believer in Germany's need to expand in Eastern Europe in order to knock out the Russian menace and establish German power on a continental basis, he was intent above all on exploiting the economic resources of the conquered territories and lamented the squandering of those resources through the premature implementation of racial programs.

Had Hitler died soon after naming Göring as his successor, German policy during the Second World War might have been very different. But Göring never had an opportunity to practice his brand of deviationism, nor did he ever significantly modify the policies of Hitler. By the time the war began, self-indulgence and drugs had taken the edge off Göring's drive and capacity for hard work. His Ministerial Council for the Defense of the Reich was never an effective policy-making instrument; it met for the last time in December 1939. In the course of the war Göring's authority steadily declined, and many of his most important economic powers were taken over by Todt, Speer, and Sauckel. Within their respective spheres these men excercised enormous influence, but their activities were restricted to immediate, practical tasks.

Far greater influence could have been exercised by Bormann, chief of the Party Chancellery and, after 1943, Hitler's personal secretary. But Bormann was an unimaginative bureaucrat, not a policy maker, and his only distinction was his single-minded devotion to Hitler and the ideology of National Socialism. "In Hitler's opinion," a secretary wrote in describing their relationship, "Bormann was the only one among his collaborators who could reduce his ideas and projects into clear and intelligible formulae." Hitler himself described Bormann as a devil for work, thorough and efficient. "Bormann's proposals are so exactly worked out that I need only say yes or no. With him I despatch [sic] in ten minutes a pile of papers over which other men would take hours of my time." That Bormann was brutal Hitler readily acknowledged, "but what he undertakes he finishes. I can rely absolutely on that. With his ruthlessness and brutality he always sees that my orders are carried out." [2]

It is possible that Bormann's brutality fostered the brutality of his leader, but Hitler needed little stimulus in this respect. Otherwise there is little indication that Bormann influenced Hitler's policies, nor did he presume to do so. "There can be no question of influencing the Führer," he wrote to his wife, "although people often babble nonsense about it." [3] Bormann's sole ambition appears to have been to remain at the center of power, to serve as the chief instrument of the Führer, and to exclude all other influences. In this he succeeded to a remarkable degree; but precisely the quality that recommended him to Hitler—his absolute agreement with the views of his leader—makes it impossible to see in him anything more than an executor of Hitler's will.

Bormann's peer in dedication to Nazi ideology was Heinrich Himmler—single-minded to the verge of idiocy, a British historian has called him, a description that could have been applied to Bormann as well. Like Bormann, Himmler appealed to Hitler because he showed such a thorough understanding of his ideas and consistently endeavored to press them to their logical conclusion, both in theory and practice.

The great difference between the two Nazi satraps was that Himmler went far beyond Bormann in developing his own organizations for carrying out Hitler's programs. With the enormous number of offices under his control and his broad authority in matters of security and race, there seemed no limit to Himmler's powers. Yet limited they were. Although the impact of Himmler's authority was felt more strongly in the occupied countries than that of any other German official, he too was circumscribed by the multitude of rival organizations in the Nazi empire, he too was caught in the maze of conflicting competencies and was ultimately obliged to appeal to the authority of Hitler.

In the last analysis, however, Hitler did not depend on labyrinthine organizations, divide-and-rule tactics, or similar devices for his power. Hitler undoubtedly possessed one of the most forceful leadership personalities in recorded history, and as a leader dedicated to effecting decisive changes in world history he accomplished what he believed essential for this purpose: He instilled in his followers fanatic faith and unquestioning loyalty, and he held sway over those followers primarily because they believed in the man and his mission. In his ultimate control of power and authority, Hitler was indeed the Führer.[4]

PART TWO

The Course of Expansion

CHAPTER 9

The Period of Preparation

The Problem of Timing

Nazi Germany was the prime mover in European international politics before the Second World War.[1] It was not that other states were without expansionist ambitions. Mussolini's ventures into Africa were clear proof to the contrary. The difference was that none contemplated so revolutionary or so immediate a change in the world power structure as did the Nazis. Britain and France, if not altogether satiated powers, were nevertheless fundamentally concerned with preserving the status quo. They had little to gain and very much to lose by change. Soviet Russia was not without a dynamism of its own. World revolution was and remained a basic principle of Soviet foreign policy. The Stalinist party, however, had considered it temporarily expedient to hold back the world revolution and to build up the power of the Soviet Union. By awaiting the fulfillment of the prophecies of Marx, the rulers of Russia might expect to be both spectators and beneficiaries of the inevitable collapse of the capitalist world.

For Hitler alone there was a desperate urgency about the present. National Socialism, for all its folkish pretensions, was a very personal faith and one whose mission Hitler believed himself personally chosen by destiny to fulfill. With his sense of Messiahship went a desperate awareness of mortality. Whatever qualities Hitler may otherwise have attributed to himself, longevity was not among them. In a few years his energy might no longer be equal to his purpose, or he might die. Hitler thus limited the time available for solving Germany's problem of *Lebensraum* to the time span of a human life, and not even an entire lifetime but his period of maximum efficiency.

Hitler's sense of personal mortality meshed with his conception of Germany's global position. Each passing year made it more difficult

81

for the German nation to subsist or to increase in proportion to the laws of nature. During these same years the peoples inhabiting the world's great land masses, inferior races though they might be, were inexorably building up the power that could, if given time, overwhelm the purest and most concentrated group of Germanic culture-bearers. Germany could not afford to wait until related Germanic peoples, confronted by a direct threat to their existence, should at last recognize the correctness of Hitler's racial theories and enter into an alliance with their German brothers. When the hordes of Asia should finally be ready to assume the offensive, the Germans might no longer be sufficiently strong to withstand the attack, and their lands would be reduced to an anguished battleground in the struggle for survival between the Asiatic and the Anglo-American forces.

Hitler's solution, as he had set forth at length in *Mein Kampf,* was to establish the Germans on a great land mass in their own right, a project which he believed could only be accomplished by expansion into the space of Eastern Europe. But his awareness of his own mortality combined with his conception of Germany's steadily deteriorating global position demanded that the conquest of *Lebensraum* should be carried out soon, at the latest within the next ten to fifteen years. Thus from the beginning, time played a major role in Hitler's calculations. To remain static or to wait for other Aryan powers to fall into line with Nazi Germany was to court disaster. National Socialism posited the alternative between expansion and annihilation. Hitler had long ago made his choice, and upon coming to power set about the task of acquiring the requisite areas.

Propaganda, Rearmament, and Diplomacy

If Hitler appeared to be a chancellor in chains when he came to power in January 1933, [2] Germany might have been considered with even better reason to be a country in chains. Its western boundaries with France and Belgium, fixed by the Treaty of Versailles, had been confirmed by the Locarno treaties of 1925, which the Germans themselves had negotiated and accepted, and which were guaranteed by Britain and Italy. In the east Germany faced a set of defensive alliances among the smaller states, most of them backed up by France, including specific treaties of mutual guarantee between France and Poland and France and Czechoslovakia. At sea Britain still ruled the waves, at least in the waters of Northern Europe; across the sea the United States, under the new leadership of Franklin Roosevelt, appeared to be emerging from its isolationism to assist in maintaining the postwar international order it had done so much to establish. [3]

Germany itself was in the throes of economic depression, its financial credit exhausted, its army and navy weak.

After the Nazis came to power Germany's international position seemed to deteriorate still further.[4] Whatever foreign sympathy the country may have enjoyed as a defeated and underdog nation was dissipated by the truculence and vulgarity of the new regime and its brutality in dealing with its opponents, particularly the Communists and the Jews. France, justifiably fearful of a revival of German militancy, was gratified by evidences of renewed willingness on the part of both Britain and the United States to co-operate in defending the existing international order. Soviet Russia, which had formed an alignment of sorts with its fellow outcast during the Weimar period, now looked to the West for support against Germany's new anti-Communist regime. In 1934 the Soviet Union joined the League of Nations after Nazi Germany withdrew, and in the following year it concluded a defensive alliance with France.[5] Elsewhere Communist parties were uniting with other parties of the left to form Popular Front governments to resist right-wing elements at home and conduct an anti-Nazi foreign policy abroad. The Little Entente powers of Czechoslovakia, Yugoslavia, and Rumania drew closer to France and strengthened their own alliances by establishing institutions to co-ordinate their political and economic policies.[6] Poland, while concluding a nonaggression pact with Germany in 1934, also extended its 1932 nonaggression pact with Russia for another ten years and tightened its diplomatic and military ties with France.[7] Even the Austrians, who since the First World War had appealed in vain to be allowed to establish closer relations with their fellow Germans, were alienated by the Nazis' anti-Catholic and anti-Socialist policies, and an authoritarian Austrian government now sought support for its independent status from Italy and Hungary. Mussolini, the head of the Italian government, was eager to provide such support. Despite Hitler's often-expressed desire for good relations with Italy and his fellow dictator, Mussolini had no desire for a German-Austrian union and the establishment of German power directly on the Italian border. During the first years of the Nazi regime he worked systematically and effectively to block an Austro-German union, which Hitler had said was the first major objective of his foreign policy, and looked with suspicion on all proposals for closer German-Italian relations emanating from Berlin.[8]

Hitler's first move to improve Germany's international position was to strengthen Germany itself, first by clandestine, then by increasingly overt programs of rearmament.[9] This rearmament was accompanied by a massive propaganda campaign to reassure the world about Germany's peaceful intentions, and to cast blame for any apparent Ger-

83

man threats to world peace on the moral deficiencies of Germany's enemies. Germany sought only justice, Hitler insisted. The disarmament clauses of the Treaty of Versailles had been violated by the makers of that treaty, who had failed to disarm according to its provisions; the League of Nations, so much revered by world public opinion, was nothing more than a front for France's political hegemony in Europe. In October 1933 he announced that because his own fervent appeals for honest disarmament had been disregarded, he was withdrawing Germany from the world disarmament conference; and because he had no desire to aid in the maintenance of France's European hegemony, he was withdrawing his country from the League of Nations as well.[10] At the same time Hitler made a vigorous public appeal for friendship with France, the great power most seriously threatened by Hitler's decision and the power that was still the most immediate threat to Germany.[11]

While steadfastly reiterating his desire for peace, Hitler took up two other principles the Western world had come to accept as almost sacred: the right of nationalities to sovereignty, and their right to self-determination. Hitler contended that the makers of the Treaty of Versailles, while solemnly proclaiming these principles, had in fact flagrantly violated them in dealing with the defeated powers. The world would have to face the fact that Germans, too, had the right to sovereignty and self-determination, and as leader of the German people he would not rest until these natural rights of his people had been secured. It was on the basis of these principles that he was to justify German rearmament, the remilitarization of the Rhineland, and subsequently the annexation of Austria and the German-inhabited regions of Czechoslovakia (the Sudetenland).[12]

Hitler's propaganda placed his opponents in a dilemma. Britain and France, which had used the principles of sovereignty and self-determination so effectively in undermining the Habsburg and Ottoman empires, found these weapons exploding in their hands as they faced revolt throughout their own empires. Moreover, influential leaders in both countries had come to believe in these principles themselves, although their governments generally saw fit to apply them only when confronted by force. Their many concessions to force were lessons not lost on Hitler, who became convinced that the overriding consideration of the ruling classes in Britain and France was the avoidance of war: They wanted to preserve the existing social and international order, so favorable to themselves, without the use of force and without paying the economic and social price that the use of force generally involved.

Consequently, even as he rearmed more and more openly, Hitler never ceased stressing his own desire for peace: Once Germany's justifiable demands had been met, once its sovereignty and self-determination had been achieved, it would become a bastion of peace and stability in Central Europe, a bulwark against Communist Russia, an ally in the struggle against the spread of Communism to other parts of the world. Opposition to Germany's demands for simple justice, on the other hand, might eventually compel him to resort to arms, a decision he would make with great regret—he himself had been a front-line soldier and was fully aware of the horrors of war—but one from which he would not flinch to secure justice for his countrymen. If he failed, he knew that neither he nor the existing order in Germany was likely to survive, but the Western powers should consider that the destruction of National Socialist Germany would probably be followed by the establishment of a Communist Germany and the formation of a German-Russian union, whose joint strength would overshadow and eventually overwhelm the continent. Between the alternatives of simple justice for Germany accompanied by European peace and stability, and a war that might well result in the Bolshevization of Europe, could the leaders of Britain and France hesitate?

Hesitate is exactly what they did do, and in their hesitation they failed to unite or take decisive action against the Nazi danger. In March 1935, on the grounds of Germany's right to sovereignty, Hitler openly announced his intention to rearm and the reintroduction of compulsory military conscription.[13] Britain and France protested, but Britain promptly undercut its ally by concluding a naval treaty with Germany in June, a foreign policy triumph for Hitler's confidential adviser on foreign affairs and ambassador at large, Joachim von Ribbentrop, who ran a semiofficial foreign office of his own called the *Dienststelle Ribbentrop*.[14] Through this treaty the British secured Germany's promise to limit its navy to 35 per cent of the British, a treaty ratio the British had sought to negotiate in vain before the First World War. The treaty was nevertheless a horrendous diplomatic blunder, for in effect it recognized Germany's right to rearm and consequently its right to break international treaties forbidding such rearmament. The naval treaty was a major breach in the entire postwar treaty system, and seriously undermined Franco-British confidence and solidarity.[15]

Hitler now received unexpected help from Mussolini. To bolster the prestige of his government, shaken by five years of economic depression, the Italian leader inaugurated a policy of restoring Rome's ancient dominion over the Mediterranean basin and northern Africa, and after an extended period of diplomatic tension he invaded Ethiopia in October 1935. The French and British governments had for some time allowed Mussolini to know that they would be willing to make concessions to him in Africa, their main concern being to retain

Italy as a potential ally against Germany. The French, in particular, feared the revival of German power far more than the bluster of the Italian dictator. But when Mussolini actually moved against Ethiopia, the outcry on the part of public opinion in France and especially in Britain was such that the governments of these countries found themselves obliged to give public support to League of Nations measures to halt Italian aggression. In order not to drive the Italian dictator into the arms of Hitler, however, they never made these measures sufficiently stringent to render them effective.[16]

While the French and British government strove, unsuccessfully, to appease Mussolini abroad and at the same time appease public opinion at home, Hitler took advantage of their preoccupation with Ethiopia to remilitarize the Rhineland, one of the boldest and most momentous gambles of his career. For with this move, which he announced on March 7, 1936, he destroyed at one blow the major strategic advantage the Allies had gained as a result of their victory in the First World War and brought about a drastic change in the European balance of power, to the benefit of Germany. Hitler's action affected France most immediately, for it meant that in the event of another conflict German forces would be poised directly on the French border, while conversely the French would be deprived of the advantage of being able to strike at Germany through a demilitarized zone which was also the heartland of Germany's industrial economy. But Hitler's action was perhaps an even greater blow to the small states of Eastern Europe, for it virtually eliminated France's ability to invade Germany in case of a German attack on France's eastern allies.

The remilitarization of the Rhineland was a clear-cut and unilateral violation of international treaties, not only of the Treaty of Versailles, which Hitler maintained had been imposed on Germany in violation of the armistice agreement, but of the Locarno treaty of 1925, which had been freely negotiated with the governments of France and Belgium and which was guaranteed by the governments of Britain and Italy. France now had every legal right and certainly every military reason to undertake another occupation of the Rhineland, which would still have been a comparatively easy task in view of France's immense military preponderance. German generals warned Hitler in the most pressing manner not to risk a move which was certain to provoke a French invasion and could only result in national humiliation or disaster. But Hitler disregarded all voices of caution, and the fact that his generals were proved wrong only increased his contempt for Germany's old-guard conservative leadership and his confidence that his judgment was better than that of his military experts.

Hitler's Rhineland action was no hastily considered leap in the dark. By now he had had ample opportunity to take the measure of his opponents. Not only were Western leaders preoccupied with Ethiopia, but their reaction to that conflict had given Hitler occasion to observe their paralysis of will and reluctance to resort to extreme and therefore dangerous measures in moments of crisis. Hitler had also chosen his time well. In France, which had been governed by a stopgap ministry since the preceding January, politicians facing new elections seemed more concerned with domestic than foreign dangers. Hitler felt confident that the present French leadership lacked the resolution and the nerve to undertake an invasion of Germany, and if the French did not move on a question so vital to their own interests, the British were not likely to do so either, especially if British public opinion could be convinced that the remilitarization of the Rhineland was a purely German internal affair and no threat to Britain or the peace of Europe.

To justify his action and allay the apprehensions of fearful foreigners, Hitler accompanied the remilitarization of the Rhineland with a massive propaganda campaign. This action had been undertaken, he said, in response to the recently ratified French alliance with Russia, which had completely upset the existing European balance of power and consequently all political and legal conditions under which the Locarno pact had been concluded. In any case, however, Germany had the right to sovereignty over its own territory; the remilitarization of the Rhineland, besides being essential to German national security, was no more than an assertion of that right and a step on the path of securing justice for Germany. Now that this step had been taken, Hitler was prepared to demonstrate his continued desire for peace by negotiating a series of new agreements, including treaties with France and Belgium providing for the demilitarization of *both* sides of Germany's western frontiers, and to conclude nonaggression pacts with all of Germany's neighbors, east and west, similar to the one already concluded with Poland. Hitler even held out the hope that, under proper conditions, Germany would return to the League of Nations.[17]

Hitler's gamble was successful. The French and British governments protested, as they had done in the previous year when he had announced his decision to rearm, but again they did nothing. Worse still, in trying to avoid alienating Mussolini, while at the same time taking a public stance against him, they not only failed to halt Italian aggression in Ethiopia but failed to mollify Mussolini as well. For, in spite of all their devious maneuvers, the Italian leader took offense at their public condemnation of his policies. In this frame of mind, his appetite whetted and his sense of reality dimmed by easy successes in Africa, he gradually succumbed to Hitler's arguments that even more might be accomplished in partnership with Germany.[18]

In *Mein Kampf* Hitler had described a German alliance with Italy as one of his major foreign policy objectives, and he remained convinced of the desirability of such a connection. As Hitler saw it, Italy, with its justifiable ambition for supremacy in the Mediterranean, was the natural enemy of France, whereas the basic interests of Germany and Italy were nowhere in conflict except in South Tyrol. This former Austrian territory south of the Brenner Pass had been assigned to Italy after the First World War for strategic reasons, despite its large German population. For the sake of friendship with Italy, Hitler was prepared to renounce all German ethnic claims to South Tyrol, and even to evacuate the German population from the region.[19]

Hitler was soon forced to recognize that the South Tyrol was not the only area where German and Italian interests diverged. A far more serious bone of contention was Austria, whose reunion with Germany had heretofore been one of the declared goals of Nazi policy. As mentioned earlier, the Italians had no interest whatever is substituting powerful Germany for weak Austria on their northeastern frontier, a change that might make for the effective revival not only of German claims to South Tyrol but also of ancient German dominion over the entire Italian peninsula.

Mussolini's involvement in Ethiopia gave Hitler the opportunity he needed to get on better terms with Italy. While giving Mussolini constant assurances of German support, he skillfully exploited the Duce's indignation against France and Britain to secure a relaxation of Mussolini's attitude on the Austrian question. Further, to reassure Mussolini about Germany's intentions, he concluded a so-called gentlemen's agreement with Austria on July 11, 1936, recognizing Austria's sovereignty and renouncing a policy of annexation.[20] One week later civil war broke out in Spain, where Mussolini's troops were to be heavily committed in yet another move to revive Roman influence in the Mediterranean. In Spain, as in Ethiopia, Hitler was the only leader of a great power to support Italian policy, support which included sending German troops to Spain (in return, to be sure, for valuable economic concessions.) [21] In October 1936 Mussolini's son-in-law, Count Ciano, Italian foreign minister since the previous June, paid a visit of state to Germany, where on October 23 he signed a secret treaty recognizing the common political and economic interests of the two countries, including their mutual satisfaction over the normalization of German-Austrian relations through the gentlemen's agreement of July 11.[22] Shortly afterward Mussolini publicly referred to the German-Italian relationship as the Rome-Berlin Axis, but it was not until May 1938 that a formal military alliance between Germany and Italy (the Pact of Steel) was concluded.[23]

It was now only a matter of time before Hitler, in return for German support of Italian expansion in the Mediterranean, should demand Italy's consent to German expansion in Central Europe. The first fruit of the Rome-Berlin Axis was the German annexation of Austria.

CHAPTER 10

Expansion in the Name of Self-Determination

Austria

None of Hitler's territorial objectives was more clearly defined than his desire to bring about the union of Germany and Austria. He began *Mein Kampf* with the words,

> Today I consider it my good fortune that Fate designated Braunau am Inn as the place of my birth. For this small town is situated on the border between those two German states, the reunion of which seems, at least to us of the younger generation, a task to be furthered with every means our lives long. German-Austria must return to the great German motherland, and not because of economic considerations of any sort. No, no: even if from the economic point of view this union were unimportant, indeed, if it were harmful, it ought nevertheless to be brought about. *Common blood belongs in a common Reich.*[1]

After he came to power, Hitler's policy toward Austria was characterized by the same subterfuge and deceit that he used to disguise so many of his purposes, but the records of his secret directives and conversations leave no doubt that he had not abandoned his goal of an Austro-German union. In the beginning, his tactics in dealing with Austria were similar to those he had employed with such success in Germany. Through the Nazi party organization in Austria, massively supported by funds and propaganda from the Reich, he proposed to win elections and eventually secure the formation of a National Socialist government by legal means. After that a gradual co-ordination (*Gleichschaltung*) of Austrian and German policies and institutions

90

could be inaugurated. Once European public opinion had become accustomed to the de facto union of the two countries, the actual annexation (*Anschluss*) of Austria to Germany might take place.[2]

Austria, until 1918 under the rule of the Habsburgs and the nucleus of an ancient empire, had a far grander historical tradition than Prussia, which in 1866 had triumphed in the struggle for supremacy in Germany. But after 1918 it seemed that Austria itself had no alternative but to seek incorporation into Germany. Its empire had been dismantled by the peace treaties following the First World War, and therewith Austria had been deprived of the greater part of its administrative and economic hinterland. With its large population of bureaucrats and an industrial complex designed to produce manufactured goods for the predominantly agricultural regions of its former empire, postwar Austria was in serious economic trouble from the time of its creation, for the new states carved out of the former Habsburg domain erected high tariff barriers to protect and build up their own economies. To become part of a viable economic unit (and of a stronger political unit as well), a democratically elected Austrian constituent assembly voted on March 12, 1919, for annexation to Germany.

Despite the fact that almost the entire population of what was left of Austria was German, the Allies refused to allow the principle of self-determination to be applied to Austria and prohibited the Anschluss. This was understandable, for the Allies had no desire to enlarge and strengthen the country they had just defeated at such terrible cost, or to make Germany the heir to Habsburg imperial traditions in Central and Eastern Europe. Even the proposal for a customs union between Germany and Austria, put forward in March 1931 as the capitalist world plunged into economic depression, was blocked by the French, who were fearful that economic union would be the prelude to political union. The French method of preventing that union, however—the withdrawal of short-term loans from Austria and Germany—created economic havoc in both countries and brought on the most serious phase of the great depression in Central Europe.

Bad as was the economic situation in Germany after 1931, it was even more desperate in Austria, where economic crises and political turmoil had been the order of the day even during the relatively prosperous period of the mid-1920s, and where extremist political parties and ideologies had already flourished in the days of the Habsburgs. Thus Austria in the 1930s seemed an even more fertile field than Germany for the dissemination of Nazi ideas and the growth of the Nazi party. The Austrian Nazis, however, lacked the leadership of a Hitler, and they encountered powerful opposition from the Roman Catholic

Church, the Socialists, organized labor—and from the Austrian government.[3]

At the time the Nazis registered their greatest gains in Germany, Austria was under the leadership of a coalition government representing the predominantly Roman Catholic and peasant population of the country. At the head of this coalition and chancellor of Austria since May 1932 was Engelbert Dollfuss, an ambitious and ruthless politician, who had observed the success of Hitler's tactics in Germany and was resolved not to repeat the errors of the Weimar Republic. As early as March 4, 1933, he suspended parliamentary government in Austria and secured the agreement of President Wilhelm Miklas to rule by emergency decree. Political assemblies and parades were forbidden, as was the wearing of uniforms by members of political parties, and freedom of the press was curtailed. Notwithstanding these measures the Nazis won nine out of twenty seats in the municipal elections in Innsbruck at the end of April 1933, whereupon the Austrian government promptly suspended all further municipal elections. Nazi agitators from Germany were expelled from the country, and on June 19 the Nazi party in Austria was declared illegal and officially dissolved, although, as usual in such cases, it continued to operate underground.

Hitler responded by putting political and economic pressure on the Austrian government and launching a massive propaganda campaign from the Reich.[4] At the end of May he imposed a one-thousand mark fee on German tourists going to Austria, thereby dealing a severe blow to the Austrian tourist industry. But Dollfuss did not give in. Instead he turned to Mussolini, who promised him military assistance in the event of a German invasion and encouraged him to reorganize his government on more authoritarian lines; above all he was to crush Marxist and Socialist organizations so as to deprive Hitler of the excuse to interfere in Austrian internal affairs in order to save the country from Bolshevism. Dollfuss also received support from Hungary, which had at least as much reason as Italy to fear a German-Austrian union and a possible revival of German imperialism in Central Europe. On March 17, 1934, the governments of Italy, Austria, and Hungary signed the so-called Rome Protocols, which provided for closer political and economic co-operation among the three states and placed Austria publicly and officially under Italian protection.

Meanwhile, in accordance with Mussolini's advice on domestic policy, Dollfuss dissolved all Austrian political parties with the exception of his own newly formed Fatherland Front. In doing so he crushed the Socialists with ruthless severity, a move of doubtful political wisdom, for by this action he permanently alienated Austria's urban workers and thereby deprived himself of what might have been his most effective domestic support against the Nazis. In April, Doll-fuss promulgated a new constitution for Austria giving himself dicta-torial powers. And on May 1, again at the advice of Mussolini, he signed a concordat with the Vatican giving the Church wide control over Austrian education.[5]

Dollfuss's turn to Mussolini was a bitter blow to Hitler, who re-garded an alliance with Italy as essential to a successful German for-eign policy. Moreover, Hitler was far from pleased by the conduct of the Austrian Nazis, who were feuding among themselves and who, like Röhm and his SA, frequently disregarded his orders and pursued policies of their own. To avoid alienating Italy further and to escape dependence on the Austrian Nazis, he decided to change his tactics and to adopt a waiting game in Austria. In March 1934, shortly before the signing of the Rome Protocols, he ordered that the use of force as well as press and radio attacks against the Austrian government should henceforth be strictly avoided. Nazi leaders were to concentrate instead on disseminating pro-Nazi and pro-Anschluss propaganda in Austria and to build up a clandestine party organiza-tion, which Hitler intended to keep under firm control from Ger-many.[6]

In June 1934 Hitler personally sounded out Mussolini on the Austrian question when the two dictators met in Venice. He reaf-firmed his permanent renunciation of German claims to South Tyrol and said he had come to realize that there could be no question of a German annexation of Austria. What he did want, however, were elections in Austria to make clear the attitude of the Austrian people and to secure a proper representation of National Socialists in the Austrian government. But Mussolini, who knew as well as Dollfuss what elections in Austria would mean, refused to make concessions on that point. "In view of the [Nazi] acts of violence against the Austrian government," he told the German ambassador to Italy, "He could not advise Dollfuss to start negotiations with the [Austrian] National Socialists." [7]

Negotiations would probably have been futile in any case, for by this time the Austrian Nazis had evidently decided to abandon the course of diplomacy in favor of a policy of direct action and were planning the violent overthrow of the Austrian government. German state and party officials knew that the Austrian Nazis were planning a coup, but Hitler's role in the entire affair has never been clearly es-tablished. According to Göring's testimony at Nuremberg, the Austrian Nazis led Hitler to believe that the Austrian army was pre-paring a coup of its own against the Austrian government if it would not agree to Anschluss with Germany, and that on the basis of this (false) information Hitler gave them permission to join the army in this undertaking and promised them the support of the party in Germany.[8] Whatever the truth of Göring's testimony, there is every reason to believe that Hitler knew about the prospective coup and that he agreed to allow the conspirators to go ahead with their plans because he assumed they would be successful.

Whether or not the Austrian Nazis had misled Hitler in the way Göring described, they had certainly misled themselves. They must have been convinced that pro-Anschluss sentiment in Austria was so intense and the existing government so weak that one bold thrust would be sufficient to accomplish its overthrow. They had not secured the co-operation of the Austrian army; they had not even secured assurances that the Austrian army or police would remain neutral in case they attempted a coup. Without such assurances and without considering the possible international repercussions of their action, they struck on July 25, 1934, seized the chancellery and murdered Dollfuss. They had no further successes to record. The Italian and Yugoslav governments, justifiably suspicious that the Austrian Nazis would not have dared to risk a Putsch without Germany's connivance, rushed troops to the Austrian frontier to forestall German intervention and if necessary to aid the Austrian government against the rebels. But no foreign aid was required. The Putsch was quickly suppressed by Austrian forces, and Kurt von Schuschnigg, the senior member of the Dollfuss cabinet, was called upon by President Miklas to form a new government. The murderer of Dollfuss and six of his associates were subsequently tried and executed by the Austrian authorities.[9]

The abortive Putsch in Austria, in which the German Nazis were inevitably implicated, represented a major foreign policy setback for Hitler and dealt a grievous blow to his relations with Austria and Italy. He was now confirmed in his resolve to suppress the agitation of the Austrian Nazis and to play a waiting game, for the events of the Putsch had made it unmistakably clear that nothing significant could be accomplished in Austria until Italian objections had been removed. On August 13, 1934, Hitler approved a new set of "guiding principles for German policy vis-à-vis Austria in the immediate future." To carry out the new policy, Franz von Papen, the Catholic conservative who had played so critical a role in Hitler's own rise to power, was appointed German ambassador to Vienna. At the same time the Austrian Nazis were assured that, although German tactics might change, the goal of Anschluss remained inexorably the same.[10]

As already noted, it was the involvement of Italy in Africa and subsequently in Spain that gave Hitler his chance in Austria. Papen, with his keen sense of opportunism, wrote Hitler shortly after Mussolini's invasion of Ethiopia. "I am convinced that the shift of power on the

94

European chessboard will quite soon enable us to take up actively the question of influencing the Southeastern area." Shortly afterward Mussolini himself confirmed the accuracy of Papen's judgment. Because of his appreciation for Germany's benevolent neutrality in the Ethiopian war, he told the German ambassador to Italy in January 1936 that

> he thought it would now be possible to achieve a fundamental improvement in German-Italian relations and to dispose of the only dispute, namely, the Austrian problem. Since we had always declared that we did not wish to infringe on Austria's independence, the simplest method would be for Berlin and Vienna themselves to settle their relations on the basis of Austrian independence, e.g., in the form of a treaty of friendship with a nonagression pact, which would in practice bring Austria into Germany's wake, so that she could pursue no other foreign policy than one parallel with that of Germany. If Austria, as a formally quite independent state, were thus in practice to become a German satellite, he would have no objection.[11]

Hitler, delighted by the prospect of better relations with Italy which he had coveted all along, did not press his advantage but accepted Mussolini's terms. On July 11, 1936, he concluded his gentlemen's agreement with Austria recognizing Austria's sovereignty and independence and renouncing a German policy of annexation. In return Mussolini consented to the participation of members of the so-called National Opposition (pro-Anschluss leaders) in the Austrian government, a concession he had denied Hitler two years before.[12]

Hitler remained cautious. He impressed on the Austrian Nazis that good relations with Italy were essential to the success of their Anschluss movement. Two more years would be needed before the German army could be used as an effective instrument of German foreign policy. Meanwhile the Nazi party in Austria would have to maintain discipline and allow itself to be guided by the leadership of the Reich.[13]

Despite Hitler's assurances to the Austrian Nazis that Anschluss remained the goal of his policy, many of them continued to disregard his orders and kept up their agitation in Austria, often encouraged by party functionaries in the Reich who were equally anxious to hasten the pace of events. To put an end to intrigues among Austrian and German party members and restore party discipline, Hitler in July 1937 gave Wilhelm Keppler, a German industrialist and economic expert, absolute authority over all relations with the Austrian Nazis. At approximately the same time he established connections with Dr. Arthur Seyss-Inquart, one of the few pro-Anschluss leaders in Austria who supported his policy of watchful waiting.[14]

Seyss-Inquart, born in a German enclave of Czech Moravia in 1892, came to Vienna at the age of fifteen and, after completing his work at the Gymnasium, studied law at the University of Vienna. In 1914 he enlisted in the Austro-Hungarian army, was wounded, decorated three times for bravery in the face of the enemy, and gained a reputation as an intrepid but cautious officer. While on leave in 1917 he passed his final examinations for a doctorate in law at the University of Vienna. After the war he established a highly successful law practice in Vienna, where his clientele included many Jews, despite his reputation for anti-Semitism. A fervent exponent of the Anschluss movement, he was a member of the executive committee of the Austro-German *Volksbund*; in 1932 he joined a nationalist movement known as the Styrian Home Guard (*Heimatsschutz*), which in the following year was taken over by the Austrian Nazi party. Although members of the Styrian Home Guard were henceforth regarded as full-fledged National Socialists, the party treasurer Franz Xaver Schwarz refused to recognize their affiliation with the Nazi party at the time of the Anschluss and compelled them to apply anew for membership. Thus Seyss did not become a member of the party officially until June 1, 1938, over two months after the Anschluss.[15]

Seyss-Inquart first achieved national prominence when, in June 1937, Chancellor Schuschnigg appointed him as the first member of the National Opposition to the Federal State Council, Austria's executive cabinet. Schuschnigg evidently believed that Seyss, with his reputation for caution and moderation, would be less dangerous and more amenable to reason than the more fanatic or violent elements in the pro-Anschluss camp.

Schuschnigg's effort to establish Seyss-Inquart as the prime representative of the National Opposition in the Austrian government was not an unqualified success, for old-guard Austrian Nazis refused to concede Seyss any such status. Seyss, however, now received support where it most counted—from Berlin. His appointment to the State Council gave Hitler the kind of strategic foothold in the Austrian government he had long been seeking, and one that he intended to exploit to extend Nazi influence until his ultimate goal had been achieved. Seyss was invited to the German capital soon after his appointment and was instructed by Hess to adhere to a policy of moderation, which Hitler regarded as the only possible one for the time being. Seyss himself grew discouraged by how little he was able to accomplish as a member of the Austrian government and his failure to secure any substantial concessions from Schuschnigg, but when he spoke of resigning toward the end of the year Göring ordered him to stay on.[16]

By this time Hitler himself had begun to step up the pace of his expansionist plans. At a notable conference on November 5, 1937, with his foreign minister and the leaders of his armed forces, he reviewed the basic ideas set forth in *Mein Kampf*, in particular Germany's pressing need for territory in Eastern Europe, and expressed "his unalterable resolve to solve Germany's problem of space at the latest by 1943–45." Hitler was by now convinced that Britain as well as France would very likely oppose his expansionist plans in Eastern Europe and that the threat of these countries would have to be removed before his final drive to the east could begin. But in order to wage war against the Western powers, it would be an enormous advantage to have Austria and Czechoslovakia eliminated beforehand and their populations and economies placed at the disposal of Germany. If, before the deadline he had set for solving Germany's problem of living space (1943–45), France should be immobilized by domestic strife or foreign war, he was determined to exploit this opportunity "to overthrow Czechoslovakia and Austria simultaneously in order to remove the threat to our flank in any possible operation against the West." The early destruction of these states was all the more desirable because their military strength was growing steadily. There would also be major positive advantages:

> The annexation of Czechoslovakia and Austria would mean an acquisition of foodstuffs for five to six million people, on the assumption that the compulsory emigration of two million people from Czechoslovakia and one million people from Austria was practicable. The incorporation of these two states with Germany meant, from the politico-military point of view, a substantial advantage because it would mean shorter and better frontiers, the freeing of forces for other purposes, and the possibility of creating new units up to a level of about twelve divisions, that is, one new division per million inhabitants.

While stressing the need to prepare for all eventualities, Hitler saw reason to hope that military action against Austria and Czechoslovakia would not be necessary. He believed that Britain, and probably France as well, had already tacitly written off the Czechs and were resigned to the fact that this question would be cleared up in due course by Germany.[17]

With regard to Austria, Hitler had known since January 1936 that Mussolini would not object if Austria were reduced to the status of a German satellite.[18] He now received specific assurances that the danger of foreign intervention would be minimal even if he took more drastic measures. Mussolini told Ribbentrop on November 6, 1937, "France knows that if a crisis should arise in Austria, Italy would do nothing. This was said to Schuschnigg, too. . . . We cannot impose independence upon Austria which, by the very fact that it was imposed, would cease to be independence." [19] A fortnight later a member of the British cabinet, Lord Halifax, assured Hitler of Britain's awareness that certain situations in the European order were subject to change, and among these he specifically named Austria, Czechoslovakia, and Danzig. Britain only hoped that these changes could be brought about through "peaceful evolution." [20] The French foreign minister, Yvon Delbos, took a similar line on November 26. "France," he said, "could naturally not declare her disinterestedness in territorial changes [in Central Europe]. On the other hand, she had no essential objection to a further assimilation of certain of Austria's domestic institutions with Germany's." [21]

Hitler could hardly have asked for more. The three major Western powers had agreed in principle to the *Gleichschaltung* of Austria; and he received similar assurances from leaders of Hungary, Poland, and Yugoslavia.[22] He now only had to deal with Austria.

Schuschnigg did his best to resist. Abandoned by Italy, he turned to France and the Little Entente; but nowhere did he receive guarantees of military support. In Austria itself he once again resorted to a policy of suppressing the Nazi party, and sought support from labor and Socialist elements, which his government had heretofore repressed. German pressure, however, was relentless, and in January 1938 Schuschnigg agreed to meet Hitler at Berchtesgaden. In the evident belief that the game was up in any case, Schuschnigg conceded all essential conditions of *Gleichschaltung* in negotiations with Seyss even before seeing Hitler.[23] Thus Hitler's task was simple when Schuschnigg finally appeared at Berchtesgaden on February 12, 1938. He imposed demands on Schuschnigg to which the Austrian chancellor had already agreed, and several additional items to speed the coordination of the German and Austrian military and economic systems.[24]

On February 15, in accordance with the terms of his agreement with Hitler, Schuschnigg brought Seyss-Inquart into his cabinet as minister of the interior with authority over the police, a move which signaled that he had lost control of his government. To Austrian Nazis who still yearned for more direct action, Hitler explained that he remained opposed to an internal revolution and that he would continue to seek a satisfactory solution to the Austrian question through an evolutionary policy.[25]

But Hitler was not to be allowed to pursue an evolutionary policy. Schuschnigg, seeing where his association with the Nazis in his government must inevitably lead, resorted to a final expedient to thwart their purposes in Austria. On March 4, 1938, he decided to hold a plebiscite which should demonstrate to Europe and the world that the Austrian people wanted to remain independent, and expose the falsity of Nazi claims that they wanted self-determination in the arms of Nazi Germany. Mussolini warned Schuschnigg that the plebiscite weapon would explode in his hands, but by this time the Austrian chancellor obviously thought he had nothing to lose. On March 6 he obtained President Miklas's consent to hold a plebiscite, and only on March 8, the day before the plebiscite was to be publicly announced, did he inform his minister of the interior of his plans.

Schuschnigg clearly intended that the forthcoming plebiscite should produce results satisfactory to himself. It was to be held on March 13, just four days after it was announced, in a country where no national election had been held since 1930, where there was no registry of persons entitled to vote, and on the basis of the proposition, "With Schuschnigg for Austria. We want a free and a German Austria, an independent and a social Austria, a Christian and a united Austria. We desire bread and peace in the country and the equality of all who stand for their people and their nation." The plebiscite ballots gave a choice of yes or no. To make perfectly certain the elections would furnish the results he desired, Schuschnigg arranged election committees to consist exclusively of members of the Fatherland Front, the Catholic-conservative political organization that had consistently supported the government's efforts to maintain Austrian independence.[26]

Schuschnigg's plebiscite proclamation forced Hitler's hand. As the Austrian leader foresaw, Hitler would have been seriously embarrassed by an anti-Anschluss vote in Austria. As he should have foreseen, Hitler could not afford to allow him to hold his plebiscite, at least not in the manner he intended. On March 10 Hitler removed his curb on the activities of the Austrian Nazis and promised them his support in anything they did. That same evening he instructed Seyss to demand that Schuschnigg postpone the plebiscite and change voting arrangements to ensure a proper representation of pro-German and Nazi sentiment in Austria. Seyss was to impress upon the Austrian chancellor that Hitler intended to take military action if Schuschnigg refused to yield.[27]

Events now moved so rapidly that none of the leading political figures was aware at all times of what was happening or retained firm control of the situation. Hitler issued orders to prepare for a military invasion of Austria, and at about the same time Schuschnigg, under extreme German pressure, agreed to call off the plebiscite. But Hitler now felt he had Schuschnigg on the run. Refusing to be satisfied with the plebiscite concession, he demanded that Schuschnigg resign and that Seyss be appointed chancellor in his place. Upon receiving information that Seyss had been made chancellor, Hitler cancelled his invasion order. But the news proved false—Schuschnigg had resigned, but President Miklas had refused the appointment of Seyss-Inquart. Hitler thereupon sent another ultimatum to Austria, but by now he himself had become alarmed by the pace of events.[28] His main concern was the attitude of Mussolini, and in considerable agitation he dispatched an emissary to the Duce to inform him that he might be compelled to undertake an armed invasion of Austria and to make certain that Italy would not oppose such a move. Upon receiving satisfactory assurances from Mussolini, Hitler decided to go through with the invasion despite the fact that just before midnight on March 11 Miklas finally gave in and agreed to make Seyss-Inquart chancellor.[29]

In all the confusion Hitler persisted in his efforts to clothe German activities in a mantle of legality. As late as the afternoon of March 11 he appeared to be satisfied that the appointment of Seyss as Austrian chancellor would lead to all the co-ordination with Germany he would need for the time being. Only Miklas's delay in appointing Seyss led to the renewal of the invasion order, and even then Hitler wanted a formal request from Seyss, as the senior member of the Austrian cabinet after Schuschnigg's resignation, for German troops to assist him in the restoration of law and order.[30]

At daybreak on March 12, 1938, German troops marched unopposed over the Austrian border. The era of Nazi territorial expansion had begun.

At 3:50 P.M. on March 12 Hitler himself crossed the Austrian frontier near Braunau am Inn, his birthplace, then drove to Linz where he was received by Seyss-Inquart, the new Austrian chancellor. Hitler still appears to have contemplated no more than the *Gleichschaltung* of Austria. But his tumultuous welcome in Linz and news of the enthusiastic reception of German troops in every part of the country evidently convinced him that he could go all the way.[31] On March 13, 1938, Austria was officially annexed to the German Reich.[32]

The annexation of Austria gave Hitler all the advantages he had foreseen. He acquired an additional German population of six and a half million, including enough men of military age to form six new divisions, and the potentially hostile force of an independent Austrian army had been eliminated. He gained control over an economy with valuable supplies of lignite, iron ore, magnesite (for aircraft production), and timber, plus foreign exchange and gold reserves valued at four hundred million Reichsmarks.

The German army economic staff, in analyzing the economic significance of the annexation of Austria, was pessimistic about the immediate value of the country to the German war economy because of the weakness of the Austrian economy as a whole, although this situation was certain to improve in the long run. The army economic staff concluded, however, that the Austrian economy itself was of minor importance compared to the advantages the country offered as a bridge to other and far more valuable resources: "As the most valuable increase in [Germany's] military-economic strength may be reckoned: a) in terms of additional resources, the *opening-up* of the *entire* Southeast *area* for supplying the German war economy; b) in terms of striking power, the vastly improved *possibilities for the economic strangulation of Czechoslovakia,* in case of need." [33] Winston Churchill saw the advantages to Germany in a similar light. In deploring the loss of Austria in the House of Commons, he stressed the importance of this country for Southeastern Europe as a whole. Vienna was the center of communications of the old Austro-Hungarian Empire, and its mastery gave Nazi Germany "military and economic control of the whole of the communications of Southeastern Europe, by road, by river, and by rail." [34]

So far as Hitler's expansionist program was concerned, the most significant result of the annexation of Austria was the improvement it afforded to Germany's strategic position. German power could now be brought to bear directly on Hungary and Yugoslavia (not to mention Italy), a territorial wedge had been driven between the countries of the Little Entente; and western Czechoslovakia, which included the country's most important industrial centers, was surrounded on three sides. In his propaganda Hitler might subsequently denounce Czechoslovakia as a menace to German security, an unsinkable aircraft carrier stationed in the heart of the Reich; but the fact of the matter was, as no one knew better than Hitler, that Czechoslovakia was now in the maw of the Nazi dragon. The annexation of Austria had put Hitler in a position to turn to the next objective mentioned in his fateful conference of November 5, 1937: the destruction of Czechoslovakia.

The Sudetenland

After the First World War the victorious powers had diverged from the principle of self-determination by giving the new state of Czechoslovakia the ancient boundaries of the provinces of Bohemia and Moravia as well as part of Austrian Silesia, a set of boundaries which it was hoped would give the country a more easily defensible frontier. In doing so, however, they included in Czechoslovakia over three million Germans, a large number of whom lived in the mountainous regions along the frontier and came to be called the Sudeten Germans after a mountain range between Bohemia and Silesia. After the many centuries of German-Austrian domination of Central Europe,

the majority of Germans in Czechoslovakia resented their subjugation to a Slavic government, and since the formation of the state of
Czechoslovakia they had agitated for a change in their political
status.[35]

National discontent was exacerbated by economic hardship, particularly after the coming of the great depression of the 1930s, a situation that contributed to the growth of a number of German nationalist parties. Already in the autumn of 1932 the Czechoslovak
government was alarmed and had initiated legal proceedings against
the leaders of these groups, a process that was sharply stepped up
after the Nazis came to power in Germany.[36] In October 1933 the
Nazi party in Czechoslovakia dissolved itself to forestall official dissolution by the Czechoslovak government, a fate that befell other German nationalist groups in the country. Many of these German nationalists now joined a newly formed Sudeten German Home Front party
(later the Sudeten German party), whose leader, a war veteran and
former bank clerk and gymnastics instructor named Konrad Henlein,
managed to avoid dissolution by keeping his party's public activities
strictly within the letter of the law.[37]

Although Henlein had never been a member of the Nazi party, his
organization adopted much of the ideology and many of the attri-
butes of German National Socialism. By 1935, despite some doubts
about Henlein's reliability and the claims of rival German nationalist
leaders, the Reich government decided to help subsidize his party's
spring election campaign. The results were impressive. In the parliamentary elections of May 19 the Henlein party won approximately 62
per cent of the German vote, and with that forty-four seats in the
Czechoslovak Chamber of Deputies as compared to twenty-two seats
for all other German parties. Subsequently, despite lingering doubts
about his political reliability, the Reich government awarded Henlein
a monthly subsidy of twelve thousand Reichsmarks as well as funds
for a party newspaper.[38]

The German subsidy was scarcely more than a token, but the German government soon took a more decisive step. In an effort to end
factional strife among German nationalists in Czechoslovakia, it
threw its entire support to Henlein. In June 1936, old Nazi party
members in Czechoslovakia were informed by the Reich leadership
"that Konrad Henlein enjoyed, now and for the future, their unre-
served confidence." It was a fortunate choice on the part of the German government, for, although factional strife among German nationalists continued, Henlein proved to be a loyal and able instrument of
German policy in Czechoslovakia.[39]

Throughout the Austrian crisis the German government was lavish
with official and unofficial assurances to Czechoslovakia that Ger-

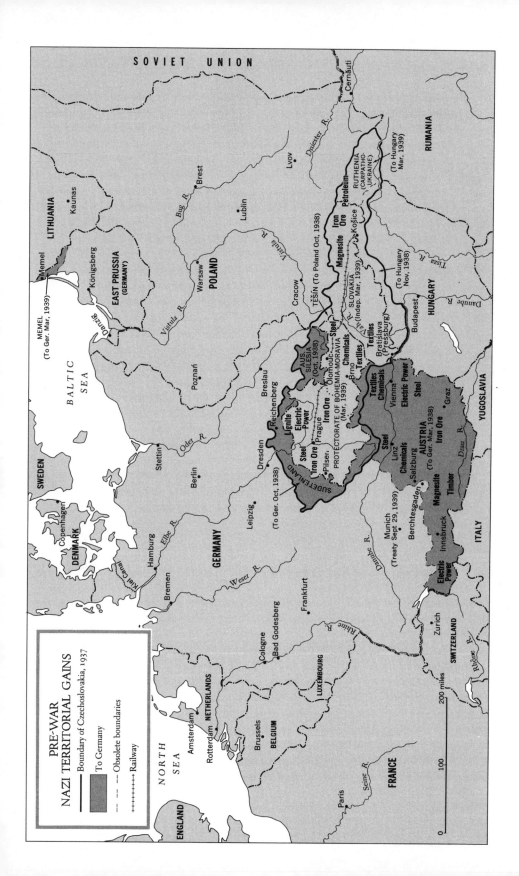

PRE-WAR
NAZI TERRITORIAL GAINS

Boundary of Czechoslovakia, 1937

To Germany

Obsolete boundaries

Railway

SOVIET UNION

LITHUANIA

Memel
MEMEL
(To Ger. Mar, 1939)

Kaunas

EAST PRUSSIA
(GERMANY)

Königsberg

Brest

Lublin

Lvov

Cernăuţi

RUMANIA

Danzig

BALTIC SEA

Poznań

Warsaw

POLAND

Cracow

Vistula R.

Bug R.

Dniester R.

RUTHENIA
(CARPATHO-
UKRAINE)
(To Hungary
Mar, 1939)

Petroleum

Iron
Ore

Magnesite

Košice

SLOVAKIA
(Indep. Mar., 1939)

TĚŠÍN (To Poland Oct, 1938)

AUS.
SILESIA
(Oct, 1938)

Steel

Steel

Olomouc

Chemicals

Brno

Textiles

PROTECTORATE OF BOHEMIA-MORAVIA
(Mar, 1939)

Iron Ore

Prague

Plisen.

SUDETENLAND
(To Ger. Oct, 1938)

Bratislava
(Pressburg)

(To Hungary
Nov, 1938)

Tisza R.

HUNGARY

Budapest

Danube R.

Textiles

Chemicals

Vienna

Electric Power

Steel

AUSTRIA
(To Ger. Mar, 1938)

Iron Ore

Graz

Drau R.

YUGOSLAVIA

Steel

Linz

Chemicals

Salzburg

Berchtesgaden

Magnesite

Timber

Innsbruck

Electric
Power

ITALY

Reichenberg

Lignite

Electric
Power

Steel

Iron Ore

Dresden

Oder R.

Breslau

Stettin

SWEDEN

Copenhagen

DENMARK

Kiel Canal

Hamburg

Bremen

Berlin

Leipzig

Elbe R.

Weser R.

GERMANY

Frankfurt

Munich
(Treaty Sept 29, 1939)

Danube R.

Zurich

SWITZERLAND

Rhône R.

Rhine R.

Cologne

Bad Godesberg

LUXEMBOURG

NETHERLANDS

Amsterdam

Rotterdam

BELGIUM

Brussels

NORTH
SEA

Paris

Seine R.

FRANCE

ENGLAND

0   100   200 miles

many had no hostile intentions toward that country. During this critical period Henlein, with considerable aid from the Reich, managed to keep German nationalists in Czechoslovakia under control. After the German annexation of Austria, however, the national enthusiasm of the Sudeten Germans could no longer be restrained, nor did Hitler make any attempt to do so. On March 28, 1938, he received Henlein in Berlin, where he confirmed him as leader of the Sudeten German movement and assured him of his determination to solve the German problem in Czechoslovakia soon. He recommended that the Sudeten Germans, for their part, adopt the tactic of always demanding so much that they could never be satisfied, and in this way keep up constant pressure on the Czech government. Their ultimate aim should be a program "which would guarantee . . . total freedom for the Sudeten Germans." [40] This program, as Hitler well knew, would deprive the state of Czechoslovakia of its most important strategic border areas and frontier fortifications, and in effect render it defenseless. Because he could hardly expect the Czechs to accept so drastic a program, he always took into account the possibility that military action might be necessary to settle the Czech question.

At his pre-Anschluss conference with his military leaders and foreign minister on November 5, 1937, Hitler had analyzed the danger that the existence of Czechoslovakia represented to Germany and had expressed his intention to eliminate that danger at the earliest possible opportunity.[41] This intention was embodied in a German military plan for an attack on Czechoslovakia (Operation Green), dated December 7, 1937: "When Germany has achieved complete preparedness for war in all fields, then the military conditions will have been created for carrying out an offensive war against Czechoslovakia, so that the solution of the German problem of living space can be carried to a victorious end even if one or other [sic] of the great powers intervene against us." The danger of a war on two fronts was clearly understood, and the point stressed that the attack on Czechoslovakia might have to be delayed for some years if the international situation did not change in Germany's favor.

> If, however, a situation arises which, owing to Britain's aversion to a general European war, through her lack of interest in the Central European problem, or because of the outbreak of a conflict between Italy and France in the Mediterranean, creates the probability that Germany will face no other opponent than Russia on Czechoslovakia's side, then operation "Green" will start *before* the completion of Germany's full preparedness for war.[42]

The annexation of Austria substantially improved Germany's military position vis-à-vis Czechoslovakia, but Hitler realized he still could not afford to resort to military action. A direct attack on Czecho-slovakia without strong justification, he told Keitel on April 21, 1938, would arouse world public opinion against Germany and lead to a dangerous international situation. Such a course could only be adopted for the elimination of Germany's last opponent on the continent. To justify an attack on Czechoslovakia, Hitler envisaged two possibilities: a period of diplomatic negotiation which gradually led to crisis and war, or lightning action as the result of an incident such as the murder of the German minister to Prague in the course of an anti-German demonstration.[43] Nevertheless, in a military directive of May 30, 1938, Hitler declared that it was his "unalterable decision to smash Czechoslovakia by military action in the near future," and he ordered that immediate preparations for an attack be made in case a suddenly favorable political or military opportunity should arise.[44] This order was restated on June 18: "The settlement of the Czech question by my own free decision stands as the immediate aim in the forefront of my political intentions. I am resolved, as from October 1, 1938, onward, to make full use of every favorable political opportunity for the realization of this aim." But the political problem remained paramount. "I shall, however, only decide to take action against Czechoslovakia if, as in the case of the occupation of the demilitarized zone [of the Rhineland] and the entry into Austria, I am firmly convinced that France will not march and therefore Britain will not intervene either." [45]

In the course of the summer of 1938, Hitler grew increasingly sanguine about the possibility of avoiding British and French intervention. At a conference with his military leaders on August 28 he pointed out that Britain at present could only intervene with five divisions and one armored brigade. The motorization of these five divisions had not yet been completed and, in any case, Germany's anti-tank defenses on the western front were formidable. As for the French, the capacity of French industry was limited, no essential changes had taken place in French armaments since 1918. "France can at most place forty divisions in the field against Germany. Therefore: 'France won't risk it.' In spite of this I am making all preparations to create the greatest possible security for us in the west." [46]

Hitler had ample evidence to support his belief that France would not risk it. Besides intelligence reports on the military weakness of the Western powers, the leaders of those powers themselves allowed him to perceive that their primary concern was still the preservation of peace. At his conference of November 5, 1937, Hitler had expressed the belief that Britain and probably France as well had already written off Czechoslovakia and were reconciled to the fact that this question would be settled in due course by Germany.[47] Just a

105

fortnight later the British statesman, Lord Halifax informed Hitler of his government's realization that certain situations in the existing European order were subject to change, and he had specifically named Danzig, Austria, and Czechoslovakia in this connection. "England was interested to see that any such alterations should come through the course of peaceful evolution, and that methods should be avoided which might cause far-reaching disturbances." [48] Prime Minister Chamberlain fully concurred with the views expressed by the British emissary, and thought Halifax's visit to Germany had greatly improved the prospects of preserving peace. "I don't see," he wrote in his journal, "Why we shouldn't say to Germany 'give us satisfactory assurances that you won't use force to deal with the Austrians and the Czechoslovakians, and we will give you similar assurances that we won't use force to prevent the changes you want, if you can get them by peaceful means.' " [49]

After the German annexation of Austria, Chamberlain noted in his journal that he no longer saw any possibility of saving Czechoslovakia from being overrun by the Germans if they wanted to do it. "I have therefore abandoned any idea of giving guarantees to Czechoslovakia, or the French in connection with her obligations to that country." [50] On March 24, 1938, he expressed the gist of these views publicly in a speech in the House of Commons: "Our object," he said, "must always be to preserve those things which we consider essential without recourse to war, if that be possible, because we know that in war there are no winners." What he considered essential, Chamberlain made clear, was little more than the defense of Britain's territories and vital lines of communication.[51]

The French were less resigned than Chamberlain to the abandonment of Czechoslovakia. Besides having concrete obligations to that country in the form of military and political alliances, they recognized in Czechoslovakia (as indeed did Hitler) the most formidable anti-German bastion in Central Europe. But in April 1938 the Popular Front government of Léon Blum gave way to the more conservative regime of Édouard Daladier, whose new foreign minister, Georges Bonnet, took his political cue from Britain. Like Chamberlain he regarded Czechoslovakia as a doomed nation, and much of his foreign policy seemed concerned with finding loopholes in France's treaty obligations to the Czechs. With the change of government in France there was also less interest in co-operation with the Soviet Union, the one major power that had consistently expressed its willingness to give concrete military guarantees to the countries threatened by Germany and that had been urging for some time the formation of an anti-German alliance. The more conservative French and British leaders had little confidence in the effectiveness of Soviet military support, nor had they any desire to aid in substituting Communist Russian for Nazi German preponderance in Central Europe, a cure they considered as bad as the disease, if not worse. In July 1938 the German ambassador reported from London of the deep understanding shown by the British government for one of the essential aspects of German policy, "namely to prevent the Soviet Union from deciding the destinies of Europe." [52]

Supplied with this kind of information about the attitude of Western leaders, Hitler realized he had only to keep up the pressure against Czechoslovakia. This he did through Henlein's Sudeten German party, propaganda, and ostentatious displays of German military might. At the end of August 1938 the Czech government, with considerable goading from Britain, expressed its willingness to concede the most extreme demands yet put forward by the Sudeten German party, including granting the Germans complete administrative autonomy and compensation for wrongs inflicted on the German minority since 1918.[53] The Czech move temporarily embarrassed the Germans, who did not want concessions but the total separation of the Sudetenland from Czech rule. In accordance with the tactics arranged with Hitler in the previous March, Henlein submitted a six-hour ultimatum to the Czech government on September 13 demanding the withdrawal of all state police in districts inhabited by a German majority and the transfer of their powers to local (German) authorities. When the Czech government failed to yield within the prescribed time, Henlein, who was operating throughout the crisis under instructions from Berlin, broke off negotiations.[54]

Meanwhile in Germany Hitler had assured an enthusiastic party rally audience at Nuremberg on September 12 that the Sudeten Germans were neither defenseless nor deserted, and indicated that a showdown in relations between Germany and Czechoslovakia was imminent.[55] Hitler had now forced the pressure to the breaking point, and Chamberlain responded according to form. He proposed to come to Germany to see Hitler personally "with a view to trying to find a peaceful solution," and his press secretary announced that he was prepared "to examine far-reaching German proposals, including [a] plebiscite, to take part in carrying them into effect, and to advocate them in public." He asked only to be given time, and that the Sudeten Germans not take any precipitate action.[56]

On September 15, 1938, Hitler received Chamberlain in Berchtesgaden, where for the first time he specifically demanded the "return to the Reich of the three million Germans in Czechoslovakia." This he intended to accomplish no matter what the cost. "He would face any war, and even the risk of a world war, for this." Chamberlain said that he personally "recognized the principle of the detachment of the Sudeten areas," but that he would have to consult his colleagues in the British government as well as the French before he could give Hitler any specific assurances. No mention was made of consulting the Czechs.[57]

Chamberlain now returned to London to convince his own government and the French of the need to compel the Czech government to grant self-determination to the Sudeten Germans, for nothing less than that could prevent a second world war. The approval of the British cabinet was secured, and Daladier reluctantly agreed that if the Czechs were un-co-operative they would have to be coerced.[58]

On September 19 the Czech government received the Anglo-French advice to give up the Sudetenland. The dangerous precedent of a plebiscite was to be avoided in favor of a direct transfer of territory, which "would probably have to include areas with over 50 per cent of German inhabitants." The hope was expressed that wherever necessary the further adjustment of frontiers could be arranged "by some international body." The first reaction of the Czech government was to reject the Anglo-French proposals, but under harsh pressure from these countries they at last gave in. On the morning of September 21 Hitler was informed that Prague had accepted unconditionally.[59]

On the following day, with the Czech surrender in his pocket, Chamberlain again arrived in Germany for conferences with Hitler, which this time took place at Bad Godesberg. To his surprise and consternation, Hitler now faced him with demands that German troops be allowed to occupy Czech areas designated by the German government immediately, a time limit he later agreed to postpone to October 1. After a certain period "for the preparation of the voting," a plebiscite should be held to determine the exact course of the new German-Czech frontiers. Hitler's new demands were manifestly designed to allow the Germans to take over all strategic frontier territory they considered militarily desirable, and to put himself in a position to advance further before the Czechs had an opportunity to construct a new defensive line.[60] Despite his annoyance, Chamberlain agreed to communicate these new demands to the Czechs, who rejected them as "a *de facto* ultimatum . . . [which] deprive us of every safeguard for our national existence." [61]

Neither Hitler's behavior nor the firm stand of the Czechs diverted Chamberlain from his efforts to conciliate the Germans. He asked the German embassy in London to assure Hitler that the Czech rejection of his demands which they had imprudently published was "not the last word"; in a radio address of September 27 he said, "How horrible, fantastic, incredible it is that we should be digging trenches and trying on gas masks here because of a quarrel in a far-away country between people of whom we know nothing. It seems still more impossible that a quarrel which has already been settled in principle should be the subject of war." [62]

While Hitler kept the pressure on, British and French diplomats continued their efforts to preserve peace. In response to their appeals, to which those of Mussolini were now added, Hitler agreed to further negotiations.[63] At his invitation the leaders of the British, French, and Italian governments met in Munich, where Mussolini put forward proposals for a peaceful solution to the crisis which had been drafted for him by the German government.[64] The agreement reached at the Munich conference on September 29, 1938, met all Hitler's demands, his only concession being that instead of occupying all the Czech areas designated by the German government on October 1, 1938, the process should be drawn out until October 10. An international commission composed of representatives of the four signatory powers was to determine the final territory to be occupied by German troops and the final Czech-German frontiers.[65]

The Munich treaty, which has since become a symbol for abject capitulation in the face of pressure, in fact did little more than provide arrangements for yielding to Hitler what he had been conceded already. The main accomplishment of Munich was to coerce the Czechs into agreeing to a speedy German occupation of the Sudetenland—they had hoped to be given time to build new frontier fortifications. On September 29 the Czech government accepted the terms of Munich. On October 1 German troops marched into the Sudetenland. By October 10 all Sudeten areas ceded to Germany had been occupied by German troops.[66]

In an annex to the Munich agreement, the signatory powers took cognizance of the problem of the Polish and Hungarian minorities in Czechoslovakia, which if not settled within three months by the powers concerned was to be the subject of another conference. The Polish government took immediate advantage of this provision to address a note to the Czechoslovak government demanding the return of Těšín (Teschen), a small bloc of territory at the northern junction of the Czech and Slovak lands. On October 1 the Czechoslovak government yielded to this demand as well, and on the following day Polish forces occupied the area.[67]

In yet another annex to the Munich agreement, the British and French governments guaranteed the new boundaries of Czechoslovakia against unprovoked aggression, a guarantee in which the German and Italian governments were to join once the question of the Polish and Hungarian minorities had been settled.

With the German annexation of the Sudetenland, Czechoslovakia lost sixteen thousand square miles of territory, 70 per cent of its iron and steel capacity, 80 per cent of its textiles, 86 per cent of its chemicals, 70 per cent of its electric power, its entire lignite industry, and important reserves of timber. A large part of the state's communications network, including the main railway line from Prague via Olomouc to Košice, was disrupted. In addition to the self-declared ethnic German population of the Sudentenland, Czechoslovakia lost approximately seven hundred thousand persons of Czech origin and another three hundred fifty thousand of Slovak origin. Most disastrous of all from the point of view of the future security of the country, Czechoslovakia, in relinquishing almost all of its frontier districts, lost virtually its entire system of frontier fortifications.[68]

CHAPTER 11

From Self-Determination to Lebensraum

The Occupation of Bohemia and Moravia

Hitler never had any intention of living up to the provisions of the Munich agreement. On October 21, a bare three weeks after Munich, he ordered the German Wehrmacht to make preparations for the final liquidation of Czechoslovakia. "It must be possible to smash the remainder of the Czech state at any time should it pursue an anti-German policy," Hitler said.[1]

There was never any question that the post-Munich Czech state would or could pursue an anti-German policy. Under heavy German diplomatic pressure, the Czechoslovak government agreed to align its foreign and economic policies with those of the Reich, and even to enact a certain amount of anti-Semitic legislation.[2] Still Hitler was not satisfied, and in March 1939 he undertook the final liquidation of the Czechoslovak state by occupying the Czech provinces of Bohemia and Moravia.

Despite the British and French guarantees of its new boundaries, post-Munich Czechoslovakia had been in trouble from the start, and already at the beginning of October 1938 the state seemed on the verge of dissolution. In Slovakia and the Carpatho-Ukraine (the easternmost section of the country), Slovak and Ukrainian political leaders formerly loyal to Prague were demanding far-reaching autonomy, while more extreme nationalists were calling for outright independence. On October 5 President Beneš, exhausted by the Sudeten crisis and by growing tensions within his own country, resigned.[3] Although the Czechoslovak constitution required the selection of a new president within fourteen days after the resignation of an incumbent, so great was the turmoil and uncertainty within the country that it was not until November 30 that a new president was elected by the National Assembly. This was Dr. Emil Hácha, a sixty-six-year-old jurist and former president of the Supreme Administrative Court, who was described by the German chargé d' affaires in Prague as "one of those men of whom no one can say anything bad . . . He has never interested himself in politics and, according to his own statement, understands very little about it." [4]

Internal difficulties in Czechoslovakia were exacerbated by foreign pressures. Poland and Hungary, which had been promised frontier rectifications along ethnic lines at the expense of Czechoslovakia, now indicated that they would be willing to go further and take all of Slovakia and the Carpatho-Ukraine under their dominion. The Hungarians were particularly eager, for these territories had formed part of the kingdom of Hungary before 1918. In Prague, where desperate efforts were being made to save what was left of the Czechoslovak state, it was recognized that the question of Slovakia was crucial. "Prague government is endeavoring to reach agreement with Slovakia as soon as possible and at any price," the German chargé d' affaires reported from the Czech capital in the first days of October 1938.[5]

The Germans, for their part, appear to have been uncertain what their own attitude toward Slovakia should be. "With regard to Slovakia we had not yet any absolutely fixed line of policy," the state secretary of the German Foreign Office told the Italian ambassador on October 4. The German government was examining the situation, but so far only one thing was certain: Germany did not intend to hand Slovakia over to Hungary. The German army opposed any settlement that would create a common Hungary-Poland frontier, and concluded that "it is in our *military interest* that Slovakia should not be separated from the Czechoslovak union but remain with Czechoslovakia under strong German influence." The German Foreign Office took the same line. In a memorandum prepared for Hitler analyzing the various alternatives for dealing with Slovakia, the Foreign Office advised that a Slovakia dominated by Hungary or Poland would be undesirable, but that Germany could tolerate an entirely independent Slovakia or an autonomous Slovakia within a Czecho-Slovak union because, in either case, Slovak policy would be oriented toward Germany. From the point of view of German foreign policy, the easiest solution would be the establishment of Slovakian autonomy within the existing Czechoslovak state.[6]

On October 6, 1938, after a succession of government crises, Czech and Slovak leaders reached an agreement at Žilina corresponding to the solution recommended by the German Foreign Office. Slovakia was granted autonomy within a Czecho-Slovak union with full control over its domestic affairs, while foreign affairs, finance, and national defense were to remain matters of common jurisdiction with Prague. On the same day Dr. Jozef Tiso, a Roman Catholic priest and acting head of the Slovak People's party (the Hlinka party), was appointed prime minister of Slovakia.[7]

In forming his new government, Tiso himself took over the Ministry of the Interior, which gave him control of the police. Dr. Ferdinand Ďurčanský, another member of the Hlinka party, was named deputy prime minister, and minister of justice, social welfare, and health. Of the three other cabinet posts, one went to a politician closely associated with the Hlinka party, and two to leaders of the Agrarian party, the second largest political organization in Slovakia. Immediately after the formation of his government, Tiso announced that henceforth Slovakia would be part of a federated Czecho-Slovak republic. "The hyphen has been officially designated to emphasize the component parts that go to make up the state." That evening the German consulate in the Slovak capital of Bratislava telegraphed to Berlin, "Slovak government formed today. Tiso prime minister. . . . Slovak government manifesto dated October 6 opposes Jewish Marxism and advocates peaceful solution of the problems at issue on the lines of the Munich agreements." [8]

Hitler had every reason to be satisfied with events in Slovakia, corresponding as they did to the recommendations of his own government. There remained the problem of dealing with the demands of the Hungarians and Poles to Slovak territory. With regard to Bratislava, which was claimed by the Hungarians, Hitler decided that the city did not belong to Germany and was therefore not Germany's to give away. "Outwardly, self-determination for Pressburg [the German name for Bratislava] is to be aimed at, and thus it will probably fall to Slovakia." On the whole, however, territorial disputes between Hungary, Poland, and Czechoslovakia were to be left to direct negotiation between the governments of these countries.[9]

Shortly after the formation of the new Slovak government, its leaders came to Germany to express their gratitude for German support in their struggle for self-determination and to contest Hungarian claims to Slovak territory, which they insisted would seriously violate the self-determination principle. Tiso told Ribbentrop on October 19 that the population statistics advanced by the Hungarians in support of their claims were based on a census of 1910 and in no way corresponded to the present ethnic situation. Even so Tiso was opposed to a plebiscite in the disputed areas. "As the Communists and Jews would vote against Slovakia, the result of a plebiscite was very doubtful," he said. Deputy Prime Minister Ďurčanský expressed himself in much the same way to Göring. He too was opposed to a plebiscite, especially in Bratislava with its large Jewish population. The Jews would vote for Hungary, Ďurčanský warned, whereas Slovakia proposed to solve the Jewish problem in the same way as Germany.[10]

By the end of October 1938 Hitler decided he could not avoid intervening in the Slovak-Hungarian boundary dispute, which threatened to disrupt the order in Eastern Europe that he was above all anxious to preserve. Appealed to by the governments of both sides, he agreed that Germany and Italy should act as arbiters, and on November 2, 1938, a German-Italian court of arbitration meeting in Vienna handed down its decision. Slovakia was left Bratislava, but otherwise the decision favored the Hungarians on almost every point. Hungary, after all, still had to be lured into the Axis camp, whereas Slovakia, desirable as its good will might be, was dependent on the Axis for its very existence.[11]

German policy favoring an autonomous Slovakia within a Czecho-Slovak union changed when Hitler decided to implement his plans for liquidating what was left of the Czech state. It is impossible to determine the precise date when Hitler made this decision, but he had certainly been considering it since early in 1939. "If they were to depart from the ethnographic line and change over to territorial principles," he told the Hungarian foreign minister in January, "Poland and Hungary would have to participate. An ingenious solution must be sought for, one planned precisely as to timing and requiring the smallest risk." [12]

Hitler's strategy now was to foment such disorder in Czecho-Slovakia that he might justify a German occupation as the only alternative to anarchy. In February the German Propaganda Ministry received orders to mount a gigantic propaganda campaign against the Prague government, which was to be accused of pursuing an anti-German policy, terrorizing its ethnic German citizens, concentrating Czech troops on the Sudeten frontier, permitting secret meetings of Communist agents on Czech territory, and continuing its tyrannical treatment of the Slovaks, who now demanded complete independence from Prague. To accompany the propaganda, German agents in the Czech provinces were instructed to provoke anti-German incidents and in general to create an impression of disorder and political instability.[13]

Neither German propaganda nor German agitation was particularly successful. No foreign power took seriously Hitler's expressions of fear about the Czech threat to Germany's national security, and in the Czech provinces themselves the people remained relatively calm. "Very great difficulty in arousing the Czechs to the necessary state of

114

provocation," one German agent reported; "more violent action required to create serious incidents." [14]

The Germans had better luck in Slovakia. While their propaganda pounded on the theme of the sufferings of the Slovak minority under Czech tyranny, on the political level the German government encouraged radical Slovak nationalists to agitate for the severance of all ties with Prague. On February 12, 1939, Hitler received one of the most rabid of these radicals, Dr. Vojtěch Tuka, and informed him that until recently he had not known of the Slovak people's burning desire for independence but that the situation was now clear to him. He advised the Slovaks to free themselves from the Czechs, who were still intriguing against Germany and whose future was dark. He could no longer guarantee the state of Czecho-Slovakia, but he would be prepared to guarantee an independent Slovakia at any time, even today. It would be a comfort to him to know that Slovakia was independent. [15]

The Slovak government took the hint from Berlin and began to put forward demands for greater independence, but Tiso was not at all anxious to stir up trouble that might result in a revival of Hungarian demands. "Tiso and Sidor [the Slovakian representative in the central Czecho-Slovak government] are said to be more inclined recently to agreement [with Prague] than to breaking away," the German chargé d' affaires in Prague reported on March 9, but the Slovak ministers had been told "that the settlement of mutual relations could serve no purpose until Prague knew whether Slovakia intended finally to remain within the state." [16] The Slovak leaders, under pressure from the Germans, were of course unable to make any promises. The inexperienced Czech president, Emil Hácha, now played into Hitler's hands. Angered by the refusal of the Slovak ministers to provide the assurances he desired, he dismissed both Tiso and Ďurčanský and jailed the leading advocates of Slovak separatism, including Vojtěch Tuka. Two days later Hácha named Sidor prime minister of Slovakia and asked him to form a new government. [17]

The crisis over Slovakia gave Hitler the excuse he needed for intervention. On March 11 he ordered the preparation of an ultimatum to the Czech government, on the following day he secured the active support of the Hungarians by promising them the Carpatho-Ukraine, and on March 13 he summoned Tiso to Berlin to press him on the question of Slovakian independence. "It was a question not of days but of hours," the Führer said; "if Slovakia wished to become independent he would support and even guarantee her efforts in this direction. If she hesitated or refused to be separated from Prague, he would leave the fate of Slovakia to events for which he was no longer responsible." Tiso understood the threat: Refusal of independence meant that Slovakia would be occupied by the Germans or turned over to Hungary and Poland. He assured the Führer that he could rely on Slovakia, and on the following day the Slovakian parliament duly proclaimed that country's independence. Tiso was restored to his position as prime minister and authorized to form a new government. At the same time, to prevent any kind of demonstration on behalf of Czecho-Slovak unity, German troops occupied Slovak territory along the Czech border as far as the river Váh.[18]

Demoralized by these events, President Hácha asked to be received in Berlin.[19] There is no doubt that the German invasion of the Czech provinces would have taken place no matter what Hácha had done, but his appeal for an audience gave Hitler a chance to confer upon the invasion an appearance of legality. He received Hácha at 1:15 A.M. on March 15, and after a long harangue presented him with an ultimatum: He was to accept a German protectorate over the Czech provinces of Bohemia and Moravia and order the Czech army and people to offer no resistance to the entry of German troops. In return Hitler promised to guarantee the Czech people "an autonomous development of their ethnic life as suited their character." Otherwise the country would be subjected to a ruthless military invasion and air bombardment, and all vestiges of Czech autonomy would be eliminated. Hácha was an elderly man suffering from heart trouble, but he put up a tenacious resistance. Several times he had to be given shots by Hitler's physician to enable him to remain at the conference table. But by 3:55 A.M. he gave in and agreed to accept the German terms.[20] At 6:00 A.M. German troops officially crossed the Czech border. On the evening of March 15 Hitler arrived in Prague.[21]

Also on March 15 Hitler acceded to Tiso's request to take the newly independent state of Slovakia under his protection. That same day, as if to underscore the value of German protection, the Carpatho-Ukraine, which like Slovakia had declared its independence from Prague on March 14, was delivered up to the Hungarians.[22]

The reaction of public opinion in the West was immediate and vehement.[23] Although both the British and French governments continued to explore means of conciliating and perhaps dividing the Axis powers, they responded to the pressure of domestic public opinion by giving military guarantees to Poland, Rumania, Greece, and Turkey, and inaugurating political and military talks with the Soviet Union. Whatever the intentions of the various government leaders concerned may have been, it was the Anglo-French guarantee to Poland that eventually brought these states into war against Germany in September 1939.

116

Hitler at the time of his attempted Munich Putsch in November 1923.
At his right is Alfred Rosenberg, editor of the Nazi party newspaper
Völkischer Beobachter.

Hitler's almost reverential behavior toward the aged President Paul von Hindenburg, shown here on the occasion of the ceremonial opening of the Reichstag on March 21, 1933, at the Garnisonskirche in Potsdam (the Day of Potsdam), convinced many Germans, and especially German conservatives, that the Nazi leader would respect old Prussian-German traditions symbolized by Hindenburg and would allow himself to be guided by the old-guard Prussian-German leadership.

Hitler the ascetic and dedicated leader, in a typical party propaganda photograph.

Hitler the demagogue.

Nazi propagandists liked to emphasize the point that, if the German people were encouraged to pull in their belts on behalf of the national cause, the Führer was also doing so. He is shown here sharing a one-dish meal (*Eintopf*) with Goebbels and other members of his entourage at the Reich Chancellery.

The signature of the Concordat with the Holy See, July 20, 1933. From left to right: Ludwig Kaas, chairman of the German Center party, papal house prelate and adviser in the Vatican on German ecclesiastical affairs; Franz von Papen, German vice-chancellor; Monsignor Giuseppe Pizzardo, under secretary of the Holy Congregation of Extraordinary Ecclesiastical Affairs; Cardinal Eugenio Pacelli, papal secretary of state, the future Pope Pius XII; Monsignor Alfredo Ottaviani, chancellor of the Holy College; Rudolf Buttmann, director of the Cultural Policy Department, Reich Ministry of the Interior; Monsignor Giovanni Battista Montini, the future Pope Paul VI; Dr. Eugen Klee, counselor at the German Embassy to the Holy See.

Scene from the Nazi party rally at Nuremberg, September 1935, which gives some idea of the regimented pageantry the Nazis were able to mount on such occasions.

Paul Joseph Goebbels.

Reinhard Heydrich inspecting a training school for police, April 1942, while acting Reich protector of Bohemia and Moravia.

Staatsbibliothek, Berlin

Staatsbibliothek, Berlin

Heinrich Himmler.

Martin Bormann, Robert Ley, and Rudolf Hess.

Wilhelm Frick, Reich minister of the interior.

Martin Bormann.

Hitler and Hjalmar Schacht, May 5, 1934, upon the occasion of laying the cornerstone of the new Reichsbank building.

Hitler and R. Walther Darré, Reich peasant leader, minister of food and agriculture, and theorist about blood, soil, and the nobility of the peasantry.

Dr. Fritz Todt, the head of Hitler's major construction organization.

Hitler, Albert Speer, and Martin Bormann inspecting a construction project.

Werner von Fritsch, Werner von Blomberg, and Hitler at army maneuvers, 1935.

Hitler with his generals and admirals, from the old era and the new. At his right, Admiral Erich Raeder.

Hitler's visit to Mussolini in Venice, June 1934. Hitler, Constantin von Neurath, the German foreign minister, Mussolini, and Ulrich von Hassell, the German ambassador to Italy and later a leader of the anti-Nazi resistance.

Mussolini and Joachim von Ribbentrop.

In view of the fateful consequences of his occupation of Bohemia and Moravia, an area already within Germany's sphere of influence and one which he could have occupied at any time, why did Hitler choose to take such a step at this particular time? For by his ostentatious violation of the Munich treaty he cast aside the principle of self-determination before its full fruits had been collected; he exposed himself to the world as a ruthless opportunist whose word could not be trusted and with whom it was useless to negotiate; and he discredited the policies of those Western statesmen who heretofore had played into his hand.

The most obvious explanation is that Hitler had no reason to expect the reaction his move would provoke in the West. At Munich, Britain and France had appeared to give him a free hand in Central Europe. By arranging that the Czech government appeal for German aid in restoring law and order, Hitler may have thought he had supplied ample legal and moral justification for his action. The West had been satisfied with even more specious explanations in the past.

There were, however, more compelling reasons for the occupation of Bohemia and Moravia at this time—reasons Hitler himself put forward to explain his move that were completely in accord with his overall plans and major policy statements. Hitler had always maintained that sooner or later he would have to fight to gain the territory he thought essential to guarantee the future of the German people. Once the inevitability of war was recognized, the main problem became one of timing, of striking while Germany's military strength was at its maximum in comparison to that of its opponents. Early in 1939 Hitler evidently decided not to wait until 1943 or 1945, the latest possible time limit he had set himself two years earlier, but to launch the military phase of his struggle in the near future.[24] German weapons were modern, the very latest in military equipment, but new inventions might quickly render such equipment obsolete. The Western powers, with the economic resources of much of the world at their disposal, were beginning to rearm. In a few years their armament might not yet be equal to that of Germany, but it was likely to be proportionately far greater than the ratio as it existed in 1939. German morale was at a peak, the German nation united in purpose. Then there was the person of Hitler himself and all the forces he represented; Mussolini in Italy, the sole guarantor of the Axis alliance; and Franco in Spain, who could be expected to be sympathetic to the Axis cause. All three dictators, however, might be removed at any time by sickness or death. The leadership of the Western powers, on the other hand, as Hitler had been able to observe personally, was notably lacking in forceful personalities. But this situation too might

117

change. From the point of view of preparedness and leadership, the opportunity for military action might never again be so favorable for Germany.[25]

In March 1939 Hitler was not sure when he would strike, or against whom, but he regarded the occupation of Bohemia and Moravia as an essential precondition to military action in any quarter. As the gateway to Southeastern Europe, the area was of prime strategic importance, but it also possessed prime economic importance as well. The incorporation of Bohemia and Moravia meant the gearing of such concerns as the Skoda munitions works to German military production, and the integration of the entire Czechoslovak economy with its important coal, iron ore, and timber resources, into that of Germany. The Germans seized ten million pounds sterling in gold in the vaults of the Czech National Bank, and the Bank of England was kind enough to turn over to the Reichsbank an additional six million pounds which the Czechs had deposited in England through the Bank of International Settlement at Basel. In addition the Germans secured 43,000 machine guns, well over 1,000,000 rifles, 2,676 artillery pieces, 469 tanks, 1,582 planes, and over 3,000,000 rounds of artillery ammunition. The German occupation also eliminated what was left of Czechoslovak military strength, removing a hostile force of twenty-one regular divisions, fifteen or sixteen second-line divisions, and freeing thirty German divisions for use elsewhere. All danger that Czechoslovak airfields might be used, however briefly, as bases for bombing attacks on German industry was likewise eliminated.[26]

Memel: Postscript to Self-Determination

On March 23, 1939, eight days after the German occupation of Bohemia and Moravia, Hitler acquired the territory of Memel from Lithuania. The old Hanseatic city of Memel, whose population consisted largely of Germans, had been placed under Allied control in 1918 but was seized by Lithuanian troops in January 1923. In February an Allied investigating commission decided to grant Lithania sovereignty over the city and its environs, but to constitute Memel an autonomous region within the Lithuanian state. The Memel Statute officially establishing this status of the Memel territory was signed by Britain, France, Italy, and Japan on May 8, 1924.[27]

Subsequent German nationalist agitation against Lithuanian rule was rigidly suppressed by the Lithuanian government which, since 1926, had been a virtual dictatorship. The Lithuanian government, however, was unable to prevent the development of underground German nationalist organizations, which in 1933 included two fac-

118

tions claiming identification with the German National Socialist movement.[28]

In the face of rising nationalist agitation in Germany after 1933, the Lithuanian government began to take more rigorous measures against the Memel Germans, especially persons associated with the Nazi movement. In March 1935 a number of German nationalists, including Dr. Ernst Neumann, the leader of the Memel Nazis, were imprisoned on the charge of plotting the reunion of Memel with the Reich. The German government did not feel it was in a position to intervene on their behalf, and its failure to do so resulted in a good deal of disillusionment with Reich leadership and increased Hitler's difficulties in keeping the Memel Germans under control. Upon being released from prison in July 1938, Neumann was enjoined by Reich authorities "to impose a stricter and more unequivocal discipline than before on the young hotheads in the Memel territory who hoped to be able to force a quick and violent solution of the Memel problem through street riots, revolts, and assassinations." Neumann's disciplinary measures were evidently unsatisfactory, for in November Heydrich urged Ribbentrop to put further pressure on the German leadership in Memel. Efforts on the part of Memel Germans to force a union with the Reich by provoking incidents might confront Germany with a situation that was "altogether undesirable . . . in view of the international political situation." As the Memel Germans remained unruly, Hitler himself at last intervened with instructions to Gauleiter Erich Koch in East Prussia demanding greater restraint on the part of Neumann and his followers, an order Koch carried out in his usual blunt fashion by threatening to have Neumann shot in case of disobedience.[29]

The restraint imposed on the Memel Germans was purely tactical and designed to keep them quiet while Hitler absorbed Austria, the Sudetenland, and Bohemia and Moravia. In March and again in October 1938 he ordered his military leadership to make preparations for the occupation of Memel.[30] In response to the demands of German diplomats, the Lithuanian government announced on October 29 the termination of the state of martial law in the Memel territory. With all legal restrictions removed, the German nationalists engaged in a succession of demonstrations against Lithuanian rule. In the Memel parliamentary (*Landtag*) elections of December 11, 1938, the German party list received over 87 per cent of the vote.[31]

For the next three months Hitler continued his efforts to impose restraint on the Memel Germans; but after the occupation of Bohemia and Moravia he felt free to make his move in Memel. On March 20, 1939, Ribbentrop pointed out to the Lithuanian foreign minister that no one could contest the fact any longer that the population of the

Memel territory desired reunion with Germany. There were now two possibilities for Lithuania: a friendly cession of the territory to Germany, in which case Germany would be generous in economic matters; or a revolt in Memel, in which case Hitler would act with lightning speed and further developments would be governed by military rather than political considerations. When the Lithuanian minister protested that he was not competent to make a decision in the name of his government, Ribbentrop demanded that a Lithuanian delegation with powers to conclude the necessary treaty be sent to Germany —within forty-eight hours.[32]

Forty-eight hours later a Lithuanian delegation duly arrived in Berlin, and that same eveining it signed a treaty providing for Lithuania's evacuation of the Memel territory and its reunion with Germany. Lithuania was to be given a free port zone in Memel, and the two signatory powers pledged to refrain from using force against one another or to support the use of force directed against either of them by third parties.[33]

Hitler, on board the battleship *Deutschland,* received the news of the Memel treaty in the early hours of March 23 and proceeded at once to the city, where he addressed a cheering population from the balcony of the municipal theater. A law for the incorporation of Memel into the Reich was promulgated that same day.[34]

Memel was only a minor episode in the course of Nazi expansion, but it was to be Hitler's last bloodless territorial acquisition. For his next territorial demands, the return to Germany of lands lost to Poland after the First World War, were rejected by the Polish government, which was supported by guarantees from Britain and France. With that Hitler was faced with the alternative of backing down or of launching the military phase of his expansionist movement. Hitler did not hesitate long. On September 1, 1939, he sent his troops into action against Poland, which was to be his first military victim in the Second World War.

CHAPTER 12

The War for Lebensraum:
The Attack on Poland

In the late eighteenth century, Prussia and Russia, with the assistance of Austria, had engaged in three partitions of Poland, putting an end to Poland's existence as a state. After the First World War, Poland was reconstituted from the territories of the countries which had taken part in its partition. The re-establishment of a Polish state was a fulfillment of the Allied pledge to grant self-determination to the peoples of Europe, but for the Allies there was the additional consideration that this new state on Germany's eastern flank, including as it did provinces that Germans had come to regard as an integral part of their own country, would almost certainly find itself obliged to become part of a coalition dedicated to the future containment of Germany. The boundaries of Poland were supposed to be drawn along ethnic lines, but because of the jumble of nationalities in East-Central Europe—and the desire of the Allies, particularly France, to make Poland as large and strong as possible—it was inevitable that the new state should include many peoples who did not regard themselves as Polish. Among these were large numbers of Germans.

By the terms of the Treaty of Versailles, Germany was obliged to cede to Poland the greater part of the provinces of Poznań and West Prussia, plus a strip of territory along the Vistula to the Baltic to give landlocked Poland an outlet to the sea. This was the so-called Polish Corridor, which separated the German province of East Prussia from the rest of Germany. The predominantly German city of Danzig at the northern end of the Corridor was made a free city within the Polish customs union to serve as a seaport for Poland. The Treaty of Versailles provided further that in Upper Silesia and parts of East Prussia, plebiscites were to be held to determine whether these territories

121

should go to Poland or remain with Germany. By far the most important of these plebiscites, which was to decide the future status of the rich industrial region of Upper Silesia, took place on March 21, 1921, and resulted in victory for Germany. But the Poles refused to accept this verdict and Polish troops moved into several districts of Upper Silesia, which the Polish government claimed because of their predominantly Polish character and because they were essential to the economy of the new state. Eventually the problem was referred to the League of Nations, which decided to divide Upper Silesia and to allot the principal mining and industrial districts, where the Polish population was in a majority, to Poland.

The manner in which Poland's territorial claims were handled fanned the hatred of patriotic Germans for the Treaty of Versailles, for the hypocrisy of the Allies and their fine principles, and for the League of Nations, which seemed to be nothing more than an instrument of Allied policy. So intense was German indignation that during the era of the Weimar Republic no German government dared abandon Germany's claims to the territories lost to Poland, and the failure of successive republican administrations to bring about a rectification of Germany's eastern frontiers gave nationalist opponents of the regime the opportunity to indulge in an orgy of abuse at the expense of the Weimar system.

In view of the general feeling among German nationalists about the Polish question, it comes as something of a surprise to find that Hitler, the most extreme of those nationalists, devoted remarkably little attention to Poland in his early speculations about Germanic expansion into Eastern Europe. This reticence was not the result of any feelings of respect or friendship for the Poles; it was simply that Hitler's attention was consistently focused on Russia, the only country he regarded as large enough to meet Germany's requirements for living space in the east. He clearly took it for granted that when Germany should at last launch its great war for *Lebensraum* against Russia, the territories of Poland, too, should come under German dominion.

Although Hitler said very little about Poland and the Poles in his prewar ideological tracts, the few things he did say fit in perfectly with his overall ideological conceptions. In 1928 he expressed the belief that the Poles, as a non-Aryan people, could never be assimilated into a Greater German Reich. The National Socialist movement, he declared, should under no circumstances annex Poles with the intention of making Germans of them some day. It should either seal off these alien racial elements to prevent the corruption of German blood, or it should remove them altogether and thereby free their lands for settlement by Germans.[1]

Hitler's ideas did not change over the years, although, after coming to power, and especially after the conclusion of the ten-year nonaggression pact with Poland in January 1934, he avoided public expressions of hostility. When it suited his diplomatic purposes he even laid particular stress on German-Polish friendship, and during the Munich crisis he invited the Poles to co-operate in the dismemberment of Czechoslovakia, which they did with considerable enthusiasm.[2]

The Poles soon learned about the dangers of supping with the devil. After the destruction of Czechoslovakia, Hitler began to direct his attention to his partner in spoliation and to voice demands for Danzig and the Corridor as he had recently demanded the Sudetenland. The German occupation of rump Czechoslovakia and the annexation of Memel on March 16 and 23, 1939, brought Poland pledges of aid from Britain and France on March 31, which were extended on April 6 into guarantees of mutual assistance. Hitler responded by declaring on April 28 that Poland's entry into a treaty relationship with Britain and France had violated the German-Polish agreement of 1934, and that his nonaggression pact with Poland was therefore null and void.[3]

Some weeks before this public declaration, however, and even before the Anglo-French pledge to Poland, Hitler had instructed his generals to work on a plan for "solving" the Polish question; on April 3 they were told that this plan should be ready to put into execution any time after September 1, 1939.[4] Although Hitler actually went to war with Poland on September 1, this order did not necessarily mean that he had definitely committed himself to a military solution of the Polish question. His instructions of April 3 were no different from similar instructions to prepare plans for the solution of the Austrian and Czech questions, and it is possible that Hitler's basic attitude toward Poland as a political entity was the same as toward these other states: He wanted to remove the Polish threat from his eastern flank before taking action in the west. As in the case of Austria and Czechoslovakia, he had reason to believe that he might succeed in eliminating Poland without war, or at least substantially improve his strategic position by securing the peaceful cession of Danzig and a route through the Corridor.[5]

In a military directive of April 11, 1939, Hitler stressed his desire to avoid disturbances with Poland, but if Poland adopted a threatening attitude "a final settlement" with the Poles might be necessary in the interest of Germany's defenses in Eastern Europe. As in previous directives dealing with Austria and Czechoslovakia, he foresaw the possibility of taking action without danger of Western intervention in the event of domestic crises in France and "resulting British restraint." "Intervention by Russia, if she were in a position to intervene, cannot be expected to be of any use to Poland, because this would mean Poland's destruction by Bolshevism." For the time being, however, "the great objectives in the reconstruction of the Wehrmacht will continue to be determined by the antagonism of the Western democracies." The military plan for an attack on Poland constituted only a precautionary complement to preparations against the West. "It is not to be looked upon in any way . . . as the necessary prerequisite for a military conflict with the Western opponents." [6]

During the next months Hitler put heavy pressure on Poland to give him Danzig and a route through the Corridor, and if these demands had been met he may have been sincere about his offer to conclude a new treaty with Poland and guarantee its remaining territory.[7] Such a treaty would have served the same purpose as the later pact with Russia in lessening the danger of a two-front war. But if this was Hitler's intention, it is difficult to see why he should have alienated the Poles by demanding Danzig and the Corridor in the first place, since neither was essential for waging war against the West. It is more likely that Hitler hoped the Western powers would allow him to destroy Poland as he had destroyed Czechoslovakia in the expectation that he would then move against Russia.

Hitler himself later explained his failure to conclude a new nonaggression pact with Poland by his lack of confidence in the Poles. They were within striking distance of vital industrial areas in eastern Germany and Bohemia, and he believed they would take the first possible opportunity to stab Germany in the back. Stalin, who in Hitler's opinion could not risk a war under any circumstances, was in that respect a safer treaty partner, as well as being several hundred kilometers farther removed from the German border.[8] Once Hitler had convinced himself he could not rely on Poland, he evidently decided Poland would have to eliminated before he took action against the West. Just when he made the decision to attack Poland, however, is difficult to determine.[9]

According to one possible interpretation of the events of 1939, it was the Anglo-French guarantee to Poland that convinced Hitler he could not expect a peaceful surrender of Danzig and the Corridor, that the days of peaceful expansion were over, and that war would be necessary to achieve his next aims.[10] But this interpretation is open to many objections. Even after the Anglo-French guarantee Hitler's military directives still emphasized that he did not wish to solve the Danzig question by force and that Germany's relations with Poland should continue to be based on the principle of avoiding any disturbances.[11] The Germans had little reason to take the Anglo-French guarantee seriously. Similar guarantees to Czechoslovakia had been disavowed with easy sophistry. In the case of the Polish guarantee, the Germans noted that it was to come into effect only when, in the judgment of Britain, German activity clearly threatened Poland's independence, and when the Polish government "accordingly" considered it vital to counter Germany's action by military resistance.[12] In diplomatic exchanges Hitler professed to be deeply disturbed by the threat of encirclement implied in the Polish guarantee and the subsequent Anglo-French treaties with Greece, Rumania, and Turkey, but there is no evidence in communications to members of his own government that his alarm was genuine. Not until the British formally reaffirmed their pledge to Poland on August 25, 1939, does Hitler appear to have believed the Western powers might actually live up to their commitments. The news of that pledge, in fact, caused him to hold off his attack on Poland in a last desperate effort to preserve British neutrality.[13]

Another possible explanation of Hitler's decision to go to war in September 1939 was his success in arranging a nonaggression pact with the Soviet Union on August 23, which, by freeing him from the danger of a major war on two fronts, gave him what amounted to a blank check for waging war against the West. Further, the economic agreements concluded with the Soviet Union in conjunction with the nonaggression pact assured Germany of vital supplies of strategic raw materials and would go far to free Germany from the throttling effect of an Allied naval blockade.

The treaties with Russia, however, do not appear to have had any more influence in fixing Hitler's decision to go to war with Poland than the Anglo-French guarantees. Neither the Germans nor the Western powers had any high regard for Russia's military capacity, which appeared to have been eroded still further by recent large-scale purges of the Soviet military leadership. Indeed, British and French lack of confidence in the effectiveness of Russia's military co-operation was one of the major reasons for their lack of enthusiasm for an alliance with Russia.[14] As for Hitler, Russia played a remarkably small role in his political and military calculations as he contemplated the prospect of war in 1938 and 1939, and there is every reason to believe that he would have resorted to military action even without the Russian treaty. In both the Austrian and Sudeten crises, while Russia was still openly hostile to Germany, Hitler had hoped and expected his opponents to give way, but in each case he seems to have been prepared to fight.

The evidence is overwhelming that throughout all these crises the question of timing remained Hitler's paramount concern. Yet, although he continued to insist on an early solution to Germany's problem of space and had firm ideas as to how that solution could best be achieved, he appears to have been very uncertain about the exact moment when he should resort to military action, or against whom.

Not until the first part of August 1939 is there reliable evidence that Hitler had definitely decided to attack Poland. At this time the Russo-German pact had not yet been concluded, nor had Hitler succeeded in neutralizing the Western powers. Important as the German negotiations with Russia appear to have been in retrospect, Hitler seems to have attached far more importance to his efforts to isolate Poland from the West.

On August 11, 1939, he discussed the Polish question with Carl Jacob Burckhardt, the League of Nations high commissioner for Danzig, and made statements he clearly intended Burckhardt to pass on to Britain and France. Upon the next instance of Polish provocation, Hitler said, he proposed to crush the Poles without warning so as to leave no trace of Poland afterward. He would strike like lightning with the full strength of a mechanized army, while leaving seventy-four divisions to safeguard German security in the west. The whole object of his policy, Hitler explained, was to gain a free hand in the east. "Everything that I undertake is directed against Russia; if the West is too stupid and too blind to grasp this, I will be obliged to come to an understanding with the Russians, to defeat the West, and then after its downfall to turn with my assembled forces against the Soviet Union." [15] With this statement Hitler obviously intended to spell out to the British and French the true objectives of his policy, to let them know they had nothing to fear from him unless they interfered with his plans in the east, and to warn them that any intervention on their part would only redound to the benefit of Russia.

On the same day that Hitler was talking to Burckhardt, Ciano noted in his diary after a conference with Ribbentrop, "The decision to fight is implacable. He rejects any solution which might give satisfaction to Germany and avoid the struggle. I am certain that even if the Germans were given more than they ask for they would attack just the same, because they are possessed by the demon of destruction." Ciano's impression about the demonic quality of German policy was confirmed on the following day in a conference with Hitler. "Hitler is very cordial, but he, too, is impassive and implacable in his decision. . . . I realize [sic] immediately that there is no longer anything that can be done. He has decided to strike, and strike he will." According to the official German record of their conversation, Hitler told Ciano that "Poland's whole attitude made it plain that in any conflict she would always be on the side of the opponents of Germany and Italy." Poland's speedy liquidation at the present moment would therefore represent an enormous advantage "in the inevitable clash with the Western democracies." The attack would have to be launched soon, no later than the end of August, for the farther autumn advanced the more difficult military operations in Eastern Europe would become.[16]

On August 14 Hitler expressed similar views to the leaders of his armed forces. As recorded in General Halder's diary, Hitler said, "Central problem is Poland. Must be carried through at all costs." Although Germany had not yet concluded treaties with the Western powers or Russia specifically providing for the isolation of Poland, Hitler was confident that Poland was in fact isolated. Owing to their military weakness Britain and France could not intervene effectively and could certainly offer no immediate support to Poland. There was nothing to force them into a war; both were aware of how much they stood to lose in a conflict, even if victorious; and neither country possessed leaders of quality. "The men I got to know at Munich were not the kind that start a new world war." Nor did Hitler believe in the sincerity of their pledges to Poland. The treaties with Poland were not yet ratified, Britain was not even giving Poland money to buy arms in other countries. "Even now England is putting out feelers to find out how the Führer envisages developments after Poland has been disposed of. All this supports the conviction that while England may talk big . . . it will not resort to armed intervention in the conflict."

In contrast to his lengthy analysis of British policy, Hitler devoted comparatively little attention to Russia, but he definitely excluded Russia from his list of possible opponents in a Polish conflict. "*Russia* has no intention of pulling England's chestnuts out of the fire and will keep out of war," Hitler said. "A lost war is as dangerous for Stalin as a victorious [Russian] army. His interests at most extend to the Baltic states." Almost as an aside Hitler discussed Germany's current diplomatic negotiations with Russia:

> Loose contacts. Began with negotiations for trade agreement. Under consideration whether we should send a negotiator to Moscow and whether or not this should be a prominent figure. [Russia] gives no thought to obligation toward the West. The Russians understand the destruction of Poland, but what about the [Polish] Ukraine? Promise to delimit spheres of interest. The Baltic? Issue is Lithuania (not Baltic). The Russians want more detailed discussions. Distrust. No common frontier. Führer inclined to meet halfway.[17]

The German nonaggression pact with Russia, under negotiation since the spring, was signed on August 23, 1939, a diplomatic success Hitler welcomed not so much for its neutralization of the Russian threat as that it seemed to eliminate all possibility of Anglo-French intervention in a German-Polish conflict.[18] Of greater practical importance for Hitler, so far as Russia itself was concerned, was the German-Russian economic agreement signed on August 19 which guaranteed Germany a substantial supply of lumber, cotton, feed grain, oil cake, lead, zinc, phosphates, platinum, raw furs, and above all petroleum. This treaty, plus the possibility of transshipment via Russia of crucial raw materials such as rubber and tin from East Asia, did much to free Hitler from the nightmare of economic blockade which haunted all Germans conditioned by the experiences of the First World War.[19]

On August 22, already assured of the successful conclusion of a nonaggression pact with the Soviet Union, Hitler reviewed the international and military situation with his supreme commanders at a conference on the Obersalzberg. Discussing the development of his decision to settle the eastern (i.e., Polish) question, he confessed that theoretically it would have been desirable to eliminate the threat of the west first, but as it became increasingly clear that Poland would stab Germany in the back the moment it became involved in difficulties in the west, he realized that the elimination of Poland was an essential precondition to a western campaign. Besides, war with Poland would give the Germans a chance to test their new weapons before the final great showdown in the west.

Once again Hitler emphasized the overriding importance of time, and the temporary advantage the Axis possessed in terms of leadership. In the field of armaments, Britain's recent rearmament program had not yet altered the situation substantially in Britain's favor. Little had been done for the army; improvements in the navy would not be felt until 1941 or 1942. Only the air force had been effectively strengthened; but, because of a lack of antiaircraft artillery Britain's vulnerability from the air was still great. France was short of manpower because of a declining birth rate, its armaments were outdated, its artillery obsolete.

On the international scene, Britain was contained in the Mediterranean by Italy, in the Far East by tension with Japan, in the Near East by tension with the Mohammedan peoples. France's eastern alliances were a shambles, its position in the Mediterranean had deteriorated. In the Balkans, Yugoslavia was tied down now that the Italians were established in Albania, Rumania's existence depended on tensions between other powers, Turkey lacked competent leadership. Hitler knew that Britain and France had attempted to make an alliance with Russia, perhaps hoping that German strength would be dissipated in the east against the combined forces of Russia and Poland. But any such hopes had been foiled by his own pact with Russia. "With this I have knocked the weapons out of the hands of these gentlemen. Poland has been maneuvered into the position we need for military success."

Of course there would be risks, but there were risks involved in all great political decisions. Germany was faced with the harsh alternative of striking now, while the chances of success were still favorable, or allowing events to take their course and facing certain annihilation in the future. "Time for a solution now ripe. Therefore strike!"

The destruction of Poland was to be the first step. The primary military objective would be the complete annihilation of Poland's armed forces, not the attainment of a specific line. Even if war broke out in the west, the destruction of Poland was to remain the priority. Hitler intended to give a propagandist reason for starting the war; it was immaterial whether this was plausible or not.

> When starting and waging a war it is not right that matters, but victory. Close your hearts to pity. Act brutally. Eighty million people must obtain what is their right. Their existence must be made secure.
> . . . New German frontier delimitation according to sound principles and possibly a protectorate as a buffer state. Military operations will not be influenced by these considerations. The wholesale destruction of Poland is the military objective. Speed is the main thing. Pursuit until complete annihilation.[20]

On August 23, with the isolation of Poland apparently assured, Hitler gave the order to launch the attack on Poland on August 26.[21] To make certain that a suitable incident would take place to justify German military action against Poland, Heydrich and his secret police arranged to stage an attack on the German frontier radio station at Gleiwitz by men dressed in Polish uniforms.[22] At the same time German diplomatic agents were instructed to prevent any possible diplomatic agreement with the Poles, and to contrive to arrange matters in such a way that "the responsibility for the breakdown [of negotiations] . . . and for all consequences fall upon Poland." [23]

With the political stage seemingly so perfectly set, Hitler was dismayed to learn on August 25 that Britain and France, instead of seeking excuses to abandon Poland, had ratified their treaties of mutual assistance with that country. That evening he postponed the date for the attack on Poland "because of the changed political situation." "Is this temporary or for good?" Göring asked. Only temporary, Hitler said, "but I must see whether we can eliminate British intervention." [24]

During the next days Hitler used all his familiar and heretofore successful tactics to prevent Western intervention. He wanted the restoration of Danzig, a route through the Corridor, and the opportunity to end the "Macedonian conditions" on Germany's eastern frontier. Afterward he would negotiate a treaty with Britain guaranteeing the integrity of the British Empire and placing the power of the Reich at its disposal.[25] On August 26 Halder wrote in his diary, "A faint hope that England might still, by negotiation, be brought to accept demands which would be rejected by Poland." Halder learned from Brauchitsch, the commander in chief of the army, that Hitler's plan was to demand Danzig, a corridor through the Corridor, and a plebiscite on the same basis as the Saar. "England will perhaps accept, Poland probably not. *Wedge between them!*" [26] Halder was less hopeful about the situation two days later. "Situation very grave. Determined to solve Eastern question one way or another. Minimum demands: return of Danzig, settling of Corridor question. . . . If minimum demands not satisfied, then war: Brutal! . . . War very difficult, perhaps hopeless. . . . Personal impression [of Hitler]: exhausted, haggard, croaking voice, preoccupied. 'Keeps himself completely surrounded by his SS advisers.'" [27]

In response to a British proposal, Hitler agreed on August 29 to enter into direct negotiations with Poland—but demanded that the British arrange for the appearance of a Polish plenipotentiary in Berlin on the following day. At midnight on August 30 the British ambassador in Berlin presented a written reply from his government saying that Britain could not advise Poland to send a plenipotentiary at once, and recommending that German-Polish negotiations be initiated through regular diplomatic channels. To this Ribbentrop answered that the failure of the Polish plenipotentiary to arrive at the stipulated time had prevented the German government from presenting its proposals to Poland. The next day, in a communiqué to the diplomatic representatives of Britain, France, Japan, the United States, and Russia, the German government declared that, in view of the nonarrival of the Polish plenipotentiary, it considered its proposals to have been rejected.[28]

At 6:30 A.M. on August 31 word was received at German military headquarters that the attack on Poland would begin at 4:45 A.M. on the following day. At 11:30 A.M. Halder wrote in his diary, "Intervention of West said to be unavoidable: in spite of this, Führer has decided to attack." Later in the day, however, he noted that according to Brauchitsch the Führer was calm and had slept well, and that he had evidently decided that Britain and France would not intervene.[29]

At dawn on September 1, 1939, German troops crossed the Polish frontier on a broad front, an action German diplomatic representatives were instructed to describe not as war but "engagements caused by Polish attacks." [30] On that day the British and French governments demanded that Germany suspend its aggressive action against

Poland, otherwise they would fulfill their military obligations to that country. The Germans denied that there had been any aggression, their troops did not suspend their activities, and on September 3 Britain and France declared war on Germany.[31] The Second World War had begun.

The German forces engaged in Poland outnumbered the Polish by almost three to one, they were headed by mechanized divisions and supported by overwhelmingly superior air power. Striking rapidly into Poland from three fronts—East Prussia, Silesia, and Slovakia— they overwhelmed the poorly equipped Polish forces before they could be effectively mobilized. This was the first example of the kind of Blitzkrieg campaign that Hitler, with the inadequate economic resources at his disposal, proposed to wage against successive opponents until final victory had been achieved. In the case of Poland, his Blitzkrieg was dramatically successful. Within four weeks all effective Polish resistance had been broken; on September 28 Russia and Germany signed a treaty dividing Poland between them; on October 6 the last Polish regular army units surrendered.[32] Hitler was now free to deal with his opponents to the west.

CHAPTER 13

Security in the North:
The Attack on Denmark and Norway

Hitler's decision to eliminate the uncertainty of Poland before attacking in the west meant that Germany was forced to leave its western flank almost unprotected, and to stake all on the successful annihilation of the Polish forces. The German generals were justly apprehensive. They had long considered the most effective Allied offensive against Germany to be a vigorous thrust into the Ruhr, the heartland of the German war economy, whose loss would mean the end of Germany's ability to wage war. A moderately competent Allied intelligence service, they reasoned, would know about the weakness of Germany's western defenses and realize that a determined push by Britain and France might well succeed in overrunning the Ruhr. At the very least the German generals expected a heavy bombardment of Ruhr industries.[1]

Instead of attacking, the Western powers stood pat behind their concrete fortifications. There was some expectation of a German collapse from within, occasioned either by political or economic crises, and there was reason to hope for a German entanglement with Russia over the spoils of Poland. But the main reason for the Allies' strategy of defense was the confident belief on the part of both British and French leaders that they had time on their side. With time they could build up overwhelming power of their own, and by a rigid application of blockade and constriction they could grind down the foe's capacity to resist. Sufficient time would obviate all need for a costly and bloody military offensive.[2]

That the advantage of time lay with the Allies Hitler was well aware, but he was also aware of Western calculations in this regard. If Britain and France saw their overall strategy in defense, Germany

132

could risk a temporary concentration of its power in the east. Hitler urged restraint on the German forces left in the west during the Polish campaign. Submarine and air activity were to be kept to a minimum. Britain and France were not to be goaded out of their defensive posture.[3]

Events proved that Hitler had gauged the Allied strategy correctly, but he allowed that strategy to go unchallenged only so long as it was to his own advantage. Immediately after the Polish campaign he swung the weight of German power to the west with the intention of ending the threat from Britain and France as soon as his troops could be moved into position for effective action. Hitler proposed to launch his attack in the west at the earliest opportunity, if possible already in the autumn of 1939, but because of bad weather the attack was postponed time after time during the next few months.[4] Then it was postponed yet again because Hitler believed a vital threat to German security had now developed in quite a different theater of operations.

When the Second World War began Hitler had no intention of undertaking a military expedition into Scandinavia. The Scandinavian people were Nordics who at some future date might be cajoled or coerced into some kind of greater Germanic political organization. But for the time being Hitler counted on the Scandinavian states to remain neutral as they had done in the First World War. He already had enough problems to cope with.[5]

Hitler's calculations with respect to Scandinavia were upset in the first instance by the Soviet Union, which immediately after the outbreak of war took advantage of the terms of its nonaggression pact with Germany to extend its defense perimeter by demanding that the Baltic states and Finland permit the establishment of Russian military bases on their territories. These demands were accepted by the Baltic states, which in August 1940 were absorbed into the Soviet Union as Soviet Socialist Republics.[6] Finland, however, refused to yield to Soviet pressure, and on November 30, 1939, the Soviet Union went to war with Finland.[7] The Finns' valiant resistance evoked widespread sympathy and admiration, but from the German standpoint the most significant aspect of the Russo-Finnish war was the possibility it offered the Allies to outflank Germany in the north.[8]

It was this danger that propelled Hitler into action in Scandinavia. As the war progressed he received increasingly alarming reports that the Allies were in fact preparing to mount a campaign in this area, and that under the cover of sending aid to Finland they proposed to occupy Norway and Sweden. Even after the Russo-Finnish war ended with Finland's surrender on March 12, 1940, news of impending British action in Scandinavia continued to be received in Berlin. Hitler was convinced that such a move had to be forestalled at all costs, for if the British succeeded in establishing themselves in Norway they would be in a position to close the entrance to the Baltic and dominate the entire German sea coast, including all German naval bases. Germany's capacity to wage submarine warfare against Britain would be paralyzed, the British would be poised to launch air and naval strikes against vital German military and ecomomic installations, or even to mount an actual invasion of German territory.[9]

Quite as serious as the strategic threat posed by a British occupation of Scandinavia was the economic threat. Germany was dependent on Sweden and Norway for 51.1 per cent of its iron ore, and Germany's ore reserves in 1939 were sufficient for only nine months of steel production at the 1938 (peacetime) level of consumption. Thus Scandinavian ore deliveries were essential to the German war economy. They were also extremely vulnerable to enemy attack or blockade. During the summer months Swedish ore could be shipped to Germany via the German-controlled Baltic sea from the Swedish ports of Lulea and Oxelösund, but in the winter the Gulf of Bothnia, on which Lulea was located, normally froze, and Oxelösund alone could deal with barely one-fifth of the ore needed by Germany. The normal export harbor for about 45 per cent of Sweden's iron ore was Norway's ice-free Atlantic port of Narvik, which was handling well over half the Swedish ore exports to Germany by the time the first war winter fully closed in.[10] These shipments from Narvik were made possible, despite Britain's naval supremacy in the Atlantic, by the geographical nature of the Norwegian coast, where a continuous fringe of islands forms an inland waterway which allowed ships to sail along the Atlantic coast without leaving Norway's neutral territorial waters until they were safely inside the Skagerrak.

Winston Churchill immediately put his finger on this vital link of the German war economy, and on September 19, 1939, he brought the British cabinet's attention to the importance of stopping shipments of Swedish iron ore from Narvik, which would become critical for Germany as soon as ice formed in the Gulf of Bothnia. Churchill ranked the effectual stoppage of ore shipments to Germany as a major military objective, and suggested as a beginning that the British navy lay a minefield across the three-mile limit in Norwegian territorial waters, as in 1918, in order to force ships into the open sea. Churchill perceived that such a British move would inevitably provoke German counterblows, but Britain could desire nothing better than to force Germany to fight in Scandinavia, for nowhere else in Europe could British sea power be brought to bear more effectively.[11]

Hitler was fully aware of Germany's vulnerability in Scandinavia. In November 1934 he had impressed on Göring and Raeder the need

THE NORTHERN STATES
AND POLAND

━━━━━ German-Russian boundary Sept 28, 1939*

To Germany

To Russia

-- -- -- -- Obsolete national boundaries
*German-Russian nonaggression
pact signed Aug 23, 1939

to strengthen the German fleet "because it would be impossible to wage war if the navy were not able to safeguard ore imports from Scandinavia." He had said much the same thing to Rauschning earlier in the year: One of his first measures in the next war would be to occupy Sweden in order to establish control over its ore mines.[12]

But when war came in 1939, Hitler showed no inclination to extend the conflict to the north. He knew as well as Churchill that on this watery battleground Germany's naval weakness would be a major, perhaps insuperable, handicap. He therefore pursued a policy of respecting Scandinavia's neutrality as the simplest and most effective means of safeguarding his ore supply.[13]

Hitler's views on Scandinavia were not shared by his naval leadership. On October 10, 1939, Admiral Raeder tried to persuade him to extend Germany's sphere of submarine operations by acquiring naval bases on the Norwegian coast, which he thought could be obtained by peaceful means if Russia joined Germany in putting pressure on the Norwegian government. Changing his tack to reinforce his case, Raeder pointed out the disadvantages should the Scandinavian coast fall to Britain. If not in itself vital to Germany, the area would be fatally critical in the hands of the enemy. Britain would then control the approaches to the Baltic, be in a position to turn Germany's flank in the north, and be able to exert decisive pressure on Sweden.[14]

"The Führer at once saw the significance of the Norwegian problem," Raeder later wrote to one of his admirals.[15] But Hitler was not yet convinced about the necessity of a Scandinavian campaign. Just the day before Raeder had presented his arguments, Hitler had sent out guidelines to his military leaders in which he had assumed the continued neutrality of the Scandinavian states and their uninterrupted trade with Germany even in the event of a long war.[16] Hitler was counting on British respect for world, or at least American, public opinion, and on Scandinavia's appreciation of the fruits of peace. He promised Raeder to consider the Norway proposal, but that was all. Nor did Hitler energetically back his navy's desire to step up U-boat warfare against Britain. The German economy would have been hard pressed to meet simultaneously the material requirements of a western offensive and a large-scale submarine building program, but Hitler's restraint with regard to Britain may not have been altogether the result of material deficiencies. His activity during this period suggests that his policy was still attuned to the possibility of a settlement with Britain. The German push in the west was now scheduled for November. Were Hitler to win a resounding victory over the French and then turn unequivocally to his objectives in the east, might he not yet convince his British cousins of his sincerity in desiring their continued dominion over a world empire? Whatever Hitler's motives, little was done at this time to strengthen Germany's weak submarine fleet or to extend its bases. From October 10 until December 11 Hitler did nothing about the navy's suggestions with regard to Norway. The Russian attack on Finland on November 30, however, by raising the specter of Allied intervention of Scandinavia, lent new force to Raeder's arguments. Shortly afterward German apprehensions were to receive nourishment from other quarters.

On the evening of December 10, 1939, the Norwegian politician Vidkun Quisling and his go-between in Germany, Albert Viljam Hagelin, appeared in Berlin, where they stayed as guests of the educational center of Alfred Rosenberg's Foreign Political Office.[17] Quisling was the founder and leader of the Nasjonal Samling (National Unification) party, an anti-Bolshevik and anti-Semitic organization which advocated the formation of an authoritarian national government independent of party politics, and a foreign policy based on close ties with other Nordic nations.

Quisling was no common political opportunist or racist fanatic. An introspective loner, opinionated and stubborn, he was a fervent patriot and something of a mystic in his Nordic nationalism. Until he dedicated himself to politics in 1933, he had enjoyed a career of highest distinction as an army officer and as a member of several humanitarian relief missions in Eastern Europe under the auspices of his fellow-countrymen, Fridtjof Nansen, and the League of Nations. An expert on Russian affairs, he served as military attaché in Leningrad and Helsinki from 1918 to 1921, and as secretary of legation in Moscow from 1927 to 1929, taking care of British interests in Russia after Britain broke off diplomatic relations with the Soviet Union. For this service he was named honorary commander of the Order of the British Empire.

While engaged in famine relief in the Ukraine, Quisling married a Russian, and he appears to have felt an early admiration for the achievements of the Russian Revolution. Gradually, however, he became obsessed with a hatred and fear of Bolshevism, a feeling that appears to have developed after Stalin came to power. Upon his return to Norway he attempted to convince his countrymen of the dangers threatening them from the east, denouncing Russian Communism and its ally, international Jewry, and calling for the establishment of a corporate state to unite the country and save it from the Bolshevik menace.

Appointed minister of defense in May 1931 in the cabinet of Peder Kolstad, the head of the Peasants party, Quisling from the first came under sustained attacks from the left, and his inept and often naïve reaction exposed him to still further abuse. Unable to secure the funds he deemed essential for Norway's military security, he found his distrust of party and parliamentary government confirmed and did much to bring down the government of Kolstad's successor, Jens Hundseid, whom he had also served as minister of defense. His subsequent efforts to take over the Peasants party as a vehicle for his own political program were unsuccessful, and in May 1933 he founded the Nasjonal Samling party.

With the example of Hitler before him, Quisling tried to attain power through the institutions of the parliamentary system he intended to overthrow. But despite the severity of the great depression in Norway, his attempt to emulate Hitler's successes at the polls was a sorry failure. A poor speaker and organizer, unable to get along with colleagues or supporters, he was a miserable party leader and the results of the elections he contested showed it. In the general elections of 1933 and 1936 his party did not win a single seat. Quisling professed not to be discouraged. "The electorate has chosen Mammon and Marxism," he told his followers after disastrous municipal elections in 1937. "But we will continue to fight. We shall do our duty. Our cause will win in the end." [18]

Wretched as was the showing of Quisling's party in Norway, the Nasjonal Samling nevertheless had a more impressive record than similar parties in other Nordic countries. By 1935 it had attracted the attention of Alfred Rosenberg, whose Foreign Political Office was attempting to foster the concept of Nordic solidarity in Scandinavia.[19] By the time the Second World War began Rosenberg was obliged to confess that, of all political and cultural groups in Scandinavia in which his organization had taken an interst, only Quisling's Nasjonal Samling was worthy of serious attention as an effective fighting body imbued with the ideal of a greater Germanic community. But the Quisling party had so few members and enjoyed so little popular sympathy that there seemed no prospect of its coming to power without outside support.[20] It was evidently to gain this support that Quisling and Hagelin came to Berlin in December 1939. Here they lent their voices to the arguments of the German navy about the need for German action in Scandinavia.

This was not the first time that Quisling and Hagelin had attempted to draw the attention of Nazi leaders to the strategic and economic importance of Norway—and of the dangers threatening Germany there. The earliest reliable evidence of such efforts is a letter from Hagelin to Göring of May 18, 1939, filled with dire warnings about the political situation in Norway. The Norwegian population was strongly pro-British, Hagelin said, the Norwegian government dominated by a Jew, Carl Joachim Hambro, the president of the Norwegian parliament (*Storting*). Hagelin assured Göring that Quisling's organization was in a position to change that situation "de-

138

cisively and in a short time," but for this purpose Quisling needed money, and Hagelin mentioned the sum of six and a half million Reichsmarks.[21]

In June 1939 Quisling paid a personal visit to Germany, where he was received by Rosenberg and by Paul Körner, the deputy director of Göring's Four-Year Plan. On this occasion Quisling restated the arguments about Norway's strategic and economic importance, and appealed for financial support for his party to counter British and Marxist-Communist influences. More effective still, of course, would be direct German intervention in Norway and the installation of a Nasjonal Samling government there, a course Quisling advocated with increasing insistence after the war began.[22]

For some time Quisling's arguments found little response in Germany. Rosenberg's influence was negligible, and Göring was well aware that Hitler's primary concern in the north was the preservation of Scandinavia's neutrality. But on his visit to Berlin in December 1939 Quisling acquired a more effective and willing sponsor in the person of Grand Admiral Raeder.[23] In a conference with Raeder on December 11, Quisling said he had convincing evidence that the British intended to occupy Norway, and that they might attempt to do so soon. To prevent this mortal threat to its strategic position, Germany would therefore have to act, and act fast. Quisling drew Raeder's attention to the fact that the present government of Norway would no longer be legal after January 11, 1940, since it had decided to extend itself for a year contrary to the provisions of the constitution. This would provide the opportunity for a political revolution. Should the occasion arise, Quisling was prepared to take over the government and to ask Germany for aid. He was also ready to discuss military plans with the German Wehrmacht.

In reporting Quisling's views to Hitler the next day, Raeder advised caution in acting on the suggestions of the Norwegian leader, whose motives were uncertain. Under no circumstances, however, could Norway be allowed to fall to the British "as this could be decisive for the outcome of the war." Britain would then be able to cut off all Scandinavian ore shipments to Germany, and to carry the war into the Baltic. The most dangerous aspect of the German occupation of Norway, Raeder said, would be the elimination of the neutral shipping zone along the Norwegian coast and the consequent disruption of ore transport from Narvik, a situation with which the German navy was not yet ready to cope. On the other hand, if Quisling were right about the imminence of a British invasion of Norway, the Germans would be totally deprived of the ore supply. Raeder therefore recommended that the High Command of the Wehrmacht be permitted to make plans with Quisling for preparing and carrying out the occupation of Norway, either by peaceful means (e.g., by persuading the Norwegian government to ask for German aid in preserving its independence) or by force.[24]

Hitler was sufficiently impressed by the seriousness of the situation in Norway to decide to see Quisling personally; if he received a favorable impression, he would sanction preparations for a German occupation of Norway as recommended by his naval leaders. He received Quisling on December 14, and that afternoon he gave orders to the OKW to assign a small staff to investigate the possibility of a German occupation of Norway. His own preference would be to have Scandinavia remain neutral, he told Quisling, but he could not tolerate having the English in Narvik. During the next four days Hitler had two further conversations with Quisling in which he continued to stress his desire for Scandinavian neutrality, but also the impossibility of allowing Britain to occupy Norway.[25]

On January 1, 1940, the preliminary OKW study on Norway was sent to Hitler, who on January 27 ordered that it be revised under his personal and immediate supervision and in closest co-operation with the overall military leadership. The study was henceforth to bear the code name *Weserübung* ("Weser exercise"), and was to be completed in the shortest possible time.[26]

Hitler was not yet completely convinced of the need for German action, nor certain of the form such action should take if it were to be carried through. He continued to hope that Scandinavian neutrality could be preserved, and explored the possibilities of putting political pressure on the Scandinavian governments to this end. German leadership was aware of the gravity of a military undertaking in the north. It meant gambling with the entire German fleet.[27]

Meanwhile Quisling informed Berlin about further British preparations in the north, particularly under the cover of aid to Finland, and of the Norwegian government's alarming willingness to condone British violations of Norway's neutrality.[28] A totally different set of impressions was recorded by the official German diplomatic representative in Oslo, who until the eve of the German invasion minimized the possibility of an attack on Norway by the Western powers.[29] On the whole Quisling's information about Allied intentions corresponded more closely to the facts of the situation than the data that trickled through German diplomatic channels. Plans for mining Norwegian territorial waters and sending aid to Finland were indeed under consideration in Britain and France. The conclusion of peace between Russia and Finland on March 12 put an end to projects to aid Finland; but soon afterward the Supreme Allied War Council resolved to mine Norwegian territorial waters. Authorization was received from the British cabinet on April 3; and early in the morning

140

of April 8 the mine fields were finally laid.[30]

Long before this had been done, Hitler had become convinced of the seriousness of the British threat in Scandinavia, and the British attack on a German supply ship *Altmark* in Norwegian territorial waters on February 16 may have provided him with a welcome pretext to take action in that area. On February 19 he pressed for more speed in the preparation of the Norwegian campaign, and two days later he summoned General Nikolaus von Falkenhorst to his headquarters and placed him in charge of the Norway project. Falkenhorst had taken part in the German campaign in Finland in 1918, and was therefore familiar with military conditions in the north.[31] Hitler was not yet certain whether to strike first in the west or in the north, but on February 28 he accepted General Jodl's recommendation that plans for campaigns in both sectors should be made so that they could be undertaken independently of each other. What he still wanted most of all, he told Rosenberg, was the preservation of Scandinavian neutrality, and he firmly opposed any political action on the part of pro-German elements in Norway. In view of Britain's behavior, however, a crisis in the north seemed imminent, and Germany should be prepared for all eventualities.[32]

A detailed Führer directive for those preparations went out to the German military leadership on March 1, 1940.

> The development of the political situation in Scandinavia, [Hitler said], requires the making of all preparations for the occupation of Denmark and Norway by a part of the Wehrmacht (*Fall Weserübung*). This operation should prevent British encroachment on Scandinavia and the Baltic. Further it should guarantee our ore base in Sweden and give our navy and Luftwaffe a wider base of operations against Britain. . . . In view of our military and political power in comparison with that of the Scandinavian states, the force to be employed in the *Fall Weserübung* will be kept as small as possible. The numerical weakness will be balanced by daring actions and surprise execution.
>
> On principle, we will do our utmost to make the operation appear as a *peaceful* occupation, the object of which is the military protection of the neutrality of the Scandinavian states. Corresponding demands will be transmitted to the governments at the beginning of the occupation. If necessary, naval and air demonstrations will provide the necessary emphasis. If, in spite of this, resistance should be met with, all military means will be used to crush it. . . .
>
> The crossing of the Danish border and the landings in Norway must take place *simultaneously*. I emphasize that the operations must be prepared as quickly as possible. In case the enemy seizes the initiative in Norway, we must be able to apply

immediately our own countermeasures. It is most important that the Scandinavian states as well as the Western opponents should be taken *by surprise* by our measures.[33]

In making his plans for Scandinavia, Hitler at no time mentioned the possibility of occupying Sweden. He evidently believed that with the occupation of Denmark and Norway, Sweden would be effectively cut off from the West and that German political pressure would suffice to ensure the necessary supplies of Swedish iron ore.

By March 3 Hitler had made up his mind to attack in the north before moving in the west. He wanted all preparations completed by March 10, so that military operations could begin on March 15. The attack in the west was to begin three days later. Secrecy was of the essence in this "most daring and most impudent undertaking in the history of warfare."[34]

Falkenhorst's military directives followed Hitler's in stressing the peaceful character of the German occupation, which was simply intended to place Scandinavian neutrality under the armed protection of Germany. Demands were to be made to the governments of Norway and Denmark to refrain from all armed resistance, to tolerate the German occupation, and to co-operate loyally with German military and civilian offices. Upon their agreement to these conditions, these governments were to be assured broad recognition of their domestic sovereignty and support in carrying on the national economy. All military resistance, on the other hand, was to be ruthlessly crushed. The military aim of the occupation was to safeguard German strategic and economic interests; to frustrate Anglo-French efforts to dominate the area; and, beyond that, to create a strong base for the conduct of German air and sea warfare.[35]

Apart from his desire to give the German seizure of Denmark and Norway the appearance of a peaceful operation, Hitler had almost no immediate or long-range plans for the occupation and administration of these countries. Such plans as were made were drawn up by the German army in conjunction with its military preparations.[36] It is evident from the first drafts of these plans that the army wanted to prevent a repetition of what had happened in Poland, where the installation of a Nazi civil government had cleared the way for the ruthless implementation of Nazi ideological programs. Building on Hitler's desire to preserve the appearance of normality in Scandinavia, the army proposed that the existing administration of Norway be allowed to continue to govern the country with a minimum of interference from German authorities; but, because Norway would also be an area of military operations, the German military commander should be assigned ultimate executive power, including the right to issue decrees and give orders to the native government and bureaucracy. "A [German] chief of the civil administration is not necessary," the army planners stated, "because the administration of the country is not to be taken over by us either in a military or civil capacity. Instead there will be a delegate [*Beauftragter*] of the Wehrmacht commander to the Norwegian government (an official of the foreign service), who will carry out the supervision of the government and administration." A second draft proposal of March 5, which contained almost identical plans for the occupation of Denmark, added the significant provision that the German occupation authorities should not concern themselves with questions of race and nationality.

Hitler accepted the greater part of the army's proposals, most of which dealt with routine administrative matters, but he refused to concede ultimate executive power to the Wehrmacht commander or supreme supervisory powers to a delegate of that commander. The assignment of the army was exclusively military, Hitler said, and military administrative activity could only be permitted when it was essential for military purposes. Otherwise all political, administrative, and economic policies and measures were to be carried out exclusively by civil authorities (*Zivilorgane*) in accordance with instructions issued by himself. To preserve the appearance of normality in the conquered territories, Hitler adopted the army's proposal to make officials of the German foreign service the chief representatives of German interests in Denmark and Norway; however, these officials were to be responsible to civilian, not military, agencies. He also agreed to allow the existing governments to remain in power, but added the provision that if these governments engaged in active or passive resistance they were to be removed and replaced by native governments consisting of persons willing to co-operate loyally with the Germans. Personnel changes were to be restricted to the top positions as far as possible; the main body of the bureaucracy was to be persuaded to go on working.

Shortly before the German attack in the north was finally launched, Hitler informed Ribbentrop that Germany's diplomatic representatives in Copenhagen and Oslo were to serve as Reich plenipotentiaries and the chief representatives of German interests with the governments of Denmark and Norway. At approximately the same time the German army was instructed to turn over to the Foreign Office all existing plans for the occupation and administration of these countries.

With the conclusion of peace between Finland and Russia on March 12, 1940, Hitler relaxed the tempo of his Scandinavian campaign, which he had previously scheduled to begin on March 15. In view of the changed situation the preparations for *Weserübung* should be completed calmly with especial attention to secrecy. By now Hitler's concern seems to have shifted from fear of an imminent British attack on Norway to the vulnerability of his northern flank when the time came to launch his campaign in the west. For the moment that Germany violated the neutrality of the Netherlands and Belgium, as envisaged in his campaign plans, the British might seize this excuse to violate the neutrality of Norway. On March 15 Raeder informed his naval commanders that the "political leadership" did not believe that the British action against Norway was imminent, but that *Weserübung* was still necessary and that preparations should continue so that it could be put into operation at the shortest possible notice. *Weserübung* would then be carried out shortly before the attack in the west.[37]

In a decisive conference with Hitler on March 26, Raeder agreed that the danger of a British landing in Norway was no longer acute, but he warned that the British would continue to interfere with German shipping in neutral waters and thereby create incidents in order to give them an excuse to take action in Norway. Sooner or later, therefore, Germany would be compelled to carry out the *Weserübung* operation. Raeder opted for the sooner alternative on the grounds that after April 15 the nights would be too short to allow German ships to make the crossing to Norway without serious danger of interception. There would be a new moon on April 7. These arguments evidently convinced Hitler, for at the conclusion of Raeder's record of the conference of March 26 he noted: 'Führer has agreed to *Weserübung* —X-day to be around the time of the new moon." [38]

On March 27 Hitler confirmed his decision to carry out *Weserübung* in a conference with General Halder, the chief of the army general staff. He wanted to launch the campaign in Scandinavia on April 9 or 10, he said, the attack in the west four or five days later, probably on Sunday, April 14.[39] On April 2 Hitler met with Falkenhorst, Raeder, and Göring. Upon their confirming that all preparations for the Scandinavian campaign were complete, Hitler gave the order to attack at dawn on April 9. The escape of the kings of Denmark and Norway was to be prevented by all means, and the acceptance of Germany's basic military demands by the Danish and Norwegian governments obtained as soon as possible to prevent unnecessary bloodshed. In case these governments refused to comply with German demands, they should be prevented from issuing orders for resistance.[40]

The German attack on Denmark and Norway began as scheduled on April 9.[41] The Danish government accepted the German conditions, although under protest, which meant that the Germans were able to occupy Denmark quickly with almost no losses in manpower.

They were not so lucky in Norway. The Norwegian government evaded capture and gave orders to the army and people of the country to engage in all-out resistance to the invader. Thus the illusion of a peaceful German occupation of Norway was shattered from the start. The superiority of German strength was overwhelming, however, and by the end of April almost all organized resistance in Norway had ceased.[42] Germany's northern flank and its supply of Scandinavian iron ore had been secured, and an extensive line of strategic bases had been acquired for carrying on naval warfare against Britain.

CHAPTER 14

Security in the West:
The Attack on France
and the Low Countries

Britain's response to the German attack on Poland in September 1939 had confirmed Hitler's worst fears about Britain's attitude with respect to Germany's continental position. He had always seen in France an irreconcilable foe of Germany and one that would have to be destroyed before Germany could enjoy security on the continent. With the racially related British, on the other hand, he had wanted not only peace but an alliance, and he had long argued that friendship with Britain should be a cornerstone of German foreign policy. After coming to power, however, he had recognized that the British as well as the French would very probably oppose the establishment of German hegemony on the continent. At the conference with his top military and diplomatic leaders on November 5, 1937, he had described Britain and France as two hate-inspired antagonists to whom a German colossus in the center of Europe would be a thorn in the flesh, and who would oppose any further strengthening of Germany's position either in Europe or overseas.[1]

After Britain's declaration of war on Germany, Hitler expressed himself even more strongly about the hostility of both Britain and France. In a memorandum to his military leaders shortly after the conclusion of the Polish campaign, he declared that ever since the Peace of Westphalia of 1648 Britain and France had sought to prevent the formation of a German union and to preserve a balance of power favorable to themselves. The central aim of the Western powers in the First World War had been the destruction of the German national state formed in 1871; it remained their primary objective in

146

the Second World War. If the German state were to survive and the German people to gain their rightful status on the European continent, they would be compelled to face a showdown struggle with Britain and France sooner or later. It was the task of German leadership to see that this struggle was waged at a time most advantageous to Germany.[2]

With the final surrender of the Polish forces on October 6, 1939, Hitler made a speech before a special session of the Reichstag offering to make peace with the Western powers and to settle all outstanding international differences by negotiation, a peace offer contemptuously rejected by Chamberlain six days later.[3] In all likelihood Hitler's peace bid was nothing more than a propagandistic maneuver designed to convince the German people that the continuation of the war was due to the recalcitrant attitude of Britain and France. For it can be taken as certain that he had no intention of concluding a permanent peace with these states while they were still in a position to threaten Germany's security. The only purpose of a peace treaty at this time would have been to give him an opportunity to divide Britain from France and thereby enable him to dispatch them separately.[4]

Desirable as such a policy might have been, Hitler was never given an opportunity to pursue it. Nor does he appear to have had any serious intention of doing so, for the time factor still played the decisive role in his calculations. As he explained to his military leaders early in October 1939, the success of the Polish campaign and the treaty with Russia had made it possible for Germany, for the first time in many years, to wage war on a single front and to throw all its strength against the west while leaving only a few covering troops in the east. This was a situation that could not be expected to endure. By no pact or treaty could the lasting neutrality of the Soviet Union be assured. At present all reason spoke against Russia's departure from a position of neutrality, but in eight months or a year this situation might change. The trifling significance of treaties, as Hitler was able to state with some authority, had been demonstrated on all sides in recent years. The greatest security against any kind of Russian intervention lay in a massive and prompt display of German military might.

Nor could Germany count on the continued neutrality of other European states, which were temporarily neutral either through fear, their lack of interest in the war, or their desire to be sure of joining the winning side. If Germany delayed its attack against the West, the neutrals' confidence in a final German victory would decline, and with it Germany's diplomatic position. What was true of other neutrals was also true of Germany's ally, Italy, whose friendship toward

Germany depended entirely on the person of Mussolini and his ability to remain in power. Should Germany show signs of weakness and indecision, Mussolini would find it increasingly difficult to pursue a pro-German course, much less join the war on Germany's side. So here, too, time was running against Germany.

Meanwhile time would permit a steady increase in the military power of Britain and France, whose war industries were able to draw on the resources of the entire world. Every increase in the strength of the Western powers would make Germany's inevitable life and death struggle with these countries more difficult. But for Hitler the conclusive argument for knocking out the threat from the west at the earliest possible moment was his recognition that Germany had an Achilles heel—the Ruhr. Ruhr industries were essential to the German war economy, and located as they were along Germany's western frontier, they were perilously vulnerable to attack. Hitler was sure that the importance and vulnerability of the Ruhr must be evident to Germany's enemies, and that, given time to build up their offensive strength, they would strike at this vital center of the German war economy. For this purpose they did not even have to undertake an actual invasion of Germany. Air attacks alone could inflict damaging blows; but more effective still would be an Allied thrust into the Low Countries, from which the Ruhr could be pulverized by long-range artillery. There was every reason to suppose the Allies would make such a move. Belgium and the Netherlands might be anxious to remain neutral, but the preservation of their colonies, their international trade, the very security of their domestic economy, depended entirely on British and French good will. With such means of exerting pressure, Britain and France could compel Belgium and the Netherlands to enter the war on their side, or at least secure permission for the passage of their troops through Belgian or Dutch territory, at any time they desired—and that without covering themselves with the odium of a breach of neutrality.

There was also the problem of the United States. The efforts of interventionists in America to involve that country in the war against Germany had so far been unsuccessful; but here, too, time might well bring changes, none of them to Germany's advantage.

Hitler concluded that attack, and immediate attack, was under all circumstances the best policy. A start could not be made too soon. The coming months would not lead to any important increase in Germany's offensive power, but only to the offensive and defensive strength of the enemy.

Hitler proceeded to define Germany's objectives in the west. The German war aim must be the elimination of the military strength of the Western powers, the destruction of their ability to oppose the consolidation and further development of the German people in Europe. Territorial gain would be of importance only to the extent to which it contributed to the destruction of enemy armies. It was imperative to be aware of the major objectives from the start and to concentrate solely on the annihilation of enemy troops and resources. If this should not be possible for reasons unknown at the moment, then the secondary objective would be the seizure of territory which offered favorable conditions for the successful conduct of a longer war.[5]

At the end of September 1939, as the Polish campaign was drawing to a close, Major Deyhle of the OKW general staff recorded in his war diary,

> *Decision of the Führer* to attack in the *West,* and that as soon as possible because the French/English army is not yet ready. Intention of attacking through Belgium and Holland (at least the southern part) is certain from the start. From the beginning it is the Führer's idea not to repeat the Schlieffen plan, but, while giving strong protection to the southern flank, to attack through Belgium/Luxembourg in approximately a west-north-west direction and to gain the channel coast.[6]

The decisive Führer order to prepare for military operations against the West was issued on October 9.[7] The major attack was to be conducted against the northern wing of the western front, through Luxembourg, Belgium, and the Netherlands, and was to be carried out with as much strength and at as early a date as possible. The purpose of this attacking operation was to crush the French mobile army and the allies fighting by its side. At the same time the objective would be to control as large an area as possible in the Netherlands, Belgium, and northern France, to be used as a base for conducting both an air and a sea war against Britain and as a protective zone for the vital Ruhr area. "The more Dutch territory we occupy, the more effective can the defense of the Ruhr be made," Keitel said in a directive of November 15. "This viewpoint must determine the choice of objectives made by the army, even if the army and navy are not directly interested in such a territorial gain." [8]

Hitler repeatedly urged haste. He was much concerned lest the Allies move into Belgium and the Netherlands before his own offensive preparations were completed. He hoped the attack might be launched early in November, but agreed with his military leaders to hold off until the full impact of German might could be brought to bear in the west, a condition that might delay the attack until mid-November or beyond. Moreover he was determined to attack only if weather permitted operations by the bomber and fighter planes of the Luftwaffe, for only then could one of Germany's most valuable trumps be used effectively.[9]

Preparations for an offensive in the west were completed early in November, as Hitler had desired, but the weather now forced a long series of postponements of the date of attack, which was first set for November 7. Throughout the winter Hitler continued to hope for a few days of clear weather, but the weather refused to co-operate and the German armies remained poised in the west in vain.[10]

Early in January 1940 a German plane with a staff officer of the German air force on board lost its way and had to make a forced landing in Belgium. The officer was carrying documents relating to the German campaign in the west, as well as a timetable of the most recent plan of attack. The Germans had no way of knowing which of these documents had fallen into the hands of the Belgian authorities before they could be destroyed, but the reaction of the Belgian government and subsequent Belgian and Dutch military preparations made it clear that the German plan of attack through the Low Countries had been discovered. As a result German plans for a western offensive, which Hitler had already ordered revised repeatedly during the delays caused by inclement weather, had to be revised once more, this time fundamentally, causing yet another delay.[11]

By March of 1940 all preparations for the campaign against the west had been completed—but by this time a further menace to German security had loomed in Scandinavia, the elimination of which became another life and death issue for Hitler. For a time he was uncertain whether he should strike first in the north or in the west; but by March 3 the situation in the north convinced him to undertake the Scandinavian campaign first.[12]

Hitler's military plans for the conquest of Western Europe had been worked out in far more detail than his plans for the occupation and administration of the territories he proposed to conquer. About his future intentions toward Western Europe Hitler was in fact strangely reticent. Security was to be won for the Germans on their western flank. So much was clear. The French threat was to be eliminated for all time, and a basis laid for a campaign against Britain should that be necessary. But once the French and British menace to German security had been destroyed, what was to be done with the peoples and territories of Western Europe?

Nazi theories on this subject were dominated as usual by considerations of race. The Dutch and the Flemish, despite their apostasy to Anglo-French ideologies, were good Germans if not true; Nazi planners agreed that these peoples should enjoy a preferred status in the Germanic realm of the future. The chief problem here would be to train these peoples to assume a position befitting their race within the National Socialist system.[13]

Beyond that the fundamentals of Nazi policy fail to emerge. How was National Socialism to handle the French and the Walloon peoples, whose contributions to European civilization were so numerous and so striking that Nazi theorists found themselves obliged to assign these Romance nations a Germanic background? Their existence could not be, or at any rate was not, so summarily dismissed as that of the Jews and the Slavs.

The fact is that Nazi racial conceptions about their Latin neighbors were fuzzy. Hitler's alliance with the Italians and his search for a more cordial entente with the Spaniards failed to clarify the issue. The Latins might be a lesser breed, but apparently they, too, were to have their place within the New Order.

In *Mein Kampf* Hitler had specifically rejected the west and south as legitimate goals of Germanic expansion, although he always took into account the possibility that Germany would have to control territory in these regions for purposes of security. By 1940, so far as one can judge from his private conversations and secret directives, he had not yet come up with any overall racial-political formula for the west. He did, of course, make plans for the occupation of Western Europe well before launching the German invasion, but the long-range programs that formed so prominent a feature of Nazi policies in the east were conspicuously absent. Seyss-Inquart summed up the problem upon leaving his post as deputy governor general in Poland to become Reichskommissar of the occupied Netherlands: "In the east we have a National Socialist mission; over there in the west we have a function. Therein lies something of a difference!"[14]

On November 4, 1939, Hitler sent out an order to the highest Reich offices on the question of the occupation and administration of Belgium, the Netherlands, and Luxembourg. At the moment of invasion, he proposed to announce the political reasons for his action and to reassure the peoples and governments of these countries about his future political intentions. Supreme administrative power in the occupied areas was to be invested in the commander in chief of the army, but every effort should be made to retain the native administration to carry on the routine business of government. Germany's policy toward the governments of the occupied countries was to be determined by their behavior. In all countries that resisted the German occupation, the male population capable of bearing arms was to be interned. The occupation armies were to live off the land, the economy was to be kept going. The local population was to be fed, the art treasures protected. All invasion plans were of course to remain top secret, but Hitler thought it necessary to inform the heads of the var-

151

ious Reich offices that would be involved in occupation government to have plans prepared and personnel ready when the time came for a German administration to be installed.[15]

Hitler's order for the administration of the occupied countries in the west of May 9, 1940, the day before the German attack, differed little from the one of the previous November. The commander in chief of the army was to set up a military administration, which was to be conducted "so as to avoid giving the impression that it is intended to annex the occupied territories." The provisions of the Hague convention on land warfare were to be observed, the population protected, and economic life maintained. But all hostile acts on the part of the local population, such as sabotage, guerrilla warfare, passive resistance, or stoppage of work as a political gesture, were to be suppressed with the utmost severity.[16]

Simultaneously with the launching of the German attack on the Low Countries, Hitler issued his proposed pronouncement on the political reasons for his action. These reasons were almost identical with those given for the occupation of Denmark and Norway. Belgium and the Netherlands, Hitler said, while publicly proclaiming a policy of neutrality, had in fact taken the side of Britain and France from the beginning, and he had conclusive evidence to prove that they intended to place their territories at the disposal of the Western powers for an attack on Germany. In this struggle for existence forced on the German people by Britain and France, the Reich government was not disposed to sit idly by while the Western powers carried the war, by way of the Low Countries, into German territory. "It has therefore issued the command to German troops to ensure the neutrality of these countries by all the military means at the disposal of the Reich."

German troops did not come as enemies of the Belgian and Dutch peoples, Hitler continued, nor did Germany intend to encroach, now or in the future, on the sovereignty and independence of the kingdoms of Belgium and the Netherlands, or on their European and extra-European possessions. Even at this late date the governments of these countries had it in their power to ensure the well-being of their peoples by ordering that no resistance be offered to German troops, and Hitler appealed to them to do so. If they failed to issue the necessary orders, they alone would be responsible for the inevitable bloodshed that would ensue, as well as all other consequences of resistance.[17]

Neither the Belgian nor Dutch governments, nor the government of Luxembourg to which a similar proclamation was addressed, responded to Hitler's appeal, with the result that when the Germans conquered the Low Countries they were obliged to set up governments of their own.[18]

At dawn on May 10, 1940, the German armies finally launched their offensive in the west, invading the Netherlands, Belgium, and Luxembourg without warning and without a declaration of war. Co-ordinating the action of mechanized units, infantry, and air power, the Germans waged a Blitzkrieg even more impressive than their campaign in Poland.

In the Netherlands German parachute and airborne troops succeeded in capturing and holding strategic bridges until their mechanized units arrived. On May 15, five days after the German attack began, the Dutch armies surrendered, but not before the queen of the Netherlands and her government had succeeded in escaping to Britain, where they set up a Dutch government in exile.

On the second day of their offensive in Belgium, the Germans captured the fortress of Eben Emael, which the Allies had presumed to be impregnable and which was the key of the Belgian defense system. They then pushed rapidly into western Belgium, as though to sweep through the flatlands of the Low Countries into France as they had done in the First World War. The drive into western Belgium was a feint, however, to draw Allied troops into a trap and divert their attention from the main German offensive, which was launched in the difficult hilly terrain of Luxembourg and the Ardennes in southern Belgium. By May 13 German troops in this sector had crossed the Meuse at several points and, in co-operation with the Luftwaffe, broke through the relatively weak western extension of France's famed defensive network, the Maginot Line, whose strongest fortifications stopped just beyond the frontiers of Luxembourg northwest of Verdun. Having effected this breakthrough, German armored units raced down the Somme valley toward the channel, reaching the coast near Abbéville on May 21. With that a major objective of their Sickle (*Sichelschnitt*) operation, the division of the Allied armies, had been achieved.

The Germans now moved rapidly to envelop and destroy the Allied forces cut off in the north. On May 28 the main Belgian army, surrounded and no longer in communication with other Allied forces, surrendered. In contrast to Queen Wilhelmine of the Netherlands, who had gone into exile, the king of the Belgians decided to go into military captivity with his troops.

Meanwhile the other Allied forces caught in the German net retreated to Dunkirk, where it seemed that they too would shortly be forced to surrender. On May 26, however, Hitler, fearful of overextending his weary armored units and of exposing them to possible enemy counterattacks in the difficult river and canal terrain of Flanders, called a halt to the German advance, confident that his Luftwaffe could complete the destruction of the Allied forces trapped

153

along the channel coast. But the Luftwaffe, hampered by bad weather and harrassed by the fighter squadrons of the Royal Air Force, was unable to do so. Two days later Hitler gave orders allowing his armored units to resume their offensive, but by that time the Allies had had an opportunity to reorganize their defenses. Behind those defenses, beginning on May 27, the British carried out a gigantic evacuation operation from Dunkirk, and by June 4 approximately two hundred thousand British and one hundred thirty thousand French and Belgian soldiers had been safely transported to Britain. The Luftwaffe, once again hampered by bad weather and the activity of the RAF, failed to halt or even seriously hinder the British rescue operation; but the principal reason for its failure appears to have been that it concentrated on bombing the troops on the beaches rather than the boats sent to rescue them, the bombs exploding in the soft sand and doing relatively little damage.

Numerous military historians, as well as several German generals, have been severely critical of Hitler's military judgment in preventing German armored units from carrying out the final destruction of the Allied armies at Dunkirk and allowing a veteran army to escape to Britain. But Hitler, who had no way of knowing the extent of his enemies' demoralization, had compelling reasons for wishing to avoid exposing his armored units to further risk (unnecessarily, as he thought), for he still needed his tanks to deal with some sixty-five French divisions which were in the field to the east and south. The theory that Hitler halted the German advance at Dunkirk as a gesture of good will to Britain or to avoid destroying the troops of another Nordic nation runs counter to all reliable evidence about his intentions at the time. It is equally unlikely that he did so to give Göring and his Nazi Luftwaffe the glory of annihilating the British while withholding that honor from his conservative generals. By now there were Nazis enough among his military commanders, especially in the armored units, and in any case the generals had already earned ample glory.

On June 5, 1940, with their right flank secured by their victories in northern France and the Low Countries, the Germans launched a major offensive into eastern and southern France. So successful were the German operations that on June 10 Benito Mussolini, convinced that Germany had won the war, finally brought Italy into the conflict in order not to be left out when it came to sharing the spoils. On June 13 the Germans entered Paris; three days later the French cabinet, which had moved to Bordeaux, voted to ask Germany for an armistice. Prime Minister Paul Reynaud, who opposed capitulation, thereupon resigned, to be succeeded by the aged field marshal, General Henri-Philippe Pétain, the hero of the Verdun campaign in the First

FRANCE, THE LOW COUNTRIES, AND BRITAIN

- To Germany
- "Vichy France"

△ △ ▼ ▼ Fortifications

SCOTLAND

Edinburgh

Belfast

IRELAND

IRISH SEA

GREAT BRITAIN

Newcastle

NORTH SEA

DENMARK

Hamburg

Manchester
Liverpool

WALES

Birmingham

ENGLAND

Cardiff

Bristol

London

Thames R.

Ramsgate

Plymouth

Southampton

PORTLAND HEAD

ISLE OF WIGHT

Strait of Dover

Dunkirk

Bremen

NETHERLANDS
(Capitulation
May 14, 1940)

Amsterdam

The Hague

Rotterdam

Chemicals

Nijmegen

Dortmund

Elec. Power

RUHR VALLEY

Essen

Antwerp

Brussels

Ghent

BELGIUM
(May 28, 1940)

Lille

Coal

Ft. Eban
Emael

Liège

Chemicals

Düsseldorf

Cologne

GERMANY

Frankfurt

May 10, 1940

May 10, 1940

Rhine R.

ENGLISH CHANNEL

Alderney

CHANNEL ISLANDS

Cherbourg

Caen

Abbeville

Dieppe

Le Havre

Somme R.

Coal

Steel

Iron Ore

Textiles

Chemicals

Elec. Power

Reims

Seine R.

Verdun

LUXEMBOURG

ARDENNES

Meuse R.

Moselle R.

May 14, 1940

Saarbrucken

West Wall
(Siegfried
Line)

Coal

Metz

Iron
Ore

Maginot
Line

Strasbourg

Steel

Mulhouse

Basel

Brest

Rennes

Paris (Occupied June 14,
armistice June 22, 1940)

Orléans

Loire R.

Nantes

Bourges

FRANCE

Dijon

Iron
Ore

Iron Ore

Iron Ore

Berne

SWITZERLAND

ATLANTIC

OCEAN

Limoges

Vichy

Chemicals

Geneva

Lyons

ALPS

ITALY

Turin

Chemicals

Bordeaux

Caronne R.

Molybdenum

St. Etienne

Textiles

Elec. Power

Chemicals

Elec. Power

Textiles

Bauxite

Nice

Bayonne

Hendaye

Toulouse

Montpellier

Marseille

Rhone R.

PYRENEES

ANDORRA

SPAIN

MEDITERRANEAN SEA

0   100   200 miles

World War, who requested an armistice on June 17. The armistice was signed on June 22 in Compiègne, in the same railway car that had been used for signing the German capitulation on November 11, 1918. Hitler's victory, and revenge, were complete.[19]

The Franco-German armistice provided that German forces should occupy three-fifths of France, including the northern part of the country, with Paris, and the entire seacoast to the Spanish border. On July 2 the French government moved to the spa of Vichy (temporarily, it was assumed at that time), where on July 9 the French parliament voted to give Pétain powers to establish an authoritarian regime.

As a result of the German military victory in the west, their occupation of the Low Countries and the greater part of France, French opposition to Germany's continental hegemony and the French threat to Germany's western flank had been eliminated. The British, however, despite the fact that their expeditionary force had been driven from the continent, had not been conquered and remained a threat to German security in the west.

CHAPTER 15

The Problem of Britain

After the German victory in the west, there is every indication that Hitler expected even the dogged British would at last be prepared to concede German supremacy on the continent, provided they could do so without losing their own position as a world power. Hitler was willing, even anxious, to accord them this status. He regarded the British as Nordic cousins, and saw in the British Empire a cornerstone of Western civilization, a monument to the state-building capacity of the Anglo-Saxon race. In his fundamental considerations on foreign policy he had consistently advocated a German alliance with Britain, and there can be no doubt of the sincerity of his expressions of regret about his inability to form one. In November 1939 he told Rosenberg that he still believed an Anglo-German understanding to be the correct policy for Germany, especially from a long-term point of view. He, for his part, had done everything possible to achieve it, but a Jewish-dominated minority in Britain had frustrated his efforts. The British would only see the light after they had been taught a terrible lesson.[1]

By June 1940 Hitler believed the British had been taught such a lesson. Their armies had been driven from the continent, and all chances for a victory over Germany seemed irretrievably lost. Now, if ever, the British might be expected to see reason, to reverse the disastrous decision of September 1939 and enter into partnership with Germany for the domination of the world. On June 2, 1940, Hitler told Rundstedt and other German generals that if Britain were now prepared to make a sensible peace, as he expected, his hands would at last be freed for his greatest and real task, the destruction of Bolshevism.[2]

On June 13, 1940, Hitler used the dramatic moment of the entry of his troops into Paris to make the first of several statements following the defeat of France about his desire for peace and friendship with Britain. In a much-publicized interview with the American journalist Karl von Wiegand, Hitler said, "All I have ever asked is that Germany should enjoy equal rights with Great Britain, and receive back its former colonies. It has never been my intention to destroy the empire." Then, in an obvious effort to undercut the Churchill government and appeal to class sentiment in Britain, Hitler continued, "One thing and one thing only will have been annihilated as a result of this war—the capitalist bloc which set itself to cause the death of millions of men for its private and ignoble interests. I am convinced, however, that not we but the English themselves will be the instrument by which the destruction of this plutocratic group is brought about." [3]

Hitler was much disturbed by the absence of any positive response to his Wiegand interview, or to his various peace overtures through diplomatic channels. At the end of June he expressed the fear that the British would probably need another demonstration of German military might before they gave in "and freed our backs for the east." But he was most reluctant to deal Britain such a blow. "If we crush England by force of arms," he told his generals, "the British Empire will fall to pieces. But this would be of no advantage to Germany. We should spill German blood only in order that Japan, America, and others might benefit." [4]

On July 19 Hitler made another public appeal to the British, this time in a speech before the German Reichstag. The only possible result of a continuation of the war, he said, would be the destruction of the British Empire, something he had never desired. He felt a sense of disgust for the conscienceless British war profiteers, most of them undoubtedly already safely relocated in Canada, who were dooming their country and people to destruction. "In this hour I feel it is my duty before my conscience to appeal once more to reason in Great Britain as elsewhere. I consider myself in a position to do this, since I am not a vanquished foe begging favors but the victor speaking in the name of reason. I can see no reason why this war need go on." [5] Hitler's public plea for peace was again accompanied by diplomatic overtures; but on July 22 the British foreign secretary, Lord Halifax, publicly rejected Hitler's peace bid, which he declared was based on no arguments except fear and threats. "The speech of Halifax has definitely destroyed our belief that a party of conciliation exists over there," the German Foreign Office representative at Hitler's headquarters wrote to a German agent engaged in negotiations with the British in Switzerland, "and the Führer does not want any further attempts to be made to build bridges for the English. If the English want their own destruction, they can have it." [6]

Hitler was disappointed by the British attitude, but he was not caught by surprise. Preparations for carrying on air and sea warfare against Britain had been in train since the beginning of the war; and since November 1939 the possibilities of an actual invasion of Britain had been under examination by German naval leaders. These possibilities were discussed with Hitler on May 21, 1940.[7] At this time he evidently had some hope that air and submarine blockades would be sufficient to compel Britain's surrender, but on July 2, on the basis of detailed recommendations from General Jodl, he ordered that preparations for an actual invasion of Britain should go forward. "All preparations must bear in mind that the plan for a landing in England has not yet taken any sort of definite shape, and that these are only *preparations for a possible operation.*" [8]

Hitler's first detailed directive to prepare for a landing in England was issued July 16, three days before his Reichstag speech appealing to the British to see reason. "Since England, despite its hopeless military position, still shows no sign of willingness to come to terms, I have decided to prepare a landing operation against England and if necessary to carry it out," Hitler said. The aim of the operation, which was given the code name Sea Lion, was to eliminate the English homeland as a base for carrying on the war against Germany, and if necessary to occupy the island completely. For this purpose Hitler planned a surprise landing operation on a broad front, approximately from Ramsgate to the area west of the Isle of Wight, in which the Luftwaffe would take the role of the artillery, the navy that of the engineers. All preparations were to be completed by mid-August. Hitler recognized that before an invasion could be attempted a number of conditions had to be met: The British air force had to be morally and physically broken so that it could no longer mount any aggressive opposition to the German crossing; the embarkation area had to be dominated by German coastal artillery; and a mine barrier had to be laid down to seal off both flanks of the Straits of Dover as well as the western entrance to the channel, approximately along a line from Portland to Alderney. Meanwhile every effort was to be made to tie down British naval forces in the North Sea and the Mediterranean, and to weaken those forces by aerial and submarine attacks.[9]

Hitler was fully aware of the difficulties of a cross-channel invasion. "A landing in England is an exceptionally daring undertaking," he said in a naval conference of July 21, "for although the passage is short, it is not merely a question of crossing a river but of crossing a sea which is controlled by the enemy. Forty divisions will be necessary. The most difficult task will be the continuous supply of materiel and foodstuffs. We cannot count on obtaining supplies of any kind in England." [10] On July 31 he called the attention of his army leaders to the enormous risks involved in transporting an army to Britain. "A crossing should only be undertaken if there is no other way open of reaching an understanding with England." Hitler wanted preparations pushed as rapidly as possible so as not to lose his military momentum, but before proceeding to extreme measures he proposed to try yet again to persuade the British to come to terms. The primary reason the British did not make peace, he believed, was their expectation that Russia and the United States might yet intervene on their side. Stalin was even now flirting with the British to encourage them to continue the war, for Russia had no interest in seeing Germany grow too powerful. As yet Hitler saw no sign of overt anti-German activity on the part of Russia, but even so he instructed his army leaders "to take the Russian problem under consideration," and to formulate plans for the destruction of Russia and therewith the elimination of Britain's last hope for support on the continent.[11]

Hitler's instructions to prepare for an attack on Russia at this early date, seen against the background of his ideological program and the policy he actually adopted, have given rise to a theory, supported by the postwar testimony of a number of German leaders, that Hitler was never serious about the invasion of Britain and that all invasion preparations were mere camouflage for the Russian campaign.[12] This theory is certainly false in so far as it applies to Hitler's policy in the summer of 1940, for there can be no doubt of the seriousness of his invasion plans from July to September of that year. During this period the entire German economy and transport system were disrupted by invasion preparations. Top priority was given to the construction of aircraft and naval vessels at the expense of production for the army, which was partially demobilized to make manpower available for production purposes; the German navy requisitioned almost all shipping facilities in German and German-occupied territories in its efforts to assemble a transport fleet.[13] It is impossible to believe that such drastic measures were undertaken merely for the sake of camouflage, or that the elaborate German invasion plans, which could not have been known to the Russians, were simply an academic exercise.

The German transport fleet was made up of craft of widely different sizes and speeds, and consisted to a large extent of unwieldy tug-drawn barges, some of which the navy, with indifferent success, was attempting to convert into motor coasters. Admiral Raeder informed Hitler that because of the unwieldy and heterogeneous composition of the transport fleet an invasion would require not only absolute security from attacks by sea and air, but a clear night and a calm sea, which meant that a crossing would have to be carried out before the autumn and winter storm season set in. Raeder pointed out further that the commandeering of the majority of tugs and barges on Europe's inland waterways had almost brought inland shipping to a

160

halt, and this at a time when Germany's coal and iron ore stockpiles were already dangerously low. The requisition of seagoing vessels would shortly affect the coal and ore trade with Scandinavia, and the utilization of the fishing fleet would seriously reduce Germany's supply of seafood. When the harvest was brought in later in the summer, the lack of bulk transport facilities would create the danger of large-scale food spoilage, and there would be difficulties in supplying the peasants with artificial fertilizer for next year's crops. For reasons of both climate and economy, therefore, the invasion preparations could not be allowed to drag on too long.[14]

Hitler agreed on the need for speed; on July 31 he set September 15, 1940, as the target date for invasion. Whether the operation could take place at that time or would have to be postponed, perhaps until the following spring, would depend on the success of the Luftwaffe in destroying British air and sea power; for without complete mastery of the air over the invasion route the operation could not be considered. The crossing, even without enemy interference, would be difficult enough. Because of the limited transport facilities, the landing forces would have to be staggered, and the army could not count on keeping its divisions together. Even after a beachhead had been established, there would be the problem of keeping the invasion forces supplied.[15]

Despite his awareness of the risks of invasion and the effects of invasion preparations on the German war economy, Hitler ordered that these preparations be kept up. "The material and personal preparations of all branches of the Wehrmacht for Operation Sea Lion have top priority until the deadline set by me," he stated in an order of August 20.[16]

To destroy British sea and air power, which Hitler considered an essential precondition for the invasion of Britain, the Luftwaffe early in August launched a major offensive against British naval and air bases, harbors, communication centers, and vital industries; on August 17 the German government proclaimed a total blockade of the waters around the British Isles. But as Hitler's deadline of September 15 drew nearer it was obvious that German submarine and air attacks had not yet broken British sea or air power, and that neither blockade nor bombardment had convinced the British government of the necessity of coming to the conference table. On September 3 the German invasion deadline was moved ahead to September 20; on September 13 Hitler considered abandoning the project altogether, but on the following day he merely ordered a new postponement, leaving open the possibility of an invasion early in October.[17] For a month Hitler's mind swayed in indecision while the German maritime and inland fleets were tied up on the Atlantic coast and the German economy continued to give priority to production for warfare against Britain. Not until October 12 did Keitel issue an order in Hitler's name definitely postponing the campaign against Britain until the following spring. Preparations for a landing in Britain were to be maintained solely as a political and military threat to prevent the British from sending their defensive forces to other sectors.[18]

Some weeks later, at a conference with Mussolini and senior German and Italian officials, Hitler explained that with respect to Britain Germany was in the position of someone with only one shot left in his rifle.

> If he misses, the situation is much worse than before. The landing cannot be repeated, since too much equipment would be lost in the case of failure. England would then not have to worry any more about a landing and could employ the bulk of its forces on the periphery wherever it pleases. So long as the attack has not taken place, on the other hand, the English would have to reckon with the possibility.[19]

Hitler was convinced by now that, barring major blunders on his part, the military situation in Europe could no longer develop unfavorably for Germany. An invasion of Britain, with the inadequate means at his disposal and the menace of Russia at his back, was precisely the kind of blunder he was determined to avoid. Having gambled so often up to this point, Hitler had begun to feel ultimate success within his grasp and no longer saw any reason to take unnecessary risks. There still existed numerous possibilities for striking at Britain, whether through blockade, bombardment, or attacks on critical outposts of the British Empire such as Gibraltar or the Suez Canal, and Hitler proposed to take advantage of them.[20] But these blows, even if successful, would merely cripple British power; they would not destroy it. Moreover, an increasingly stringent blockade of Britain would run the risk of bringing the United States into the war, thereby placing America's sea power and productive capacity at Britain's disposal.

In his search for a means to strike a decisive blow, Hitler explored many possibilities; but more and more he leaned to the view that, before proceeding with military undertakings that involved any serious risk, he must knock out the menace of Russia, which stood athwart his economic lifelines in Eastern Europe. Franco's refusal early in December 1940 to enter the war,[21] a step which would have enabled the Germans to undertake the capture of Gibraltar and the closure of the western Mediterranean to the British, may have fixed his decision, for on December 18 Hitler issued the decisive directive to prepare for a campaign against Russia—which was launched on June 22, 1941.

This decision was made all the more easily because Hitler thought the conquest of Russia would be a relatively simple undertaking, an opinion shared by the majority of his military advisers.[22]

In resolving to shift the focus of his military endeavor from west to east, Hitler may also have been influenced by a continuing desire to avoid what he regarded as a racial civil war with Britain. One top-ranking member of the Nazi hierarchy at least seems to have believed that this was Hitler's intention. Shortly before the German invasion of Russia, Rudolf Hess, the Führer's deputy and head of the Nazi party organization, flew to Britain in an effort to convince influential persons in that country to come to terms with Germany. There is no evidence that Hitler himself had anything to do with the Hess mission, and his anger about this futile gesture and dangerous blow to German prestige was almost certainly genuine.[23] Hitler himself appears to have abandoned all expectation of successful negotiation with Britain while the British still had reason to hope for support from the United States or Russia.[24] In a long letter to Mussolini of June 21, 1941, he explained that he lacked the means to eliminate the United States, but he could eliminate Russia. If, after the defeat of Russia, Britain still failed to bow to the realities of the military-political situation, then, with security at his back and the resources of the entire continent at his disposal, he could consecrate himself to the task of removing this last and most persistent opponent of Germany's continental supremacy.[25]

It was only after December 1940 that German preparations for an invasion of Britain became primarily a question of camouflage for the preparations being made against Russia, which were now to be represented as camouflage for the invasion of Britain. Actually the preparations against Britain were not altogether camouflage, for Hitler believed that even after the defeat of Russia an invasion of Britain might still be necessary, in which case the camouflage preparations would serve as a nucleus for the real thing.[26] Already by mid-July 1941, in the belief that the war with Russia was won, Hitler ordered a redirection of Germany's economic emphasis to aircraft and submarine production; an order of August 5 stipulated "that the bases for Operation Sea Lion were to be retained and the material preparations for it were to be continued." [27] By the end of August German optimism about the Russian campaign had begun to wane. According to an order of August 31, the preparations for landing in Britain to disguise Germany's intentions in the east "had fulfilled their purpose completely," but now the troops employed in these preparations were needed for other tasks. All other preparations were to be abandoned "until further notice." Military and economic plans for an invasion of Britain were essentially completed, and everything was ready to go as soon as the signal for resuming serious invasion preparations was given.[28]

But that signal never came. In March 1942 Jodl issued a directive that at least a year's notice would be given if Sea Lion plans were to be resumed, a directive that in effect postponed the operation permanently.[29]

CHAPTER 16

Security in the Southwest:
Spain and North Africa

With the growing realization that the invasion and conquest of Britain would not be feasible in the summer or autumn of 1940, the German leadership began to consider seriously other means of striking at Britain. Among these the conquest of Gibraltar and the subsequent closure of the entrance to the western Mediterranean to British sea power was one of the most obvious as well as one that seemed to offer a great possibility of success.

But a campaign in the southwest, valuable as it might be in crippling Britain, did not become a pressing concern for Hitler until Italian defeats in Greece and North Africa forced him to recognize the vulnerability of the Axis in this area. The British might not yet be capable of striking a mortal blow, but it rapidly became evident that, from their bases in the Mediterranean and North Africa, they might undertake the conquest of the Italian and French colonial empires; that they could launch air and naval operations against southern Europe, including the Rumanian oil fields; and that they could assemble expeditionary forces to attack any point along the extended and almost unprotected coastlines of southern France, Italy, and the Balkans. North Africa, too, would be the most likely place for the landing of an American expeditionary force in case the United States decided to intervene in the war in Europe. If Germany's southern flank were to be secure, it would be necessary to control the entrances of the Mediterranean and thereby render it impossible or at least far more difficult for the British to deploy their sea power in the Mediterranean or make use of their Mediterranean and North African bases.

The key to the success of any such endeavor was Spain; for because of his own lack of sea power, Hitler could not move effectively against Gibraltar or undertake the closure of the Mediterranean except by land, and Spain was the only overland route available. Accordingly, as Hitler became increasingly aware of his vulnerability in the southwest, he made steadily greater efforts to enlist Spain's active participation in the war on the side of the Axis in order to safeguard his southern flank, a problem that became even more critical after he made his decision to attack Russia.[1]

Spain

With Franco's victory in the Spanish civil war, achieved with the diplomatic and military support of Germany and Italy, it appeared that an ancient diplomatic situation had been renewed.[2] France was surrounded by continental enemies as in the golden age of Habsburg power. Hitler had apparently achieved what Bismarck had been forced to renounce: the establishment of a pro-German government in Madrid. The family of dictators, bound together by common interests, seemed to have spun around France a net more firm than any family of crowned heads had ever succeeded in weaving.

Hitler, however, knew something of the dependability of international friendships. Franco's debt of gratitude to Germany and Italy, even if underwritten by opportunism, was not necessarily a guarantee of a reliable Spain. Hitler had questioned the desirability of a 100 per cent Franco victory during the Spanish civil war, believing that once firmly established in power the Caudillo would attempt to play off Germany and Italy against Britain and France. A dependent Franco seemed to him a more dependable Franco.[3]

The Franco who emerged victorious from the civil war in March 1939 was certainly dependent enough. By secret treaties with Germany of March and July 1937, Spain promised to maintain close diplomatic and economic ties with Germany, to seek German co-operation in the reconstruction of its economy and the development of its raw materials, and to permit maximum participation by German firms and private citizens in Spanish economic life. A treaty of friendship between Spain and Germany of March 31, 1939, reaffirmed previous diplomatic and economic ties between the two countries, and by treaties of December 22, 1939, Spain agreed to reserve the greater part of its exports for Germany, in particular iron ore, zinc, lead, mercury, wolfram, wool, and hides.[4]

Until the fall of France, Hitler could have expected no more from Spain than benevolent neutrality; but with the extension of German

166

power to the Pyrenees he was in a position to impose direct pressure on Spain to meet his political and economic demands. The Spaniards were eager to please. With the defeat of Britain seemingly imminent, their great concern was to share in the spoils of the French and British empires.

In a letter to Hitler of June 3, 1940, Franco explained his previous neutrality on the grounds of Spain's economic weakness and the vulnerable position of its offshore islands.[5] On June 13, three days after Italy entered the war, Spain changed its official status from neutrality to nonbelligerency, and on the following day Spain occupied the international zone of Tangier "to ensure [its] neutrality." [6] On June 19 the Spanish government sent the Germans a memorandum declaring that the further existence of the French Empire in North Africa was intolerable for Spain and demanding the territory of Oran, French Morocco, an extension of Spanish territory in the Sahara to the twentieth parallel, and an extension of Spain's coastal territory in Africa between the mouth of the Niger and Cape Lopez. If Britain should continue to fight after French resistance had ceased, Spain would be prepared to join in the war against Britain, in which case Spain would need to be supplied with food and fuel, war materials, and submarines to aid in the defense of the Canary Islands.[7]

The Germans did not hasten to ensure Franco's entry into the war against Britain by immediately conceding to all his territorial demands. They had their own territorial aspirations in Africa, they had to deal with the large and often conflicting claims of the Italians, but most important of all they had to avoid alienating Vichy France, which still exercised nominal authority over the greater part of the French Empire and the French fleet. For, if the Germans now engaged in a premature division of France's African empire, which they did not yet control, they might expect the French colonies and the French fleet to go over to the British without further ado. Moreover the Germans saw reason to hope that the French, embittered by their apparent abandonment and betrayal by Britain, might be persuaded to make common cause with Germany against perfidious Albion, in which case Germany would have gained a far more valuable ally than either Italy or Spain. In response to Spain's demands, therefore, the German government promised "to take cognizance of Spain's territorial desires in North Africa," but nothing more.[8]

Hitler's own great hope was that the British would make peace and relieve him of the necessity of undertaking a hazardous invasion or participating in the destruction of the British Empire. When the British still showed no sign of coming to terms during the summer of 1940, Hitler informed his generals on July 13 that he now counted on

167

the need to use force and that he wanted to bring Spain into the picture "in order to build up a hostile front against England from the *North Cape* [of Norway] to *Morocco.*" [9]

While Hitler still saw reason to hope that an invasion of Britain could be carried out, or that the British could be starved into submission by an aerial or naval blockade, he devoted scant attention to Spain or to plans being made by his military leaders for the conquest of Gibraltar. But as the prospects for a successful invasion or siege of Britain declined, his interest in striking at Britain through the Mediterranean grew. After a conference with Hitler on September 14, 1940, General Halder recorded in his diary, "*Gibraltar:* No specific orders; only the expression of intention to promise the Spaniards everything they want even if we cannot provide it all." [10] Hitler explained his views somewhat more fully in a letter to Mussolini three days later. It was necessary to be prepared for unforeseen circumstances, he said. "I am therefore convinced that it can be important to make it possible for Spain to enter the war." The Spanish government had approached Germany with numerous military and economic requests, some of which would require a serious sacrifice on Germany's part, but under the circumstances Hitler believed he would be justified in giving the Spaniards what they wanted. He feared that the French colonies in North Africa, with or without the connivance of Vichy, might go over to the British, an action that would give new impetus to the British cause, at least temporarily. "But as soon as there is a reliable bridge to North Africa via Spain I would no longer consider this danger to be very great. For Spain, too, a clear decision in this direction means increased security." [11]

On September 17 Hitler put these same arguments to Ramón Serrano Suñer, Franco's brother-in-law and Spanish minister of the interior, who had been commissioned by the Caudillo to bring about "a clarification of the conditions under which Spain was ready to fight the war together with Germany." Serrano Suñer informed Hitler that Spain could enter the war immediately as soon as its supply of food and war materials was secure. For reasons of domestic and external security, he sought assurances concerning Spain's "known territorial demands," to which he now added a demand for a frontier rectification along the Pyrenees. Hitler promised to provide for all Spain's military and economic needs, and to aid in the defense of Spain's Atlantic islands and coastline. He also promised the Spaniards Gibraltar; but with respect to Spain's demands in North Africa and along the Pyrenees he remained noncommittal. To clarify any problems that might be at issue between Germany and Spain, he suggested a personal meeting with Franco at the Spanish-French border, an invitation the Spanish dictator immediately accepted.[12]

SECURITY IN THE SOUTHWEST

Despite his overtures to the Spaniards, Hitler was not yet certain of his political course. After the indefinite postponement of plans for a direct invasion of Britain on September 14, Admiral Raeder urged him to strike at Britain by every other means "before the USA could intervene effectively," and to clear up the Mediterranean question during the winter months through the capture of Gibraltar, the Suez Canal, and a drive through Palestine and Syria to the Turkish border. Hitler told Raeder that he agreed in principle. "After the conclusion of the alliance with Japan [13] he intended to confer immediately with Mussolini and possibly also with Franco. He had to decide whether collaboration with France or Spain offered the greater advantage: probably with France, since Spain demanded much (French Morocco), but offered little." [14]

On September 28 Hitler told Ciano of his desire to meet with Mussolini to discuss the general situation, especially the Spanish question, before making any far-reaching decisions. From experiences gained during the Spanish civil war, he was convinced that no progress could be made with the Spaniards without concrete and detailed agreements. The main thing for Germany and Italy was to win the war in the shortest possible time. If victory could be hastened by bringing Spain into the war, Hitler was prepared to make every effort to do so; but he had some doubts as to whether Spanish participation would be worth the cost involved. The Spanish proposals to Germany, somewhat crudely expressed, were that during the coming year Germany was to supply Spain with four to seven hundred thousand tons of grain, all of its fuel, all military equipment which the Spanish army now lacked, including heavy artillery and aircraft, and that special weapons and German troops be made available for the conquest of Gibraltar. In terms of territory Spain demanded all of Morocco, Oran, and an extension of territory south of Rio de Oro. In return for all this, Spain agreed to promise Germany—its friendship. Hitler thought it essential to consider very carefully whether the advantages to be gained by these vague assurances of Spanish friendship were worth the sacrifices entailed. For the time being it might be better if the French remained in Morocco and defended it against the British rather than to hand it over to the Spaniards, who in the event of a British attack would probably be as dilatory as during the civil war and call upon Germany and Italy for aid. Hitler restated most of these arguments when he met with Mussolini at the Brenner Pass on October 4, 1940. His doubts about the desirability of Spanish participation were great, the Spanish price high, the risks of paying it many, especially with regard to the French.[15]

In the final week of October Hitler met with Franco and the leaders of the Vichy government for talks he hoped would give him a clear indication of his future political course in Southwestern Europe. In his conference with Franco at Hendaye on October 23, he stated frankly that his primary purpose at this time was to put together as large a coalition against Britain as possible, but the territorial claims of Spain and the hopes of the Vichy government were obstacles in his path. There was the danger that if the French were explicitly told that they were certain to lose a number of their African colonies, these colonies would go over to the British with the concurrence of the Vichy government. He therefore considered it essential to promise the French that, by co-operating in the defeat of Britain, they might hope to retain a highly valuable colonial empire. The purpose of his trip to Hendaye, Hitler said, "was to examine the possibility of co-operation with France on this basis." What Hitler proposed was the signature of a secret protocol between Germany and Spain, to which Italy would adhere, which would take into account the problem of France and France's African colonies.[16]

The Spaniards refused to play this game. Serrano Suñer expressed his surprise to Ribbentrop that a new course was evidently to be followed in Africa, and that Germany's policy toward France had changed. He understood the reasoning behind Germany's position, but wondered what reward Spain would receive for entering the war. It now appeared as though the compensations for France might be even greater than those awarded to Spain. "Spain, in order to justify the entry into the war to its own people, had to be able to define the rewards of victory more exactly." [17]

After much haggling, the Germans and Spaniards agreed upon the text of a protocol that provided for Spain's accession to the Treaty of Friendship between Germany and Italy of May 22, 1939, and Spain's future accession to the Tripartite Pact between Germany, Italy, and Japan at a date to be set by all four powers. Spain was to join in the war against Britain after the Axis powers had supplied Spain with all necessary military equipment, food, and raw materials, but even then only "at a time to be set by common agreement among the three powers." As for territorial rewards,

> in addition to the reincorporation of Gibraltar into Spain, the Axis powers state that in principle they are ready to see to it, in accordance with a general settlement which is to be established in Africa and which must be put into effect in the peace treaties after the defeat of England—that Spain receives territories in Africa to the same extent as France can be compensated by assigning to the latter other territories of equal value in Africa, but with German and Italian claims against France remaining unaffected.

The protocol was to remain strictly secret.[18]

Hitler was not so disturbed by the inconclusive results of the Hendaye meeting as might have been expected. He was still far more concerned with bringing France into the war against Britain than Spain and, for the time being, had no intention of meeting Spain's territorial demands because of their possible effect on French opinion. "If France were brought into the anti-English front," Hitler told Mussolini on October 28, "then French West and North Africa would be secured, new bases against England acquired, and Gibraltar taken with a very small force; with her help, the one gateway to the Mediterranean could be sealed off, while the other exit, the Suez Canal, could be closed just as effectively by new German mines." The Spaniards, on the other hand, would be incapable of defending their own territories, much less the French North African empire. So low was Hitler's opinion of Spain's military capacity that he wondered whether the announcement of Spain's adherence to the Axis should not be postponed until it was absolutely certain that Britain could not land in Spain or on Spain's Atlantic or Mediterranean islands. Despite these reservations, however, Hitler proposed that all preparations for Spain's entry into the war should be continued.[19]

As late as October 28, then, Hitler does not appear to have envisaged or desired Spain's immediate entry into the war. But on that very day Mussolini launched an attack on Greece which was to change the situation completely.[20] Had the Italians overrun Greece quickly, as Mussolini was confident they would, the Greek campaign would have been no problem. But the Italian offensive bogged down almost from the beginning, and the establishment of a front in Greece opened the way for British military intervention in the southern Balkans, where they would be within bombing range of the Rumanian oil fields. It was the danger to the Axis position resulting from Mussolini's ill-conceived and disastrous Greek campaign that convinced Hitler he must now make every effort to bring Spain into the war, capture Gibraltar, and close the western entrance of the Mediterranean to the British.

On November 4 Halder recorded in his diary that Hitler had received a letter from Franco promising to carry out the agreements he had made orally, "i.e., to enter in on our side. The Führer now intends to press for Spain's entrance into the war." On that same day Hitler told his naval leaders that he was now determined to occupy Gibraltar as soon as possible. "Franco is obviously prepared to enter the war on Germany's side in a short time; army general staff has already made preparations to send the necessary troops." [21]

On November 12 Hitler issued his first major directive calling for military action in Southwestern Europe and North Africa. Significantly, the first section of this directive dealt with France.

> The aim of my policy toward France, [Hitler said], is to co-operate
> with this country in the most effective way for the future prosecution
> of the war against England. For the time being France will have the

role of a "nonbelligerent power" which will have to tolerate German military measures on her territory, in the African colonies especially, and to give support, as far as possible, even by using her own means of defense. The most pressing task of the French is the defensive and offensive protection of their African possessions (West and Equatorial Africa) against England and the de Gaulle movement. From this task the participation of France in the war against England can develop in full force. [With respect to Spain Hitler said], Political measures to induce the prompt entry of Spain into the war have been initiated. The aim of *German* intervention in the Iberian Peninsula (code name *Felix*) will be to drive the English out of the western Mediterranean. For this purpose: a) Gibraltar should be taken and the Straits closed; b) the English should be prevented from gaining a foothold at another point of the Iberian Peninsula or of the Atlantic islands.

For the preparation and execution of these undertakings Hitler was sending reconaissance parties to Spain to conclude the preparations already in progress for the operation against Gibraltar, which was to be carried out by German troops. German troops were also to be held in readiness to march into Portugal in case the British tried to gain a foothold there, and the German navy and Luftwaffe were to study how the Spanish defense of the Canaries might best be supported, and how the Portuguese Cape Verde Islands, Madeira, and the Azores might be captured. The Italian offensive against Egypt was to be supported, if at all, only when the Italians had reached Mersa Matrûh.[22]

Hitler explained the reason for his sudden demand for Spain's immediate entry into the war in personal conferences with Ciano and Serrano Suñer at the Berghof on November 18, and in a letter to Mussolini of November 20.[23] He made no effort to disguise the fact that he considered Italy's precipitate attack on Greece at so unfavorable a season of the year a catastrophic blunder. The political consequences had been serious. Bulgaria, which had shown little enough desire to accede to the Tripartite Pact before, was now completely averse even to considering such a step. It had become more difficult to divert Russian attention from Eastern Europe to the Middle East. On the contrary, Molotov on his recent visit to Berlin had shown an increased interest in the Balkans.[24] The attitudes of Yugoslavia, Turkey, and France had in each case been adversely affected. But if the political consequences were serious, the military and economic consequences might well be disastrous. The crucial problem was the Rumanian oil supply. The British were now establishing air bases in Crete and Greece which brought them within striking distance of the oil fields of Ploesti. "I hardly dare think about the consequences," Hitler said, "for one thing is certain, Duce, there is no effective protection for oil fields." Southern Italy and all of Albania were now within range of enemy bombers, and to destroy enemy air bases was a difficult if not impossible task. "From the military standpoint this situation is threatening. From the economic standpoint, as far as the Rumanian oil fields are concerned, it is positively terrifying."

In view of the new situation in the Mediterranean resulting from Italy's Balkan campaign, Hitler proposed to Mussolini that Spain should be prevailed upon to enter the war in the first week of January to enable German forces to seize Gibraltar and close the Mediterranean from the west. At the same time German troops would move into Spanish Morocco to secure the area against a possible British offensive. With the Straits of Gibraltar under Axis control, the British would be forced to send their transports around South Africa, the pressure in the eastern Mediterranean would be relieved, and the danger of the defection of France's North African colonies lessened. Hitler urged Mussolini for his part to make every effort to reach the Egyptian stronghold of Mersa Matrûh and establish an air base there from which bombers could drive the British fleet from Alexandria and mine the Suez Canal. "The Mediterranean question must be settled this winter. . . . In the spring, by the beginning of May at the latest, I should like, however, to get back my German forces, so that this alone indicates the suitable time for our action." 25

Mussolini agreed that the time had come to play the Spanish card, and volunteered to exert the necessary pressure on the Spanish government. Franco expressed his willingness to co-operate. He agreed to speed Spanish military preparations, but pointed out that the time required for this could not be determined with any precision. For in addition to the attack on Gibraltar, preparations had to be made to meet any number of other military contingencies such as British attacks on the Spanish coast or Atlantic islands. To deal with these problems, Franco requested the dispatch of German military and economic experts to Spain, as well as an officer who enjoyed the Führer's special confidence.26

The officer Hitler chose to conduct what he hoped would be final negotiations for Spain's entry into the war in December 1940 was Admiral Wilhelm Canaris, the chief of Germany's counterintelligence department, who was thoroughly familiar with conditions in Spain and who had already been engaged in numerous reconnaissance missions there. From Hitler's point of view his choice of emissary could hardly have been more unfortunate, for Canaris was an opponent of the Nazi regime. He was to be deeply involved in the plot against Hitler of July 20, 1944, and was later executed for his part in the affair. According to the postwar testimony of his closest associates, Canaris had been warning Franco for many months against joining forces with the German dictator. Exactly what Canaris told the Spaniards will probably never be known—it is doubtful whether the Spaniards were so indiscreet as to keep a record of his remarks, and he himself certainly kept none—but he must have given them ample reason for gratitude, because after the war the Spanish government granted his widow a pension. Perhaps Canaris did no more than hint that Spain could safely refuse Hitler's demands, but such a hint from such a source was sufficient.

According to Canaris's report on his interview with Franco on December 7, 1940, he had, in accordance with his instructions, impressed on the Caudillo in the most forceful possible manner the necessity for Spain's prompt entry into the war. Franco, however, had replied that the state of Spain's military preparations would not admit its entry into the war on the deadline demanded by the Führer. Spain still lacked adequate supplies of food, fuel, and military equipment. The Canary Islands, even if adequately protected by artillery, had only enough food to withstand a siege of six months. "It was to be feared that, after the conquest of Gibraltar, Spain would prove a heavy burden for the Axis powers." [27]

Hitler would no longer tolerate evasions. Canaris was instructed to demand that Franco name the earliest possible deadline for an attack on Gibraltar and Spain's entry into the war. Still the Spanish leader refused to commit himself. He could fix no deadline since this depended on the future economic development of Spain, which could not be perceived today, as well as on the future development of the war against Britain. "General Franco made it clear," Canaris said, "that Spain could enter the war only when England was about ready to collapse." [28]

Canaris's reports evidently convinced Hitler that there was nothing more he could do about Franco, for on December 11 he ordered that Operation Felix was not to be carried out because the necessary political prerequisites no longer existed. All reconnaissance missions already in progress were to continue until their completion, but all other preparations should cease. The batteries earmarked for reinforcing the defense of the Spanish islands and coasts were not to be delivered. On December 18 Hitler issued the directive to initiate intensive preparations for Operation Barbarossa, the campaign against Russia. [29]

Hitler was filled with anger and resentment about what he regarded as Franco's shortsighted policy and ingratitude. On December 31 he told Mussolini that if German troops had been allowed to enter Spain on January 10, as he had planned, Gibraltar would have been in Axis hands by February and all problems in the Mediterranean area would have been solved. [30] Nevertheless, for a month after receiving Canaris's discouraging reports Hitler did nothing about Spain. On January 9, 1941, however, he informed his military leaders that despite Spain's unpromising attitude he would try again to persuade Franco to enter the war.[31] Mussolini was urged to use his influence with the Caudillo,[32] and the Germans themselves now applied the most brutal combination of pressure and threats. On January 21 Ribbentrop instructed his ambassador in Madrid to tell Franco verbatim that "unless the Caudillo decides immediately to join the war of the Axis powers, the Reich government cannot but foresee the end of Nationalist Spain." The Spaniards countered by accusing the Germans of failing to deliver essential supplies as they had promised, so that they could be considered coresponsible for Spain's failure to enter the war. Ribbentrop seethed with frustration. He demanded to know whether his ambassador had delivered the Reich government's message to Franco word for word, for surely such direct threats could not have failed in their effect. Ambassador Stohrer replied that Ribbentrop's threats had been communicated as ordered, but that Franco had brought forward so many arguments against Spain's entry into the war that these could be regarded as a de facto rejection of the German demands.[33] On February 6 Hitler followed up Ribbentrop's threats with a rather more subtle appeal; Mussolini added his arguments in a meeting with Franco on February 12. But all to no avail.[34] The Spaniards still protested their need for further supplies. In addition, they now insisted that Spanish troops alone should carry out the conquest of Gibraltar, since Spanish honor would not admit the conquest of this Spanish territory by foreigners. "From this position taken by the Spaniards," Ribbentrop telegraphed to Madrid on February 21, "it is quite evident that Franco has not the least intention of entering the war, because the conditions stated actually postpone *ad calendas Graecas* this entry into the war." [35] "The gist of the long Spanish speeches and written explanations," Hitler wrote to Mussolini a week later, "is that Spain does not want to enter the war and will not do so either. This is very regrettable, since this eliminates, for the time being, the simplest possibility of striking at England through her Mediterranean position. But the Spanish decision is also to be regretted because it deprives us of the best opportunity of putting an end to France's seesaw policy." [36]

In refusing to yield to the demands of Hitler, who had heretofore crushed all opposition with ruthless determination, Franco was taking a desperate risk. But as Canaris may have told him, and as he himself must have realized, his decision presented Hitler with the alternative of leaving Spain under the leadership of a benevolent neutral or of conquering a hostile nation. What Franco had in fact succeeded in doing was to convert the weakness of Spain, and his own weakness within Spain, into sources of strength for dealing with the Germans. He confronted Hitler with the image of a Ferdinand VII and a Joseph Bonaparte, and forced the Führer to consider the winning of Gibraltar against the background of another Peninsular War. Hitler cannot have avoided seeing the comparison. Too many other similarities with Napoleon's experiences must have oppressed his imagination already.

Even in the face of these considerations, Hitler might have attempted to compel Franco to join his war. He had gambled before on human nature, and he might have played on Franco's desire to rule, even as a Nazi puppet, against the threat of annihilation by German might. But, as in the case of Britain, this was not Hitler's season for gambling. He also had numerous other reasons for staying his hand in Spain. In the first place, he recognized the correctness of the Caudillo's warning that Spain at war would be a permanent and severe drain on the German economy, and that this drain would occur at just those points where the German economy could least afford a further bloodletting. The end of Spanish neutrality would also mean the need to defend Spanish territory with German troops. Like Italy, Spain would become a military as well as economic burden.

Operation Felix was only postponed temporarily. Toward the end of February 1941, with preparations for the attack on Russia well under way, Hitler ordered that preparations for the capture of Gibraltar continue so that an attack could be carried out directly after the successful conclusion of the Russian campaign.[37]

Plans for an attack on Gibraltar soon gave way to other considerations. Hitler feared that the British might take advantage of Germany's involvement in the east to land an army in Spain or Portugal, and on May 1 he ordered that preparations be made to meet this contingency.[38] The result was Operation Isabella, whose aim was the destruction or expulsion of British forces that landed on the Iberian Peninsula, the German occupation of the most important Spanish and Portuguese harbors on the Atlantic coast, and the creation of favorable conditions for a later attack on Gibraltar.[39]

In the spring of 1942, when it had become obvious that Germany was not about to score a quick victory over Russia, Isabella was reworked into an essentially defensive operation for holding the passes of the Pyrenees and was given the new code name of Ilona, which was later changed to Gisela because an SS officer lost a briefcase containing the plans for Ilona. Gisela, which underwent many modifications including a change in the code name to Nürnberg in June 1943, remained operative until the Allied landings in Normandy in June 1944, which finally removed the Iberian Peninsula from the sphere of German military calculations.[40]

North Africa

The refusal of Franco to enter the war and the consequent cancellation of plans for the capture of Gibraltar forced the Germans to consider a more costly and far less certain method of combatting British influence in the Mediterranean, namely the support of Italian military operations in North Africa. In his directive of November 12, 1940, for the preparation of Operation Felix, Hitler had stated that the commitment of German forces in the Italian offensive against Egypt would come into consideration, if at all, only when the Italians had reached Mersa Matrûh.[41] By January 11, 1941, when the Italians had not only failed to advance but were in full retreat in both North Africa and the Balkans, Hitler ordered that for strategic, political, and psychological reasons Italy should be given German help in the Mediterranean area. The German army was to prepare a unit to aid the Italians in the defense of Libya, an operation subsequently given the code name Sunflower (*Sonnenblume*).[42] After conferences with Mussolini on January 19 and 20, it was agreed that this unit should be sent to Tripoli as soon as possible;[43] but before the Germans could reach Tripoli the Italian retreat in North Africa had turned into a rout. The British captured Tobruk on January 22, Derna on January 24, and Bengasi, the capital of Cyrenaica, on February 7. In a campaign of just over two months, the British forces had captured over 114,000 Italian prisoners at a cost of 3,000 casualties of their own.[44]

By this time Hitler had decided that only large-scale German intervention could save the Italians in North Africa; German defensive support was no longer enough. "The arrival of a German unit makes sense only if *by its strength and by its composition* it is really capable of bringing about a turn of fate," he wrote Mussolini on February 5. An armored unit had to be thrown against the British which could destroy them in a battle of movement, and naval and air operations had to be conducted against the British fleet to prevent it from establishing new supply bases for Britain's advancing motorized ground forces. If these procedures were not adopted, Italian North Africa could not be held. Hitler was prepared to place the necessary German forces at Mussolini's disposal, and in case his proposals were approved, to send General Rommel, "the most daring general of armored forces whom we possess in the German army," as commander of the German troops in North Africa. Hitler could only regret yet again that Franco's irresolution had prevented the attack on Gibraltar, for if the western entrance of the Mediterranean had been closed to the British these operations in North Africa would probably never have been necessary.[45]

Mussolini approved Hitler's proposals. His commander in Libya,

Marshal Graziani, who favored a defensive strategy, was relieved of his duties, and Mussolini agreed to place all Italian as well as German mobile units under the command of General Rommel.[46] The first contingent of German troops arrived in Tripoli on February 11, a second contingent on February 14. On February 18 Hitler ordered that German forces in Africa under Rommel were henceforth to be known as the German Africa Corps, and that Rommel be reinforced with a full armored division and the Fifth Light Infantry division, including its armored regiment.[47]

On March 30 Rommel launched a counterattack against the British in Libya, and by the end of May Axis forces had reached the Egyptian frontier. But Rommel was never given the manpower or equipment to sustain the Axis offensive. Britain's control of the sea lanes in the Mediterranean proved a formidable obstacle to reinforcing and supplying Axis troops in Africa, and the bulk of Germany's military power was soon to be employed in campaigns in the Balkans and Russia. Rommel launched a second offensive against Egypt in May 1942, but early in July he was halted at El Alamein, sixty miles west of Alexandria. Despite his growing supply problem, Rommel remained optimistic about his chances in North Africa. If his army could break through the enemy positions at El Alamein, he still expected to be able to conquer Egypt.[48]

Already German plans for the administration of Egypt were being discussed through diplomatic channels, and the king of Egypt let it be known that he would be happy to remain in his present position under Axis auspices. On July 2 Hitler expressed his belief that the king of Egypt should be urged to withdraw as quickly as possible from British protection and wait for the Axis to invite his return and restore him to his throne. "As regards the future of Egypt," he said, "it is clear that Italy must retain a vital interest therein. Their possessions in Eritrea and Abyssinia alone render it essential that they should receive the Suez Canal; and they can guarantee the security of the Suez Canal only by maintaining garrisons in Egypt." Hitler advised that the Italians should avoid getting involved in minor problems in Egypt. "In the things that matter—irrigation, road construction, and the like—I am quite sure that the Italian colonists, who work like bees, will achieve marvels under the leadership of the Duce." [49]

But the Italians were never given the opportunity to demonstrate their colonizing prowess in Egypt. On October 23, 1942, the British launched a major offensive from El Alamein, and on November 8 an Anglo-American force landed in French North Africa. By May of the following year all Axis resistance in North Africa had come to an end, and the opportunity for capturing either Gibraltar or Suez was irretrievably lost.

178

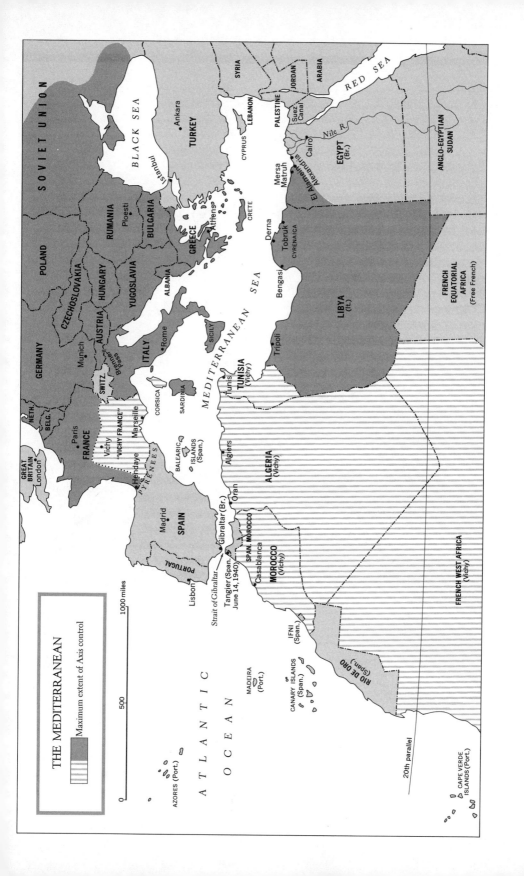

THE MEDITERRANEAN

Maximum extent of Axis control

0   500   1000 miles

ATLANTIC OCEAN

AZORES (Port.)

MADEIRA (Port.)

CANARY ISLANDS (Span.)

CAPE VERDE ISLANDS (Port.)

20th parallel

RIO DE ORO (Span.)

IFNI (Span.)

Casablanca

MOROCCO (Vichy)

SPAN. MOROCCO

Tangier (Span.) June 14, 1940)

Strait of Gibraltar

Gibraltar (Br.)

Lisbon

PORTUGAL

Madrid

SPAIN

Oran

Algiers

ALGERIA (Vichy)

BALEARIC ISLANDS (Span.)

Marseille

Vichy

"VICHY FRANCE"

Hendaye

PYRENEES

Paris

FRANCE

GREAT BRITAIN

London

NETH.

BELG.

GERMANY

Munich

Brenner Pass

SWITZ.

AUSTRIA

CORSICA

SARDINIA

ITALY

Rome

SICILY

Tunis

TUNISIA (Vichy)

Tripoli

MEDITERRANEAN SEA

FRENCH WEST AFRICA (Vichy)

LIBYA (It.)

Bengasi

CYRENAICA

Tobruk

Derna

CRETE

GREECE

Athens

ALBANIA

YUGOSLAVIA

HUNGARY

CZECHOSLOVAKIA

POLAND

RUMANIA

Ploesti

BULGARIA

BLACK SEA

Istanbul

Ankara

TURKEY

SOVIET UNION

CYPRUS

LEBANON

SYRIA

PALESTINE

JORDAN

ARABIA

Alexandria

El Alamein

Mersa Matruh

Cairo

Nile R.

Suez Canal

RED SEA

EGYPT (Br.)

ANGLO-EGYPTIAN SUDAN

FRENCH EQUATORIAL AFRICA (Free French)

CHAPTER 17

Security in the Southeast: Hungary and the Balkans

North Africa was not the only region where Hitler was diverted from his main expansionist course by the failures of the Italians. In the spring of 1941 he once again felt himself obliged to come to the aid of his Italian allies, this time in Southeastern Europe, where he believed vital German interests were now at stake.

Hitler had not wanted to get involved in Southeastern Europe, which he and his more orthodox followers had never regarded as more than a *Flügelstellung zum deutschen Lebensraum,* a sort of right wing of Germanic expansion.[1] The Nazis expected to dominate the area and to exploit it; but within the foreseeable future they did not plan to occupy or annex it. Until a German peasant should require a plot of Hungarian or Balkan soil for living purposes, these countries and their peoples might continue to exist. Their long particularist traditions would prevent their becoming a threat to German security and would facilitate the maintenance of German political and economic supremacy.

Before the Second World War the states of Southeastern Europe faced the choice of uniting in a strong federation to avoid exploitation as pawns of the great powers, or of scrambling individually to make bargains with the powers at the expense of their neighbors and at least cost to themselves. Until war finally engulfed them all, they tried hard not to exclude either possibility. The fear of being despoiled was balanced by the desire to despoil each other, and the menace of a great power was weighed with its value as an ally. The situation was a cruel test for the political leaders involved, and one from which not many emerged with distinction.

In this complicated and vicious political arena, Nazi Germany gradually won a favored position. Britain would have been a safer patron; its geographical location and general policy rendered its friendship less dangerous than that of other powers. But in proportion as Britain lost in threat, it lost in value as an ally. Britain was useless in implementing a revisionist program, and for purposes of defense was in a poor geographical position to render effective aid. France, too, was in a poor geographical position, but until the Munich crisis France continued to be regarded as the most reliable protector of the new states of Eastern Europe.[2] After Munich, and especially after the final dismemberment of Czechoslovakia, these states lost confidence both in France's ability and will to provide them with effective support.

In contrast to Britain and France, Russia was conveniently located for purposes of rendering effective aid; but, if any principle can be said to have inspired Balkan leadership in this era, it was fear of the social as well as political implications of the Soviet Union. This did not mean that Russia was excluded from consideration as an ally. Bulgaria in particular was sympathetic to the land of its fellow Slavs, and the presence of non-Slav Rumania between them suggested many happy possibilities. Italy, too, was conveniently located, but like Russia was generally regarded far more as a threat than a protector.

Germany had the natural advantage an industrial country always possesses in a predominantly agricultural region. Its economy complemented that of the lands of Southeastern Europe, which had long formed an agricultural hinterland for German manufacture. The establishment of close economic ties with Southeastern Europe had been fostered by leaders of both the Habsburg Empire and the Second Reich, not only for the obvious economic advantages involved, but in the expectation that economic influence would bring with it proportionate political influence. This expectation figured prominently in the policies proposed by officials of the Third Reich.

Hitler himself showed little interest in Southeastern Europe as such, but he was fully aware of the region's economic significance, above all as a major source of raw materials that could not be cut off by a naval blockade. Unlike some of his economic experts, however, he had little confidence that economic ties alone would lead to political ascendancy or otherwise ensure Germany's access to the raw materials of this region in time of crisis. As long as Hungary and the Balkan states retained the power to make independent political decisions, there was always the danger that they might line up with other powers to thwart German purposes. In Hitler's view, then, Germany could never be certain of the economic resources of Southeastern Europe without a large measure of political control, exercised either directly or through his Italian allies; at the same time he recognized the grim fact that without these resources a German war economy would not be able to function.[3]

The fundamental consideration was the Rumanian oil supply. As a result of Nazi autarchic measures, the annual German production of a half million tons of natural oil had been increased by two and a half million tons of synthetic oil, giving Germany a total annual production of approximately three million tons. Even in peacetime this oil supply had to be supplemented heavily by imports. In wartime Germany's oil requirements were certain to be appreciably higher— twelve to twenty million tons annually, according to the estimates of Dr. Ferdinand Friedensburg, the most highly regarded German authority on the subject. Even if production of synthetic oil were substantially increased, there could be no question of satisfying wartime needs completely or even in any considerable part from this source for many years, if ever. Dr. Friedensburg concluded that Germany would have to establish a secure outside source of oil; for this purpose he suggested Poland, Rumania, as well as the Caucasus and the Near East, all of which might be dominated by German land power. The Polish and Rumanian sources were the most readily accessible, but Poland's annual production of natural oil was a mere half million tons. As the possibilities of controlling the Caucasus and the Near East were as yet remote, the seven million ton production of Rumania appeared to be crucial.[4]

The critical requirements of a German war economy were not confined to oil. Germany produced only limited supplies of bauxite, whereas Hungary and Yugoslavia produced an estimated 13 and 10 per cent respectively of the world's supply in 1939. Germany produced no chrome or antimony. In this case Turkey produced approximately 20 per cent of the world's chrome, Yugoslavia 10 per cent of the world's antimony. Yugoslavia produced substantially more copper than Germany, and almost as much lead as Germany and Austria combined. In the field of raw textiles, which Germany had always imported in large quantities, cotton was supplied by Bulgaria and Greece, flax by Rumania and Hungary, silk by Bulgaria and Yugoslavia, and significant quantities of wool and hemp by all the countries of this area. Germany was also a large importer of food. Before the war almost half of its livestock and cereals came from Southeastern Europe, and it had absorbed almost half of the region's food exports. If a blockade should sever Germany's access to other markets, the Nazis counted on the availability of the other half of those food exports.[5]

Hitler's lack of confidence that economic influence alone would bring Southeastern Europe into the German security orbit did not mean that the Nazis neglected the use of the pocketbook as an instrument of politics. Nazi leadership left no means untried to attach the states of this region more closely to Germany. During the heyday of peaceful Nazi economic expansion the proportion of German trade with these countries grew significantly, the greatest increment coming after the annexation of Austria and Czechoslovakia.[6] But while the Nazis labored to reduce Southeastern Europe to subservience, the resistance Hitler had expected began to take shape. Hungary and the Balkan states, fearing the fate of Austria and Czechoslovakia and seeking to escape excessive economic dependence on Germany, initiated policies to loosen their ties with Germany and entered into closer political and economic relations with Germany's rivals. By 1939 it was evident that economic pressure alone was proving far from decisive in guaranteeing Germany the resources of Southeastern Europe.[7] This guarantee was not forthcoming until political pressures began to force the issue.

The Nazis did not lack intrinsic political appeal. Their revisionist bait was tempting, their claim to be the only reliable bulwark against the Bolshevik menace was convincing. But Hungarian and Balkan leaders were, on the whole, far too wary to bind themselves to the fortunes of any single state. As long as it was possible to do so, they kept their chips on every color of the international board and nervously awaited the spins of fate.

Hungary

The Treaty of Trianon of 1919 had relegated the Hungarians, who had long dominated a large part of Central and Southeastern Europe, to a position of equality or worse in relation to peoples over whom they had once held sway. On every frontier they could see former possessions, including many with large Hungarian populations. Revisionism—the recovery of some or all of these territories by revising or overthrowing the postwar treaties—was a program that appealed to a large proportion of the Hungarian people, and one on which their leaders could always rely for popular support.[8]

Hitler recognized in Hungary a natural ally in his own attacks on the postwar treaty system, and he conducted his diplomatic negotiations with that country accordingly.[9] Relations with Hungary were not always easy. In 1934 the Hungarian government had been as alarmed as Italy and Yugoslavia about the prospect of a German annexation of Austria, and had joined these countries in opposing an Anschluss. The Hungarians were no more enthusiastic about an Anschluss in 1938; but by this time Hitler had overcome the opposition of Italy and could afford to disregard Hungarian objections. Nor did he do anything to coat the pill for the Hungarians, for he promptly quashed their requests for the Burgenland, Austrian territory that had been part of the kingdom of Hungary before 1918. In his subsequent campaign against Czechoslovakia, however, Hitler successfully played on Hungarian revisionist aspirations to lure Hungary into the Nazi camp.[10]

The Munich agreement of September 30, 1938, met not only Germany's demands on Czechoslovakia, but provided for the settlement of the Polish and Hungarian minority questions as well. If within three months no final settlement had been reached among the states concerned, another meeting between the leaders of the four signatory powers was to take place to deal with the question. The Poles secured their share of the booty almost immediately by submitting a virtual ultimatum to the Czechoslovakian government, but the Czechs proved more obdurate in dealing with the Hungarians. Eventually they were forced to yield to Hungarian demands as well, not by all four signers of the Munich treaty but solely by Germany and Italy. On November 2, 1938, a German-Italian court of arbitration meeting at Vienna awarded Hungary a broad strip of southern Slovakia and Ruthenia.[11] In March 1939, when the Germans broke up what was left of Czechoslovakia, the Hungarians sank still deeper into their debt by acquiring the remainder of Ruthenia (the Carpatho-Ukraine). Admiral Horthy, the head of the Hungarian government, expressed his thanks for this vital headwater region in advance. "On Thursday, the sixteenth of this month," he wrote to Hitler on March 13, "a frontier incident will take place to be followed by the big thrust on Saturday. I shall never forget this proof of friendship, and Your Excellency may rely at all times on my unshakeable gratitude." [12]

During this same period Hungarian foreign policy was brought into line with that of the Reich. On February 24, 1939, Hungary joined the Anti-Comintern Pact,[13] on April 11 it left the League of Nations. In its domestic policies, too, the Hungarian government sought to ingratiate itself with Germany by introducing legislation modeled on the Nazi example, including stringent anti-Semitic measures. After the outbreak of war in September, the Germans endeavored to keep Hungary in order by closely supervising the actions of the Hungarian government, while Hitler impressed on Hungarian leaders their dependence on Germany in acquiring—and holding—their new territories.[14]

Control over Hungary, however, was but one facet of Hitler's principal concern in Southeastern Europe: the maintenance of peace and order to prevent any disruption in the flow of supplies from this region to Germany. In June 1940 this peace and order appeared to be seriously jeopardized when Russia occupied the Rumanian provinces

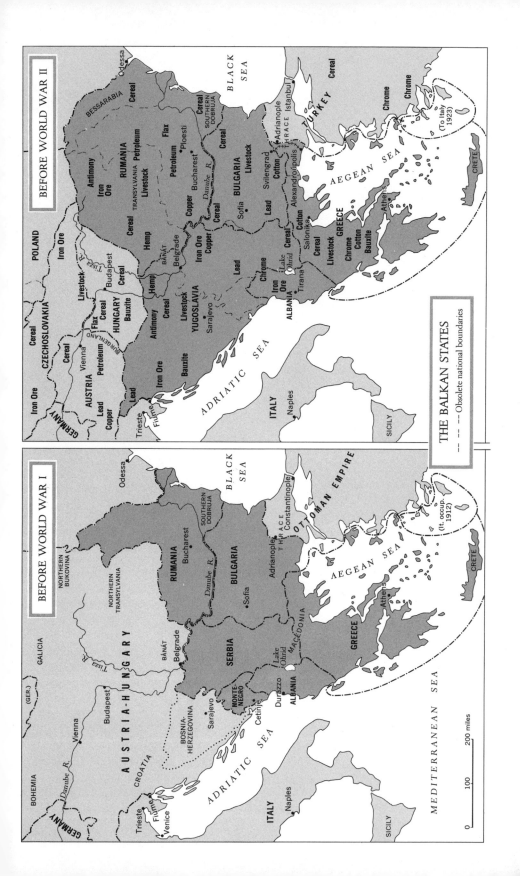

BEFORE WORLD WAR I

GERMANY
BOHEMIA
GALICIA
(GER.)
Vienna
Danube R.
Budapest
AUSTRIA-HUNGARY
Tisza
BÁNAT
Belgrade
CROATIA
BOSNIA-HERZEGOVINA
Sarajevo
MONTE-NEGRO
Cetinje
Durazzo
ALBANIA
Trieste
Fiume
Venice
ITALY
Naples
SICILY
ADRIATIC SEA
MEDITERRANEAN SEA
0   100   200 miles
Odessa
NORTHERN BUKOVINA
NORTHERN TRANSYLVANIA
RUMANIA
Bucharest
SOUTHERN DOBRUJA
Danube R.
SERBIA
Sofia
BULGARIA
Lake Ohrid
MACEDONIA
BLACK SEA
Adrianople
THRACE
Constantinople
OTTOMAN EMPIRE
AEGEAN SEA
GREECE
Athens
CRETE
(It. occup. 1912)

BEFORE WORLD WAR II

GERMANY
Iron Ore
Cereal
CZECHOSLOVAKIA
Cereal
Cereal
Vienna
AUSTRIA
Petroleum
Lead
Copper
Iron Ore
Lead
Trieste
Fiume
Iron Ore
Bauxite
Livestock
Budapest
BURGENLAND
Flax
Cereal
HUNGARY
Bauxite
Hemp
Cereal
Tisza
BÁNAT
Belgrade
Hemp
Antimony
Cereal
Livestock
YUGOSLAVIA
Sarajevo
Iron Ore
Copper
Lead
Chrome
Iron Ore
ALBANIA
Tirana
Lake Ohrid
ITALY
Naples
SICILY
ADRIATIC SEA
POLAND
Iron Ore
Odessa
BESSARABIA
Cereal
Antimony
Iron Ore
RUMANIA
Petroleum
TRANSYLVANIA
Livestock
Flax
Petroleum
Ploesti
Bucharest
Danube R.
Cereal
Copper
Cereal
Cereal
SOUTHERN DOBRUJA
Cereal
Sofia
BULGARIA
Livestock
Lead
Cotton
Svilengrad
Cereal
Alexandropolis
Cotton
Salonika
Cereal
Livestock
GREECE
Chrome
Cotton
Bauxite
Athens
BLACK SEA
Cereal
TURKEY
Adrianople
THRACE
Istanbul
Chrome
Chrome
(To Italy 1923)
AEGEAN SEA
CRETE

THE BALKAN STATES
— — — Obsolete national boundaries

of Bessarabia and Northern Bukovina. The Russian action set off Hungarian and Bulgarian demands for Rumanian territory inhabited by their national minorities, and the governments of these states threatened to use force to make good their claims.[15] Alarmed lest the Hungarian and Bulgarian demands lead to further Russian moves at the expense of Rumania and endanger their Rumanian oil supplies, the Germans held off the Hungarians until the conclusion of their campaign in France. They then imposed a territorial settlement on Rumania similar to the one previously dictated to Czechoslovakia. On August 30, 1940, a second German-Italian court of arbitration meeting at Vienna awarded Hungary the Rumanian territory of Northern Transylvania.[16] One month later the Hungarian government agreed to the passage of German troops through their country to provide a visible guarantee of what was left of Rumania—and to guard the oil fields in Germany's interest.[17]

In October 1940 Mussolini launched his ill-fated attack against Greece. On March 25, 1941, prior to coming to the aid of the Italians in the Balkans, Hitler pressured the Yugoslav government into adhering to the Tripartite Pact. Two days later the Yugoslav government that had signed this pact was overthrown by a coup d'état, and Hitler began making preparations for a military campaign against Yugoslavia.[18]

The Hungarians had been disturbed by Germany's negotiations with Yugoslavia, and when they received news of Yugoslavia's accession to the Tripartite Pact they begged the Germans not to forget their revisionist claims against that state.[19] To this request the Germans made no reply. The coup d'état in Yugoslavia changed the situation. On March 27 Hitler told the Hungarian minister to Germany that in the event of war with Yugoslavia, Hungary would have a unique opportunity to obtain territorial revisions for which it would perhaps otherwise have had to wait for many years; for this purpose "it would be appropriate if Hungary took certain military measures." The next day the German general Friedrich Paulus was sent to Budapest to arrange military co-operation with the Hungarians.[20]

Although the Hungarians had only recently signed a pact of friendship with Yugoslavia, they agreed to join the German attack on that country.[21] Early in April, following the collapse of Yugoslav military resistance, they were rewarded with sizable strips of territory along their southern border. The Hungarians were not at all satisfied with these concessions. They had assumed that they would be given all Yugoslav territory that had been part of the kingdom of Hungary before 1918, and they were indignant that they were not allowed to occupy the Bánát area east of the Tisza River. Hitler assured the Hungarians that this territory would eventually be turned over to them, but he pointed out that the Rumanians also laid claim to it. As he did not want to jeopardize the position of the present government in Rumania, which had succeeded in maintaining order despite the recent cessions of Rumanian territory, he proposed to keep the Bánát under German military occupation for the time being.[22]

Long before arranging for Hungarian co-operation against Yugoslavia, the Germans had been making preparations for their campaign against Russia, which was to be launched in the spring of 1941. The Hungarians were not officially involved in these preparations until the final week before the attack on Russia took place. Hitler had little enough confidence in the Hungarians' loyalty, but none at all in their discretion. On March 22, 1941, he ordered his generals not to count on Hungary as an ally in the Russian campaign beyond its present status. There were to be no preparatory discussions which would give the Hungarians any indication of German plans with regard to Russia. On May 1, in discussing the participation of other states in the Russian campaign, he considered initiating military talks with the Hungarians in the last part of May, but it was not until June 15 that he actually informed the Hungarian government of his decision "to clarify German-Russian relations unequivocally." [23]

Immediately prior to his attack on Russia, Hitler thanked Horthy "for the understanding measures of the Hungarian armed forces, which by the mere fact of having strengthened their frontier defenses will prevent Russian flank attacks and tie down Russian forces." On June 26, after an alleged Russian bombing attack on Hungarian territory, the Hungarian government informed the Germans that it considered itself to be at war with the Soviet Union.[24]

Rumania

In contrast to Hungary, Rumania had been the beneficiary of the post–World War I peace treaties, which had either provided for or confirmed large-scale increases in Rumanian territory. As these increases had inevitably taken place at the expense of neighboring countries, there were few sections of Rumania that were not regarded as irredenta by somebody else. Hungary laid claim to Transylvania, Bulgaria to Southern Dobruja, Russia to Bessarabia, and the Rumanians were well aware that little restraint could be expected on the part of any of these states should opportunities for territorial revision present themselves. The Rumanian government therefore worked hard for the success of the Balkan Entente and for some kind of Balkan federation.[25] When it became clear that Rumania could no longer count on previous treaty or alliance systems and that revisionist countries threatened the very existence of the Rumanian state, the Rumanian government saw no alternative but to commit itself to a powerful ally. Out of this necessity Hitler fashioned another diplomatic victory.[26]

The establishment of predominantly German influence in Rumania began with the final dismemberment of Czechoslovakia and the formation of close political ties between Germany and Hungary. With the most stable bastion of the Little Entente removed and Hungary a partner in Axis aggrandizement, the Rumanians were justifiably fearful that they might soon share the fate of Czechoslovakia and thought it expedient to make their own bargain with Berlin. The breach of the Munich treaty had exposed the worth of Hitler's bond, to be sure; but for purposes of Rumanian security it had demonstrated even more clearly the uselessness of British and French guarantees. Russia, the only other great power to which Rumania might have turned, was known to covet Bessarabia, and to many Rumanian leaders its system of government seemed an even greater threat than its territorial ambitions. Nazi Germany, whatever its other drawbacks, was not directly on Rumania's border, it did not claim any Rumanian territory, and it was belligerently anti-Communist.

On March 23, 1939, almost immediately after the final dissolution of Czechoslovakia, Rumania concluded an economic treaty with the Reich providing for German co-operation in the development of Rumanian agriculture, mining, and industry, its transportation and communication systems, its banks and its petroleum resources. In return Germany was to supply the war material and equipment needed by the Rumanian armed forces and armaments industry. By this agreement the Nazis succeeded in imposing their supervision over the entire Rumanian economy and military establishment.[27]

Even now the Rumanian government refused to burn its bridges. It accepted British and French guarantees of Rumania's territorial integrity and independence on April 13, 1939, and concluded economic agreements with France on March 31 and Britain on May 11. There still remained the possibility that a bloc might be formed in the southern Balkans which, supported by Britain and France and with the participation of Turkey, might discourage further revisionist efforts in that area.

The Nazi-Soviet pact of August 1939 might have been expected to end all Rumanian confidence in Germany. Instead it convinced Rumanian leaders that they had nowhere else to turn. The British and French governments confessed their inability to render effective aid to Rumania, and Russia posed a greater threat than ever. "Only [German] protection could now limit and contain, if not halt, the danger

188

of the Soviet thrust," the Rumanian foreign minister wrote later in describing the Rumanian attitude.[28]

From September 1939 the Rumanian government made increasingly generous concessions to Germany in the economic field, and, especially after Germany's victories in the west in the spring of 1940, it emphasized its desire for closer political collaboration.[29] The moves to establish closer relations with Germany did not save Bessarabia, which together with Northern Bukovina was occupied by the Russians on June 27, nor did they save the territories demanded by Hungary and Bulgaria. More than ever, however, Rumanian leaders were convinced that only the protection of Germany could preserve what was left of their country. On the evening of June 29, 1940, the Rumanian government informed the Germans of its intention to renounce the Anglo-French guarantees and henceforth to conduct a definitely pro-German policy. Three days later King Carol sent a message to Hitler appealing for his protection and requesting that he send a German military mission to Rumania.[30] Hitler held off until Rumania had yielded to the territorial claims of Hungary and Bulgaria, but on August 30, the day Rumania formally accepted the territorial settlement imposed by Germany and Italy at Vienna, Germany and Italy formally guaranteed Rumania's new frontiers.[31] "The Axis powers," the Rumanian foreign minister announced, "have offered absolute safety to the Rumanian state. . . . At the slightest attempt upon the integrity or inviolability of Rumanian territory, the German armies will shoot. By this guarantee we tie ourselves indissolubly to the Axis powers. Henceforth our policy will know no other than that of the Axis, in which we place all our hopes." [32]

Still the Germans were not satisfied. They did not trust King Carol, with his Jewish mistress and pro-Western entourage; nor did they think the king had the authority to carry out the unpopular cessions of territory without provoking revolution or civil war. In the belief that only a strong hand could avert chaos in Rumania, they turned to General Ion Antonescu, who on September 4 had been appointed Rumanian minister president and who appeared to have control over the Rumanian army. At the urging of the Germans, Antonescu on September 5 forced King Carol to sign decrees giving up the authoritarian powers he had exercised since 1938 and transferring these powers to the minister president. Antonescu assured the German minister in Bucharest that he had the army firmly in hand, and that Germany "could depend on him absolutely to restore order and complete the carrying out of the Vienna Award according to plan." He adhered to the king's request to send a German military mission to Rumania, and in every respect desired the closest possible collaboration with Germany.[33] King Carol abdicated on September 6 and was succeeded by

189

his young son Michael; but for the next four years the real leader of the government was to be General Antonescu.

On September 14, 1940, Hitler ordered General von Tippelskirch to go to Bucharest to make preparations for the German military mission to Rumania. "I have the definite impression," Tippelskirch reported to Berlin soon afterward,

> that General A[ntonescu] places great value on the early arrival of German troops in the country. He believes that a Russian attack may occur at any time and does not feel safe from Hungary, either. He told me when I left: Just give me two months of peace for the internal reorganization of the country, then I believe I can vouch for Rumania. He thinks he would have that security only after a practical demonstration of the German guarantee by the presence of German troops in the country.[34]

On September 20, the day after receiving Tippelskirch's report, Hitler ordered that a German division should be sent to Rumania as early as possible. In addition, in response to Antonescu's requests for German personnel and instruction units, the army and Luftwaffe were to send military missions to Rumania. "Their ostensible tasks," Keitel wrote in a top secret order of the same day,

> will be to instruct our friend Rumania in organizing and training her armed forces. . . . Their *real tasks*, which must not become apparent either to the Rumanians or our own troops, are: a) to protect the oil fields from seizure by a third power and from destruction; b) to enable the Rumanian army to carry out definite tasks in accordance with an effective plan worked out with special regard to German interests; c) in case a war with Soviet Russia is forced upon us, to prepare for the commitment of German and Rumanian forces from the direction of Rumania.[35]

Early in October German military units began arriving in Rumania in force. On November 23 Rumania adherred to the Tripartite Pact.[36] German control over Rumania—and the Rumanian oil fields— seemed assured.

Mussolini's attack on Greece in October upset German plans in Rumania as in every other political and military sector, but it did give Hitler an excuse to heavily reinforce German troops in Rumania on the pretext that they were needed to prevent the British from gaining a foothold in the Balkans. In mid-January 1941 Antonescu was informed that in the next weeks more than half a million German soldiers would be arriving in Rumania. There is no question that Hitler did, in fact, fear a British move in the Balkans—above all, air or commando attacks on the Rumanian oil fields—but by this time the major objective of these massive German troop concentrations in Rumania was to extend the field of German military deployment against Russia.[37]

Hitler was impressed by Antonescu's success in maintaining order in Rumania and satisfied with his attitude toward Germany, so much so that in January 1941 he backed him in suppressing a revolt by the Iron Guard, an anti-Semitic and anti-Marxist paramilitary organization, whose leaders had counted on German support in their bid to take over the government. The Guard leaders had some justification for this expectation; for many years they had been encouraged by the Nazis to stir up trouble against anti-German regimes in Rumania. Because of the Guard's ideological orientation it still enjoyed the support of prominent Nazi leaders, Himmler among them; but Hitler now needed order in Rumania, not trouble, and he looked upon Antonescu as the chief of state most likely to provide it. "He really is a personality," Hitler said after meeting Antonescu in mid-January. "He is inspired by glowing fanaticism, is ready to do battle for his country, and will wage it with, without, or if necessary even against the Legion [i.e., the Iron Guard]." [38]

Despite his alleged regard for Antonescu, Hitler did not take him into his confidence about his future military plans. In making preparations for the campaign against Yugoslavia, he did not envisage any role for Rumania other than that of protecting its frontiers against Yugoslavia and Russia, in which its task was to be supported by the German military mission. Not until 11:30 P.M. of April 5 was the German chargé d'affaires in Bucharest instructed to inform Antonescu that the German attack on Greece and Yugoslavia would begin at dawn on the following morning. Hitler's reticence about Yugoslavia may have been due to the fact that both Rumania and Hungary claimed a portion of Yugoslav territory, the Bánát. To avoid a possible clash between his two allies and a blow to the prestige of the Antonescu government, he prevented either from entering the disputed area, which was instead occupied by German troops. The Rumanians were informed that the definitive division of Yugoslav territory would take place only after the final restoration of peace in Europe.[39]

Hitler was more forthright about his intentions in Russia. On May 23 General von Schobert was appointed to succeed General List as commander of the German forces in Rumania with the task of preparing defensive and subsequent offensive arrangements for the attack on Russia. These operations were to be explained to Antonescu as measures to counter the large-scale concentration of Russian troops on the German border. Schobert was to evade all questions as to whether Germany expected war with Russia or would, if need be, attack Russia.[40]

191

Hitler met Antonescu personally on June 11, 1941. Although he did not inform him outright of his intention to attack Russia, he discussed at length Russia's hostile moves against Germany and stated that an explosion might occur at any moment. In that event Hitler did not intend to ask Rumania for assistance; he merely expected that Rumania in its own interest would do everything to facilitate a successful conclusion of the conflict. Afterward "Rumania would receive indemnities which, as far as Germany was concerned, had no territorial limitations." When Hitler raised the question whether, in the event of war with Russia, Rumania should stay out temporarily for its own safety, Antonescu declared that "he himself wanted to join in the struggle from the first day." [41]

With that assurance Hitler made his final plans for German operations against Russia via Rumania. On June 18 he informed Antonescu that he felt compelled to attack the Soviet Union "soon." [42] The attack took place on June 22. True to his promise, Antonescu immediately declared war on Russia, and Rumanian troops crossed the Russian frontier at the same time as the Germans.

Bulgaria

Bulgaria, which had taken the side of the Central Powers during the First World War, had emerged from that conflict with its territory considerably trimmed and its sovereignty limited. Like Hungary, it was a state ready to succumb to revisionist temptations. During the final years of the 1930s, the fearful members of the Balkan Entente had attempted to promote Balkan solidarity by restoring Bulgaria's status to full sovereignty. By the Salonika agreement of July 31, 1938, Bulgaria signed a pact of mutual nonaggression with the members of the Balkan Entente, and the Entente in return renounced the clauses of the Treaty of Neuilly limiting Bulgaria's armaments and the clauses of the Treaty of Lausanne demilitarizing certain zones along the Bulgarian frontier.

A policy of harshness in time of strength and concessions in time of weakness worked no better in the Balkans than elsewhere in Europe. Bulgarian revisionists immediately began to clamor for restoration of their "old frontiers," a program that proved to be a major obstacle to the formation of a neutral Balkan bloc.

At the beginning of the Second World War popular sentiment in Bulgaria fixed its hope on Russia, whose return to the imperialist field augured well for a revival of Panslavic expansionism. Feelings of Slavic brotherhood had created a pro-Russian sympathy in Bulgaria quite apart from political considerations, but Slavic sympathies were by no means decisive—Bulgaria, after all, had fought on Germany's side in the First World War—and they were certainly not powerful enough to persuade the wily King Boris III, virtual dictator of Bulgaria since 1935, to commit himself to a pro-Russian course. Bogdan Filov, an archaeologist and scholar of some renown, became minister president of Bulgaria on February 16, 1940. He announced his foreign policy to be the attainment of Balkan solidarity, and waited for war to bring with it opportunities—and offers.

The Russian occupation of Bessarabia and Northern Bukovina at the end of June 1940 boded well to inaugurate a general reapportionment of Balkan territory. Bulgaria promptly entered its claim to Southern Dobruja, which was still part of Rumania, and turned to Russia for support. King Boris's chief counselor was sent as minister to Moscow, a special Bulgarian mission to Russia was formed, and the Bulgarian government initiated measures to increase Bulgarian trade with Russia.

June passed into July and July into August, but still the Russians had made no definite move to satisfy Bulgarian territorial ambitions. During this same summer the Germans had began to show more promise. They had crushed France in a lightning campaign and driven the British expeditionary force from the continent. Toward the end of July Filov and his foreign minister Ivan Popov paid a visit to Germany, where Hitler informed them he would support Bulgarian claims to Southern Dobruja. By September 7, 1940, the territory was in Bulgarian hands.[43]

Hitler lost no time in presenting his claims for services rendered. At the end of September Bulgaria was invited to accede to the Tripartite Pact, which King Boris refused to do on the grounds that such an action might provoke an attack by Turkey or Greece, or lead to a rapprochement between Turkey and the Soviet Union.[44] This was to be Bulgaria's last rejection of German wishes. Early in November the Germans compelled the Bulgarian government to permit the dispatch of a small group of German specialists to Bulgaria to strengthen Balkan air defenses. On November 18 King Boris was received by Hitler, who informed him of his intention to come to the aid of the Italians in the Balkans and secured his agreement to send German troops through Bulgaria to attack Greece. The Bulgarian army was not to take an active part in military operations, but, supported by German units, was to provide flank protection against Turkey.[45]

The Bulgarians were not slow to present their own bill. In return for their co-operation they demanded the Greek province of Thrace. The Germans agreed to give them this territory with the exception of a narrow strip of land along the Turkish border, which they proposed to keep under their own control to discourage any possible Turkish

193

intention to intervene in the Balkans. On March 1, 1941, on the occasion of Bulgaria's accession to the Tripartite Pact, Germany gave Bulgaria a formal promise of Thrace.[46]

Meanwhile German secret reconnaissance missions had thoroughly investigated Bulgarian transportation facilities and operational conditions, German commando units had taken over key strategic points, and staff talks between German and Bulgarian military leaders had worked out the details of their military co-operation. Conscious of Russian sensitivity with regard to Bulgaria, which the Russian government claimed as part of the Russian security sphere, the Germans delayed as long as possible in sending large numbers of troops to Bulgaria. On February 27, however, they informed the Russians that British action in Greece compelled them to take countermeasures via Bulgaria. On March 1 the first of 680,000 German troops moved into Bulgaria.[47]

Hitler had not asked for active Bulgarian military support against Greece, but he thought such support would be desirable against Yugoslavia. On March 27 he announced his intention to persuade the Bulgarians to intervene actively against Yugoslavia by promising them the Yugoslav part of Macedonia. The Bulgarians accepted the bait. When giving his final orders for the attack on Greece and Yugoslavia on April 3, Hitler counted on the Bulgarians not only to hold his flank against Turkey but to engage actively in the attack on Yugoslavia.[48]

As it turned out, the Germans did not need Bulgarian aid against Yugoslavia, and their delay in permitting Bulgarian troops to enter Macedonia aroused considerable uneasiness in Sofia. On April 17, however, with the capitulation of the entire Yugoslav army, the Germans paid off the Bulgarians by allowing them to occupy Greek Thrace and Yugoslav Macedonia to the Svilengrad-Alexandroúpolis line in the east, and (by May 15) to Lake Ohrid on the west.[49]

As Bulgaria was not on the Russian frontier, it played little part in German plans for the attack on Russia. In making their diplomatic preparations prior to that attack, the Germans sent a request to Bulgaria not to reduce to any large extent the units stationed for security reasons along the Turkish frontier, but no effort was made to bring that country into the war against Russia. Hitler was aware of the strong popular sympathy for Russia among the Bulgarians, but calculated that by having them partners in the spoliation of Greece and Yugoslavia he had bound them to the German cause. He was content with Bulgarian neutrality and government promises to send him the raw materials he needed from Bulgaria and its occupied territory. In December 1941 Bulgaria declared war on Britain and the United

States, but it never severed diplomatic relations with the Soviet Union.[50]

The Italian Attack on Greece

Hitler's steady success in building up a diplomatic empire in Southeastern Europe was halted by Mussolini, who was as disturbed as any of the declared opponents of Germanic expansion by the increase of Nazi influence in that area. Each diplomatic triumph increased the prestige of the junior member of the Axis and correspondingly diminished the stature of the Duce. From the position of equal partner, Mussolini was rapidly being reduced to an unwilling spectator in the resounding successes of Adolf Hitler.

Confidence between the Axis leaders was most seriously shaken when Germany occupied Czechoslovakia in March 1939 without consulting or even informing the Italians. Mussolini quite rightly feared the added leverage the possession of this territory would give Hitler in the affairs of Southeastern Europe. The Italians had their own ambitions in the Balkans, and had long hoped to make this region part of the Italian sphere of influence.

To compensate for the German gains in Czechoslovakia and to recoup his own prestige, Mussolini seized Albania on April 7, 1939. Hitler, probably with real sincerity, expressed his approval of the Italian move. He foresaw Albania being made into a stronghold from which Italy would inexorably dominate the Balkans. As the Balkans were not in themselves desirable to Hitler, he may have been quite willing to accord Mussolini the task of securing his southeastern flank. In this connection he spoke to Ciano shortly before the outbreak of the war. He proposed that the Axis powers eliminate uncertain neutrals one after the other, and that they cover each other in the process. He himself was implacable in his determination to crush Poland, Hitler said. Then, either to show the Italians his good faith about sharing the spoils or in the belief that Italy would be able to control the Balkans, he suggested that "Italy might well regard Yugoslavia as a neutral of this kind." [51]

Mussolini was a cautious gambler, and he declined to balance the German successes in Poland with an Italian move against Yugoslavia. There was still a French army to be defeated before Mussolini would confidently strike out in his own cause. As Ciano expressed it, "If the democracies attack, we should be able to free ourselves 'honorably' from the Germans; if the democracies simply swallow it, without fighting back, we should take advantage of it to settle accounts once and for all with Belgrade." [52]

195

With France on the verge of military collapse, Italy entered the war on the side of Germany on June 10, 1940; but Mussolini was not satisfied with his share of the glory and the spoils, and he remained deeply suspicious of German activities in the Balkans. To ensure Italian influence in that area, he issued an ultimatum to Greece on October 28, 1940, demanding strategic bases on Greek soil. Greece, backed by a British guarantee which had been given when Italy occupied Albania in April 1939, rejected the Italian demands, and war in the Balkans began.[53]

The Italian action had been set off by the movement of German troops into Rumania early in October 1940.[54] Mussolini, who as usual had not been informed, raged in impotent fury against this further increase of German influence. "Hitler always presents me with a *fait accompli*. This time I am going to pay him back in his own coin. He will find out from the papers that I have occupied Greece. In this way the equilibrium will be re-established." On October 14, 1940, Mussolini fixed October 26 as the date for the attack on Greece. On October 28 Greece rejected the Italian ultimatum, and Mussolini was forced to expose his hopelessly inadequate military hand.[55]

Hitler was caught by surprise by the Italian move. Only two months before Mussolini had earnestly begged him to leave the Balkans out of the conflict because Italy intended to direct its military effort against Egypt and had no desire to defend its back against British attacks based on Greece.[56] Hitler must have been gratified by this attitude. Germany was involved in delicate negotiations with the Balkan states which Hitler undoubtedly hoped would end in a bloodless Axis victory over the entire peninsula. He was also busy with plans for Spain, an invasion of Britain, and the campaign against Russia.

The Germans were not sure that a military campaign in the Balkans might not eventually be necessary, but the Italian move at the time at which it came was defined by Hitler as a "regrettable blunder." The Italian attack was launched at an unfavorable season, without adequate manpower or equipment, and the Germans recognized at once that it would in all probability bog down. The German air force was brought into position to counter possible Greek—and British—air attacks against the Rumanian oil fields, and ten German divisions were placed in readiness for any eventuality, including a threatening attitude on the part of Turkey. Hitler rejected concomitant plans for offensive action against Turkey for the purpose of breaking through to the Suez Canal from the east. "This would be a very lengthy operation and would involve great difficulties," he said.[57] The German preparations were made solely to defend the po-

Mussolini and Hitler. Behind Hitler are Count Ciano, and, in the white
uniform jacket, Hermann Göring.

Chancellor Engelbert Dollfuss of Austria.

The successor of Dollfuss as chancellor of Austria, Kurt von Schuschnigg. At his right, his erstwhile protector Benito Mussolini, on the occasion of a meeting of the heads of the Austrian, Hungarian, and Italian governments, March 31, 1936.

Hermann Göring (back to camera) being received by Arthur Seyss-Inquart (with glasses) at the Reichsbrücke in Vienna, March 27, 1938, soon after the Anschluss. To the right of Seyss-Inquart, with his arm raised in salute, Reinhard Heydrich; behind Seyss-Inquart, also wearing glasses, Theodor Habicht, leader of the Austrian Nazis.

Konrad Henlein, leader of the Sudeten German party.

The principal figures at the Munich conference, September 1938: Neville Chamberlain, Édouard Daladier, Hitler, Mussolini, Count Ciano.

The public jubilation of the Austrian population at the time of Hitler's entry into Vienna after the Anschluss.

The reaction of the population of Prague as German troops occupy the city in March 1939.

The signature of the Hitler-Stalin pact, August 23, 1939. At the table, Vyacheslav Molotov. Behind him, from left to right, General Boris Shaposhnikov, chief of the Soviet General Staff, Joachim von Ribbentrop, Stalin, and Secretary of Embassy Perlow.

Emil Hácha, the successor of Beneš as president of Czechoslovakia who stayed on as nominal head of the Czech government after the German occupation.

Vidkun Quisling.

←—《 Hitler before the Reichstag, September 1, 1939, announcing the opening of hostilities against Poland. Behind Hitler is Hermann Göring, the president of the Reichstag; seated in the front row, at the left of the picture, are Paul Joseph Goebbels, Fritz Todt, Joachim von Ribbentrop, and Rudolf Hess.

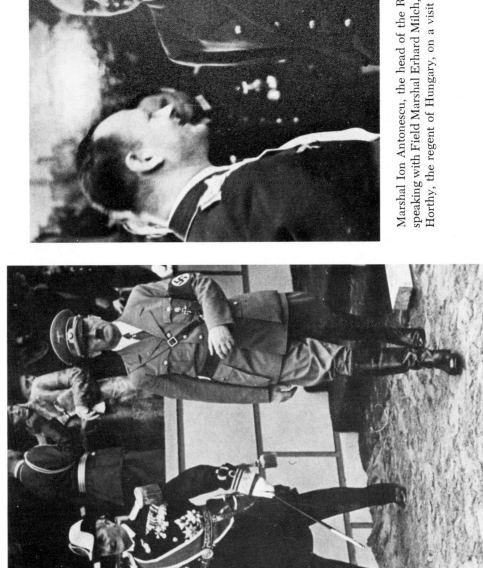

Marshal Ion Antonescu, the head of the Rumanian government (on the right), speaking with Field Marshal Erhard Milch, February 1942. *Left*: Admiral Miklós Horthy, the regent of Hungary, on a visit to Hitler in Berlin, August 25, 1938.

Hitler's meeting with Franco at Hendaye, October 1940.

General Erwin Rommel.

sition in the southeast, whose extreme vulnerability Hitler described in detail in a letter to Mussolini of November 20.

Hitler had wished to persuade his ally to await a more favorable season; in any case, until after the elections in the United States. "The Greek situation bears heavily on the diplomatic preparations which were in full swing," Hitler wrote. "In a general way we feel the consequences in the form of an accentuated tendency of certain nations to avoid making definite commitments to us, and to await the march of events." Bulgaria, Hitler said, had already demonstrated slight inclination to join the Tripartite Pact, and was now completely opposed to such a decision. It was impossible to tell at the moment what impression the Italian attack had produced in Yugoslavia, but the Axis could not afford a hostile attitude there. Most serious of all was the effect of Italy's action on the military and economic situation. Greece might now become a British air base, a direct threat to southern Italy and only five hundred kilometers from the Rumanian oil fields. "One thing is certain, Duce, there is no effective protection for the oil fields." Antiaircraft guns constituted a danger as great as assailing aircraft. "Should the oil refineries be destroyed, the damage would be irreparable." Already the British had occupied Crete. Hitler predicted that they would take other islands for use as air bases. "From the military point of view, this situation is dangerous. From the economic standpoint, as far as the Rumanian oil fields are concerned, it is positively terrifying." [58]

On November 12 Hitler ordered his staff to make preparations to occupy the Greek mainland north of the Aegean in case of need, a plan that was built around the protection of the Rumanian oil fields. By December Hitler recognized that the Italian military situation in Greece was sufficiently serious to demand German intervention. His military strategy was to form a slowly increasing task force in Rumania. After favorable weather had set in, probably in March, this force was to occupy the Aegean north coast by way of Bulgaria, and if necessary the entire Greek mainland. The support of Bulgaria against Greece was expected, but was not yet certain. Hitler expected Turkey to remain neutral. The position of Yugoslavia remained to be determined.[59]

The German Attack on Yugoslavia

After his success in persuading the Rumanian and Bulgarian governments to permit the passage of German troops through their countries, Hitler could have moved against Greece without involving Yugoslavia. Three to four hundred kilometers of strategic railroad line through Bulgaria to the Greek frontier ran within twenty kilometers of the Yugoslav border, but it was hardly to be expected that Yugoslavia alone would suddenly pounce on the communications of the Wehrmacht. The need to secure Yugoslavia was part of Hitler's policy of making absolutely certain of his Balkan flank before pushing into Russia. Bombers based on Yugoslav airfields were as dangerous to Rumanian oil refineries as bombers based in Greece. To eliminate or at least minimize this danger, Hitler did everything in his power to entice Yugoslavia into the Axis alliance system.

Yugoslavia, like Czechoslovakia and Rumania, had benefited from the redistribution of territory that followed the First World War. As the kingdom of the Serbs, Croats, and Slovenes, it included not only these Slavic peoples but Germans, Hungarians, Turks, as well as other Slavic nationalities; much of its territory was made up of lands recently ruled by Austria-Hungary, Bulgaria, and Turkey. Although even now some Yugoslav leaders were not satisfied with the extent of their territories, they were by and large defenders of the post–World War I treaties and supporters of the various alliances designed to defend those treaties. The great weakness of Yugoslavia was the lack of any real sense of solidarity among its various peoples, whose traditional national hostilities were exacerbated by cultural and religious differences. The Croats, for example, were by and large Roman Catholic and used the Roman alphabet; the Serbs were Greek Orthodox and used the Cyrillic alphabet; within both groups there was a strong admixture of Moslems. States hostile to Yugoslavia did what they could to make the situation worse. The Italians, in particular, periodically fostered the growth of a Croat independence movement hoping that the breakup of Yugoslavia would allow them to extend their own influence in the Balkans.[60]

The principal object of the Germans in Yugoslavia, as in the other states of Southeastern Europe, was to ensure their access to the economic assets of the country and prevent its use as a base of operations by hostile powers. German economic policy in Yugoslavia was a distinct success. In January 1938 the economic policy department of the German Foreign Office reported that since the conclusion of the German-Yugoslav economic agreements of 1934 the volume of trade between the two countries had trebled, and that Germany now held first place in Yugoslav exports and imports.[61] German political influence in Yugoslavia also appeared to be growing. Under King Alexander, who had imposed an authoritarian regime on Yugoslavia in 1929, the Yugoslav government had joined Italy in taking a firm stand during the Austrian crisis of July 1934 to prevent any move on the part of Hitler to annex Austria to the Reich. But Alexander was assassinated in October 1934 by members of Macedonian and Croatian terrorist organizations who demanded freedom for their peoples from Serbian rule; and, in June 1935, Milan Stojadinović, who had done much to bring about closer economic relations with Germany as Yugoslavia's finance minister, was appointed minister president and foreign minister. Stojadinović now proceeded to seek closer political ties with Germany as well. A few months after his appointment the Yugoslav minister to Berlin informed the Germans that the leaders of his government were "quite determined to continue in the policy, already pursued by them, of political and economic rapprochement with Germany. . . . Furthermore they were determined to loosen existing ties." [62] In succeeding years Stojadinović resisted French and Czechoslovak efforts to develop the Little Entente into a general mutual assistance program, and attempted to safeguard Yugoslavia's security through treaties with Bulgaria and Italy. At the time of the Austrian crisis in 1938, Stojadinović assured Germany that he regarded the Austrian question as a purely internal affair.[63]

The policies of Stojadinović were most welcome to the Germans, who encouraged him to stabilize the situation in Southeastern Europe still further by concluding a nonaggression pact with Hungary. [64] But within his own country Stojadinović's policies were not so warmly received, and his refusal to yield to the demands for greater autonomy on the part of the Croats and other national groups aroused widespread opposition. Anxious to avoid a crisis and fearful of Stojadinović's personal ambitions, Prince Regent Paul appointed a new government in February 1939 with Dragiša Cvetković as minister president and the former Yugoslav minister to Berlin, Aleksander Cincar-Marković, as foreign minister. Both men protested their personal sympathy for Germany, but well-informed Germans were convinced that German interests in Yugoslavia had suffered a serious blow. The German minister to Belgrade reported that the dismissal of Stojadinović meant the removal of the only personality capable of carrying on a strong authoritarian regime, and the beginning of a policy of conciliation in dealing with national minorities. As the Croatians would henceforth undoubtedly play a greater role in the formulation of Yugoslav policy, the German minister recommended that his government gradually relax its restraint in dealing with Croatian nationalist leaders and exploit every opportunity for winning their friendship.[65]

The fall of Stojadinović resulted in a resurgence of Italian activity on behalf of the Croatian nationalist movement, which also received support from a number of Nazi offices.[66] Hitler himself, however, persisted in his efforts to work through the Yugoslav central government. The breakup of Yugoslavia could only lead to disorder in the Balkans which he had no interest in promoting. In talks with the new Yugoslav foreign minister and with the prince regent in April and June 1939, Hitler sought to persuade them to dissociate themselves from the Western powers and join forces with the Axis, a policy that would at a stroke consolidate Yugoslavia's domestic and international position. The Nazi party office dealing with ethnic Germans abroad was given strict orders to keep the Germans in Yugoslavia quiet, and in July 1939 a secret economic treaty was signed granting the Yugoslav government credit to purchase war materials in Germany.[67]

The Yugoslav leaders did not commit themselves. They had seen the worth of Hitler's word in Czechoslovakia, they feared Axis revisionist policies, and because of their geographical position they felt more immediately threatened by Germany and Italy than by Russia, which had frightened other states of Eastern Europe into the Axis camp. Accordingly, while attempting to maintain cordial relations with the Axis, they evaded closer political ties. Instead of relying on Axis support to consolidate their domestic situation, the Serbs concluded a treaty with the Croats granting them a large measure of autonomy and bringing their most influential political leader, Vladko Maček, into the government as deputy minister president. In foreign affairs the Yugoslav government resumed diplomatic relations with the Soviet Union on the eve of the Russian occupation of Bessarabia, and even after the great German victories in the west in the spring of 1940 it maintained its attitude of reserve toward the Axis.[68]

Hitler continued to pursue a policy of cautious restraint in dealing with Yugoslavia, and he put pressure on Mussolini to do the same. It was not until Italian defeats in Greece began to threaten the entire Axis position in the Balkans that he felt compelled to force the pace of Axis policy in Yugoslavia. Once again he attempted to attain his goals by negotiation with the central government rather than with revolutionary nationality groups. In conversations with the Yugoslav foreign minister in November 1940, he offered to guarantee Yugoslavia's domestic and international position in return for its accession to the Tripartite Pact. Recognizing that fear of Italy was a major obstacle to accession, he made it clear that such a guarantee would also protect Yugoslavia from the Italians, for it would put an end to Italian demands for Yugoslav territory and undercut their efforts to support Yugoslavia's national minorities. Finally, in return for Yugoslavia's co-operation in the consolidation of Europe, Hitler offered Yugoslavia the Greek harbor of Salonika and therewith an outlet to the Aegean. If Yugoslavia rejected these offers, Hitler indicated that he could not vouch for the policy of Italy.[69]

The Yugoslavs remained evasive, but Hitler kept the pressure on. In February 1941 the Yugoslav minister president and foreign minister were invited to Germany; in March it was the turn of Prince Regent Paul. In talks with all three leaders Hitler renewed the offers made in the previous November. The Yugoslavs drove a hard bargain. They demanded a written guarantee of Yugoslavia's sovereignty and territorial integrity, a written statement that neither Italy or Germany would demand the passage or transportation of troops through Yugoslav territory or any other kind of military assistance, and a written statement that "in the new settlement of the frontiers in the Balkans the interests of Yugoslavia in a territorial connection with the Aegean Sea, through the extension of its sovereignity to the city and harbor of Salonika, are to be taken into account." Hitler and Mussolini accepted these conditions, and on March 25, 1941, the Yugoslav minister president and foreign minister signed the documents of Yugoslavia's accession to the Tripartite Pact.[70] With that, Germany's flank for the forthcoming attack on Greece via Bulgaria, which was scheduled to be launched on April 1st, seemed secured. Hitler appeared to have scored another major diplomatic victory.

In this instance, however, Hitler had miscalculated. In his haste to conclude a treaty with the Yugoslav government, he had neglected to take into account the fact that the leaders with whom he had negotiated did not control the Yugoslav army. When Yugoslavia's accession to the Tripartite Pact was announced, patriotic army leaders were convinced they had been sold out and they gave full credence to rumors that the army was to be demobilized and disarmed. Fearful that their country was about to share the fate of Czechoslovakia and Rumania, Yugoslav officers on the night of March 26–27 carried out a coup d'état overthrowing the existing regime. Prince Regent Paul was ousted; King Peter, although not yet of legal age to ascend the throne, was installed as nominal chief of state; and a new government was formed under General Dušan Simović, the principal organizer of the coup.[71]

The Simović administration announced its intention of remaining on friendly terms with Germany, but the new government immediately opened negotiations with Britain and Russia, and on April 6 a Yugoslav pact with Russia was signed in the presence of Stalin.[72] Simović obviously had no intention of trusting his country's fortunes exclusively to the Germans.

Upon receiving Simović's assurances of his desire for good relations with Germany, including his willingness to adhere to the Tripartite Pact, Ribbentrop was in favor of attempting to negotiate with the new Yugoslav government. "Is that how you size up the situation?" Hitler asked him. "The Yugoslavs would swear black is white. Of course they say they have no hostile intentions, and when we march into Greece they will stab us in the back." [73] Hitler's time was running short. Greece had to be disposed of early in April to allow time for deployment for the Russian campaign. Neither Hitler nor his staff believed the attack on Greece could be militarily justified so long as the Yugoslav attitude remained ambiguous and its army could threaten Germany's lengthy line of communications. They were convinced, moreover, that the Simović government had received promises of British and Russian support. Before these promises could be put into effect, Yugoslavia would have to be crushed.

On March 27, 1941, Hitler explained to his generals the overall situation and the rationale of the Yugoslav campaign. Yugoslavia was an uncertain factor in the action against Greece and even more so with regard to the Russian campaign later on. Serbs and Slovenes were never pro-German. Their governments never sat securely in the saddle because of the nationality problem and because an officers' clique was always ready for a coup d'état. Had such a coup occurred after the main German armies were engaged in Russia, the consequences to the German military situation would have been considerably more serious. Hitler was therefore determined, without waiting for possible loyalty declarations from the new government, to destroy Yugoslavia militarily and as a state. The blow was to be delivered with unmerciful harshness and lightning speed. The political effect would deter Turkey from intervening and influence favorably the campaign against Greece.

> We will try to get the neighboring states to participate in a suitable way. Actual military support against Yugoslavia is to be asked of Italy, Hungary, and in certain respects of Bulgaria too. Rumania's principal task is to provide cover against Russia. . . . It is to be expected that the Croats will take our side when we attack. They will be assured of political treatment (autonomy later on) in accordance with this. The war against Yugoslavia presumably will be very popular in Italy, Hungary, and Bulgaria, as these states are to be promised territorial acquisitions; the Adriatic coast for Italy, the Bánát for Hungary, and Macedonia for Bulgaria.

Southern Yugoslavia was to be used as a base for further operations against Greece. The army was to make every effort to reopen the Danube to navigation as soon as possible and to secure the copper mines at Bor, which were "all-important economically." [74]

At dawn on April 6, 1941, German troops invaded Yugoslavia. Organized resistance lasted only eleven days. The Yugoslav armies surrendered unconditionally on April 17. By April 23 Greece, too, was crushed. Southeastern Europe lay at Hitler's feet.

Hitler announced to the German people that the military action in the Balkans was a defensive measure taken to counter a British thrust in that area.[75] The defensive motive, quite apart from the continued necessity to maintain appearances vis-à-vis Russia, was undoubtedly a strong one. But Nazi purposes were not concentrated on defense. Southeastern Europe was now open to complete economic exploitation and was available as a base for military operations against Russia. It was organized as such by the Nazis.

CHAPTER 18

The Final Drive for Lebensraum:
The Attack on Russia

The German attack on Russia in 1941 has been called the greatest blunder of the Second World War. That Nazi ideology as expounded in *Mein Kampf* demanded the conquest of Russia and the destruction of Bolshevism was one thing, but ideology had never fixed a time limit for these accomplishments. Why, then, did Hitler defy another political principle laid down in *Mein Kampf* and gratuitously plunge his country into a war on two fronts while Britain, backed by the United States, remained a threat in the west?

The explanations from the Nazi point of view are numerous, but they all hinge on the belief that Russia would never tolerate a definitive German victory in the west. With this point established, a question formed itself automatically for the Nazi leaders: Were the Russians in a position to prevent or seriously hinder that German victory? The march of events since September 1939 convinced Hitler that they were.

The Rationale and Timing of the German Attack

Hitler never had any confidence in Russia's good faith. "No treaty or pact can guarantee the lasting neutrality of Soviet Russia," he told his generals after the successful conclusion of the Polish campaign. "For the moment everything argues against the abandonment of this neutrality. In eight months, a year, or certainly in several years things may be different. The trifling value of treaties has been demonstrated on every hand in recent years." [1]

Hitler reverted to the same theme a few weeks later. "Treaties are kept only so long as they are useful. Russia will keep this one only so long as Russia itself considers it to its benefit. . . . Russia still has far-reaching goals, above all the strengthening of its position in the Baltic. We can only oppose Russia when we are free in the west." [2]

The great difficulty for Germany, of course, was that it was not free in the west; but a relative freedom was achieved in the summer of 1940, after the fall of France, which allowed Hitler to consider the possibility of removing the danger in the east before finally settling with Britain.

By the summer of 1940 the danger from the east had begun to seem very great indeed. Hitler's primary reason for concluding a nonaggression pact with the Soviet Union had been to avoid a major war on two fronts; but as the price for Russia's neutrality he had been forced to surrender a large part of Eastern Europe to the Russian sphere of influence.[3] While the Germans were overrunning their share of Poland and Western Europe, the Russians proceeded to take over the areas allotted to them.

In the autumn of 1939, after occupying their half of Poland, they compelled the Baltic republics of Estonia, Latvia, and Lithuania to accept "mutual aid" treaties which permitted the establishment of Red Army garrisons in these countries.[4] By August 1940 all three states had been incorporated into the Soviet Union as Soviet Socialist Republics. This step had been necessary, Molotov told the Germans, in order to put a stop to British and French intrigues in the Baltic area.[5]

Early in November 1939 Finland turned down a similar Russian offer of a mutual assistance pact as well as a demand for Finnish territory that accompanied it.[6] The Russians thereupon attacked Finland on November 30, and after 105 days of fighting forced the Finns to sign a treaty in Moscow on March 12, 1940, ceding about 10 per cent of their territory, including a strip in the northeast, the Karelian Isthmus, and the entire Finnish shore of Lake Ladoga. In addition, the Russians secured a thirty year lease to Finland's naval base on the Hanko peninsula and transit privileges across Petsamo, where Europe's most important nickel mines were located. With the successful conclusion of the Finnish campaign, the Russians were in control of the entire eastern littoral of the Baltic sea.[7]

While extending their sphere of influence in the north, the Russians attempted to do the same thing in the south by bringing heavy diplomatic pressure to bear on Rumania, Bulgaria, and Turkey.[8] On June 23, 1940, Molotov informed the Germans that a solution of the Bessarabian problem could no longer be delayed. He successfully commandeered German aid in putting pressure on Rumania, and on June 27 Soviet troops occupied Bessarabia. At the same time the Russians occupied the Rumanian territory of Northern Bukovina, which Hitler had not specifically conceded.[9] These territories gave the Russians control of the principal overland route into the Balkans and of the mouth of the Danube—and brought them within one hundred miles of the Rumanian oil fields of Ploesti.

During the spring and summer of 1940 the Germans received a steady flow of reports about Russian troop concentrations in these newly occupied provinces and along Germany's own new eastern frontiers.[10] Fearful that these troop movements portended further Russian advances, Hitler sent troops into Rumania in September to secure the oil fields and to back up a German guarantee of what was left of Rumanian territory.[11] The German move prompted the Russians to seek a similar status for themselves in Bulgaria and to sound out the Germans about the possible annexation of all of Finland.[12] Hitler successfully blocked both Russian efforts, but by this time he was thoroughly alarmed.

Even more ominous for Germany than the strategic threat represented by Russia's territorial annexations was the Russian economic threat. Germany had entered the war with a perilously narrow economic margin. Conquests in Eastern and Western Europe had improved its economic position, but the lack of critical raw materials remained Germany's greatest weakness.[13] The significance of the Russians in this connection lay in the fact that they either supplied the Germans with the bulk of the raw materials they needed from abroad, or covered their routes of access to them. The Russian territorial advances since September 1939 had made that coverage almost airtight. From Finland to the Balkan passes there was not an economic cord in the east which the Red Army could not have severed or seriously endangered.

Since their victory over Finland in March 1940 the Russians had control over the routes to the Petsamo nickel mines, whose output was essential to Germany's war industries. "The Russians promise to supply us with the quantities of nickel required," Hitler told his generals in January 1941, "but only so long as they please." Russia was now threatening to take over Finland altogether, a move which if successful could place it in a strategic position to cut off Germany's supplies of Swedish iron ore.[14]

The Russian occupation of the Baltic countries, small as they were, had been another blow to the German economy. Since 1939 Germany had made secret agreements with all three states to take over 70 per cent of their total exports.[15] Although in no way decisive to the German economy, these exports had amounted yearly to some two hundred million Reichsmarks, almost as much in monetary value as Germany was scheduled to receive from Russia over the next two years as a result of economic treaties concluded in 1939. To Germany, whose grain reserve had been almost entirely depleted in 1940, the Baltic supplies of grain, hogs, butter, eggs, flax, and seeds were very valuable indeed. More important still was the oil in Estonia. The oil shale deposits in that country were uneconomical to exploit and only a hundred forty thousand metric tons had been produced in 1938, but the deposits themselves were estimated at from three and a half to five billion tons. The Russian annexation ended German hopes of tapping these oil resources and meant that all other exports from this area would form part of the promised Soviet deliveries.[16]

Most serious of all was the Russian threat to German imports from the Balkans. For many years Balkan grain had formed a large part of Germany's cereal imports, and now that war had severed its access to grain from the Western Hemisphere the supplies from the Balkans were more necessary than ever. Absolutely decisive, however, were the Rumanian oil fields, which were now within easy striking distance of the Red air force. As already noted, oil was the most critical item in Germany's war economy, and well over half of its supplies came from Rumania.[17] The destruction of the Rumanian oil fields would have dealt a disastrous blow to the German war effort. "Now, in the era of air power," Hitler told his generals in January 1941, "Russia can turn the Rumanian oil fields into an expanse of smoking debris . . . and the life of the Axis depends on those oil fields." [18]

Finally there was the importance of Russia itself to the German economy, both with respect to its own exports and its transshipment of goods from East Asia. Imports from Russia based on the trade agreements concluded since August 1939 had gone far to compensate Germany for the loss of supplies from the Western Hemisphere.[19] Russia's grain shipments were half again as large as previous German imports from Argentina and approximately equal to the annual consumption of the Wehrmacht. The nine hundred thousand tons of oil Russia promised to deliver almost equaled previous imports from the United States and amounted to about 25 per cent of Germany's military requirements. In addition, the Russians agreed to supply Germany annually with five hundred thousand tons each of phosphates and iron ore, three hundred thousand tons of scrap and pig iron, a hundred thousand tons of chrome ore, as well as platinum, manganese ores, and eighty million cubic meters of timber.[20] Across Russia lay Germany's only connection with East Asia. From this area Russia contracted to transport one million tons of soy beans to Germany, as well as crucial supplies of rubber and tin.[21]

The importance of Russia to Germany's war economy makes the attack on that country seem very much like killing the goose that lays the golden eggs, and so in a way it was. From Hitler's point of view, however, there were two serious flaws in these trade agreements: The

Russians could cut off deliveries to Germany at any time that suited their political or military convenience; and they demanded prompt payment for them of a kind most embarrassing to a nation at war, namely in war materials.[22]

German difficulties in filling Russian orders began almost immediately, and they increased steadily during the build-up of their campaign against France. The Russians for their part kept up their pressure for payments, so much so that on March 30, 1940, Hitler was obliged to order that Russia receive priority in armament deliveries over German troops to ensure the continued flow of raw materials from the Soviet Union.[23]

Russian pressure relaxed briefly after the German victories in Scandinavia and France, but Hitler did not forget the lesson of this experience.[24] It was after the victory over France in July 1940 that he ordered initial preparations for a military campaign against Russia; at approximately the same time he ordered a revision of the German armaments schedule to give German requirements absolute priority.[25] As German deliveries to the Soviet Union began to lag, the Russians warned that if a balancing of accounts were not achieved soon a suspension of Russian deliveries to Germany was to be expected. This warning, delivered in September 1940, forced the Germans to agree to step up their payments,[26] but by now Germany's top leadership realized that all arms sent to Russia would very probably be used against themselves. Everything was done, therefore, to avoid or delay shipments of arms, including the sale in January 1941 of a strip of Lithuania which had been ceded to Germany by the secret treaty of September 28, 1939. In exchange for this territory Germany received thirty-one and a half million Reichsmarks credit in the Soviet Union.[27]

In Hitler's view the Russians' threat to Germany's vital supply lines and their demand for armaments in exchange for raw materials essential to the German war economy made for an impossible situation. His solution to the problem was characteristically direct. "What one does not have, but needs, one must conquer," he said two days before the attack on Russia.[28] The conquest of Russia would in one blow eliminate the threat to Germany's economic lifelines and ensure German access to Russia's natural resources without the need to pay for them. Hitler realized that military action might result in a large-scale destruction of Russian economic assets, but he was confident that the speed of Germany's conquest could prevent excessive damage and that direct German control would make for vastly greater deliveries of food and raw materials than the trade agreements with the Soviet Union had provided.[29]

For the timing of Hitler's Russian campaign, the decisive factor was the refusal of Britain to surrender in the summer ot 1940. His various peace feelers met with no response, and his "final appeal to common sense" of July 19, 1940, was contemptuously rejected.[30] "Something has happened in London!" Hitler remarked to his generals a few days later. "The English were entirely 'down,' now they are up again." The reason for this change of attitude, Hitler was convinced, was Russia. There had been secret telephone conversations between Moscow and London which German agents had monitored. Nothing of importance had been said, but the fact that this contact had been made at all showed clearly that Russia was unpleasantly impressed by the quick developments in Western Europe.

> Russia need say no more to England than that she does not want Germany to be great. Then the English, like a drowning man, will have reason to hope that things will be entirely different in six to eight months. *Should Russia, however, be smashed, then England's last hope is extinguished.* The elimination of Russia would also eliminate Britain's other great hope, the United States, because the Americans would then be left alone to face the enormously increased power of Japan in the Far East.

On the basis of these calculations Hitler came to a decision at the end of July 1940. *"In the course of this conflict Russia must be eliminated. Spring '41. The sooner we smash Russia the better."* Hitler would have preferred to settle with Russia immediately, but there was no longer enough good weather left during the summer and autumn of 1940 to ensure success. *"Operation only makes sense if we smash the state heavily with one blow,"* he said. "Winning a certain amount of territory does not suffice. A standstill during the winter hazardous. Therefore better to wait, but decision definite to dispose of Russia. . . . May '41. Five months' time for carrying it out." [31]

This decision, made on July 31, 1940, was not absolutely definite or irrevocable. Hitler continued to consider a variety of possibilities for getting at Britain, including plans for an actual invasion, stepped-up air and submarine warfare, an attack on Gibraltar to seal off the Mediterranean, as well as campaigns in North Africa and the Near East. Had Britain shown signs of cracking, had any military plans given promise of a quick and decisive victory over Britain, he would almost certainly have moved in for the knock-out blow before doing anything about Russia. But all the military plans with the exception of the actual invasion of Britain lacked the quality of decisiveness, and an invasion without absolute air or naval superiority appeared excessively hazardous while Russia remained a threat in the east.

To his naval commanders, who favored carrying on the war against Britain in one form or another, Hitler pointed out that the loss of a

German expeditionary force in the channel or a serious setback in any other sector would be the signal for Russian intervention. An adequate build-up of German naval and air power would take time, which the British, Russians and Americans could use to build up their own power—and their political relationships. "Under all circumstances the last opponent on the continent must be eliminated before it can get together with England," Hitler said. Russia's entry into the war while Germany was deeply involved elsewhere would constitute a very grave danger. *"Therefore every possibility of such a threat must be eliminated beforehand.* With the elimination of the Russian menace we can continue the war against England under thoroughly favorable circumstances." Germany would no longer have to fear a stab in the back, its lines of supply would be secure, it would be able to exploit the economic resources of Russia, and the large number of German soldiers immobilized on the eastern front by the fact of Russia's existence would be made available for duty elsewhere. Hitler estimated that once the Russian army had been destroyed and the state dissolved, fifty or sixty German divisions—and not necessarily first-class divisions—would be sufficient to control the occupied eastern territories.[32]

Great as were Hitler's expectations as to the strategic and economic advantages to be derived from the conquest of Russia, the clinching argument for the timing of the operation was his certainty that Russia could be defeated quickly and completely. He had nothing but contempt for the Red Army and its leadership, an opinion that seemed fully borne out by Russia's miserable showing in the war against Finland. The Russian army, he believed, could be destroyed with a few decisive blows, and the Bolshevik state itself would collapse the moment the first German troops marched into Russia.[33]

Hitler's ignorance about the real strength of Russia was shared to a remarkable degree by statesmen of other countries; but in his case ignorance was compounded by his racial-political ideas. According to the precepts of his racial theology, Bolshevism had robbed the Russian people of those Germanic organizers who had created the Russian state and replaced them with that ferment of decomposition, the Jews. The collapse of Russia would be the most powerful substantiation of the correctness of what Hitler called the folk theory of race.[34]

The folk theory of race never seems to have overwhelmed the calculations of the German generals, but the military leadership, too, was convinced of Russia's weakness. According to German intelligence reports the Red Army's communications and transportation systems were poor; the principles of leadership good, but the leaders themselves too young and inexperienced; the fighting qualities of the Russian troops in a heavy battle dubious; the commitment of the masses on which the Russians depended no match for an army with modern equipment and superior leadership. The Finnish war had revealed that the Russian tank forces were not able to cope with the demands of a modern war of movement, or to stand up to a well-equipped, boldly led enemy.[35]

There were sceptics among the German generals, but there had been military sceptics at every stage of the spectacular achievements of the Nazi era; and at every stage they had been proved wrong. By now the more sober German generals had become mistrustful of their own judgment, and the words of caution that some of them still dared to voice were swept aside by a high command drunk with success and obsessed with a belief in its own invincibility. Brauchitsch, the commander in chief of the army, estimated that there would be up to four weeks of heavy fighting, after which the war would be little more than a mopping-up operation.[36] Before the invasion of Russia had even begun, the generals were busy with plans for new campaigns and had set up a timetable for the conversion of the German military economy to production of the naval and air power that would be needed to defeat Britain and defend the German continental empire.[37]

By the end of 1940 all prospects for a quick and decisive defeat of Britain were at an end, and at approximately the same time Hitler appears to have made the final and definite decision to attack Russia.[38] On January 9, 1941, he summed up his arguments for the attack in a speech to his generals, concluding with the confident prediction that the conquest of Russia would make Germany impregnable.[39]

In deciding to launch the campaign against Russia, Hitler was well aware, as he had been in all his previous military enterprises, that he was gambling with the fate and future of the German people.[40] His arguments in arriving at that decision, however, made it seem not only the best of the various courses open to him, but less hazardous than many of the gambles he had risked during his previous seven years of power.

Preparations for the Occupation and Administration of Russia

The importance of Russia in Hitler's calculations was reflected in the detailed planning for the occupation and administration of Russia before the German invasion was launched.

Hitler's first orders to his military leadership to prepare for a possible invasion of Russia were issued on July 22, 1940.[41] Nine days later he announced his decision to carry out this invasion in the following spring and outlined his theories about strategy and military objectives.[42] By the end of October a draft of the military plans for the Russian campaign had been worked out by the army high command; it was extensively reworked by Hitler and finally approved by him in December.[43]

According to the December plan, the military objective was the annihilation of the Red Army and the centers of Russia's industrial power. The territorial objectives were the capture of Russia's principal industrial and agricultural areas; penetration deep enough to prevent Red air force attacks on economic areas vital to Germany, while giving the Luftwaffe bases from which to destroy the last Soviet industrial centers; and the establishment of a defensive barrier against Asiatic Russia along the Volga-Archangel line. The main strategic emphasis was surprise and speed. The mass of the Red Army was to be destroyed in giant encirclement operations so as to prevent the retreat of battle-ready troops into the wide spaces of the interior. For this purpose the largest possible number of German troops were to be employed.[44]

German military planners foresaw little danger of a large-scale Russian retreat to avoid encirclement and annihilation such as had been carried out when Napoleon invaded Russia in 1812. According to their calculations the Russians could not afford to give up the Baltic states, the Leningrad and Moscow areas, or the Ukraine, all of which were vital to the Red Army for supply reasons and would have to be defended. Mindful of their own supplies, the German generals planned to send one and a half divisions to secure the Petsamo nickel mines, and an equal number of troops to help the Finns protect their northern industrial area. A strong German force was to operate out of Rumania to protect the oil fields.[45]

On April 30, 1941, following the delay occasioned by the campaign in the Balkans, Hitler fixed on June 22 as the date the attack on Russia should begin.[46]

Hitler left his military commanders in no doubt about the type of war he intended to wage against Russia. The forthcoming campaign would be no ordinary conflict, he told them in March 1941, but a life and death struggle between two races and two ideologies; between German and Slav; between National Socialism and the criminal code of Jewish Bolshevism, which constituted the greatest threat to the future of civilization. In this struggle the German soldier was not to be bound by laws of war, nor was there any room for chivalry or out-of-date concepts about comradeship between soldiers. The ultimate objective of this war was not only the destruction of the Red Army in the field but the final elimination of the Russian-Bolshevik menace. The military power of Russia was to be broken for all time, the entire

RUSSIA

- Axis powers and associated states on the eve of the attack on Russia, June 22, 1941
- Maximum extent of Axis invasion
- Obsolete national boundary
- Trans-Siberian Railway

ARCTIC OCEAN

ATLANTIC OCEAN

Petsamo
Nickel
Iron Ore
White Sea
Timber
Archangel
SWEDEN
FINLAND (Allied with Germany June 23, 1941)
Timber
NORWAY
Oslo
Iron Ore
Stockholm
Helsinki
Flax
Lake Ladoga
Leningrad
Chrome
Iron Ore
URAL MTS.
SIBERIA
Asbestos
Platinum
Iron Ore
Timber
Railway
DEN.
BALTIC SEA
ESTONIA
Flax
Riga LATVIA
Livestock
LITHUANIA
Grain
Flax
Volga R.
Kalinin
Moscow
WHITE RUSSIA
Grain
Grain
Petroleum
Berlin
E. PRUSS.
Grain (To Germany)
Warsaw Grain (To Russia)
GERMANY
POLAND
Prague
Volga R.
Ural R.
Dnieper R.
Kiev
Kharkov
Don R.
Stalingrad
NORTHERN BUKOVINA
UKRAINE
Vienna
AUSTRIA
Budapest
HUNGARY
Grain
Iron Ore
Manganese
Grain
Rostov
Grain
Astrakhan
CASPIAN SEA
BESSARABIA
Petroleum
RUMANIA
Odessa
Iron Ore
Ploesti
Petroleum
Bucharest
Danube R.
YUGOSLAVIA
Belgrade
Sofia
BULGARIA
BLACK SEA
Petroleum
Batum
CAUCASUS MTS.
Manganese
Baku
Petroleum
ITALY
ALBANIA
Istanbul
GREECE
Ankara
TURKEY
Athens
IRAQ
IRAN
SYRIA
0   500 miles

SOVIET UNION

ENGLAND
FRANCE
GERMANY
SOVIET UNION
SIBERIA
Moscow
URAL MTS.
Vladivostok
MANCHURIA
JAPAN
ITALY
TURKEY
OUTER MONGOLIA
IRAN
AFGHAN-ISTAN
CHINA
PHILIPPINES
PACIFIC OCEAN
AFRICA
INDIA
FRENCH INDO-CHINA
NETHERLANDS EAST INDIES
AUSTRALIA
INDIAN OCEAN

- Principal Axis powers
- Soviet Union
- Trans-Siberian Railway

0   2000 miles

Bolshevik-Jewish intelligentsia and all Communist political leaders were to be wiped out. For this was to be a fight to the finish, a war of extermination, which would have to be waged with unprecedented, unmerciful, unrelenting harshness.[47]

Hitler also made it clear that he was not indulging in mere rhetoric. Immediately after expressing these views he ordered his military leaders to draw up official directives for the conduct of German troops in the east. These provided for the summary execution of Communist political leaders, who were not to be regarded as prisoners of war but as criminals. Cases of captured officials or hostile civilians were not to be handled by regular military or civil courts, but were to be brought before an officer who should decide on the spot whether the prisoner in question should be shot. When the persons responsible for hostile actions against the German forces could not be discovered, collective reprisals might be undertaken. The troops were to take ruthless action against Bolshevik agitators, guerrillas, saboteurs, and Jews, and against any hostile activity on the part of the native population so as to ensure the total elimination of all active and passive resistance.[48]

Of necessity, Hitler assigned the army an important administrative role during the first stage of the German occupation. Behind the fighting lines of each of the three main German army groups, to a depth of approximately two hundred kilometers, military administrative districts (*Rückwärtige Heeresgebiete*) were to be established. Although the military commanders of these districts were to remain part of the military hierarchy, they were to be appointed by Hitler and their orders were to be drawn up according to his general directives. In carrying out their principal task of pacifying and establishing order in the territory under their jurisdiction, they were to be aided by troops of the Reichsführer SS and chief of the German police. These troops, however, were not to be under military command but under their own SS and police officers.

As the fighting front was pushed forward, the conquered territory to the rear of the two hundred kilometer zone was to be removed from military and placed under civil administration, for which special provisions were to be made.[49]

Apart from the staff work of the army, the earliest and most elaborate preparations for the Russian campaign were in the field of economics. In November 1940 Göring informed the Reich's senior economic officials about the proposed invasion of Russia. At his orders a staff of experts was assembled to prepare a detailed study of the economy of the Soviet Union and the problems involved in its invasion and occupation.

214

These experts came to the conclusion that German conquests could not be restricted to the Volga-Archangel line, as envisaged by Hitler, but would have to include the Caucasus, whose oil fields were "indispensable for the exploitation of the conquered territories." Even if this were accomplished, the economic success of the campaign would depend on capturing intact Russia's major industrial installations and supplies of raw materials, solving the transport problem, and securing the co-operation of native labor in both industry and agriculture. This would still leave Germany with the problem of finding adequate supplies of rubber, tungsten, platinum, tin, asbestos, and manila hemp after the severance of trade with the Far East. In sum, the invasion of Russia would involve immense and possibly insoluble economic difficulties.[50]

While agreeing about the need to conquer the Caucasus oil fields, Göring brushed aside most of the other difficulties envisaged by his economic planners. "He as well as the Führer was of the opinion that the whole Bolshevik state would collapse as soon as German troops marched into Russia, and that therefore no large-scale destruction or total elimination of supplies and railroads was to be expected." Göring thought that the interruption of rubber and tin deliveries from the Far East would be a short-term problem which could be solved by reaching agreement with the Japanese to reopen the Trans-Siberian railway as soon as possible after the Russian collapse. The only serious danger he anticipated was a breakdown of the transportation and supply systems, which he believed had been the chief reason for the defeat of Napoleon. He therefore urged Hitler to commit more transport facilities to the Russian campaign and to reduce the number of combat divisions.[51]

Convinced as he was of a quick German victory, Göring was not so much concerned with the difficulties of the Russian campaign as he was with how that country might best be exploited in the German interest—and how he might ensure maximum influence there for himself. In presenting his ideas to Hitler he argued that far more effective methods of economic exploitation were needed in Russia than had been employed in Poland and the west, especially during the critical invasion period. For this purpose he persuaded Hitler to withdraw responsibility for economic affairs from all military and civil economic authorities and to entrust it instead to an economic office under his direction, which would co-ordinate and supervise the economic exploitation of the conquered territories according to a carefully prepared plan.[52]

By March 1941 Göring had set up his office to supervise economic affairs in the east. The chain of command was to run from Göring through an Economic Leadership Staff East (*Wirtschaftsführungsstab*

Ost), which was to co-ordinate the wishes of all other Reich departments. The directives of the Economic Leadership Staff would then
be carried out by an Economic Staff East (*Wirtschaftsstab Ost*)
which was to operate in the occupied territory and maintain its headquarters in the immediate vicinity of military headquarters.

Elaborate plans were drawn up for the organization of economic
offices in the field to correspond with the various stages of the German occupation, from battle zone, to military administration, and
eventually to civilian government; but in every case the economic officials were to have full authority over all economic activity. During
the period of military operations, the care and feeding of the troops
was to have priority, and economic officers were to co-operate in
every way with military commanders for this purpose. At the same
time technical and industrial experts were to accompany the troops
into the front lines to secure articles and raw materials most needed
by the German war economy and to expedite their shipment to the
Reich.

Behind the combat zone the conquered territory was to be divided
for purposes of economic administration into economic inspectorates,
economic commands, and a variety of subordinate offices to correspond to the administrative zones established by the military government. The organization of the economic administration in areas under
civil government remained to be determined.[53]

According to the orders of the Führer as transmitted by Göring, the
emphasis in all sectors was to be on short-term economic gains, "the
immediate and maximum exploitation of the occupied territory to the
benefit of Germany." Of overriding importance in this regard were
foodstuffs and oil, whose seizure was to be the main goal of German
economic activity. Other resources were to be secured only when
technically feasible. No effort was to be made to restore the economic
productivity of the conquered territory, not even the armaments industry. Reconstruction was to be undertaken only in areas where a
significant yield of grain or oil might be expected.

In the realm of agriculture the first task should be to enable the
German army to live off the country in order to ease the food situation in Europe and the burden on the transport system. In making agricultural shipments to Germany, the emphasis should be on food-oil
products and grain. So as not to jeopardize agricultural production
by changes in ownership or organization, the Soviet economic system
was to be maintained, including the administrative machinery, price
structure, and the state and collective farms.

Otherwise the German economic staff should concentrate on maintaining the lines of transport and communication, especially the railroads, which did 90 per cent of Russia's long-distance hauling.[54]

According to the estimates of German economic experts, it was quite possible that as a result of the proposed German economic policies in the Soviet Union millions of Russians would starve to death. This was an eventuality which the Nazi leadership was evidently perfectly willing to face.[55]

Hitler came late to the practical problem of administering the lands he expected to conquer from Russia.

During the period of military operations, the army was to exercise supreme political as well as military authority in the combat zone. But once the enemy had been thrown back, the question of a more permanent administration of the conquered territories would arise. Two major objectives were to be achieved: the control of Russian space, and the permanent elimination of the Slavic-Bolshevik menace.[56]

Hitler himself was not altogether certain how this was to be done. When he first mentioned the possibility of an invasion of Russia in July 1940, he spoke of a partition of the western part of the country, with the Baltic states, White Russia, and the Ukraine going to Germany, and an extension of Finnish territory to the White Sea.[57] Nine months later, with the plans for invasion well advanced, he had decided to deal with the Bolshevik menace by the simple expedient of wiping out the Bolshevik leadership. To eliminate the Slavic menace he was considering the break-up of the country into small states, each with its own government, which would be dependent on Germany and afford an effective means of controlling Russian space with a minimum investment of German military power. The main problem here would be to find native leaders for the new political units.[58]

All these were political questions which Hitler considered to be too difficult to entrust to the army. He therefore ordered that as soon as the military situation would allow, the zone of military operations was to be delimited in the rear and German civil administrations were to be set up under Reich commissars, who would receive their instructions directly from himself. A military commander responsible for military security was to be assigned to each civil administrative zone. Although he was to remain part of the military hierarchy, the military commander, too, was to receive orders drawn up according to Hitler's general directives. He was to co-operate closely with the Reich commissar, support him in his political role, and aid in the exploitation of the country for the German war economy.[59]

Among the questions Hitler considered too difficult to entrust to the army was the elimination of the ideological menace represented by Russia's Jewish-Bolshevik leadership. In March 1941 he had informed his generals of the need for drastic measures and had ordered them to draw up directives for putting them into effect.[60] But he had

217

no confidence that his generals fully appreciated the necessity for ruthlessness.

To make certain that problems of security and ideology, which in his mind were inseparably linked, were handled with appropriate severity, Hitler gave orders that SS, police, and other selected forces under the overall command of Heinrich Himmler were to accompany the troops of the regular army into Russia to carry out "special tasks" assigned them by the Führer. These tasks, as Hitler explained to Keitel, stemmed from the nature of the forthcoming conflict: a fight to the finish between two peoples and two political ideologies. They included the investigation and suppression of all persons and activities hostile to the Reich so as to ensure absolute security within and behind the combat zone, but they were also designed to prepare the occupied territories for their future political and administrative reorganization under German leadership. "Within the framework of these tasks the Reichsführer will act independently and on his own initiative." Himmler's forces in the field were to be under the command of senior SS and police officers directly responsible to himself.[61]

Hitler's order allowing Himmler's forces to operate in the combat zone independently of the army high command aroused serious objections among the German generals, but Keitel as usual did nothing to contest the Führer's decision. Instead he reached agreement with Himmler on May 1, 1941, that in the event of military emergency all Himmler troops should come under army command, and that senior SS and police officers should keep local military commanders informed of their principal assignments. Otherwise the army was to exercise no control over them whatever. Once the zone of military operations had been delimited, a senior SS and police officer with his staff and troops was to be attached to each civil administration to continue the work of pacification and rooting out the champions of Bolshevik doctrine.[62]

In assigning independent powers to the Wehrmacht, Göring, and Himmler, Hitler had in effect provided for the establishment of three separate and autonomous administrative organizations in the east. With the pacification of the conquered territory, still more administrative offices were to be set up in the form of Reich Commissariats.

Despite Hitler's fondness for divide and rule tactics, even he foresaw that the administrative confusion and conflict to which this proliferation of authority would almost certainly give rise might prove dangerous. His directives were filled with injunctions calling for harmonious co-operation among his various administrative agencies, and they provided that all misunderstandings not settled locally be referred to the Reich Chancellery for arbitration by himself.

Hitler, however, was unable to resist the temptation to organize further. On April 2, 1941, he established an agency to supervise and co-ordinate the policies of all Reich departments in the east. This was the Rosenberg office, later the Reich Ministry for the Occupied Eastern Territories, which despite its alleged co-ordinating functions proved to be nothing more than another rival administrative organization.[63]

It is hard to believe that Hitler intended to confer any real power on Alfred Rosenberg when he entrusted him with the formation of a Central Political Bureau for the East on April 2, 1941. Rosenberg had long been out of favor with Hitler, and he had no friends in influential positions who were likely to push his cause. Considered by most Germans and foreigners to be the official philosopher of the Nazi movement, he enjoyed no such status among Nazi leaders. Hitler called his most famous work, *The Myth of the Twentieth Century*, "plagiarized, pasted together, preposterous nonsense! Bad [Houston Stewart] Chamberlain with a few trimmings!" Goebbels dismissed it more briefly as an "ideological belch." Both descriptions were apt enough. Rosenberg's writings demonstrated an acquaintance with a massive literature of pseudoscience on racial problems which he had assimilated uncritically and regurgitated with ponderous pretentiousness. Hitler admitted he had never been able to read Rosenberg's books, and it is doubtful whether many other Nazi leaders had done so.[64]

Among his colleagues Rosenberg was disliked for his aloof manner, which may well have hidden a consciousness of personal inadequacy among the forceful personalities of Hitler's entourage. Despite his slavish loyalty to the Führer, he was never elevated to a top post in party or government. Even after the war began, despite Germany's desperate need for administrators, he remained in political limbo.

When preparations for the conquest of Russia were initiated, Rosenberg may have regained a certain status with Hitler by impressing him with his knowledge of Russian affairs. Born in Reval, Estonia, Rosenberg had spent part of his youth in Russia; and for all the superficiality of his understanding of the country there is no doubt that he knew more about it than most Nazi leaders. In making plans for the occupation of Russia, Hitler may well have consulted Rosenberg, for the proposals he outlined to his military leaders in March 1941 for the ethnographic partition of Russia bore a strong resemblance to Rosenberg's theories on the subject.[65]

On the day of his appointment as head of the Central Political Bureau for the East, Rosenberg presented Hitler with a detailed memorandum on the future occupation and administration of Russia. The gist of his thinking was that Russia west of the Urals consisted of

219

seven national and geographical units with their own political and cultural traditions, each of which should be handled in a manner corresponding to its unique characteristics and according to the political goal Germany hoped to attain.

To elaborate on these ideas and make certain that Germany pursued political goals corresponding not only to German desires but to the conditions obtaining in Russia, Rosenberg proposed the establishment of a permanent office for the central direction and co-ordination of German policy in the east. This office, working in close co-operation with other Reich authorities, was to be given the power to issue binding political instructions to German administrators in the east and to regulate the fundamental political and economic questions in the occupied eastern territories.[66]

Hitler responded favorably to Rosenberg's proposal. On April 20, 1941, he named him his deputy (*Beauftragter*) for the unified treatment (*zentrale Bearbeitung*) of questions connected with the east, and authorized him to set up an office for carrying out the tasks connected with this appointment. The supreme Reich authorities, in the first instance the plenipotentiary of the Four-Year Plan, the minister of economics, and the chief of the OKW, were instructed to give Rosenberg the closest possible co-operation, and to name a permanent liaison official to his office.[67]

Rosenberg immediately set to work to prepare a detailed program for German administration and policy in the east, and to confer with other Reich authorities about his plans. "As a result of these conferences, conducted for the most part by myself," he wrote soon afterward, "continuous consultation and organizational preparation is under way through my office and through the liaison men designated by other offices of the party and state. I may say that all work, insofar as it is at all possible under the present circumstances, is in full swing." [68] By mid-June plans for the entire public administration of the occupied eastern territories had been drawn up, and Rosenberg's office had been temporarily organized into departments of political affairs, economic-political co-operation, law, finance and administration, enlightenment and the press. A department for culture and science was as yet unstaffed "since the development of this question does not appear urgent." By the time the invasion of Russia began, Rosenberg believed that a satisfactory groundwork for the future German administration of Russia had been laid.[69]

Hitler's diplomatic preparations for the war against the Soviet Union were almost entirely devoted to improving Germany's strategic position in Eastern Europe and safeguarding its access to vital raw materials.

Special attention was devoted to Finland and Rumania because of their obvious strategic importance on the northern and southern flanks of the operation, and because the nickel of Finland and the oil of Rumania were essential to the German war economy. Negotiations were complicated by the fact that the Germans could not reveal their intention to attack Russia prematurely, especially not to the Rumanians whom they considered unreliable.[70] Yet they needed permission to concentrate large bodies of troops in both countries so as to be able to use their territories as bases for military operations and to protect their natural resources. There was the further complication that the Russians regarded Finland and Rumania as part of their own sphere of interest, nor would they be diverted from either area by German efforts to encourage their expansion at the expense of Britain in the Persian Gulf or in the Middle or Far East.[71]

As so often in dealing with the countries of Eastern Europe, the Germans were aided by the fact that the leaders of these states feared Russia more than Germany. Both Finland and Rumania were recent victims of Russian spoliation, and both looked to Germany as the only power capable of affording them protection against further territorial violations.[72]

In September 1940 the Germans secured Finland's permission to transport German troops and war material across Finnish territory, and with Finland's connivance they proceeded to build up their forces in the area north of Petsamo to protect the nickel mines. The Russians protested, but short of again going to war against Finland, and presumably now against Germany as well, there was nothing they could do but accept the situation. According to the testimony of German generals, military talks with the Finns also began in September 1940 and Hitler's military plans of December assumed their active participation in the Russian campaign, but it was not until April of the following year that he gave his consent to a discussion of joint operations with the Finnish high command.[73]

In Rumania the Germans were confronted not only by Russian interests but by those of their allies, Hungary and Bulgaria, whose demands for the return of their territories ceded to Rumania after the First World War became increasingly importunate during the summer of 1940. To deal with this awkward situation the Germans acted with bold decisiveness. They compelled Rumania to accept a treaty of arbitration yielding the territories demanded by Hungary and Bulgaria; but at the same time they promised to provide a visible guarantee of what was left of Rumanian territory. This was done by sending German troops into Rumania in September 1940. Once again the Russians were faced with the alternative of accepting the German action or of going to war, and once again they did nothing.[74]

The Italian war in Greece and Germany's own Balkan campaign provided the excuse for heavily reinforcing German troops in Rumania and for integrating the Rumanian and German air defenses. These moves necessitated co-operation between German and Rumanian military leaders; but as late as May 1941 Hitler insisted that military discussions with the Rumanians about operations against Russia be "as late as possible." The Germans relied instead on their own commanders in Rumania to prepare defensive measures and to co-ordinate the activity of the troops in that country in the overall German offensive.[75]

The Balkan campaign, itself primarily an effort to ensure security on Germany's southern flank, gave the Germans an opportunity to send troops into Hungary and Bulgaria as well as Rumania, and thereby to ensure their control over the governments, the economic assets, and above all the transportation networks of these states. When the attack on Russia began, the Germans were able to secure the active participation of Hungary and Rumania, as well as that of their satellite state of Slovakia.[76]

The neutrality of Turkey was temporarily assured by a German-Turkish friendship treaty of June 18, 1941, which was supplemented by a joint statement expressing willingness to further economic relations for their mutual benefit. For the Germans this meant a chance to negotiate for the purchase of Turkish chromium, another article in short supply in the German war economy. In addition the Turks promised to co-operate with Germans in preventing the passage of Soviet ships through the Straits.[77]

In the north the Germans hoped that sympathy for Finland would lead to active Swedish participation in the war against Russia. For the time being, however, they were satisfied with promises to permit the transport of German troops and equipment across Swedish territory and the right to purchase Swedish arms and raw materials.[78]

So confident were the Germans of victory that they neither sought nor desired the aid of Japan, whose participation in the war against Russia might have given Hitler the quick victory he expected. The aim of German diplomacy was to persuade the Japanese to pursue a more active policy in East Asia so as to tie down British forces and focus American attention on the Pacific. The Japanese were to be given no hint of the Russian operation.[79]

At dawn on June 22, 1941, the German armies opened their offensive against Russia. By the autumn of that year German forces had pushed to the gates of Leningrad in the north; they had laid siege to Moscow, overrun the Ukraine, and advanced into the valley of the Don in the central sector; and they had entered the Crimea on the southern end of this gigantic front. But an early winter and unexpectedly tenacious Russian resistance halted the German advance. On December 1 the Russians recaptured Rostov near the mouth of the Don; by the following week they had relieved the pressure on Moscow; on December 16 they recaptured the strategic communications center of Kalinin on the Moscow-Leningrad line.

With the German forces in Eastern Europe reeling under the impact of Russian counterattacks and the entire German front in Russia in danger of cracking, the continued presence of Britain in the field on Germany's western flank now became something more than a disagreeable irritant which could safely be ignored until final victory over Russia was achieved. Already British bombing attacks on German cities and British victories in Africa were having a detrimental effect on German morale. Far more serious than the menace of Britain itself, however, was the fact that behind Britain loomed the immense potential power of the United States, whose government was pursuing policies which clearly indicated a determination to join Britain in the conflict with Nazi Germany at the earliest possible opportunity.

It was primarily as a counterweight to Britain and the United States that Japan now assumed decisive importance in Hitler's calculations.

CHAPTER 19

The Japanese Alliance

With all his ideological emphasis on race, Hitler had always felt a certain sympathy for the Japanese. Although he did not credit them with the ability to be creators of culture, he classified them among the world's culturebearers, meaning that they were able to make use of the cultural achievements of the Aryan peoples and thus keep step with the general development of human progress. In *Mein Kampf* he recalled how as a youth he had cheered the victories of the Japanese over the Russians in the war of 1904–05, because "in the defeat of the Russians I also saw a defeat of Austria's Slavic nationalities." [1]

Hitler's admiration for the Japanese was stimulated anew when Japan invaded Manchuria in 1931, for here was an example of a people determined to secure their future by the conquest of living space which corresponded exactly with his own ideological conceptions. As chancellor he welcomed Japan's decision to withdraw from the League of Nations in May 1933 as a blow against an instrument designed to support the postwar treaty settlements, and throughout the 1930s he encouraged every kind of cultural and technical exchange between the German and Japanese peoples. [2]

On November 25, 1936, allegedly in response to the program of the Communist International (Comintern) to forge a world-wide alliance against the anti-Communist powers and the formation of the Franco-Soviet alliance of May 2, 1935, the German and Japanese governments signed the so-called Anti-Comintern Pact. Both powers evidently regarded this treaty as a basis for further political and eventual military co-operation against Russia, although its secret protocols provided for no more than benevolent neutrality in case one of the contracting parties actually became involved in war with Russia. [3]

Although Hitler had acclaimed the Japanese invasion of Manchuria in 1931, his government was not at all happy about the renewed Japanese invasion of China in July 1937. Besides jeopardizing the Germans' own interests in China, which they had attempted to further by supplying arms and advisers to the Chinese government, they feared the Japanese action would drive China into the arms of the Soviet Union and seriously lower the value of Japan as a counterweight to Russia. When German efforts to mediate between China and Japan failed, however, the Hitler government resolved to take an unequivocal stand on the side of the Japanese, because by this time they appeared to be natural allies in his campaign to destroy the international order established after the First World War. At Japan's request the Germans withdrew their military and technical advisers from China, stopped their deliveries of war materials, and recalled their ambassador from Peking. In February 1938 Germany recognized the Japanese puppet state of Manchukuo. Having made these gestures, the Germans were annoyed that the Japanese, for their part, persistently turned down German requests for economic concessions in China. But an even greater blow was Japan's reluctance to conclude a military alliance directed not only against Russia but against Britain.[4] Such an alliance had been envisaged by Ribbentrop early in 1938, his idea being that if Japan were to tie down British forces in East Asia, Britain would find it impossible to guarantee support for France in Europe. With Britain thus neutralized, France too would be neutralized, and Germany would have a free hand to pursue its objectives in Eastern Europe.[5]

By the spring of 1939 Hitler evidently decided that all efforts to entice Japan into the kind of military alliance desired by Germany were futile. While continuing to negotiate with Japan, he entered into negotiations with the Soviet Union and on August 23, 1939, concluded the notorious Hitler-Stalin pact, which he hoped would put an end to any intentions the British or French governments may have had to honor their treaty commitments to Poland.[6]

The Nazi-Soviet treaty, concluded without consulting the Japanese and in apparent violation of the Anti-Comintern Pact, produced shock and consternation in Tokyo. The Japanese were all the more concerned because, since early 1938, their troops had been engaged in costly border clashes with the Russians, and the Nazi-Soviet agreement, while seemingly giving Germany a free hand against Poland and the west, appeared to give Russia similar freedom to pursue a more active role in East Asia.[7]

The bitterness of the Japanese toward Germany did not prevent them from trying to exploit German victories in the west by entering claims to French and Dutch colonial territories in East Asia.[8] Such claims were not at all welcome to Hitler, who wanted to use these territories as bargaining counters in securing the co-operation of the defeated European states in his war against England, and who was in any case reluctant to give up European colonial possessions. But what Hitler wanted more than anything else at this time was a peace treaty with Britain which would make further military action against Britain unnecessary. Japan's pretensions only reinforced his reluctance to move against Britain and thereby contribute to the destruction of the British Empire, which he had no desire to do. "We would achieve with German blood something which would only benefit Japan, America, and others," he told his generals in July 1940.[9]

The stubborn refusal of the British to make peace, however, left Hitler no choice but to pursue every possibility for striking at Britain and to seek whatever allies he could find. While exploring means for involving Spain, Vichy France, and even Russia in the conflict with Britain, his attention inevitably turned to Japan, which was in a position to tie down British forces in East Asia and might also be used to neutralize the United States.[10]

It was in considering the relationship of the Anglo-American powers and Japan that Hitler first suggested that the solution to his dilemma about Britain might lie in Russia. *"England's hope is Russia and America,"* he told his generals on July 31, 1940. *"If hope in Russia is eliminated then America too will be eliminated,* because the elimination of Russia would result in an enormous increase in the influence of *Japan* in East Asia. *Russia is England's and America's sword against Japan in East Asia."* [11] Five months were to go by before Hitler finally made up his mind to attack Russia, but as one possibility after another for compelling the British to come to terms was eliminated in the course of the summer and autumn of 1940 his freedom of choice became more and more restricted.

Meanwhile the government of Japan was pursuing policies which were rapidly depriving that country, too, of its freedom of choice. The great problem facing Japan at this time was a shortage of strategic raw materials, a shortage so severe that it threatened to put an end to Japan's ability to continue its war with China. This situation was exacerbated by American measures to restrict shipments to Japan in order to compel the Japanese to withdraw from China. American pressure, however, only made the Japanese more desperate and brought more extreme exponents of Japanese expansion to the fore. On July 17, 1940, a new Japanese cabinet was formed under Prince Fumimaro Konoye which included General Hideki Tojo, the former chief of staff of the Kwantung army in China, as minister of war, and Yosuke Matsuoka, who had led the Japanese delegation out of the League of Nations in 1933, as foreign minister. But even before the formation of the new government, the Japanese Foreign Office, army, and navy had reached agreement that Japan must seek to overcome its shortage of raw materials by gaining control of the oil and bauxite of the Netherlands East Indies and the rubber of French Indo-China. As both France and the Netherlands were now under German occupation, the Japanese proposed to the Germans that in return for Germany's consent to an extension of Japanese control over French and Dutch territories in Southeast Asia, Japan would exert greater pressure on the British in East Asia.[12]

Once Hitler was convinced that no negotiated peace with Britain was possible, he agreed to consider the Japanese proposals, and early in September 1940 a personal representative of Ribbentrop arrived in Tokyo to conduct the necessary negotiations. The Germans soon made it clear that they were not so much concerned about Japanese pressure on Britain as about securing a treaty with Japan "for the purpose of neutralizing America," a clear and unequivocal demonstration of the solidarity and strength of purpose existing between Japan and the Axis powers which would deter America from intervening either in Europe or East Asia. If Japan would conclude such a treaty, Germany as a matter of course would recognize Japan's political leadership in Greater East Asia and ask for nothing more in this region than a few economic concessions which could be negotiated later. The essential thing at the moment was that Japan should join the Axis in the fullest sense of the word; for, although the present phase of the war might be over soon, the struggle against Anglo-Saxondom (the British Empire plus America) might go on for decades in one form or another. Germany, Italy, and Japan should therefore resolve now to stand together until the final great aim was achieved.[13]

Hitler stressed these same points in urging a Japanese alliance on Mussolini. Close co-operation with Japan, he said, was "the best way either to keep America entirely out of the picture or to render its entry into the war ineffective."[14]

The result of the negotiations with Japan in September 1940 was the Tripartite Pact, signed by the governments of Germany, Italy, and Japan on September 27, 1940, which provided for co-operation among the signatory powers in establishing new orders in Greater East Asia and the "regions of Europe." The crux of the treaty lay in Article 3 whereby the three powers agreed to co-operate and assist each other with all political, economic, and military means when one of the contracting parties was attacked by a power not involved in the European war or the Sino-Japanese conflict.[15]

In a letter to the Japanese foreign minister which was not intended for publication, the German ambassador stated that the question of whether an attack had taken place within the meaning of the pact was to be determined through joint consultation among the three contracting parties—a reservation that seriously detracted from the effectiveness of the pact as a defensive military alliance.[16] But the Germans were not so much concerned about the workings of the pact. Their prime object from the first had been to secure a public alliance with Japan which should serve as a deterrent to the United States, and with the signature of the Tripartite Pact they thought they had secured it. In his diary entry for September 27, 1940, General Halder described the pact as an "undoubted political success and a warning to America." [17]

The actual effect of the Tripartite Pact on American policy was a bitter disappointment to the Germans. Instead of being bluffed back into isolationism, the United States took a firmer line than ever in dealing with Japan and the Axis. So uncompromising was the American attitude that the Germans now began to fear that their pact might boomerang, and that Japan rather than the United States might be deterred from further intervention in the war. The great danger for Germany in this situation was that Japan, bogged down in China and at the end of its economic tether, might decide to come to terms with the United States, thereby leaving the Americans free to concentrate the bulk of their power against Germany in Europe. German fears were intensified when in February 1941 Admiral Kichisaburo Nomura, well known as an advocate of better relations with the United States, was sent as Japanese ambassador to Washington.[18]

German apprehensions about the possibility of a Japanese-American rapprochement brought about a change in Germany's policy toward Japan. After having previously assured the Japanese that they were not seeking their active aid against Britain, they now encouraged Japan to attack British positions in East Asia. Japan's entry into the war against Britain would put added military pressure on the British; but far more important for Germany was the calculation that it would almost certainly put an end to all prospects for the success of Japan's negotiations with the United States.[19] The object of German policy was spelled out by Hitler in a directive of March 5, 1941. "The *aim* of the co-operation initiated by the Tripartite Pact must be *to bring Japan into active operations in the Far East* as soon as possible. This will tie down strong English forces and the focal point of the interests of the United States of America will be diverted to the Pacific. . . . The quick defeat of England is to be designated as the common aim in the conduct of the war, thereby keeping the U.S.A. out of the war." In this same directive Hitler ordered that the Japanese were to be given no hint about Germany's forthcoming campaign against Russia.[20]

Considering the crucial necessity of a quick victory over Russia for the success of all of Hitler's plans, his refusal to inform the Japanese about the Russian campaign and failure to do anything to secure Japanese co-operation of any kind prior to the German invasion must be regarded as a major blunder. There is no specific evidence to account for Hitler's extraordinary attitude on this question. The most plausible explanation is that his contempt for Russian military power was such that he was convinced he could do without Japanese assistance, and that any efforts to involve Japan would jeopardize the secrecy of German military plans and curtail his freedom of action.

Hitler's reticence toward Japan is all the more surprising in view of Japanese policy at this time. For in April 1941 the Japanese government, without consulting Germany, concluded the equivalent of a nonaggression pact with Russia which freed Japan to move into Southeast Asia just as the previous German pact with Russia had freed Hitler to move against Poland and the west. With Germany's own attack on Russia scheduled to take place within the next two months, the Japanese agreement with Russia came at a singularly inauspicious time for the Germans and reminded them that Japan was capable of conducting an independent policy which might not be at all in line with German interests.[21]

Not until their invasion of Russia had begun did the Germans abandon their efforts to persuade the Japanese to attack Britain and urge instead that they join in the war against the Soviet Union, but now they did so with considerable vigor. In glowing terms Ribbentrop described the immense advantages for Japan as well as Germany that would result from the destruction of Russia. Germany, with Russia's natural resources and immense oil reserves at its disposal, would be able to move with decisive effect against Britain in the west, thus eliminating at the source what remained of British power in East Asia. While Japan, permanently freed from the Russian menace in the north, would be able to settle the China question at its leisure and then move south when all preparations to guarantee success had been completed. "The need of the hour," Ribbentrop telegraphed the Japanese foreign minister on July 1,

> is for the Japanese army to seize Vladivostok as soon as possible and penetrate as deeply toward the west as possible. The goal of these operations should be to have the Japanese army in its march to the west meet the German troops advancing to the east halfway, even before the cold season sets in; then to establish a direct connection between Germany and Japan over Russian territory, both by way of the Trans-Siberian railway and by air; and finally to have the whole Russian question settled by Germany and Japan jointly in such a way as to eliminate for all time the Russian threat to both Germany and Japan.

Ribbentrop argued that the problem of the United States, too, would be solved with the conquest of Russia. "As far as America is concerned, I hope that after Russia has been brought to its knees, the weight of the Tripartite Pact nations . . . will suffice to paralyze any tendency toward intervention in the war that may still arise in the United States." [22]

On the basis of what is now known of the Russian military situation in the autumn of 1941, it seems possible that a Japanese invasion of Russia from the east coinciding with German blows from the west might have brought about the collapse of the Soviet Union, which in turn might have been decisive for the outcome of the entire war. Japan's refusal to join in the German attack on Russia may therefore have been an even greater blunder than Hitler's failure to secure Japanese co-operation prior to that attack, especially since Japan's alternative policy of expansion toward the south was to lead to war with the United States and ultimate disaster. That the Japanese did not join in the attack on Russia was certainly not due to respect for their recently concluded nonaggression pact, nor to any lack of awareness of the advantages for Japan which would result from the destruction of Russia—there were in fact several Japanese leaders who put forward convincing arguments in favor of a Russian campaign. They were overruled, however, because there seemed even more valid reasons for remaining aloof from the conflict.[23]

In the first place, the most critical problem for Japan was still its shortage of strategic raw materials, and there was no prospect that the most serious of these shortages would be relieved by the Japanese conquest of Siberia. The Germans, to be sure, promised to provide the Japanese with everything they might require; but even if the Germans could live up to those promises, which was doubtful, the Japanese would have been placed in a position of dependence which would have allowed the Germans to exert a decisive influence on the conduct of Japanese policy as a whole. This was a situation the Japanese were evidently determined to avoid.

Apart from economic considerations, the Japanese had important strategic motives for refusing to join Germany in the war against Russia. The Japanese, after all, had considerable reason to fear a rapid and decisive German military victory over Russia. Such a victory would have brought the Wehrmacht to the frontiers of the Japanese sphere of influence and would have substituted German for Russian power in East Asia. On the other hand, if the Germans did not win a quick military victory, the Japanese would have found themselves involved in a conflict painfully similar to the one they were already waging in China—with their problem of strategic shortages still unresolved. Moreover a Japanese attack on Russia and the stoppage of shipments to Vladivostok might have been as likely to provoke

American intervention as a Japanese drive to the south, and that at a time and place chosen by the Americans.

Had the Germans won the quick victory over Russia they so confidently expected, then the Japanese, following the example of the Russians in Poland and the Italians in France, could still have invaded Siberia to safeguard their interests on the Asiatic mainland. Until the Germans were clearly on the verge of such a victory, however, they decided to remain on the sidelines and pursued policies which indicate that they may even have desired a military stalemate in Russia. For they can hardly have avoided seeing that the establishment of a balance of power between Germany and Russia might be the most effective means of gaining some measure of security on their western flank.

So it was that during the summer and autumn of 1941 the Japanese leaders, while not altogether excluding the possibility of war against the Soviet Union, continued to explore alternative political courses, including a settlement with the United States. Early in September 1941 the first shipments of American military supplies for Russia arrived in Vladivostok without interference of any kind from the Japanese navy. In reporting this fact to Berlin, the German chargé d'affaires in Washington noted that there was general satisfaction in America "over the successful intimidation of the Japanese." [24]

The Germans did not give up their attempts to involve the Japanese in the war against Russia. Ribbentrop in particular continued to urge the desirability of this course. So long as Russia remained in the field, he argued, even the most grandiose conquests in Southeast Asia would leave Japan in a precarious strategic position; only by joining Germany in the destruction of Russia could Japan guarantee its national security and therewith solve all its other problems simultaneously. If Japan did nothing else, it should prevent the shipment of American supplies to Russia via Vladivostok, either by stopping (not sinking) American ships, or by following the American example and creating a security zone for East Asia comparable to the Pan-American security zone. [25]

The principal German concern, however, remained the possibility of a Japanese-American rapprochement; when they saw their efforts to secure Japan's participation in the war against Russia were getting nowhere they felt they had no alternative but to encourage Japanese expansion in other sectors as a means of wrecking the Japanese-American negotiations, even if this meant provoking American intervention. For if the Americans intervened in the war at all, and by the autumn of 1941 it seemed increasingly likely that they would do so, then it would be far preferable for Germany that the cause of such intervention should arise in the Pacific—and with Japan as an active ally instead of neutral.[26]

To overcome Japanese hesitations about striking out boldly on a new expansionist course, the Germans did everything they could to convince them that the Americans had neither the strength nor the will to intervene effectively. Ribbentrop drew their attention to the fact that America's only response to determined aggressive action in the past had been economic reprisals. Even now, with all their blustering and threats, the Americans clearly considered themselves too weak to oppose Japan militarily and were making desperate efforts to prevent further Japanese expansion by means of insincere negotiations. It was common knowledge among military experts, Ribbentrop said, that the American army and air force were not yet prepared for war, and that the American navy was distinctly inferior to that of Japan. Within America itself isolationist sentiment was still supreme, the vast majority of the American people staunchly opposed to war. Thus Japan still had freedom to act, but the longer it waited the more the ratio of forces would shift to its disadvantage. In November Ribbentrop pointed out to the Japanese that the American military economy was still pitifully weak, as was demonstrated by the inability of the United States to supply either Britain or Russia adequately, and he urged the Japanese to take advantage of that weakness while there was still time. "Perhaps never in history has a state been so favored by fate as Japan at this hour. Japan can now, without the risk of armed American intervention, hazard any thrust in the area of the east, as long as American territories (the Philippines) are not affected by such an action." [27]

To the alarm and dismay of the Germans, however, the Japanese continued their negotiations with the United States. Had the Americans yielded to Japanese demands to be given a free hand in China and the mainland of Southeast Asia at this time, there can be little doubt that the Japanese would have concluded the kind of treaty with the United States which the Germans most feared, namely one which would have permitted the Americans to focus their attention on Europe and eventually bring the bulk of their power to bear against Germany. But the Americans did not yield. On the contrary, in an effort to discourage further aggression on the part of Japan and compel them to withdraw from China, they imposed increasingly severe restrictions on their trade with Japan. In July they froze all Japanese assets in America; in August they placed an embargo on the shipment of all strategic war materials to Japan.[28]

America's economic policy faced the Japanese with the alternative of submitting to American pressure to withdraw from China, or of extending the war by conquering territories where the raw materials essential to their war economy could be obtained. Once again there were differences of opinion among Japanese leaders as to which course to pursue, but by September 6 the various factions within the government had agreed on a sort of compromise. Negotiations with the United States were to continue, as desired by Prime Minister Konoye and other more cautious elements; but at the same time military preparations were to be accelerated to make the country ready for a major extension of the war by the end of October. "If by the early part of October there is no reasonable hope of having our demands agreed to in the diplomatic negotiations . . . we will immediately make up our minds to get ready for war against America (and England and Holland)." [29]

By the first part of October all "reasonable hope" appears to have been abandoned in Japan. Konoye resigned on October 16, to be succeeded by the more militant General Tojo, who retained his position as minister for war. By this time the Japanese had entirely ruled out an attack on Russia as being too risky and too unprofitable. With strategic economic shortages still their most critical problem, they decided that if the United States persisted in its economic boycott the only possible course for Japan would be to relieve those shortages by a policy of conquest in Southeast Asia. Between the islands of Japan and the southeastern sources of raw materials, however, lay America's Philippine Islands. The fateful question before the Japanese now was whether they could hazard a major drive to the south with the Americans lying athwart their main lines of communication. The decision they reached in answer to this question was that they could not: If they undertook a drive to the south, the threat represented by the American presence in the Philippines would have to be eliminated. This would mean war with the United States.

Strategic considerations, too, played a part in the Japanese decision to risk war with the United States. Japanese planners proposed to extend their conquest beyond the Philippines to include the most important British and American bases in the western Pacific. Once in control of these territories, they intended to build up a network of strategic bases so formidable that the materialistic Americans would not consider it worth their while to challenge Japan's supremacy in East Asia; or if they did challenge it, that they would find the Japanese defenses impregnable. [30]

The final decision on the future course of Japanese policy was made at a government conference in the Imperial Presence on November 5: If the current negotiations with the Americans did not lead to a result satisfactory to Japan by the first part of December, hostilities against the United States were to begin. [31]

In the wake of this decision, the Japanese once again sought closer relations with Germany. Early in November they put out discreet feelers to elicit a promise from Germany not to conclude a separate armistice or peace in the event of a war between Japan and the United States. The Germans, their policy still determined by fear of a Japanese-American agreement, did not hesitate to give the Japanese the assurances they requested. In case Japan or Germany became involved in war with the United States, no matter for what reason, it was considered a matter of course in Berlin that no separate armistice or peace would be made. If any doubts existed in Japan on this score, Germany was prepared to conclude a special agreement to cover all possible contingencies. After expressing their gratification about this assurance, the Japanese pressed their advantage further. If Japan should open hostilities against the United States, would Germany also consider itself at war with America? Once again the Germans answered in the affirmative. "Should Japan become engaged in a war against the United States," Ribbentrop informed the Japanese ambassador on November 28, "Germany would of course join the war immediately. There is absolutely no possibility of Germany's entering into a separate peace with the United States under such circumstances. The Führer is determined on this point." [32]

The timing of this assurance must have been particularly welcome to the Japanese, for already on November 26 the Pearl Harbor striking force had left the Kuril Islands on its way to Hawaii.

The Germans kept their promises. On December 5 Ribbentrop sent the Italians the draft of a treaty with Japan providing that in case of war between Japan and the United States, Germany and Italy would immediately consider themselves to be at war with the United States as well and would carry on that war with all the means at their command; nor would either country sign a separate armistice or peace with the United States or Britain except by full mutual agreement among the signatory powers.[33] It is indicative of the eagerness of the Germans to commit the Japanese to military action against the Western powers at any cost that their draft treaty made no mention whatever of Russia.

Immediately after the Japanese attack on Pearl Harbor on December 7, 1941, the Japanese ambassador in Berlin called on Ribbentrop asking in the name of his government that Germany and Italy honor their pledge to Japan by issuing formal declarations of war against the United States at once. Ribbentrop replied that Hitler was at that very moment studying means for making such a declaration so as to make the best possible impression on the German people and Germany's allies. Already he had sent out orders to the German navy to attack American ships whenever and wherever they might meet them.[34]

The final treaty between Germany, Italy, and Japan, pledging co-operation in the war against the United States and promising not to conclude a separate armistice or peace was signed on December 11, 1941.[35] On that same day Germany and Italy declared war on the United States.

Still the Japanese were not satisfied. On December 15 they presented the Germans with the draft of a military convention which provided for a division of the world into spheres of military operations along the seventieth degree of longitude, with Germany and Italy responsible for the territory west of that line, Japan for the territory to the east. The draft included provisions for mutual aid in either sphere when circumstances seemed to warrant it.[36]

The Germans disliked the Japanese proposal. German diplomats feared that the division of the world into operational spheres was an attempt to establish a precedent for a subsequent delimitation of political spheres, while German military leaders regretted the absence of any specific Japanese commitments regarding Russia. The treaty made no mention of Japan's entry into the war against the Soviet Union or even of halting the American shipment of supplies to Russia via Vladivostok. The army office of military economy (Wi-Rü Amt) noted that the longitudinal line proposed by the Japanese cut through territories which constituted organic economic units whose parts were mutually dependent on each other. Instead of an arbitrary division of operational spheres, the Wi-Rü Amt proposed a division following existing international boundaries, and suggested a line running along the eastern frontier of Iran, which would then follow the boundaries of India, Afghanistan, and Russia as far as Tannu-Tuva; after that it would turn north through Russia and follow the Yenisei River to the Arctic Ocean. Such a line, while conceding all of India and Pakistan to Japan, would give the Germans a better frontier in Russia and assure German control of the Kuznetsk industrial basin.

Despite their reservations about the Japanese proposal, the Germans decided not to haggle. They believed that the essential thing was to engage the Japanese against Britain to the greatest possible extent, and that the best means for doing so was to leave them maximum prospects for conquest at the expense of the British Empire. The military treaty designating their mutual fields of operation which was signed on January 18, 1942, by the German, Italian, and Japanese governments corresponded almost exactly to the original Japanese draft. Not until after the signature ceremony did the Germans express the hope, and that only orally, that the Japanese would endeavor to stop American shipments to Russia via Vladivostok and that they would do everything possible to tie down Russian forces in Siberia to prevent their withdrawal for use on the western front.[37]

The Japanese did not fulfill German hopes in either regard. Shipments to Russia continued to arrive in Vladivostok without Japanese interference of any kind, and the Japanese took no effective steps to tie down Russian forces in East Asia. Russian troops transferred from Siberia in the months after the conclusion of the Russo-Japanese neutrality pact may have been the decisive factor in checking the German drive on Moscow in December; and the troops which continued to be transferred from East Asia appear to have played an important role in sustaining Russian counterattacks during the rest of the winter.[38]

CHAPTER 20

Hitler's Declaration of War on the United States

The attack on Pearl Harbor opened the way for the Japanese to acquire the raw materials and strategic bases they deemed essential for their national survival. Yet their act of aggression against the United States can only be regarded as a monumental blunder, for in one blow it overcame the still powerful isolationist sentiment in America and united the American people, as they might never have been united otherwise, in support of a war to halt Japanese expansion in East Asia.

But if Japan's Pearl Harbor attack had an understandable rationale and actually brought about a substantial improvement in Japan's strategic and economic position, what can be said for Hitler's declaration of war on the United States, an act which brought Germany no appreciable military or economic advantages and one which cancelled out the greatest single benefit to Germany of the Japanese attack, namely its diversion of American attention from Europe to the Pacific? Once Japan had committed itself to war with the United States and all danger of a Japanese-American rapprochement had been removed, Hitler might surely have found excuses to procrastinate about fulfilling his pledge to join Japan in that war. At the very least he might have demanded Japanese support against Russia in return for German support against America, if only a promise to stop American shipments to Russia via Vladivostok.

Hitler certainly seemed to have every reason to procrastinate. For, after Japan's dramatic act of aggression, the American government, however much it might regard Germany as the more dangerous enemy, would have had difficulty in convincing the American public that an attack by Japan should be answered by an American attack on Germany. By delaying his own declaration of war on the United States, therefore, Hitler might have gained several months of grace before the Roosevelt government could find cause to direct any large proportion of American power against Germany. Those months might have given him time to defeat Russia or at least stabilize the Russian front, in which case he would have been in a far more favorable position to face the Anglo-American challenge. As it was, by throwing down his own gauntlet to the United States he gratuituously placed Germany on an equal footing with Japan in the ranks of America's enemies. In doing so he put an end once and for all to every possibility of a quick German military victory and thereby created a situation which virtually guaranteed Germany's ultimate defeat.

In attempting to explain Hitler's castastrophic decision to declare war on the United States, analysts of Nazi policy have placed a good deal of emphasis on Hitler's ignorance about America and his apparent contempt for American military capacities.[1] The evidence about Hitler's low estimate of American power must be treated cautiously, however, for his comments about American weakness were generally intended to instill courage into people justifiably fearful about America's strength. Certainly Hitler's actual policies, in contrast to many of his statements, appear to have been determined by a very realistic respect for American power and by a constant fear that America might intervene in the war before Germany's position on the European continent had been consolidated, an attitude that was to be expected from a man as obsessed as Hitler with the experiences and lessons of the First World War.

Hitler's references to the United States in *Mein Kampf* are sparse, but the few comments he did make reveal a thorough appreciation of the power and security of a state established on a continental territorial base—exactly the kind of territorial base, in fact, he intended to acquire to ensure Germany's security. Hitler devoted far more attention to the United States in his unpublished second book, in which he discussed the possibility that the growth of American power and its consequent threat to the world power position of Britain might make the British more amenable to an alliance with Germany. In both works Hitler expressed admiration for American racial policies, in particular immigration legislation which excluded unhealthy and racially inferior peoples.[2]

Hitler's regard for America declined sharply after 1929, his views evidently strongly influenced by reports about the impact of the great depression on the United States. After coming to power he frequently spoke about the pernicious effect of Jewish-capitalist influences in America, and warned American visitors that they could only solve their economic and social problems by solving their racial problems, and that they would eventually find themselves compelled to expel the Jews and send the Negroes back to Africa.[3] It is, of course, possible that Hitler's derogatory comments about the United States at this time were largely motivated by the patent hostility of the Roosevelt regime toward his own government, or by his desire to contrast National Socialism's success in solving unemployment and other economic problems with the sorry record of a country to which most Europeans still looked as the land of unlimited opportunity.

Whatever his real opinions may have been, Hitler's policies in dealing with the United States were characterized by caution.[4] With the coming of war in 1939, this attitude of caution toward the United States became a cardinal principle of German foreign policy. The Nazi press received strict orders to avoid all statements that might give offense to the Americans and even to desist from attacks on President Roosevelt, heretofore a favorite target of Nazi polemicists. When these orders were not immediately or strictly enough observed, Nazi journalists received further instructions on September 18 expressly charging them "to treat all questions concerning the United States with even more caution than hitherto." Directives along similar lines were sent to all branches of the German government and armed forces, a policy to which the German government adhered until the eve of Hitler's own declaration of war on the United States.[5]

The most numerous and certainly the most stringent of the directives concerning the United States were issued to the German navy. Clearly aware that Germany's submarine warfare had been the most important single factor leading to American intervention against Germany in 1917, Hitler instructed the navy to avoid any kind of provocation of the United States at sea, and he consistently rejected the many appeals of his admirals to be allowed greater freedom in waging submarine warfare. "The attempt of certain circles in the U.S.A. to lead the entire continent into a position of hostility toward Germany," Hitler told the leaders of his armed forces on October 9, 1939, "has so far been unsuccessful, but may in the future still accomplish the result they desire. . . . The primary danger for Germany lies in the fact that, in the event of a long war, other states may be drawn into the enemy camp either for economic reasons or because of a threat to special interests." [6]

In October Hitler turned down his navy's plea for an all-out naval and submarine blockade of Britain. Two months later he ordered that even those American ships that entered the combat zone were not to be attacked. In February 1940 he refused to authorize German submarines to patrol the Canadian coast off Halifax, an important center for the formation of British convoys, because of the "psychological effect that any such step might have on the United States." On March 5 the navy was sent a categorical order not to stop, capture, or sink American ships wherever they might be. During the great German offensive in the west in the spring of 1940 this order was relaxed somewhat to give the navy "complete operational freedom in the combat zones off the English and French coasts," but in confirming these instructions Hitler specified that intensified naval warfare was to be confined to the combat zones which President Roosevelt himself had defined in a declaration of November 4, 1939, and which placed those zones out of bounds to American ships.[7]

The refusal of the British to come to terms with Germany in the summer of 1940 enormously increased the importance of both the United States and Japan in Hitler's calculations. The German estimate of the American danger was, on the whole, fairly realistic and accurate. In July 1940 German military experts predicted that the United States could not fully train and equip a million-man army before the summer of 1941, and they thought it unlikely that America would have a large, effective force ready for use in Europe before the summer of 1942. In December 1940 Hitler told Jodl that Germany would have to solve all continental problems in the course of the following year, "because in 1942 the United States will be ready to intervene." German experts agreed that, in the event of a long war, American intervention would be a very serious danger indeed, but that for the time being the great question about America was whether it could send sufficient aid to Germany's enemies to extend the conflict into a long war.[8] It was to discourage America from sending war materials abroad and if possible to neutralize America altogether that the Germans concluded the Tripartite Pact with Japan on September 27, 1940, but they never felt certain of Japanese loyalty, and until the attack on Pearl Harbor they feared that Japan's usefulness as a counterweight to America might be vitiated through a Japanese-American agreement.[9]

Thus the Germans found themselves confronted with three main problems in dealing with America: to keep American aid to Germany's enemies at the lowest possible level; to prevent an American agreement with Japan; and, above all, to prevent direct American intervention in the war in Europe.

In dealing with the first of these problems, the Germans were caught in the dilemma of having to restrict their submarine warfare to avoid provoking outright American intervention. Even so, their rate of sinking ships of other nations bearing supplies to Britain was formidable. After they invaded Russia they attempted, though without success, to persuade the Japanese to stop American shipments to the Soviet Union through a naval blockade of Soviet ports.[10]

In seeking to prevent a Japanese agreement with America,

the Germans formed their own agreement with Japan in September 1940. After that, as we have seen, they attempted to engage Japan in the war against Britain and Russia, and finally they thought it necessary to go so far as to pledge Japan their support in a war against the United States.[11]

To prevent direct American intervention in Europe, the Germans employed the same methods they had been using since the beginning of the war. The German navy was instructed to co-operate with the government's policy of keeping the United States out of war and "under no circumstances" was it to become involved in incidents which might give the American government excuses for further intervention.[12]

In the realm of propaganda, the German government soon realized that the Americans paid no attention whatever to what was said about their country in the German press, so that the policy of restraint in commenting about the United States in Germany was gradually abandoned in the months before Pearl Harbor. With respect to German propaganda in America, however, restraint remained the order of the day. German agents were instructed to support isolationist elements and to work against Roosevelt's election to a third term, but in doing so they were to avoid compromising isolationist or anti-Roosevelt forces by obvious signs of German support or by associating them in any way with a pro-German policy. To bolster American isolationist sentiment, German agents were to describe the New Order being created in Europe as a political and economic union comparable to the union of American states, a bloc of two hundred fifty million people who desired nothing from America but to be left alone to work out their own problems and who certainly had no desire to interfere in the affairs of the Western Hemisphere. The theory that the New Order in Europe was or ever could be a threat to American security was to be represented as a product of British propaganda, American interventionists to be pictured as the dupes of Britain or in the pay of munitions makers who stood to profit from a continuation of the war.[13]

Hitler himself attempted to contribute to molding America's image of his New Order. In an interview with the Hearst correspondent Karl von Wiegand, he pointed out that Germany was one of the few countries that had never made any attempt to meddle in American affairs, and to reassure those Americans alarmed by reports of Nazi activities in Latin America he said, "Germany has never had any territorial or political designs on the American continent, and has none at present." [14]

In considering the American problem in terms of world power politics, Hitler believed that American as well as British policy toward Germany was decisively influenced by the hope of Russian intervention. In July 1940 he had expressed the opinion that the destruction of Russia might be the most effective means of preventing American intervention "since the elimination of Russia would mean a considerable strengthening of Japanese power in the Far East." In January 1941, after the decision to attack the Soviet Union had been made, Hitler was even more definite on this point. "The smashing of Russia will enable Japan to turn against the United States with all its forces," he told his military leaders. "This will prevent the latter from entering the war." [15]

On the eve of the German attack on the Soviet Union, Hitler forcefully restated the arguments for avoiding incidents with the United States and his belief that the defeat of Russia would discourage American intervention because of the increased threat that would be posed by Japan. Until the development of the Russian campaign had become clearer, that is until Germany had achieved the expected decisive victory over Russia, "the Führer desires absolutely to avoid any possibility of incidents with the U.S.A." The navy and Luftwaffe were forbidden to attack all naval vessels, whether inside or outside the "closed area," with the exception of ships definitely recognized as belonging to the enemy, from the cruiser class upward. In a subsequent order he forbade all attacks on American merchant ships, including those that sailed into the combat area. Hitler was confident that the collapse of the Soviet Union would have a decisive effect on both Britain and America; therefore it was "absolutely essential that all incidents with the United States should be avoided. . . . Germany's attitude toward America is therefore to remain as before: not to let itself be provoked, and to avoid all controversy." [16]

The American government did not make it easy for Hitler to adhere to his policy of restraint. Roosevelt had never made any secret of his loathing for the Hitler regime or of his desire to aid the opponents of Nazism. For purposes of sending such aid, however, he was severely handicapped initially by the American Neutrality Act, which was stoutly defended by American isolationists. Even before the German invasion of Poland he had attempted to secure the repeal or at least the amendment of those provisions of the act which forbade the sale or shipment of arms in American ships to all countries involved in war. In November 1939 the Neutrality Act was in fact amended to permit the sale of arms to the Allies, but only on a cash and carry basis. American isolationists, recalling the lessons of the First World War, wanted to make it impossible for any belligerent to run up debts in the United States which might give the American government a motive to intervene to save American investments. Nor did isolationists want arms sent abroad on American ships, which would

242

then become legitimate targets of enemy attacks and lead to incidents which would also create a demand for intervention. To ensure the passage of the cash and carry amendment, Roosevelt was obliged to define the combat zone beyond which American ships would not be allowed to go. It was the area beyond this zone which Hitler shortly afterward declared out of bounds to German air and submarine attacks.[17]

As German victories in the spring and summer of 1940 made Americans more conscious of the magnitude of the Nazi menace, Congress approved Roosevelt's request for a billion dollars to strengthen America's armed forces and to step up the pace of American aircraft production. Isolationist sentiment remained powerful, however, and the Roosevelt administration was unable to secure the passage of any major measures to help the hard-pressed British. To circumvent the isolationists in Congress, he concluded an executive agreement (which did not require congressional approval) with the British on September 2, 1940, which gave the British fifty overaged American destroyers for convoy duty in exchange for a ninety-nine year lease on British naval bases in Newfoundland and the Caribbean. The transfer of these bases in itself gave further aid to Britain, for it relieved British forces stationed at these bases for duty elsewhere.[18]

In September 1940 the first peacetime military conscription was introduced in the United States; in October Congress approved the expenditure of over seventeen billion dollars for military purposes; in November Roosevelt was elected to an unprecedented third term as president of the United States. On December 17 Roosevelt announced his decision to secure approval of a Lend-Lease Act to aid all countries fighting to preserve freedom, and on December 29 he made a fervent public appeal for support of the Lend-Lease program in which he described the United States as the Arsenal of Democracy. The Lend-Lease Act submitted to Congress on January 10, 1941, asked for seven billion dollars in credits to nations whose defense was considered vital to the United States; despite the determined opposition of isolationist forces the act was passed on March 11.[19]

So far, despite the appeals of his admirals, Hitler had reacted to American moves to aid Britain with tough-minded and most unusual restraint. But now, "to counter the expected effects of America's aid-to-England law," he announced that Germany would henceforth consider the waters off Iceland as being within the combat area, and that this area was to be regarded as extending to the boundaries of the Pan-American security zone; within this combat area German naval and air forces were to be allowed to operate without restriction.[20]

Hitler soon recognized that he had made a mistake, for in extending the combat area he had simply given the Americans an excuse to give further aid to Britain. In response to Hitler's announcement, the Americans declared that henceforth British warships as well as merchantmen might be repaired in American docks. On March 30 all Axis as well as all Danish ships in American ports were seized; on April 4 the Americans announced the extension of the Pan-American security zone to the east coast of Greenland. On that same day American forces occupied Greenland, a possession of German-occupied Denmark, allegedly to prevent Greenland from falling into the hands of the Germans but in fact to use it as an advanced base for sending aid to Britain.[21]

Hitler at once pulled in his horns. On April 20 he publicly recognized America's new definition of the neutrality zone off the North American coast, and on April 25 he once again ordered German naval forces in the Atlantic to do everything possible to avoid incidents with American vessels.[22]

The Americans, however, kept up the pressure. In a major speech on foreign policy on May 27, 1941, Roosevelt stressed the danger to the entire Western Hemisphere if the Germans were to control the Atlantic and stated that the United States would do everything in its power to prevent this from happening. "Our patrols are helping now to ensure delivery of the needed supplies to Britain. All additional measures necessary to deliver the goods will be taken." The United States, the president declared, was now in a state of unlimited emergency.

On June 14 the United States froze all Axis assets in America; two days later the State Department ordered all German consular officials and the employees of other German offices still operating in the United States to leave the country by July 10. On July 8 the Americans took over from the British the defense of Iceland, a strategic point in the convoy routes across the Atlantic; a week later they extended the definition of the territorial waters of the Western Hemisphere to include Iceland. In August Roosevelt and Churchill joined in the promulgation of the Atlantic Charter, a document expressing the determination of the United States to co-operate with Britain in securing a just and lasting peace and which could only be interpreted as an assurance to Britain that, if necessary, the United States was prepared to co-operate in defeating the Axis powers.[23]

Soon afterward there occurred the type of incident Hitler had so strenuously sought to avoid. A German submarine became involved in an engagement with the American destroyer *Greer*—whether the submarine attacked the American vessel or the *Greer* first attacked the submarine has never been definitely established.[24] Roosevelt, however, used the incident to issue an order that henceforth all American ships on convoy duty were to "shoot on sight" on all Axis

244

ships encountered in the American neutrality zone. In October he called for the repeal of that section of the Neutrality Act which prohibited the arming of American merchant vessels, and in November Congress repealed almost all the remaining restrictive provisions of the act.[25]

With each new American provocation the German navy appealed to Hitler to be allowed to take countermeasures, but Hitler adhered to his policy of restraint. Even if the American Neutrality Act were repealed in its entirety, he said, he intended to do everything possible to avoid incidents, and in fact orders to this effect continued to be issued until December 2, 1941.[26]

Hitler's restraint was entirely tactical and was certainly not due to any affection for the United States or respect for the rights of neutrals. For while giving his own forces orders to avoid incidents with the United States, his government was encouraging Japan to attack British possessions in East Asia, even if this might lead to war between Japan and America. In playing this dangerous game Hitler's primary purpose, as we have seen, was to prevent a Japanese-American rapprochement, to maintain Japan as a counterweight to the United States, and to focus American attention on East Asia.[27]

Part of this purpose was fulfilled, and with a vengeance, when Japan attacked Pearl Harbor on December 7, 1941. But Hitler's hope that Japanese action in the Pacific would divert American attention to East Asia did not appear to have been realized by the Japanese attack. For on December 9, two days after Pearl Harbor, Roosevelt announced that he considered Germany just as guilty as Japan for the bombing of Pearl Harbor and that a diversion of American forces from the Atlantic to the Pacific was not to be expected.[28] On that same day Hitler issued orders for German submarines to begin an immediate all-out attack on American ships wherever they might be. On December 11 he declared war on the United States.[29]

By declaring war on America while the greater part of his army was still bogged down in Russia Hitler sealed his fate, and for that reason alone this action must be considered the greatest single mistake of his career. But by now he was inextricably caught up in processes he himself had set in motion, and in the context of these processes his declaration of war not only becomes more understandable but even assumes a quality of inevitability.

For some time already Hitler had been convinced, and in this he was certainly correct, that Roosevelt was only waiting for an opportunity to intervene in the European war. He had already moved America a long way from a status of neutrality, and his shoot-on-sight order to American ships would probably have produced an incident in the near future which would have given him the pretext he needed for intervention. Hitler must therefore have calculated that any delay on his part in honoring his pledge to Japan to join immediately in the war against the United States would accomplish nothing more than a brief postponement of his own inevitable clash with that country. The failure to honor his pledge, on the other hand, might irreparably damage Germany's relations with Japan and permanently end all prospects of Japanese co-operation against Russia. Moreover, in view of America's steady and obvious abandonment of a status of neutrality, further German delay in responding to American acts of provocation might create the impression that Germany was afraid of the United States and seriously lower Germany's prestige in the eyes of its satellites and the uncommitted nations. These and similar dangers could all be avoided by an immediate declaration of war, which would have the additional advantage of allowing German aircraft and submarines to strike at American shipping before America's defenses had been properly organized.

After the terrible anxieties the Germans had felt about the course of Japanese policy and the possibility of a Japanese-American rapprochement, there can be no doubt that Japan's final commitment to war against the United States came as a great relief, " a deliverance," "a new lease on life." Hitler frankly acknowledged his own vast sense of relief. The Russian campaign had bogged down, his compatriots seemed convinced that the United States would enter the war against them sooner or later no matter what course Germany pursued, so Japan's entry into the war did much to lift German morale at a critical moment. "For the first time we have on our side a first-rate military power," Hitler said. Giving Japan a free hand in East Asia was admittedly a turning point in history. "It means the loss of a whole continent, and one must regret it for it is the white race which is the loser." But Hitler would not concede that his alliance with Japan represented a betrayal of National Socialist principles. To win, he said, "we are quite prepared to make an alliance with the devil himself." [30]

It should be remembered that Hitler still counted on a short war. If Japan could hold America in check for just a year, then the Russian campaign would be over (if it were not, Hitler must have realized the war would be lost in any case) and Germany could once again shift the bulk of its military might toward the west, backed by all the resources of Europe—and Asia. Surely, then, both Britain and America would realize that the task of defeating the Axis powers and Japan was hopeless, but if they still refused to come to terms Germany could calmly build up its strength to knock out first one, then the other, at the appropriate moment.

Culmination

As the German armies drove deep into Russia in the summer and autumn of 1941, Hitler appeared to be fulfilling the last and most important phase of his ideological program: the conquest of Lebensraum in Eastern Europe. What he had already achieved by way of fulfilling that program, however, seemed nothing short of miraculous. Without wealth, without social status, without experience in government and diplomacy, he had within just over ten years built an insignificant extremist party into the most powerful political organization in Germany, secured control of the German government, and eliminated all rivals to his personal authority. To gain the kind of support he deemed essential to any ruler who aspired to make decisive changes in world history, he had employed every device available to modern totalitarian leaders for manipulating public opinion to inspire his followers with fanatic enthusiasm and unquestioning loyalty. As head of the German government he had abrogated the provisions of the Treaty of Versailles restricting Germany's sovereignty and freedom of action, remilitarized the Rhineland, reintroduced compulsory military service, and made Germany once again a major military power. Through skillful and ruthless diplomacy he had acquired Austria and the Sudetenland for Germany without having to fire a shot. In the process he had destroyed the state of Czechoslovakia, the most formidable anti-German bastion in Central Europe. After having made the decision for war, which he had always believed would be necessary to realize his objectives in Eastern Europe, he had conquered Poland, eliminated the French threat in the west, driven the British expeditionary forces from the Continent, and secured his northern and southeastern flanks. And he was now engaged, apparently successfully, in the removal of the last threat to German security in Europe and the acquisition of land and economic resources which he confidently expected would make Germany impregnable.

247

By the autumn of 1941 German forces controlled a territory extending from the North Cape of Norway to the deserts of North Africa, from the Channel Islands in the Atlantic to the outskirts of Moscow and the Crimea. Altogether it was an area considerably larger than that of the United States, most of it in a temperate climatic zone, rich in natural resources, and for its size the most economically productive region in the world. This high level of productivity was due in large measure to the population of the area under German dominion, which, without counting the inhabitants of European Russia, was well over twice as large as that of the United States. Far more important than the size of the population, however, was its quality. The people of Europe were among the most highly educated in the world; they were also part of a society and culture which encouraged inventiveness and industry and which was responsible for the majority of scientific and technological developments of the industrial age. In almost all the European countries which came under German control there was a large reservoir of skilled labor capable of producing and using the most sophisticated scientific and technological equipment, together with a corps of civil servants trained to operate the complicated administrative mechanisms essential to the functioning of an industrial society.

Through the intelligent and efficient exploitation of the men and resources of continental Europe, and especially by taking advantage of the good will initially accorded the Germans in many parts of Russia as liberators from Bolshevik tyranny, Hitler might still have succeeded in overthrowing the Stalin regime, stabilizing the Russian front, and achieving a stalemate in the west. But, as we have seen in the chapters dealing with the Nazi government of Germany, intelligence and efficiency were not among the more prominent features of Nazi rule.

The Nazis prided themselves on having created a united Europe, but the Europe under their control was in many ways far more fragmented than before the German conquest. Apart from Himmler's police and racial offices, which can hardly be said to have contributed to a sense of European unity, the Nazis signally failed to provide Europe with unifying ideas or institutions. Many of the conquered states, for example Czechoslovakia, France, and Yugoslavia, had been broken into smaller governmental or administrative units. In each of the conquered territories not actually annexed to the Reich, a different German administration had been established: a Protectorate in the Czech provinces of Bohemia and Moravia, a Government General in rump Poland, a Reichskommissariat in Norway, another Reichskommissariat in the Netherlands, a military government in Belgium, to name only a few.

248

Meanwhile, within each of these administrative satrapies, there was the same administrative overlapping, the same empire building, the same vicious infighting between the multitude of Nazi offices and officials that characterized Nazi rule in Germany; only in the occupied countries the difficulties were compounded by the problems of wartime and the fact that the Nazis were ruling over foreign and, for the most part, hostile peoples. In the vast administrative maze that constituted the Nazi government of Europe, the only unifying authority was Hitler, who to the end of the war retained ultimate responsibility for determining all major lines of policy and for making all major political decisions. The problems of governing Europe, however, were simply too numerous and too complex to be supervised and dealt with effectively by a single man, no matter how great his talents and energies, and the Nazi empire suffered accordingly.

Serious as were the inadequacies of the Nazi administration of Europe, a far more disastrous feature of the Nazi empire was Hitler's insistence on implementing his ideological program while the war was still in progress and before a final German victory had been assured. Nazi ideological policies were so grotesque, so perverse, and so self-defeating that they defy credulity and seem to belong to a realm of sadistic fantasy. Tragically, the horrors perpetrated by the Nazis in the name of nation and race were all too real. With savage fanaticism, and often with complete disregard for the political, military, or economic consequences, Hitler and his henchmen proceeded to establish the Nazi New Order on the basis of the racial-national principles propounded in *Mein Kampf.* These principles, which had been applied in Germany since 1933 in dealing with the Jews, provided the guidelines for Nazi policy in all the occupied territories, but they were put into practice on the greatest scale and most fatefully in Russia, where they transformed a population which in many areas had greeted the Germans as liberators into a people inspired with determination more fanatic than that of the Nazis themselves, because more desperate, to repel the German invaders.

The manner in which the New Order was established unquestionably contributed to the weakening of Hitler's empire; it may even have been the decisive factor in his defeat. A strong case can be made that it was above all the continued resistance of the Russians that gave the United States the time and opportunity to intervene effectively. Hitler himself had always recognized time to be one of his major adversaries, but in this case there is the final ironic twist that his own racial policies provided time for refugee scientists in America, despised and driven from Hitler's Europe on racial or ideological grounds, to develop weapons which made a final Hitler victory impossible.

However great the effect of Hitler's racial policies on the outcome of the war, from the point of view of his arm aims they provide striking confirmation of the literal nature of his ideological concepts and his determination to put them into effect. As we have seen in the present volume, however, the exigencies of military and economic security, real or imagined, had compelled Hitler to extend his dominion over areas and peoples that had played little or no part in his original ideological program. Besides Jews and Slavs, the Nazi empire included Norwegians and Greeks; Walloons and Magyars; and, by 1943, Italians and Albanians as well. Not even for the French, whose conquest he deemed essential to future German security, did Hitler have any precise, or even general, future plans.

How all these peoples were organized under Nazi rule, the guidelines Hitler laid down for their treatment, the policies he pursued, the mutations in those policies caused by the shifting fortunes of war and local resistance movements—these and similar problems provide further and perhaps the most authoritative evidence about the ultimate nature of Hitler's war aims and are the subject of the second volume of this book, *The Establishment of the New Order.*

Appendices

A Note on the Spelling

The political and national upheavals that have taken place in Europe in the twentieth century have made the spelling of proper and geographical names a difficult as well as sensitive problem.

In the spelling of proper names, I have tried to use the spelling commonly used by the bearers of those names. When transliteration was required, I have adopted the system in most general use among contemporary American scholars.

In dealing with geographical names, I have used the spelling found in American atlases published during the period when the events described in this book were taking place. Thus I have used the name in common use in 1939 for Danzig, not the Polish Gdańsk; the Italian names for cities in the South Tyrol, for instance, Bolzano instead of Bozen; the Slovakian name for Bratislava instead of the German Pressburg or the Hungarian Pozsony. In some cases, however, I have used the German spelling of place names, with the local spelling in parentheses. The name Auschwitz, for example, loses much of its emotional impact when rendered by the Polish Oświeçem.

Whenever in doubt about spelling, I have tried to be clear rather than consistent.

Abbreviations

ADAP Akten zur deutschen auswärtigen Politik, 1918–1945 (Baden Baden and Göttingen). German text of *Documents on German Foreign Policy*, a series still in the process of publication.

AO   Auslandsorganisation. Organization for Germans Abroad.

DAF   Deutsche Arbeitsfront. German Labor Front, the organization of all German workers including entrepreneurs and managers.

DDP Dokumente der deutschen Politik (Berlin, 1937–44). A Nazi government document publication.

DGFP Documents on German Foreign Policy, 1918–1945 (Washington, 1949–). A publication of captured German documents.

DUT   Deutsche Umsiedlungs-Treuhandgesellschaft. German Resettlement Trusteeship Corporation.

EWZ   Einwandererzentralstelle. Central Immigration Office.

HSSPF   Höherer SS-und Polizeiführer. Senior SS and police officer.

IMT International Military Tribunal, *Trial of the Major War Criminals before the International Military Tribunal. Proceedings and Documents,* 42 vols. (Nuremberg, 1947–49). The published records of the main Nuremberg trials.

NCA Nazi Conspiracy and Aggression, 8 vols and 2 suppl. (Washington, 1946–48). A selection in English translation of documents presented in evidence at Nuremberg.

NG, NI, NID, NO, NOKW   Prefixes of numbers of documents collected for the Nuremberg trials, most of them unpublished.

NS   National Socialist or Nazi.

NSDAP   Nationalsozialistische Deutsche Arbeiterpartei. National Socialist German Workers party.

OKW   Oberkommando der Wehrmacht. High Command of the Armed Forces.

OSS   Office of Strategic Services, Research and Analysis Branch. Under the auspices of this office, a large number of valuable studies of the German government, the Nazi party, and the countries under German occupation were prepared.

OT   Organisation Todt. The armaments and construction organization under Dr. Fritz Todt.

ABBREVIATIONS

PS   Prefix of numbers of documents collected for the Nuremberg trials. See NG above.

RAD   Reichsarbeitsdienst. Reich Labor Service.

RFSS   Reichsführer SS. The title of Heinrich Himmler, head of the SS.

RGBl   Reichsgesetzblatt. The official publication of German laws and treaties.

RHDGM   Revue d'Histoire de la Deuxième Guerre Mondiale. A journal containing many useful articles and bibliographies on the Nazi era.

RKFDV   Reichskommission für die Festigung des deutschen Volkstums. Reich Commission for the Consolidation of the German People. Himmler's main office for racial questions. The initials may, however, also refer to the position of Himmler himself as head of that office: Reichskommissar für die Festigung des deutschen Volkstums, Reich commissar for the consolidation of the German people.

RSHA   Reichssicherheitshauptamt. The Central Office for Reich Security. Another major office under Himmler, this one in charge of all state and party police organizations.

RuSHA   Rasse-und Siedlungshauptamt. Central Office for Race and Re-settlement.

SA   Sturm Abteilung. The Nazi storm troops, or more literally attack or assault division. Brown shirts.

SD   Sicherheitsdienst. The Security Service of the RFSS, the intelligence service of the SS.

Sipo   Sicherheitspolizei. Security Police.

SS   Schutz Staffel. Literally "guard echelon," the elite guard of the Führer under the command of Himmler. Black shirts.

T   Code letter prefix for microfilm serial and frame numbers of captured Nazi documents filmed at Alexandria, Virginia. The films are now on deposit in the National Archives, Washington.

TWC   Trials of the War Criminals before the Nuernberg Military Tribunals under Control Council Law N-10, 15 vols. (Nuremberg, 1946–49). Includes trial records and documents in evidence of other Nuremberg trials.

UWZ   Umwandererzentralstelle. Central Office for Evacuation.

VfZ   Vierteljahrshefte für Zeitgeschichte. A journal containing many useful articles and bibliographies on the Nazi era.

VoMi   Volksdeutsche Mittelstelle. Liaison Office for Ethnic Germans.

WF   Whaddon Film. Code letters I have used as a prefix to microfilm serial and frame numbers of captured Nazi documents filmed at Whaddon Hall, England. The films are now on deposit in the Public Record Office, London, and the National Archives, Washington.

Wi-Rü   Amt. Wehrwirtschaft-und Rüstungsamt. The German army's Military Economy and Armaments Office.

ZBA   Zentralbodenamt. Central Land Office.

Biographical Sketches

ALEXANDER I. King of Yugoslavia, 1921–34; assassinated in Marseille, October 9, 1934.

ALTENBURG, DR. GÜNTHER. Head of Political Department of the German Foreign Office dealing with Austria and Czechoslovakia, 1938; afterward in charge of Ribbentrop's personal secretariat; head of the Information Department of the Foreign Office, 1939; Reich plenipotentiary for Greece, 1941–43; head of the *Dienststelle Altenburg* in Vienna (dealing with Balkan questions), 1944–45.

ANTONESCU, MARSHAL ION. Rumanian general; minister president, September 4, 1940; chief of state, September 14, 1940–44.

ANTONESCU, MIHAI. Rumanian lawyer; minister of justice, September 14, 1940–January 27, 1941; minister of state attached to the minister president's office from January 27, 1941; deputy minister president, 1942–44.

BACKE, HERBERT. State secretary in the Reich Ministry of Food and Agriculture, 1933–43; chief of the food division and member of the general council of the Four-Year Plan; acting Reich minister of food and agriculture, 1943–45.

BECK, GENERAL LUDWIG. Chief of the general staff of the German army, 1935–38; resigned October 31, 1938; committed suicide July 20, 1944, after the failure of the plot to assassinate Hitler.

BELOW, COLONEL NICOLAUS VON. Luftwaffe adjutant to Hitler, 1937–45.

BENEŠ, DR. EDUARD. Czechoslovak foreign minister, 1918–35; president of Czechoslavakia, December 18, 1935–October 5, 1938.

BLOMBERG, FIELD MARSHAL WERNER VON. Reich defense minister, January 30, 1933–35; Reich war minister and commander in chief of the Wehrmacht, 1935–February 4, 1938.

BLUM, LÉON. French minister president, June 1936–37; vice-president of the cabinet, June 1937–January 1938; minister president and minister of the treasury, March–April 1938; president of the French Socialist party.

BOHLE, ERNST WILHELM. Gauleiter and head of the *Auslandsorganisation*

(AO) of the Nazi party, May 1933–45; state secretary in the Foreign Office, November 1937–November 1941.

BONNET, GEORGES. French foreign minister, April 1938–September 1939.

BORIS III. King of Bulgaria, 1918–43.

BORMANN, MARTIN. Deputy chief of the Office of the Deputy of the Führer, 1933–41; head of the Party Chancellery 1941–45; personal secretary to the Führer, April 1943–45.

BRANDT, ANTON. SS *Obersturmbannführer;* SS and police officer for Poznań, 1939–45.

BRAUCHITSCH, GENERAL WALTHER VON. Commander in chief of the German army, February 1938–December 1941.

BRÄUTIGAM, OTTO. Staff member, German Embassy in Paris, 1936–39; official in Economic Policy Department, Foreign Office, 1939–40; consul general in Batum, 1940; liaison officer of the Reich minister for the occupied eastern territories to the High Command of the Army, June 1941–45; deputy head of the Political Department, Reich Ministry for the Occupied Eastern Territories, 1941–45.

BÜLOW, BERNARD WILHELM VON. State secretary in the German Foreign Office; died June 1936.

BURCKHARDT, CARL J. Swiss historian; League of Nations high commissioner in Danzig, February 18, 1937–September 1, 1939; president of the International Committee of the Red Cross, 1939–45.

BURGSDORFF, DR. KURT VON. Under state secretary in the Office of the Reich Protector of Bohemia and Moravia.

BUSCHENHAGEN, COLONEL ERICH. Chief of staff of the German army in Norway.

CANARIS, ADMIRAL WILHELM. Chief of the German counterintelligence (*Abwehr*) of the OKW, 1938–44. Hanged in March 1945 for complicity in the July 20, 1944, plot to assassinate Hitler.

CAROL II. King of Rumania, 1930–40.

CHAMBERLAIN, NEVILLE. British prime minister, May 28, 1937–May 10, 1940.

CHURCHILL, WINSTON. First lord of the Admiralty, September 5, 1939–May 10, 1940; prime minister, May 10, 1940–July 1945.

CIANO DI CORTELLAZZO, COUNT GALEAZZO. Son-in-law of Mussolini; Italian foreign minister, 1936–43.

CINCAR-MARKOVIĆ, ALEKSANDER. Yugoslavian foreign minister, February 1939–March 27, 1941.

CREUTZ, RUDOLF. Deputy head of the central office of the RKFDV.

CVETKOVIĆ, DRAGIŠA. Yugoslavian minister president, February 1939–March 27, 1941.

DALADIER, ÉDOUARD. French minister president and minister of national defense, 1938–40; minister of war and foreign affairs, 1939–40.

DALUEGE, KURT. SS *Obergruppenführer;* chief of the *Ordnungspolizei,* 1936–44; acting Reich protector of Bohemia and Moravia, June 1942–August 1943.

257

BIOGRAPHICAL SKETCHES

DARRÉ, R. WALTHER. Reich minister of food and agriculture, 1933–45; Reich peasant leader, 1934–45; head of the Reich Food Estate, 1934–45; chief of the Central Office for Race and Resettlement (RuSHA), 1931–38.

DELBOS, YVON. French foreign minister, 1936–38.

DEYHLE, MAJOR. Adjutant of General Jodl.

DIELS, DR. RUDOLF. First chief of the Gestapo.

DIETRICH, DR. OTTO. Press chief of the Nazi party, 1932–45; press chief of the Reich government, 1937–45; state secretary in the Reich Ministry of Propaganda, 1937–45.

DIRKSEN, DR. HERBERT VON. German ambassador to the Soviet Union, 1928–33; to Japan, 1933–38; to Great Britain, 1938–39.

DOLLFUSS, ENGELBERT. Federal chancellor of Austria, 1932–July 25, 1934.

ĎURČANSKÝ, DR. FERDINAND. Member of the Slovak People's party; deputy minister president and minister of justice, social welfare, and health in the autonomous Slovak government, October 1938–March 10, 1939; Slovak foreign minister, March 14, 1939–July 1940; minister of the interior, October 1939–July 1940.

EBERT, FRIEDRICH. President of the German Republic, 1919–25.

EICHMANN, ADOLF. SS *Obersturmbannführer;* chief of the department in charge of Jewish affairs in the RSHA.

EPP, GENERAL FRANZ XAVER, RITTER VON. Reichsstatthalter of Bavaria, 1933–45; head of the Colonial Office of the Nazi party; minister for colonies, 1941–45.

FALKENHORST, GENERAL NIKOLAUS VON. Commander in chief of the German armed forces in the Norwegian invasion and occupation.

FILOV, BOGDAN. Bulgarian archaeologist; minister president, February 1940–September 1944.

FRANCO Y BAHAMONDE, FRANCISCO. Chief of state, president of the government, and generalissimo of the armed forces of Spain from October 1936.

FRANK, HANS. Bavarian minister of justice, 1932; president of the Academy of German Law; governor general of occupied Poland, 1939–45.

FRAUENFELD, ALFRED E. Member of the Austrian Nazi party and active on behalf of the Anschluss; later named *Generalkommissar* in occupied Russia.

FRICK, DR. WILHELM. Early member of the Nazi party; minister of the interior and of education in Thuringia, January 1930–April 1931; Reich minister of the interior, 1933–43; Reich protector of Bohemia and Moravia, 1943–45.

FRITSCH, GENERAL WERNER VON. Commander in chief of the German army, 1935–February 1938.

FUNK, DR. WALTHER. Reich press chief and under state secretary in the Ministry of Propaganda, 1933–37; Reich minister of economics, February 1938–45; president of the Reichsbank, January 1939–45; plenipotentiary general for military economy, February 1938–45.

BIOGRAPHICAL SKETCHES

GAFENCU, GRIGOIRE. Rumanian foreign minister, December 1938–June 1940.

GAMELIN, GENERAL MAURICE. Allied commander in chief, September 1939–May 1940.

GISEVIUS, HANS BERND. Gestapo official who later joined the anti-Nazi opposition movement.

GOEBBELS, DR. PAUL JOSEPH. Gauleiter of Berlin; Reich minister of propaganda, 1933–45; Reich plenipotentiary for total war effort, 1944–45.

GÖRING, HERMANN WILHELM. President of the Reichstag, 1933–45; minister president of Prussia and Reich minister for air, 1933–45; commander in chief of the Luftwaffe, 1934–45; plenipotentiary for the Four-Year Plan, 1936–45; acting Reich minister of economics, December 1937–February 1938.

GRAZIANI, GENERAL RODOLFO. Commander of the Italian forces in North Africa until February 1941.

GREIFELT, ULRICH. SS *Oberführer;* head of the office of the RKFDV; head of the Executive Office for Immigrants and Repatriates.

GREW, JOSEPH C. American ambassador to Japan, 1932–41.

HÁCHA, DR. EMIL. President of the Supreme Administrative Court of Czechoslovakia, 1925–38; president of Czechoslovakia, November 1938–March 1939; head of the Czech administration in the Protectorate of Bohemia and Moravia, 1939–45.

HAGELIN, ALBERT VILJAM. Quisling's representative in Germany, 1939–40; minister of commerce in Quisling's Norwegian government, April 1940; head of the Norwegian Department of the Interior, September 1940–45, with title of minister from September 25, 1941.

HALDER, GENERAL FRANZ. Chief of the general staff of the German army, December 1938–September 1942.

HALIFAX, EDWARD WOOD, VISCOUNT. British foreign secretary, February 1938–December 1940; ambassador to the United States, 1941–46.

HAMBRO, CARL JOACHIM. President of the Norwegian Storting, 1926–40.

HASSELL, ULRICH VON. German ambassador to Italy, 1932–38; later a member of the anti-Nazi resistance; executed in September 1944 for participation in the plot to assassinate Hitler.

HAUSHOFER, DR. GEORG ALBRECHT. Son of Karl Haushofer, the authority on geopolitics; professor of geopolitics at the University of Berlin; at one time a Nazi closely associated with Hess and Ribbentrop, he later joined the opposition to Hitler; hanged after the abortive July 20, 1944, assassination attempt.

HENDERSON, SIR NEVILE. British ambassador in Germany, 1937–39.

HENLEIN, KONRAD. Founder of the Sudeten German *Heimatsfront*, 1933, renamed the Sudeten German party in 1935; Reichskommissar for the Sudeten German territories, October 1, 1938; Gauleiter of the Sudetengau and Reichsstatthalter, May 1, 1939–45.

HESS, RUDOLF. Early member of the Nazi party; deputy of the Führer, 1933–41; head of the Central Party Committee (later called the Office of the Deputy of the Führer), 1932–41; flew to Britain in May 1941 in futile effort to persuade the British to make peace and interned for the duration of the war.

HEYDRICH, REINHARD. SS Obergruppenführer; chief of the SD from 1931; chief of the Sipo and SD, 1936–42; deputy chief of the RSHA, 1939–42; acting Reich protector of Bohemia and Moravia, 1941–42.

HIERL, KONSTANTIN. Reich labor leader, 1933–45.

HILDEBRANDT, RICHARD. SS Obergruppenführer; SS and police officer for the Vistula district, 1939–43; chief of the RuSHA, April 1943–45.

HIMER, GENERAL KURT. German military plenipotentiary in Denmark, April 1940.

HIMMLER, HEINRICH. Reichsführer of the SS, 1929–45; Reichsführer SS and chief of the German police, 1936–45; Reichskommissar for the consolidation of the German people, 1939–45; Reich minister of the interior, August 25, 1943–45.

HINDENBURG, GENERAL PAUL VON. President of the German Republic, 1925–August 2, 1934.

HLINKA, ANDREJ. Roman Catholic priest; founder and leader of the Slovak People's party; died August 1938.

HOFMANN, OTTO. SS Obergruppenführer; chief of the RuSHA, December 1939–April 1943.

HORTHY DE NAGYBÁNYA, MIKLÓS. Admiral in the Austro-Hungarian navy; regent of Hungary, 1920–October 16, 1944.

HÖTTL, DR. WILHELM. Official in the Foreign Intelligence Department of the RSHA.

HOSSBACH, FRIEDRICH. Adjutant to Hitler, 1937; later served in the regular army.

HUGENBERG, DR. ALFRED. German publisher and industrialist; leader of the German Nationalist party; Reich minister of economics and food and agriculture, January 30–June 27, 1933.

JODL, GENERAL ALFRED. Chief of the Wehrmacht Operations Staff of the OKW, October 1939–45.

KALTENBRUNNER, DR. ERNST. SS Obergruppenführer; state secretary for security in Seyss-Inquart's cabinet in Austria, March 1938; chief of the SS in Austria, 1935–38; senior SS and police officer in Vienna, 1938–43; chief of the Sipo and SD, 1943–45; chief of the RSHA, 1943–45.

KEITEL, GENERAL WILHELM. Chief of the OKW, February 4, 1938–45.

KEPPLER, WILHELM. German industrialist; economic adviser to Hitler and the Nazi party from 1932; adviser to Göring as plenipotentiary of the Four-Year Plan; specialist for raw materials in the Four-Year Plan; given absolute authority by Hitler over Reich relations with the Austrian Nazis, July 1937; state secretary for special duties in the Foreign Office, March 1938–45; Reichskommissar in Vienna, March–June 1938; chief of the Office for Soil Research, Reich Ministry of Economics, 1939–45.

KERSTEN, DR. FELIX. Swedish physiotherapist; doctor, masseur, and confidant of Himmler.

KILLINGER, MANFRED VON. SA Obergruppenführer; minister in Slovakia, July 1940–January 1941; in Rumania from January 24, 1941.

KOCH, ERICH. Gauleiter of East Prussia, 1928–45; *Oberpräsident* of East Prussia 1933–45; Reichskommissar for the Ukraine, 1941–44.

KONOYE, PRINCE FUMIMARO. Japanese prime minister, July 16, 1940–October 17, 1941.

KÖRNER, PAUL. State secretary in the Prussian Ministry of State, 1933–45; state secretary and chairman of the Central Office of the Four-Year Plan; deputy chief, Economic Executive Staff East; chairman of the supervisory board of the Hermann Göring Werke.

LAHOUSEN, GENERAL ERWIN. Official of the German counterintelligence (Abwehr).

LAMMERS, DR. HANS. State secretary in the Reich Chancellery from January 1933; chief of the Reich Chancellery, 1934–45.

LEY, DR. ROBERT. Founder and chief of the German Labor Front, 1933–45.

LIST, GENERAL WILHELM. Commander of an army in the Polish and western campaigns; commander of the German army in Rumania until May 21, 1941; commander in chief in the southeast, June–October 1941.

LOEB, GENERAL FRITZ. Head of Goring's special staff to study the German raw materials and foreign exchange situation, May 1936; head of the Office for Raw and Synthetic Materials, Four-Year Plan, October 1936–38.

MAČEK, VLADKO. Leader of the Croatian Peasant party; deputy minister president of Yugoslavia, August 26, 1939–April 7, 1941.

MATSUOKA, YOSUKE. Japanese foreign minister, July 17, 1940–July 16, 1941.

MEISSNER, DR. OTTO. Chief of the Presidential Chancellery, 1920–45.

MEYER-HETLING, KONRAD. Chief of the planning section in the Central Office of the RKFDV.

MICHAEL I. King of Rumania, September 6, 1940–December 30, 1947.

MIKLAS, WILHELM. President of Austria, 1928–March 1938.

MILCH, GENERAL ERHARD. State secretary in the Reich Air Ministry, 1933–45; inspector general of the Luftwaffe, 1939–45; Central Planning Board, Four-Year Plan, 1942–45.

MOLOTOV, VYACHESLAV. Chairman of the Council of People's Commissars of the Soviet Union; people's commissar for foreign affairs from May 1939.

MUSSOLINI, BENITO. Founder and head of the Italian Fascist party; head of the Italian government, prime minister, and commander of the armed forces.

NAUJOCKS, ALFRED HELMUTH. Officer in the SS and SD.

NEUMANN, DR. ERICH. Secretary to the General Council, Four-Year Plan,

1938–39; state secretary in the Central Office, Four-Year Plan, 1938–42; director general, German Potash Syndicate, 1942–45.

NEUMANN, DR. ERNST. Leader of the Memel Nazis.

NEURATH, CONSTANTIN VON. Reich foreign minister, 1932–February 4, 1938; Reich protector of Bohemia and Moravia, March 18, 1939–August 20, 1943.

NOMURA, ADMIRAL KICHISABURO. Japanese foreign minister, September 1939–January 1940; ambassador to the United States, February–December 1941.

OSHIMA, GENERAL HIROSHI. Japanese ambassador to Germany, November 1938–December 1939; again February 1941–45.

OTT, GENERAL EUGEN. German military attaché to Japan, 1934–38; ambassador, 1938–43.

PANCKE, GÜNTHER. SS *Gruppenführer;* chief of the RuSHA, 1938–December 1939; senior SS and police officer for Denmark, November 1943–45.

PAPEN, FRANZ VON. Reich chancellor, June 1–December 2, 1932; vice-chancellor, January 30, 1933–July 1934; Reichskommissar for Prussia, January–August 1933; special plenipotentiary for the Saar, November 1933–June 1934; negotiated Concordat with the Vatican, signed July 20, 1933; minister extraordinary and plenipotentiary on special mission to Austria, August 16, 1934–March 13, 1938; ambassador to Turkey, April 1939–August 1944.

PAUL. Prince Regent of Yugoslavia, October 9, 1934–March 27, 1941.

PAUL-BONCOUR, JOSEPH. French foreign minister, March 13, 1938–April 10, 1938.

PAULUS, GENERAL FRIEDRICH. Deputy chief of the Operations Section, Army General Staff; surrendered with remains of his sixth army at Stalingrad, February 1943.

PÉTAIN, GENERAL HENRI-PHILIPPE. Chief of state in the Vichy government of France, June, 1940–44.

PETER II. King of Yugoslovia, 1934–45 (with Prince Paul as regent until March 27, 1941; in exile following the German invasion in April 1941).

PICKER, DR. HENRY. Representative of the Reich Ministry of the Interior at Hitler's headquarters, 1942.

POPOV, IVAN. Bulgarian foreign minister from February 16, 1940.

QUISLING, VIDKUN. Norwegian defense minister, 1931–33; founder and leader of the Nasjonal Samling party, 1933–45; chief of the Norwegian government, April 1940; minister president of Norway, February 1942–45.

RAEDER, ADMIRAL ERICH. Commander in chief of the German navy, May 1935–January 1943.

RAINER, FRIEDRICH. Leader in the Austrian Nazi party before the Anschluss; Gauleiter of Salzburg, 1938–41; Reichsstatthalter for Salzburg, 1940–41; Gauleiter and Reichsstatthalter of Carinthia, 1941–45; chief of the civil administration of Upper Carniola, 1941–45.

RAUSCHNING, HERMANN. President of the Danzig Senate, June 20, 1933–November 24, 1934.

RIBBENTROP, JOACHIM VON. Adviser to Hitler on foreign affairs and head of the Dienststelle Ribbentrop; ambassador to Britain, October 1936–February 1938; Reich foreign minister, February 1938–45.

RÖHM, ERNST. Chief of staff of the SA; killed June 30, 1934.

ROMMEL, GENERAL ERWIN. Commander of the German Afrika Korps, December 1941–May 1943; commander in chief in northern Italy, 1943; commander of Army Group B in France, November 1943–July 1944.

ROOSEVELT, FRANKLIN DELANO. President of the United States, March 1933–April 12, 1945.

ROSENBERG, ALFRED. Editor of the Nazi party newspaper, *Völkischer Beobachter*, 1921; Reichsleiter and head of the party office for foreign affairs, the *Aussenpolitisches Amt;* Reich minister for the occupied eastern territories, 1941–45.

RUNDSTEDT, GENERAL GERD VON. German army group commander during occupation of the Sudetenland; also during the Polish, western, and Russian campaigns; commander in chief in the west, July 1942–July 1944; Sept. 1944–March 1945.

SAUCKEL, FRITZ. Gauleiter of Thuringia, 1927–45; Reichsstatthalter of Thuringia, 1933–45; plenipotentiary for labor, March 1942–45.

SCHACHT, HJALMAR. President of the Reichsbank, December 1923–December 1930; March 1933–January 1939; acting minister of economics, August 1934–December 1937; plenipotentiary general for military economy, May 1935–December 1937; minister without portfolio, November 1937–January 1943.

SCHIRACH, BALDUR VON. Reich youth leader, 1933–45; Gauleiter and Reichsstatthalter of Vienna, July 1940–45.

SCHLEICHER, GENERAL KURT VON. Reich defense minister, June–December 1932; Reich chancellor, December 1932–January 1933; murdered June 30, 1934.

SCHMITT, KURT. Reich minister of economics, June 1933–August 1934.

SCHNURRE, KARL. Deputy chief, Economic Policy Division, German Foreign Office.

SCHOBERT, GENERAL EUGEN RITTER VON. Commander of the German forces in Rumania, May–September 1941.

SCHUSCHNIGG, KURT VON. Austrian minister of justice, 1932–34; minister of education, 1933–34; federal chancellor, minister of defense and of foreign affairs, July 27, 1934–March 11, 1938.

SCHWARZ, FRANZ XAVER. Nazi party treasurer, 1925–45.

SELDTE, FRANZ. Founder and leader of the Stahlhelm veterans organization; Reich labor minister, 1933–45.

SERRANO-SUÑER, RAMÓN. Spanish minister of the interior, January 1938–October 1940; foreign minister, October 1940–September 1942.

BIOGRAPHICAL SKETCHES

Seyss-Inquart, Arthur. Austrian lawyer; councilor of state, May 1937; minister of the interior and security, February 16, 1938–March 15, 1938; chancellor, March 11–15, 1938; Reichsstatthalter of the Ostmark, March 15, 1938–May 1, 1939; Reich minister without portfolio, May, 1939; deputy governor general of Poland, October 1939–May 1940; Reichskommissar of the Netherlands, May 1940–45.

Sidor, Karol. Member of Slovak People's party; minister without portfolio representing Slovakia in the Czecho-Slovak government, December 1938–March 1939; minister president of the autonomous Slovak government, March 12–14, 1939; minister of the interior in the Slovak government, March 14–15, 1939; Slovak minister to the Holy See, June 1939–45.

Simović, General Dušan. Commander in chief of the Yugoslav air force 1936–38, 1940; chief of the General Staff, 1938–39; led coup d'état against the government of Prince Regent Paul, March 27, 1941; minister president, minister of the interior, and commander in chief of the armed forces, March 27–April 17, 1941.

Speer, Albert. German architect; Reich minister for armaments and munitions and head of the OT, February 1942–45.

Stalin, Josef Vissarionovich. Secretary General of the Central Committee of the Communist party of the Soviet Union and member of the Politburo; chairman of the Council of Ministers and commissar of defense from 1941.

Stohrer, Dr. Eberhard von. German ambassador to Spain, September 19, 1937–January 1, 1943.

Stojadinović, Dr. Milan. Yugoslav minister president and foreign minister, June 24, 1935–June 1939.

Strasser, Gregor. Early member of the Nazi party and a leader of the radical left wing of the movement; resigned as head of the party's Political Organization Department, December 1932 over disagreements with Hitler; murdered June 30, 1934.

Strasser, Dr. Otto. Joined Nazi party in 1925; founded a radical wing of the party, 1930; fled from Germany in 1934.

Stuckart, Wilhelm. State secretary in the Reich Ministry of the Interior, March 1935–45; chief of staff of the plenipotentiary for the administration of the Reich, 1939–45.

Thomas, General Georg. Chief of the Military Economics Staff of the German armed forces (later the OKW), November 1934–39; chief of the Military Economy and Armaments Office of the OKW, 1934–January 1943; general for special assignments with the chief of the OKW, January 1943–44; after failure of attempt to assassinate Hitler in July 1944, sent to a concentration camp.

Tippelskirch, General Kurt von. Deputy chief for intelligence of the Army General Staff.

Tiso, Dr. Jozef. Roman Catholic priest; leader of the Slovak People's party from August 1938; minister president of the autonomous Slovak government, October 1938–March 10, 1939; minister president of Slovakia, March 14–October 26, 1939; president of Slovakia, October 26, 1939–45.

TODT, DR. FRITZ. Inspector general for German highways, 1933–42; founder and chief of the OT; plenipotentiary-general for construction, Four-Year Plan, 1938–42; Reich minister for armaments and munitions, March 17, 1940–42; killed in air crash, February 8, 1942.

TOJO, GENERAL HIDEKI. Japanese minister of war, July 17, 1940–44; prime minister, October 17, 1941–July 18, 1944.

TUKA, DR. VOJTĚCH. Member of the Slovak People's party; deputy minister president of Slovakia, March 14–October 26, 1939; minister president, October 27, 1939–September 1944; foreign minister, July 1940–September 1944.

VEESENMAYER, EDMUND. Member of the Austrian Nazi party; assistant to Wilhelm Keppler, 1933–44; German minister and Reich plenipotentiary in Hungary, March 1944–45.

WEIZSÄCKER, ERNST VON. Head of the Political Department, German Foreign Office, August 1936–38; state secretary, April 1, 1938–April 1943; ambassador to the Holy See, 1943–45.

Notes

PAGE

xi

1. Eberhard Jäckel, in his intelligent analysis of the development of Hitler's ideas (*Hitlers Weltanschauung. Entwurf einer Herrschaft* (Tübingen, 1969), goes so far as to say that "hardly anyone, and perhaps actually no one, among Hitler's followers and contemporaries took the trouble fully to understand this ideology" (p. 159). Some historians still question its importance. E. M. Robertson, for example, writes in *Hitler's Pre-War Policy and Military Plans, 1933–1939* (London, 1963): "Hitler seldom looked more than one move ahead; the view that he had tried to put into operation a programme, carefully formulated in advance, is quite untenable" (p. 1). On this entire problem, see Karl Lange, *Hitlers unbeachtete Maximen. "Mein Kampf" und die Öffentlichkeit* (Stuttgart, 1968), which contains an appendix listing the various publications of *Mein Kampf* abroad. It is interesting—and significant—that no substantive changes were ever made in the many German editions of *Mein Kampf*. Hermann Hammer, "Die deutschen Ausgaben von Hitlers 'Mein Kampf,'" *VfZ* 4 (1956): 161–78; Werner Maser, *Hitlers Mein Kampf. Entstchung, Aufbau, Stil, Anderungen, Quellen, Quellenwert, kommentierte Auszüge* (Munich, 1966).

In a revealing letter of February 6, 1933, one week after the Nazis came to power, Bernhard von Bülow, the state secretary of the German Foreign Office and an intelligent and perceptive observer, wrote to Herbert von Dirksen, the German ambassador to Russia,

> I already realized from your telephone call that there is unrest in Moscow as a result of the Nazis coming to power on January 30. I believe that they overestimate there the importance in terms of foreign policy of the change of government. When they have the responsibility the National Socialists are naturally different people and pursue a different policy than they proclaimed before. It was always like this, and it is the same with all parties. . . . Things are still boiled in water here like everywhere else (*DGFP*, C, 1: 21–22).

xii

2. In a speech to invited representatives of the German press of April 4, 1941, Goebbels explained Nazi tactics with astonishing candor.

> Until now we have succeeded in leaving our opponents in the dark about the real goals of Germany, just as our domestic opponents did not know

266

what we were aiming at until 1932 and that our oath of legality was only a stratagem. We wanted to gain power through legal means, but we did not intend to use it legally. . . . They could have suppressed us; it would not have been so difficult. But they did not. . . . In 1925 they could have put a few of us in jail and everything would have been finished. No, they let us slip through the danger zone. It was exactly the same with foreign policy. . . . In 1933, a French minister president should have said (and if I had been a French minister president I would have said it): the man has become Reich chancellor who wrote the book *Mein Kampf* which says thus and so. Such a man cannot be tolerated as a neighbor. Either he goes, or we march. That would have been thoroughly logical. But it was not done. They left us alone, they allowed us to slip through the danger zone without hindrance, we were able to circumvent the dangerous reefs, and when we were ready, well armed, better than they were, they started the war.

Quoted in the admirable work of Andreas Hillgruber, *Hitlers Strategie. Politik and Kriegsführung, 1940–1941* (Frankfurt am Main, 1965), p. 14, n. 5.

xiii

3. The conclusions reached by H. R. Trevor-Roper on this subject in his article "Hitlers Kriegsziele," *VfZ* 8 (1960): 121–33, seem to me completely convincing. For a sampling of British historical opinion on this controversial problem, see E. M. Robertson, ed., *The Origins of the Second World War: Historical Interpretations* (London, 1971). In his memoris Albert Speer, Hitler's architect and later minister of munitions, wrote that Hitler never revealed to his intimate entourage how literally he took his dream of world dominion, and that some of his advisers thought his ideas had changed by 1938. Speer says,

It seems to me, on the contrary, that Hitler's plans and aims never changed. Sickness and the fear of death merely made him advance his deadlines. His aims could only have been thwarted by superior counter-forces, and in 1938 no such forces were visible. Quite the opposite: the successes of that year encouraged him to go on forcing the already accelerated pace (*Inside the Third Reich* [New York, 1970], pp. 127–28).

4. See Speer's memoirs, *Inside the Third Reich*, especially chapters 5 and 6.
5. This is the central thesis of Edward N. Peterson's work, *The Limits of Hitler's Power* (Princeton, N.J., 1969), which is thoroughly valid for many levels of the German government, but seems to me to attach too little significance to Hitler's ultimate authority as the maker of the big political decisions.

INTRODUCTION

xxv

1. Fritz Fischer, *Germany's Aims in the First World War* (New York, 1967). See also the same author's *Krieg der Illusionen. Die deutsche Politik von 1911 bis 1914* (Düsseldorf, 1969), and Karl-Heinz Janssen, *Macht und Verblendung. Kriegszielpolitik der deutschen Bundesstaaten, 1914–1918* (Göttingen, 1963).
2. Already on November 5, 1916, the Germans had announced the formation of an independent Polish state. After the Bolshevik revolution, Finland, the Baltic states (Estonia, Latvia, Lithuania), and the Ukraine proclaimed their independence from Russia. The Central Powers recognized the independence of the Ukraine on February 1, 1918, and concluded a separate treaty of peace with the Ukraine at Brest-Litovsk on February 9. See Fritz Fischer, *Germany's Aims in the First World War*, chaps. 18–21, and John W. Wheeler-Bennett, *Brest-Litovsk: the Forgotten Peace, March 1918* (London, 1938).

xvi

3. A work comparable to that of Fritz Fischer dealing with the war aims of the Allies is badly needed. A. .J. P. Taylor's article, "The War Aims of the Allies

in the First World War," in *Essays Presented to Sir Lewis Namier*, ed. Richard Pares and A. J. P. Taylor (London, 1956), is suggestive but slight.

xxx

4. Albrecht Mendelssohn-Bartholdy, *The War and German Society* (New Haven, 1927) provides an excellent description of German hopes and disillusionment.

5. Germany's request for peace on the basis of Wilson's Fourteen Points was granted by an Allied note of November 5, 1918.

xxxi

6. That this bill was later drastically reduced and most of it never paid at all could of course have no effect on how Germans felt aboout the reparations problem at the time.

7. This failure was due in part to the refusal of the Germans to submit to an Allied demand that they make their merchant fleet available to a world shipping pool directed from London as a precondition for the delivery of food to Germany. The Germans feared that this would mean the loss of their merchant fleet. They were to lose the greater part of their merchant fleet anyway as a result of the Versailles treaty. See S. L. Bane and R. H. Lutz, eds., *The Blockade of Germany after the Armistice, 1918–1919* (Stanford, Calif., 1942), and Klaus Epstein, *Matthias Erzberger and the Dilemma of German Democracy* (Princeton, N.J., 1959), pp. 293–94.

xxxii

8. Alan Bullock's biography, *Hitler: A Study in Tyranny* (paperback, New York, 1964), is masterful. Franz Jetzinger, *Hitler's Youth* (London, 1958), contains much valuable information, which has been ampified and in some cases corrected in the more balanced work of Bradley F. Smith, *Adolf Hitler: His Family, Childhood, and Youth* (Stanford, Calif., 1967).

xxxiii

9. In his memoirs, written under the sentence of death in Nuremberg, Hans Frank, at one time Hitler's foremost legal adviser and, after 1939, governor general of occupied Poland, stated that at Hitler's request he had conducted investigations into the Führer's ancestry in 1930 in response to a threat of blackmail. In the course of those investigations, Frank says, he discovered that Hitler's father was the illegitimate son of Maria Anna Schicklgruber and a Jew named Frankenberger. Frank's story, however, is so full of demonstrable errors and contradictions that it cannot be considered even as hypothetical evidence, valuable though this might be as a psychological explanation for Hitler's anti-Semitism. In his final remarks on this subject, for example, Frank says, "That Adolf Hitler certainly had no Jewish blood in his veins seems to me so strikingly demonstrated by his entire manner [*scheint mir aus seiner ganzen Art dermassen eklatant erwiesen*] that nothing further needs to be said on the subject." He does so nevertheless, and in the same paragraph goes on to say, "I must therefore say that it is not altogether impossible that Hitler's father was consequently a half-Jew, the product of the illegitimate relationship of the Schicklgruber and the Jew from Graz" (*Im Angestcht des Galgens. Deutung Hitlers und seiner Zeit auf Grund eigener Erlebnisse und Erkenntnisse* [Munich, 1953], pp. 330–31.) Bradley Smith is almost certainly correct in dismissing Franz Jetzinger's curiously uncritical and extravagant faith in Frank's story. (Adolf Hitler, 157–60.)

10. William A. Jenks, *Vienna and the Young Hitler* (New York, 1960).

xxxiv

11. Wilfried Daim, *Der Mann, der Hitler die Ideen gab. Von den religiösen Verirrungen eines Sektierers zum Rassenwahn des Diktators* (Munich, 1958).

12. *Mein Kampf* (New York, 1939). While citing from the American (Reynal and Hitchcock) translation of *Mein Kampf*, I have frequently used my own translation of quoted passages on the basis of the 1934 German edition of Hitler's book.

The autobiographical sections of *Mein Kampf* are often inaccurate and deliberately misleading; Hitler's ideology was by no means completely developed at this time, as Eberhard Jäckel (*Hitlers Weltanschauung. Entwurf einer Herrschaft* [Tübingen, 1969]) has convincingly demonstrated. Yet there is no reason to doubt the strength of the impressions Hitler formed during his Vienna years.

xxxvii

13. With respect to Hitler's emphasis on the power of the will, Ulrich von Hassell, who became a member of the anti-Nazi resistance, recorded in his diary a joke circulating in Germany in 1941 about an imaginary conversation between Albert Speer, Hitler's architect, and the conductor Wilhelm Furtwängler:

> FURTWÄNGLER: "It must be splendid to be able to build in the truly grand manner according to one's own ideas!"
> SPEER: "Just imagine if someone said to you: 'It is my unshakeable will that from now on the Ninth Symphony is to be performed exclusively on a mouth organ'" (*Vom andern Deutschland* [Zürich, 1946], 185).

xli

14. Speech in Posen, April 10, 1943. *IMT*, 1919-PS 29:110–73.

1. THE IDEOLOGY OF EXPANSION

3

1. The major sources for the study of Hitler's ideology are his writings in which he purposefully set out to explain that ideology to his followers. The most important of these are the two volumes of *Mein Kampf*, written between 1924 and 1926, in which he endeavored to "set down in permanent form" the basic elements of his doctrine, and a sequel to *Mein Kampf*, written in 1928, which restates most of the arguments set forth in the first two volumes, but which Hitler never published, presumably because he did not feel that the year 1928 was an opportune time for doing so. This volume was discovered among the captured Nazi documents after the war by Gerhard L. Weinberg, and was subsequently published in Germany as *Hitlers zweites Buch. Ein Dokument aus dem Jahre 1928* (Stuttgart, 1961) and in America as *Hitler's Secret Book* (New York, 1961).

Hitler's extraordinary adherence to the principles set forth in *Mein Kampf* can be seen in his secret speeches and policy directives to the highest officials of his government: for example his speech to leading generals and admirals of Feb. 3, 1933 (the literature on this meeting is reviewed by Gerhard L. Weinberg, *The Foreign Policy of Hitler's Germany: Diplomatic Revolution in Europe, 1933–1936* [Chicago, 1970], pp. 26–27); the minutes of a ministerial meeting of February 8, 1933 (*DGFP*, C, 1:35–37); his speech to a group of German industrialists of February 20, 1933 (*IMT*, 203-D, 35:42–48); his conferences with army leaders of February 27–28, 1934 (Weinberg, *Foreign Policy*, p. 178); his memorandum for Göring, written in 1936, about the need for an economic Four-Year Plan ("Hitlers Denkschrift zum Vierjahresplan, 1936," ed. Wilhelm Treue, *VfZ* 3 [1955]:184–210; see below, pp. 64–66); his exposition of his future plans to his senior military and diplomatic officials on November 5, 1937 (the famous Hossbach memorandum, *IMT*, 386-PS, 25:402–13; for a critical examination of this document, see below, p. 97, n. 17); and his speech to his military leaders of August 22, 1939 (for the literature on this document, see below, p. 129, n. 20).

The same ideological continuity can be observed in the records of Hitler's wartime conversations kept by Dr. Henry Picker, an official assigned to Hitler's wartime headquarters (*Hitlers Tischgespräche im Führerhauptquartier, 1941–1942*, ed. Percy Ernst Schramm, Andreas Hillgruber, and Martin Vogt, [Stuttgart, 1965]). Even more valuable, because they cover a longer period of time, are the records of Hitler's conversations preserved by his private secretary Martin Bormann (*Hitler's Secret Conversations, 1941–1944* [New York, 1961]). Although only English and French translations of these Bormann records are available, I do not share the view of Professor Schramm that they cannot be accepted as reliable historical evidence. They correspond closely to the Picker records, on which some of them were almost certainly based. Bormann undoubtedly edited his notes of Hitler's conversations (as did Picker), and upon occasion he used them as a basis for drawing up orders in Hitler's name. In doing so, he almost certainly placed his own interpretation on Hitler's views, yet it was precisely because of Bormann's ability to interpret his ideas and intentions so accurately that Hitler cherished Bormann's services. From everything that is known about Bormann personally, it would appear that he was too much the creature of Hitler and himself too stolid and unimaginative to have formulated policies of his own which ran counter to Hitler's intentions, or to have inserted anything significant of his own in his chronicle of Hitler's views. In comparing both the Picker and Bormann records with the large amount of other contemporary evidence available dealing with the material they cover, I have found no reason to suspect the reliability of either.

More dubious are the fascinating records of Hermann Rauschning, the president of the Danzig Senate from June 1933 to November 1934, of his conversations with Hitler between 1932 and 1934 (*Hitler Speaks* [London, 1939]; American ed. *The Voice of Destruction* [New York, 1940]) which appear to have been edited to make them more relevant to the events surrounding the outbreak of the war.

Hitler's public speeches and official conversations, geared as they were to the needs and audiences of the moment, are valuable chiefly for the study of Hitler's tactics.

2. *Mein Kampf,* pp. 358, 403, 574, 579–81, 592–602, and elsewhere; *Hitler's Secret Conversations,* pp. 103–4, 215, 252.

3. On this subject, see the documents and illustrations assembled by George L. Mosse, ed., *Nazi Culture: Intellectual, Cultural and Social Life in the Third Reich* (New York, 1966); and Hermann Glaser, *Spiesser-Ideologie. Von der Zerstörung des deutschen Geistes im 19. and 20. Jahrhundert* (Freiburg, 1964).

4. *Mein Kampf,* pp. 124, 224.

5. This idea was not always quite so categorically stated. Hitler occasionally conceded that lesser breeds might produce lesser cultures. But see *Mein Kampf,* p. 581: "In this world human culture and civilization are inseparably bound up with the existence of the Aryan. His dying-off or his decline would again lower upon this earth the dark veils of a time without culture." And p. 594: "It is only the Aryan who is endowed with the glorious, creatively active ability."

4

6. Hitler, although contemptuous of Christianity, was nevertheless profoundly aware of the importance of faith in human affairs. "The great masses of people do not consist of philosophers, and it is just for them that faith is frequently the sole basis for a moral view of life" (*Mein Kampf,* pp. 364–65).

7. *Der Mythus des 20. Jahrhunderts* (Munich, 1930), pp. 114, 278–79, 539, 681–84, and elsewhere. To critics of the *Mythus,* Rosenberg replied that the essential message for his epoch would retain its validity "even if the whole *historical* proof were to be refuted at every point." (*An die Dunkelmänner unserer Zeit* [Munich, 1935], p. 6.) Hitler himself had nothing but contempt for Rosenberg's book, which he insisted should not be regarded as an expression of official party doctrine, in the first place because its title gave a completely false impression. Far from being the myth of the twentieth century, National Socialism should be regarded as a scientific answer to the myths of the nineteenth century (*Hitler's Secret Conversations,* p. 400).

8. *Mein Kampf,* pp. 895, 899, 902.

5

9. *Mein Kampf,* pp. 899–900, 902, 974, and elsewhere; *Hitler's Secret Book,* pp. 125, 127–29, 132, 141, and elsewhere.

10. *Mein Kampf,* pp. 959 ff.

11. *Mein Kampf,* pp. 141, 171; *Hitler's Secret Book,* pp. 8, 10, 12, 18, and elsewhere.

12. *Mein Kampf,* 172–74, 177, 935, 944; *Hitler's Secret Book,* pp. 15, 96, and chap. 9; Hossbach memorandum of Hitler conference of November 5, 1937, *IMT,* 386-PS, 25:404–5. In an article of January 1938, Herbert Backe, state secretary in the Reich Ministry for Food and Agriculture, wrote, "In our fight for increased production we are now approaching that point (perhaps we have already reached it) at which any further increase in agricultural production, as necessary as it is from a national standpoint, no longer strengthens but weakens our agricultural undertakings" ("Die agrarpolitische Lage," *Die deutsche Volkswirtschaft,* Jan. 1938).

6

13. *Mein Kampf,* pp. 172–74, 177, 935, 944; *Hitler's Secret Book,* pp. 15, 96; *The Goebbels Diaries, 1942–1943,* ed. Louis P. Lochner (New York, 1948), pp. 357–59.

14. *Mein Kampf,* pp. 177, 888–91, 935, 950, 962, and elsewhere; Hossbach memorandum, *IMT,* 386-PS, 25:402 ff.

7

15. *Mein Kampf,* pp. 178, 187, 944, 950; *Hitler's Secret Book,* pp. 14, 71, 139.

16. *Mein Kampf,* pp. 181, 949–50, 965–66, 978–79; *Hitler's Secret Book,* chaps. 5–8.

17. *Mein Kampf,* pp. 951–52.

8

18. *Mein Kampf,* pp. 178, 534, 552–57, 944, 951–52, 955, 964, and elsewhere.

19. It will be recalled that by Germanization Hitler did not mean the Germanization of Jews or Slavs, which he believed to be impossible, but the elimination of all such alien races and the Germanization of only those peoples the Nazis could classify as Germans but who might have forgotten or repudiated their Germanic heritage after generations of living under foreign rule.

The idea also worked the other way round. A German could not escape his commitments. In a speech at the 1936 Nuremberg party congress, Gauleiter Ernst Bohle said, "The Führer had to come in order to hammer into all of us the fact that the German cannot choose and may not choose whether or not he will be German but that he was sent into this world by God as a German, that God thereby had laid upon him as a German duties of which he cannot divest himself without committing treason to providence" (*NCA* 2:472).

20. *Mein Kampf,* pp. 403, 591; *Hitler's Secret Book,* pp. 44–48; Hossbach memorandum, *IMT,* 386-PS, 25:402 ff.

9

21. *Mein Kampf,* pp. 182, 594–96, 888, 944; *Hitler's Secret Book,* pp. 12, 34, 46–47; Hossbach memorandum.

22. *Mein Kampf,* pp. 187–88; Hossbach memorandum.

23. *Mein Kampf,* chaps. 13–15; *Hitler's Secret Book,* chaps. 14–16; Walter W. Pese, "Hitler und Italien, 1920–1926," *VfZ* 3 (1955): 113–26; Klaus Hildebrand, *Deutsche Aussenpolitik, 1933–1945. Kalkül oder Dogma?* (Stuttgart, 1971).

24. By the time of the conference of November 5, 1937, recorded by Colonel Hossbach (*IMT,* 386-PS, 25:402 ff.), Hitler was definitely counting on British opposition to a German drive to the east. His pessimism about Britain was undoubtedly reinforced by Joachim von Ribbentrop, his ambassador to London from October 1936 to February 1938, whose crude efforts to bring about an alliance were a sorry failure and whose attitude toward Britain was permanently soured as a result. Ribbentrop became German foreign minister in February 1938. On this question, see Hildebrand, *Deutsche Aussenpolitik,* pp. 55–63.

10

25. *Mein Kampf,* p. 893.

26. *Mein Kampf,* p. 994; Hossbach memorandum, *IMT,* 386-PS, 25:402 ff.

27. *Mein Kampf,* p. 599.

11

1. Hitler order of January 11, 1940, *Fuehrer Directives and Other Top-Level Directives of the German Armed Forces, 1939–1941*, vol. 1 (Washington, 1948), p. 81; also Hitler's conference of May (?) 1939, *IMT*, 079-L, 37:556. Although the date of this document is suspect (see below, p. 124, n. 9), there is no reason to doubt that the conference itself took place. See also Lammers's testimony, *IMT*, 11: 91, 102.

12

2. This intention was most sharply emphasized in dealing with the heads of the German occupation governments. A circular from Lammers, the head of the Reich Chancellery, to the heads of the governments of the German-occupied territories of June 15, 1940, informed them of Hitler's desire for monthly political and economic reports. At the specific instructions of the Führer, however, these reports were not to be sent to any other Reich or party offices. The heads of the occupation governments were directly responsible to the Führer and consequently not subject to the authority of other Reich agencies (Nuremberg document NG 1273). See also Lammers to the Reich minister of the interior, June 17, 1940 (Reich Chancellery file 1343, WF, serial 5246H, frame E311797), and the government memorandum of October 7, 1941, listing the powers delegated to the various individuals and agencies in all German-occupied territories and the decrees by which this power was delegated (NG 1151).

3. Germany was a federal union of states (Länder) that had been independent before 1871, e.g., Prussia, Bavaria, Württemberg, Baden.

4. On this problem, see the brilliant work of Ernst Fraenkel, *The Dual State: A Contribution to the Theory of Dictatorship* (New York, 1941).

13

5. See below.

6. *Mein Kampf*, pp. 579, 592–96; Ernst Rudolf Huber, *Verfassungsrecht des grossdeutschen Reiches* (Hamburg, 1939), pp. 164–66. The term *Volk* as used by the Nazis implies more than the English words *folk* or *people*, and embraces the general concept of a racial-national ethnic group.

14

7. See, for example, M. Eichler, "Die nationalsozialistische Rassenpolitik," *Du bist sofort im Bilde* (Erfurt, 1939), pp. 37, 54; *Mein Kampf*, pp. 628–30; *Hitler's Secret Conversations* (New York, 1961), p. 109.

8. The member of a *Volk*, in this case of the German racial-national community; a "fellow countryman," or more literally, "racial comrade."

9. *Organisationsbuch der NSDAP* (Munich, 1940), p. 466; E. R. Huber, *Verfassungsrecht*, pp. 361, 366.

10. Alfred Rosenberg, *Mythus des 20. Jahrhunderts* (Munich, 1930), p. 477.

11. Gottfried Neesse, *Die Nationalsozialistische Deutsche Arbeiterpartei. Ver such einer Rechtsdeutung* (Stuttgart, 1935), pp. 139–40.

15

12. *Mein Kampf*, pp. 134, 460, 465, 480, 595; *Hitler's Secret Book* (New York, 1961), chap. 3.

13. *Mein Kampf*, pp. 224, 582.

14. Conception of the world, or as used by Hitler, an intrinsic racial-national philosophy or spirit.

15. *Mein Kampf*, pp. 479–89.

16. Joseph Goebbels, *Wesen und Gestalt des Nationalsozialismus* (Berlin, 1934), p. 6; Otto Gauweiler, *Rechtseinrichtungen und Rechtsaufgaben der Bewegung* (Munich, 1939), p. 2; Herbert Scurla, *Die Grundgedanken des Nationalsozialismus und das Ausland* (Berlin, 1938), pp. 9, 13; Neesse, *NSDAP*, pp. 126, 131; *Organisationsbuch der NSDAP*, pp. 486–87.

16

17. *Mein Kampf,* pp. 465, 480; Huber, *Verfassungsrecht,* pp. 293–96; Neesse, *NSDAP,* pp. 139–40.

18. *Mein Kampf,* p. 468; Baldur von Schirach, *Die Hitler Jugend. Idee und Gestalt* (Berlin, 1934), p. 17.

19. *Mein Kampf,* p. 636. In his book *The German Dictatorship: The Origins, Structure, and Effects of National Socialism* (New York, 1970), Karl Dietrich Bracher writes: "The earliest visible breakthrough [of the Nazi party] was accomplished among the students. Here generational problems and activist enthusiasm for radical solutions, anti-Republican attitudes of many student groups, and poor future prospects coalesced. . . . To stand outside and against the 'system' was considered good form" (p. 164). See also his section on The New Education and the World of Knowledge, pp. 259–72, with its excellent references.

3. THE ATTAINMENT AND CONSOLIDATION OF POWER

17

1. Two encyclopedic volumes have been written on the fall of the Weimar Republic and the triumph of Nazism. Karl Dietrich Bracher, *Die Auflösung der Weimarer Republik. Eine Studie zum Problem des Machtverfalls in der Demokratie* (Villingen, 1960); and Karl Dietrich Bracher, Wolfgang Sauer, and Gerhard Schulz, *Die nationalsozialistische Machtergreifung. Studien zur Errichtung des totalitären Herrschaftssystems in Deutschland 1933/34* (Cologne, 1962). See also the excellent chapters in Alan Bullock, *Hitler: A Study in Tyranny* (New York, 1964); Bracher's briefer work, *The German Dictatorship: The Origins, Structure, and Effects of National Socialism* (New York, 1970); and Eliot Barculo Wheaton, *The Nazi Revolution, 1933–1935: Prelude to Calamity* (New York, 1969).

2. Kurt Ludecke, *I Knew Hitler: The Story of a Nazi Who Escaped the Blood Purge* (New York, 1937), pp. 234–35.

18

3. "Was wollen wir im Reichstag?" *Der Angriff,* Apr. 30, 1928; see also his *Wesen und Gestalt des Nationalsozialismus* (Berlin, 1934), pp. 12–13.

4. Published in the *Frankfurter Zeitung,* Sept. 26, 1930. Quoted in Bullock, *Hitler,* pp. 161–62.

5. Ernst Rudolf Huber, *Verfassungsrecht des grossdeutschen Reiches* (Hamburg, 1939), p. 31.

6. *Hitler's Secret Conversations, 1941–1944* (May 21, 1942) (paperback, New York, 1961), p. 467.

19

7. These and subsequent statistics may be found in *Schulthess' Europäischer Geschichtskalender* for the appropriate years, and the works of Bracher, Bullock, and Wheaton, cited above.

20

8. Raymond J. Sontag believes the drop in the Nazis' vote may have been due to Reich Chancellor Papen's efforts to discipline them for their failure to respond to his conciliatory gestures; the flow of contributions from industrialists and other nationalists declined sharply, and the courts showed new harshness in punishing Nazi excesses (*A Broken World, 1919–1939* [New York, 1971], pp. 162–63).

9. J. Goebbels, *My Part in Germany's Fight* (London, 1938), p. 189.

21

10. Bracher, *Die Auflösung,* chap. 10; Wheaton, *Nazi Revolution,* chaps. 6–7. Papen's memoirs, *Der Wahrheit eine Gasse* (Munich, 1952), fail to live up to their title and are generally misleading. For Hitler's version of these events, see *Hitler's Secret Conversations,* pp. 466–72.

11. *Hitler's Secret Conversations,* p. 467; on the importance of "legality" for German public opinion, see Bracher, *German Dictatorship,* p. 192, and the superb analysis of Bullock, *Hitler,* pp. 253 ff.

22

12. Presidential order to dissolve the Reichstag, February 1, 1933, *RGBl* (1933) 1:45.

13. *My Part in Germany's Fight*, p. 211.

14. *RGBl* (1933) 1:35.

15. *RGBl* (1933) 1: 43.

16. The best available biography of Göring is Roger Manvell and Heinrich Fraenkel, *Göring* (New York, 1962); there is an interesting brief sketch in Joachim C. Fest, *The Face of the Third Reich: Portraits of the Nazi Leadership* (New York, 1970), pp. 71–82; Göring's own testimony at Nuremberg (*IMT* 9) is very revealing, as are the notes of the prison psychologist G. M. Gilbert, *Nuremberg Diary* (New York, 1947).

23

17. Quoted in Willi Frischauer, *Goering* (London, 1950), p. 13.

24

18. Konrad Heiden, *A History of National Socialism* (New York, 1935), pp. 236–7; Göring testimony, *IMT* 9:251.

19. Hermann Rauschning, *The Voice of Destruction* (New York, 1940), p. 77. "Revisionist" interpretations of the Reichstag fire make a convincing case that the fire was not, in fact, started by the Nazis (Fritz Tobias, *The Reichstag Fire* [New York, 1964] and Hans Mommsen, "Der Reichstagsbrand und seine politischen Folgen," *Das Parlament* 46 [1964]:3–46). The evidence is reviewed in Wheaton, *Nazi Revolution*, pp. 251–64, and Bracher, *German Dictatorship*, p. 199 and n. 14.

20. *RGBl* (1933) 1:83; E. Fraenkel, *The Dual State: A Contribution to the Theory of Dictatorship* (New York, 1941), p. 20; Werner Best, *Die deutsche Polizei* (Darmstadt, 1941), p. 24.

21. Bracher, *German Dictatorship*, pp. 207–8, 428, 465.

25

22. The Enabling Act was passed March 23, published March 24, *RGBl* (1933) 1:141; renewed January 20, 1937 and January 30, 1939, *RGBl* (1937) 1:105; (1939) 1:95. For a review of the extensive literature on the passage of the act, see Wheaton, *Nazi Revolution*, pp. 295–300, 526–27.

23. This was to be the case, for example, with Austria, the Sudetenland, Eupen, and Malmédy, as will be seen in the second volume of this work.

24. *RGBl* (1933) 1:479, 723.

25. *RGBl* (1934) 1:747–52, 785, 973, 1235.

26

26. *Gleichschaltung*, a term stemming from the science of electricity, meant more than "co-ordination" or "synchronization" when used in a political context; it implied a sort of leveling process, and when used in connection with foreign countries it meant the gearing of those countries to German needs and practices.

27. *RGBl* (1933) 1:153, 173, 225, 233, 293, 736.

28. *Gau* is an old German word for province or district, and was used by the Nazis to describe their party (not state) administrative districts. The Gauleiter was the head of such party districts. See below, pp. 29–30.

29. *RGBl* (1933) 1:233.

30. *RGBl* (1934) 1:75. The Nazis called this the Second Organic Statute of the Third Reich. See Carl Schmitt, *Das Reichsstatthaltergesetz* (Berlin, 1934).

31. The Third Organic Statute of the Third Reich, *RGBl* (1935) 1:65.

27

32. *RGBl* (1935) 1: 49.

4. THE INSTRUMENTS OF CONTROL: THE NATIONAL SOCIALIST PARTY

28

1. Dr. Robert Ley, head of the German Labor Front, quoted in *Der Angriff*, April 9, 1942.

29

2. E. R. Huber, *Verfassungsrecht des grossdeutschen Reiches* (Hamburg, 1939), pp. 194–98, 213–14, 223, 288, 410; G. Neesse, *Die Nationalsozialistische Deutsche Arbeiterpartei. Versuch einer Rechtsdeutung* (Stuttgart, 1935) pp. 59, 143, 146; *Organisationsbuch der NSDAP*; Hans Lammers, "Die Staatsführung im Dritten Reich," *Reichsverwaltungsblatt*, 59, no. 28 (Berlin, July 9, 1938).

3. OSS, *Civil Affairs Handbook. Germany*, section 2; *Government and Administration*, Army Service Forces Manual M356–2 (Washington, D.C., 1944), pp. 48–49; hereafter cited as OSS, *Germany*.

4. When the period of Nazi territorial expansion began, new Gaus (called *Reichsgaue*) were created. There was also a special nonterritorial Gau, the Organization for Germans Abroad (*Auslandsorganisation*, or AO), which embodied the concept that ethnic Germans who had been forcibly deprived of their German statehood or who had emigrated abroad were still members of the German national community and should be represented by a party organization.

5. Administrative districts of the ancient German Empire (the First Reich), a term which remained in use during the Second and Third Reichs.

6. A group of small administrative units, usually towns and villages; a term invented by the Nazis.

7. The Zell was a party organization of persons within the army, police, factories, or offices; whereas the Block, like the Gau or Kreis, was a territorial administrative unit.

30

8. OSS, *Civil Affairs Handbook. Germany*, section 2A, suppl., *The National Socialist Party*, Army Service Forces Manual M356–2A (Washington, D.C., 1944); hereafter cited as OSS, *National Socialist Party*. See also *Organisationsbuch der NSDAP*; K. D. Bracher, *The German Dictatorship: The Origins, Structure, and Effects of National Socialism* (New York, 1970), Part 5; Lammers testimony, *IMT* 11:36–37, 93; Stuckart testimony, *IMT* 8:736 ff.

31

9. There is a brief summary of Hess's career in *IMT* 1:282. Hitler's order of July 27, 1934, giving Hess authority to participate in the drafting of legislation, *IMT* (138-D) 35:16–17; also orders of April 6, 1935 and April 17, 1938 (140-D) 35:19–20. Further definitions of the position of Hess, laws of September 24, 1935 and January 26, 1937, *RGBl* (1935) 1:1203; (1937) 1:39. On the functions of Hess, Lammers testimony, *IMT* 11:36–37; E. R. Huber, *Verfassungsrecht*, pp. 223 ff.

Hess's actual influence was never so great as his position and powers would suggest. See the brief appraisal in J. C. Fest, *Face of the Third Reich: Portraits of the Nazi Leadership* (New York, 1970), pp. 187–97. The most recent biography is J. Bernard Hutton, *Hess: The Man and His Mission* (New York, 1971.)

10. On Hess's flight to Scotland, see James Douglas-Hamilton, *Motive for a Mission: The Story behind Hess's Flight to Britain* (New York, 1971), by the son of the duke of Hamilton whom Hess approached about a peace settlement. Various medical opinions have been collected by J. R. Rees, *The Case of Rudolf Hess: A Problem in Diagnosis and Forensic Psychiatry* (New York, 1948.)

On the change in the status of the Party Chancellery, see the decrees of May 29, 1941, and January 1, 1942, *RGBl* (1941) 1:295; (1942) 1:35; also Nuremberg document D-141; National Archives document T454/20/898; and Lammers testimony, *IMT* 11:92–93.

11. On Bormann's personal life, the most illuminating documents are *The Bormann Letters: The Private Correspondence between Martin Bormann and His Wife, from January 1943 to April 1945*, edited by H. R. Trevor-Roper (London, 1954.) See also Joseph Wulf's biography, *Martin Bormann. Hitlers Schatten* (Gütersloh, 1962); the sketch in Fest, *Face of the Third Reich*, pp. 125–35; H. R. Trevor-Roper, "Martin Bormann," *Der Monat*, no. 68, May 1954; and Albert Speer's trenchant comments (*Inside the Third Reich*, [New York, 1970] pp. 103–4). The as yet unpublished memoirs of General Reinhard Gehlen, former head of the West German intelligence service, are said to contain information that Bormann was in fact a Soviet agent, and that he escaped to Russia at the

end of the war (*New York Times*, September 5, 1971). It is possible that Bormann negotiated with the Russians toward the end of the war, as did other Nazi leaders, but all existing evidence about Bormann and the entire record of his life makes the Russian spy story seem most improbable.

32

12. Hitler decree of January 16, 1942, *RGBl* (1942) 1:35; Bormann circular of April 2, 1942, on the functions of the Party Chancellery, *IMT* 40:1–3; Lammers testimony, *IMT* 11:92–93; Burgsdorff testimony, *IMT* 12:57–58. See above all Bormann's records of Hitler's table talk, collected in *Hitler's Secret Conversations, 1941–1944* (paperback, New York, 1961).

13. The Storm Troops, or more literally, Assault or Attack Division.

14. The Guard Echelon.

15. On the SA, see K. D. Bracher, W. Sauer, and G. Schulz, *Die nationalsozialistische Machtergreifung* (Cologne, 1962), pp. 829 ff., with comprehensive references. Also Heinrich Bennecke, an early member of the organization, *Hitler und die SA* (Munich, 1962.)

33

16. The story of the formation and operation of the Göring-Himmler alliance is obscure and veiled in rumor, as is the case with most political intrigues. The version of Hans Gisevius, at one time a member of the Gestapo and the German counterintelligence (*Abwehr*) is plausible but not necessarily reliable. *To the Bitter End* (Boston, 1947), pp. 109–10, 116, 166, 173.

17. It will probably never be possible to write a full biography of Himmler dealing with all his machinations and organizations. The work of Roger Manvell and Heinrich Fraenkel, *Heinrich Himmler* (London, 1965) does an excellent job with the materials available.

34

18. See the fascinating records of Himmler's doctor-masseur Felix Kersten, *The Kersten Memoirs, 1940–1945* (London, 1956). The American edition of this work is so poorly edited as to make it worthless.

19. How Himmler achieved this control remains one of the great puzzles in the history of the Third Reich. Even the exhaustive work of Bracher, *Die nationalsozialistische Machtergreifung*, does no more than list the dates when Himmler gained control of the various state (Länder) police departments (p. 539).

35

20. For more detailed accounts and references to the massive literature on this subject, see Bracher, ibid., pp. 897 ff.; and E. B. Wheaton, *The Nazi Revolution, 1933–1935: Prelude to Calamity* (paperback, New York, 1969), pp. 479 ff.

21. On the SS, see Bibliography, 8. The Himmler Organizations. Himmler delivered innumerable and interminable speeches on the history and functions of the SS. See for example his speech of January 1937, *IMT*, 1992(A)-PS, 29:206–34; of January 19, 1935, National Archives film T175/89/2611516–35; of February 18, 1937, T175/89/2611828–906.

22. *Völkischer Beobachter*, January 30, 1935.

23. *Hitler's Secret Conversations* (January 3–4, 1942), p. 178.

36

24. See George H. Stein, *The Waffen SS: Hitler's Elite Guard at War, 1939–45* (Ithaca, N.Y., 1966); Hitler's comments of August 6, 1940, on the Waffen-SS as a postwar security police troop, *IMT*, 665-D, 35:355–58; Keitel testimony, *IMT* 10:496–97, 535–37; Jodl testimony, *IMT* 15:442–43, 559–60.

25. *RGBl* (1933) 1:1016; also law of March 29, 1935, *RGBl* (1935) 1:502.

26. *Mein Kampf*, p. 479.

27. "The party must always continue to represent the hierarchy of National Socialist leadership. This minority must always insist upon its prerogative to control the state." Goebbels, *Wesen und Gestalt des Nationalsozialismus* (Berlin, 1934), p. 19; 0. Gauweiler, *Rechtseinrichtungen und Rechtsaufgaben der Bewegung* (Munich, 1939), p. 9.

37

28. Lammers testimony, *IMT* 11:93.
29. Quoted in *Deutsche Justiz*, 1935, p. 73.

5. THE INSTRUMENTS OF CONTROL: THE STATE

38

1. E. R. Huber, *Verfassungsrecht des grossdeutschen Reiches* (Hamburg, 1939), pp. 223, 230, 410.

39

2. Meissner's memoirs, *Staatssekretär unter Ebert-Hindenburg-Hitler. Der Schicksalsweg des deutschen Volkes von 1918–1945, wie ich ihn erlebte* (Hamburg, 1950), provide little insight into the actual operation of the Nazi government. More revealing is Meissner's affidavit of July 8, 1946, *IMT* 40:401–5, 408–15.
3. Lammers testimony, quoted in *TWC* 12:976–83; also Lammers affidavit, Nuremberg document NG 1364.

40

4. *TWC* 12:301–10.
5. See below, pp. 53–54.

41

6. See below, pp. 53–54.
7. As minister of food and agriculture by the Nazi agrarian theorist R. Walther Darré; as minister of economics, first by Kurt Schmitt, then by acting minister Hjalmar Schacht, by Göring, and finally by Walter Funk. See below, pp. 67–68.
8. Lammers testimony, *IMT* 11:54–55; Göring testimony, *IMT* 9:367. A list of the members and associates of Hitler's cabinet is provided in *TWC* 12:120–25.

42

9. OSS, *Germany*, pp. 141–45.
10. *RGBl* (1933) 1:175. On this entire question, see Hans Mommsen, *Beamtentum im Dritten Reich. Mit ausgewählten Quellen zur nationalsozialistischen Beamtenpolitik* (Stuttgart, 1966).
11. *RGBl* (1937) 1:39.

43

12. There is surprisingly little literature on Frick, who refused to testify at Nuremberg and who wrote no memoirs.
13. *DDP* 2:118–21.

45

14. Prosecution statement on Stuckart, *TWC* 12:204–8; defense statement, 316–32; Globke affidavit, Nuremberg document NG 3540; Stuckart affidavit, NG 3710; Lammers testimony, *IMT* 11:56–61. On the Reich Ministry of the Interior in general, see OSS, *Germany*, pp. 76 ff.
15. See Bibliography, 8. The Himmler Organizations, and K. D. Bracher, W. Sauer, and G. Schulz, *Die nationalsozialistische Machtergreifung* (Cologne, 1962), pp. 427 ff., 536 ff., with its copious references.
16. H. Göring, *Germany Reborn* (London, 1934), p. 121.
17. *RGBl* (1933) 1:83; see above, p. 24.
18. Bracher, *Die nationalsozialistische Machtergreifung*, pp. 434–35.

46

19. *Preussische Gesetzsammlung*, 1933, pp. 122, 413; 1934, p. 143; 1936, pp. 21–22; Gisevius testimony, *IMT* 12:171.
20. Bracher, *Die nationalsozialistische Machtergreifung*, pp. 434–35, 539 ff., with references; Diels affidavit, *IMT* 30:547–49, 569–71. See Himmler's account of the history and development of the political police, March 5, 1936, National Archives film T175/89/2611660–707; the exchange of letters between Heydrich and Daluege on the position of the political police, T175/123/2648591–615; an official memorandum on the same subject, Nuremberg document NO 4272; and H. Gisevius, *To the Bitter End* (Boston, 1947), pp. 114 ff.
21. *RGBl* (1936) 1:487–88; (1937) 1:653.
22. Lammers testimony, *IMT* 11:59–60.

23. On Heydrich there is a somewhat impressionistic biography by Charles Wighton, *Heydrich: Hitler's Most Evil Henchman* (Philadelphia, 1962); and the sketch in J. C. Fest, *The Face of the Third Reich: Portraits of the Nazi Leadership* (New York, 1970), pp. 98–110, 335–39.

47

24. Cited in the party decree of December 14, 1938, *IMT*, 3385-PS, 32:250–51; Höttl affidavit, *IMT* 11:228–29.

48

25. See Fest, *Face of the Third Reich*, pp. 100–101, 335–37, with references.
26. "10 Jahre Sicherheitspolizei und SD," *Die deutsche Polizei*, February 1, 1943, as reproduced in *IMT*, 1680-PS, 27:441 ff.
27. Himmler decree of August 28, 1936, cited in "10 Jahre Sicherheitspolizei und SD," pp. 444–45; further orders on the powers and functions of the Gestapo, Sipo, and SD are printed under *IMT*, 1723-PS, 27:492–500.
28. *Preussische Gesetzsammlung*, 1936, pp. 21–22; *IMT*, 29:253–54, 255–56.

49

29. Circular of the Prussian Ministry of the Interior, September 20, 1936. *Reichsministerialblatt*, 1936, p. 1343.
30. Helmut Krausnick, Hans Buchheim, Martin Broszat, and Hans-Adolf Jacobsen, *Anatomy of the SS State* (New York, 1968), p. 197.
31. Himmler order of September 27, 1939; Heydrich orders on organization of September 23 and 27, 1939, *IMT*, 361-L, 38:102–10.
32. Decree of September 26, 1939. Cited in Krausnick, *Anatomy of the SS State*, p. 175.
33. Kaltenbrunner testimony, *IMT* 11:237, 262, 305, 317, 415; Gisevius testimony, *IMT* 12:259–60.
34. Krausnick, *Anatomy*, pp. 176 ff.

50

35. Krausnick, *Anatomy*, pp. 213 ff.; Hitler orders on the duties of the HSSPF, April 21, 1941, T175/123/2648762; see also the memorandum of January 8, 1943, on the division of tasks and responsibilities of Himmler's central offices and the senior SS and police officers, T175/119/2644859 ff.
36. Cited in Krausnick, *Anatomy*, pp. 189–90.
37. See Bibliography, 9. The Armed Forces, for a sample of the enormous literature on this subject.
38. E. B. Wheaton, *The Nazi Revolution 1933–1935: Prelude to Calamity* (paperback, New York, 1969), p. 441. There were, to be sure, many officers, especially the younger men, who were sympathetic to the Nazi regime, which may have been a major consideration in paralyzing the activity of those who despised the Hitler movement and desired its overthrow. See K. D. Bracher, *The German Dictatorship: The Origins, Structure, and Effects of National Socialism* (New York, 1970), pp. 236–47.

51

39. *RGBl* (1934) 1:747, 751, 785. Hans Gisevius described the reaction of German officers to this oath (*To the Bitter End*, pp. 278–79).
40. See Bibliography, 11. Society and Culture, the Churches, and the Resistance.
41. *RGBl* (1935) 1:375, 609.
42. This was the conference recorded in the famous memorandum of Colonel Friedrich Hossbach, *IMT*, 386–PS, 25:402–13; see also Hossbach's memoirs, *Zwischen Wehrmacht und Hitler, 1934–1938* (Wolfenbüttel, 1949), pp. 186–94, 207–20. For a critique of this document, see below, p. 97, n. 17.
43. Robert J. O'Neill, *The German Army and the Nazi Party* (London, 1966), pp. 140–41, with references; John W. Wheeler-Bennett, *The Nemesis of Power: The German Army in Politics, 1918–1945* (paperback, New York, 1964), p. 362.

52

44. The story of the Blomberg-Fritsch crisis has often been told. There are good brief accounts in O'Neill and Wheeler-Bennett, cited above. The problem is treated in greater detail in J. A. G. von Kielmansegg, *Der Fritschprozess, 1938. Ablauf und Hintergründe* (Hamburg, 1949); and in H. Foertsch, *Schuld und Verhängnis. Die Fritsch-Krise im Frühjahr 1938 als Wendepunkt in der Geschichte der nationalsozialistischen Zeit* (Stuttgart, 1951.) See also Gisevius's memoirs, *To the Bitter End*, pp. 219 ff.; Hossbach, *Zwischen Wehrmacht und Hitler*, pp. 99 ff.; and especially Walter Hagen (pseudonym for Wilhelm Höttl, a department chief in the intelligence department of the RSHA), *Die geheime Front* (Linz, 1950).

53

45. R. J. O'Neill, *German Army and Nazi Party*, p. 145. On March 23, 1938, Fritsch informed his friend Baroness von Schutzbar-Milching that he had been acquitted despite the fact that Göring had been a member of the military court. The verdict, Fritsch said, had been unavoidable in view of the facts, for by some miracle his defense had been able to locate the man who had been forced into impersonating Fritsch in the affair. Confronted with this witness, the man who had denounced Fritsch and on whose evidence the entire case was based confessed that he had acted as the agent of Himmler and Heydrich and that all his statements about Fritsch had been false. Nuremberg document NG 5809A.

46. It seems likely that Fritsch, in his disgust with the "new" Germany, had actually sought death on the battlefield. This was the opinion of Gisevius, *To the Bitter End*, p. 265.

47. Decree of February 4, 1938, *RGBl* (1938) 1:111. Lammers testimony, *IMT* 11:29; Keitel testimony, *IMT* 10:472–73, 477–78; Keitel affidavit, *IMT* 40:365–85, 423–32.

48. Whereas Blomberg's nickname in the officers corps was Rubber Lion (*Gummilöwe*), Keitel's was *La-Keitel*, a pun on the German word for lackey.

54

49. J. Wheeler-Bennett, *Nemesis of Power*, pp. 372–73.

50. *RGBl* (1938) 1:112; Göring testimony, *IMT* 9:290; Keitel testimony, *IMT* 10:487; Lammers testimony, *IMT* 11:23.

6. THE INSTRUMENTS OF CONTROL: RACIAL OFFICES

55

1. Not to be confused with the RSHA (Reichssicherheitshauptamt). Founded in 1931 by R. Walther Darré, the Nazi soil and race theorist, as a special research branch of the SS to determine the racial standards required to constitute a genuine German, to examine the racial credentials of candidates for the SS, their wives, and fiancées, and to conduct programs of physical and moral training. Darré was pressured out of this office by Himmler in 1938 and was succeeded by Günther Pancke, who later became the HSSPF for occupied Denmark. Pancke was succeeded in December 1939 by Otto Hofmann, formerly head of the race section of the RuSHA, and in April 1943 by Richard Hildebrandt.

In a memorandum of September 3, 1935, Himmler claimed that the creation of a new German peasantry was one of the ideological and political tasks of the SS, and that the carrying out of all measures necessary for this program was the exclusive prerogative of the RuSHA (Nuremberg document NO 4114). On May 25, 1940, Pancke wrote Himmler proposing that the RuSHA be given exclusive responsibility for the actual selection and eradication (*für die praktische Auslese und Ausmerze*) in the Old Reich and the occupied territories, as well as for the recruitment of workers for the Reich, a proposal which Himmler warmly seconded (NO 2791). See also a memorandum (unsigned) of November 6, 1941, on the tasks of the RuSHA (NO 2576); the memorandum of Otto Hofmann of November 26, 1941, for talks with Himmler about the future tasks and organization of the RuSHA (NO 2577); and a memorandum of Hildebrandt of August 20, 1943, on the division of responsibility between the RuSHA and the RSHA (NO 1761).

2. A Himmler circular of August 8, 1936, on the co-operation between the SS and Lebensborn, defines the purpose of the Lebensborn association (NO 2884). A set of the statutes of the association, dated February 10, 1938, is signed by Himmler (NO 3498). See also the directive of the central office of the RKFDV to political and educational offices in Germany and the east on the Germanization of Polish orphans, February 19, 1942 (NO 1615; T175/194/2733126); and a letter of SS *Sturmbannführer* Brandt to SS *Brigadeführer* Janowsky, April 15, 1942 (NO 3731).

3. By a Hitler order of July 2, 1938, the VoMi was assigned responsibility for ethnic and border area questions (*Volkstums und Grenzlandfragen*), for Germanic minorities abroad, and for foreign minorities within Germany (NG 4948). By the time the RKFDV (see below) was founded, Himmler had brought the VoMi organization under his control. *IMT* 26:362–64; 29:273.

4. See above, p. 49.

56

5. Hitler draft order, September 28, 1939, and final order of October 7, 1939, *IMT*, 686-PS, 26:255–57; T175/194/2732985–87. SS *Untersturmführer* Gerhard Folkerts, "Die Aufgaben des RFSS als RKFDV," dated February 15, 1941, is an account of Himmler's activities as RKFDV replete with statistics, T175/94/2733378–97. On this organization, as well as for all other Himmler offices mentioned in this section, see Robert L. Koehl, *RKFDV: German Resettlement and Population Policy, 1939–1945: A History of the Reich Commission for the Strengthening of Germandom* (Cambridge, Mass., 1957). The initials RKFDV could refer either to the Reich Commission as an office, or to Himmler personally as the head of that office: *Reichskommissar für die Festigung des deutschen Volkstums*. The difficulty in studying the Nazi race offices caused by their proliferation and constant restructuring is vastly increased by the fact that Nazi officials, in their feuds and power struggles, frequently defined the powers and functions of their offices to suit their own purposes, with the result that these definitions are often confusing and contradictory.

6. Koehl, *RKFDV*, pp. 55, 64, with references. See also Greifelt's memorandum, "Die Festigung des deutschen Volkstums als zentrale Ostaufgabe," written in late 1941 (NO 4817); the affidavit of Rudolf Creutz, Greifelt's deputy (NO 4718); of Konrad Meyer-Hetling, the head of the planning section of the RKFDV (NO 4726); and of Hans-Joachim Götz, the head of the organization's legal department (NO 5321).

7. NO 3078. Published in translation by Koehl, *RKFDV*, pp. 249–50. See also Himmler's directive to the Reichsstatthalters and heads of the administration (*Oberpräsidenten*) in the east of December 6, 1939 (NO 2526).

8. Greifelt memorandum of December 15, 1939, NO 5720–21; see also his memorandum, "Die Festigung des deutschen Volkstums als zentrale Ostaufgabe," NO 4817.

57

9. The documents on the establishment and tasks of the ZBA are published in *Documenta Occupationis Teutonicae*, 7 vols. (Poznań, 1945–59), 5:183–88; see also Koehl, *RKFDV*, p. 60.

10. Draft instructions for setting up the immigration office, undated (NO 3495); Koehl, *RKFDV*, pp. 54, 64, 104–7.

11. Keppler letter of November 3, 1939, thanking Himmler for founding the DUT (NO 2407); Himmler letter, undated, on reasons for founding the DUT (NID 15359.) A document of July 31, 1941, describes the entire structure of the organization and lists its personnel (T74/16/388084–86). See also the affidavits of Dr. Alfred Kulemann, the administrative chief of the DUT (NO 5243), and of Kurt Kleinschmidt, the deputy administrative chief (NO 5245).

12. Originally called the Office for the Evacuation of Poles and Jews, the name was changed in May 1940 to the more euphemistic Umwandererzentralstelle (Martin Brozsat, *Nationalsozialistische Polenpolitik, 1939–1945* [Stuttgart, 1961], p. 87).

13. In October 1939 Eichmann, who had built up a central office for the evacuation of Jews in Prague, was appointed executive director of a Reich Central Office for Emigration, which was nominally under the authority of the Reich Ministry of the Interior but whose chief was Reinhard Heydrich. Soon afterward Eichmann was transferred to the RSHA, where in January 1940 he took over as chief of Department IV D 4 for Emigration and Evacuation, which was subsequently renamed Department D IV B 4 for Jewish Affairs and Evacuation. H. Krausnick, H. Buchheim, M. Brozsat, and H.-A. Jacobsen, *Anatomy of the SS State* (New York, 1968), pp. 47–48, 582–83.

14. Established by a decree of February 2, 1940, *RGBl* (1940) 1:355; its authority further defined in an unpublished decree of the same date (NI 4267).

15. Established by a Himmler order of January 21, 1941, in his capacity as RKFDV (NO 4129).

16. Affidavit of Dr. Franz Riedweg, a foreign SS volunteer assigned to the Germanische Leitstelle, April 12, 1947 (NO 2957).

7. THE INSTRUMENTS OF CONTROL: THE ECONOMY

59

1. See Bibliography, 10. The Economy, Rearmament, and Raw Materials.

2. For a sample of Nazi theorizing on this matter, see Hans Buchner, *Grundriss einer nationalsozialistischen Volkswirtschaftstheorie* (Munich, 1931); Herbert Hart, *Das dritte Reich, wie es sein wird. Eine neue Wirtschaftsordnung für Deutschland* (Hamburg, 1932); Ernst Posse, *Umschichtung der Wirtschaft und der Wirtschaftsauffassung* (Hamburg, 1934); Jens Jessen, *Volk und Wirtschaft* (Hamburg, 1935); and Otto Gauweiler, *Rechtseinrichtungen und Rechtsaufgaben der Bewegung* (Munich, 1939).

60

3. *RGBl* (1933) 1:487–88. On this subject see Theodor Becker, "Die Kartellpolitik der Reichsregierung," *Rechtsfragen der Wirtschaft*, vol. 2 (Berlin, 1935); and Werner Kreutz, *Der Zwangskartellierung in der gewerblichen Wirtschaft der Gegenwart* (Berlin, 1936).

4. *RGBl* (1934) 1:185, 565; *DDP* 2:185–86, 189.

5. *RGBl* (1934) 1:1194; (1935) 1:1169; (1936) 1:918; *DDP* 2:185, n. 1; *TWC* 12:92–93.

6. The word *Wehrwirtschaft*, often translated as "war economy," is in fact a far more ambiguous term and at this time was used to suggest the defensive nature of German rearmament.

61

7. On the Four-Year Plan, see below, pp. 64–67. There is a brief outline of the changes in the Nazi economic leadership in *TWC* 12:91 ff.; see also Schacht's memoirs, *Account Settled* (London, 1949), and *Confessions of the Old Wizard* (Boston, 1956); also Schacht's testimony at Nuremberg, *IMT* 12:417 ff.

8. Nazi proclamation of May 2, 1933, on taking over the unions, *DDP* 1: 139–41; *IMT*, 2220-PS, 29:349–52. Hitler's decree on the German Labor Front of October 24, 1934, *DDP* 2:158–160. See also Will Decker, *Die deutsche Arbeitsfront* (Berlin, 1941), and Hans-Gerd Schumann, *Nationalsozialismus und Gewerkschaftsbewegung. Die Vernichtung der deutschen Gewerkschaften und der Aufbau der "Deutschen Arbeitsfront"* (Hanover, 1958).

9. *RGBl* (1934), 1:45; *DDP* 2:140.

10. *RGBl* (1935) 1:311.

62

11. *RGBl* (1935) 1:769; *DDP* 3:249–54.

12. *RGBl* (1938) 1:652; *DDP* 6:542–43.

13. Law establishing the Reichskulturkammer, September 22, 1933, *RGBl* (1933) 1:661; *DDP* 1:315.

14. *RGBl* (1933) 1:1015; *DDP* 1:145, 277, 349, 369. For more of the literature on these crucial problems, see Bibliography, 7. General Works, the Nazi Party and Government.

15. The text of the concordat with the Holy See is printed in *DDP* 1:350–61. Documents of the negotiations leading up to the concordat are in *DGFP*, C, 1:266 ff., with an analytical list of these documents on p. lviii. See also Bibliography, 11. Society and Culture, the Churches, and the Resistance.

63

16. Laws of July 15, September 13, and December 8, 1933, and of February 16, 1934, *RGBl* (1933) 1:495, 626, 1060; (1934) 1:100; changes under the Four-Year Plan, *RGBl* (1937) 1:422; *DDP* 1:217–19, 244–47; 2:249; *TWC* 12:99.

64

17. *RGBl* (1933) 1:685, 749, 1096; *DDP* 1:215–25. See also the Law for the Reconstitution (*Neubildung*) of the German Peasantry, July 14, 1933, *RGBl* (1933) 1:517, with later changes, *RGBl* (1934) 1:568; (1935) 1:295; the Law on the Bank for Agricultural Resettlement, September 18, 1933, *RGBl* (1933) 1:647; the Laws for Residential Resettlement of September 22, 1933, and July 3, 1934, *RGBl* (1933) 1:659; (1934) 1:568; the Law for Territorial Planning (*Raumordnung*) of February 15, 1936, *RGBl* (1936) 1:104; and the Laws for the Setting-up of Local Courts, *RGBl* (1934) 1:349, 594; (1935) 1:9; etc.

Despite all the emphasis the Nazis placed on the preservation and proliferation of the German peasantry, the farm population of Germany actually declined during the Nazi years. K. D. Bracher, *German Dictatorship: The Origins, Structure, and Effects of National Socialism* (New York, 1970), p. 336.

18. On this subject, see Hans Grimm's influential work, *Volk ohne Raum*, 2 vols. (Munich, 1926); and the writings of R. Walther Darré, Reich minister of food and agriculture and Reich peasant leader, *Das Bauerntum als Lebensquell der nordischen Rasse* (Munich, 1929); *Im Kampfe um die Seele des deutschen Bauern* (Munich, 1934); *Neuadel aus Blut und Boden* (Munich, 1930); *Um Blut und Boden* (Munich, 1942.)

19. Analysis of the organization and functions of the Four-Year Plan by Dr. Erich Neumann, state secretary in the Central Office of the Four-Year Plan, *TWC* 12:543–48; Georg Thomas (chief of the army's Office of Military Economy), *Geschichte der deutschen Wehr-und Rüstungswirtschaft (1918–1943/45)*, edited by Wolfgang Birkenfeld (Boppard am Rhein, 1966), pp. 111–12 (an important source); Göring testimony, *IMT* 9:282 ff.; Körner testimony, *IMT* 9:152 ff.

20. "Hitlers Denkschrift zum Vierjahresplan, 1936," ed. W. Treue, *VfZ* 3 (1955):184–210. The memorandum appears to have been written in August, but the exact date has not been established.

66

21. Minutes of a ministerial council meeting of September 4, 1936, at which Göring read and discussed Hitler's memorandum on the Four-Year Plan, *IMT*, 416-EC, 36:488–91; Hitler's public announcement is printed in the *Völkischer Beobachter* of September 10, 1936; his official decree in the *RGBl* (1936) 1:887, 927.

22. Decree of October 22, 1936, *TWC* 12:447–52; G. Thomas, *Geschichte der Wehr-und Rüstungswirtschaft*, pp. 113 ff.

23. See the Neumann memorandum on the organization and functions of the Four Year Plan, *TWC* 12:543–48.

67

24. There is a brief description of Göring's industrial enterprises in *TWC* 12:108–14.

25. On the Göring-Schacht controversy, see the documents printed in *IMT* 36:233 ff. (Göring to Schacht, November 26, 1936; Blomberg to Hitler, February 22, 1937; Schacht to Blomberg, July 8, 1937; etc.); Thomas, *Geschichte*, p. 115; Schacht testimony, *IMT* 12:520 ff.; and Schacht's memoirs, *Account Settled* and *Confessions of the Old Wizard*.

26. On the changes in the Reich Ministry of Economics, see *TWC* 12:91–92, 529–30; Göring's decree on the reorganization of the ministry, February 5, 1938, *TWC* 12:482–88; Funk testimony, *IMT* 13:100 ff.

68

27. Göring decree of December 7, 1939. *TWC* 12:529–30; Funk-Lammers correspondence, March 1938 to January 1939, *IMT* 13:153–54; Lammers testimony, *IMT* 11:66; Funk testimony, *IMT* 13:101, 105, 189; Posse testimony, *NCA* 8A:629–31; *IMT* 13:158.

28. Article by Körner, Göring's deputy, in the journal *Der Vierjahresplan*. *TWC* 12:489–92.

29. *TWC* 12:502–3. See also the listing of offices of the plenipotentiaries within the Four-Year Plan, *TWC* 12:531–32.

30. Decree of October 18, 1940, *RGBl* (1940) 1:1395.

69

31. *RGBl* (1940) 1:513.

32. On the changes in Göring's personal position, see the R. Manvell and H. Fraenkel biography, *Göring* (New York, 1962).

33. See Thomas's own history of this organization, *Geschichte der Wehr-und Rüstungswirtschaft;* also the brief outline in *TWC* 12:98–99.

70

34. Thomas, ibid. About his own role in the vicious infighting between the various Nazi economic offices, Speer has remarkably little to say in his memoirs, *Inside the Third Reich* (New York, 1970).

35. W. Kumpf, *Die Organisation Todt im Kriege* (Oldenburg, 1953).

36. *RGBl* (1940) 1:513. Alan S. Milward, "Fritz Todt als Minister für Bewaffnung und Munition," *VfZ* 14 (1966):40–58. On Todt, see Speer, *Inside the Third Reich*, pp. 232–33.

71

37. Speer, *Inside the Third Reich*, pp. 189 ff., 234, 242, 328. Far more authoritative are the actual records of Speer's conferences with Hitler, *Deutschlands Rüstung im zweiten Weltkrieg. Hitlers Konferenzen mit Albert Speer, 1942–1945,* ed. Willi A. Boelcke (Frankfurt am Main, 1969).

38. Unsigned memorandum dated March 24, 1942, on a staff conference with the chief of the army's armaments office (Thomas), *IMT*, 1439-PS, 27:219–20.

39. September 2, 1943, *RGBl* (1943) 1:529.

40. *RGBl* (1942) 1:179–80. The protectorate was the Protectorate of Bohemia and Moravia, the predominantly Czech provinces of Czechoslovakia occupied by the Nazis in March 1939 (see below, p. 116); the Government General was the territory of rump Poland, also occupied by the Germans. The most important German decrees relating to the recruitment, allocation, and exploitation of labor are collected in *Handbuch für die Dienststellen des G. B. A.* [i.e., the plenipotentiary-general for labor] *und die interessierten Reichsstellen im grossdeutschen Reich und in den besetzten Gebieten,* ed. Friedrich Didier (Berlin, 1944).

72

41. Göring order of March 27, 1942, *IMT*, 1666-PS, 27:433.

42. Sauckel testimony, *IMT* 14:617 ff.; Körner testimony, *IMT* 9:153 ff.; Göring testimony, *IMT* 9:236 ff. For the sections relating to labor in this testimony, see the index in *IMT* 23.

43. April 20, 1942, *IMT*, 016-PS, 25:57.

44. On this problem, see J. H. E. Fried, *The Exploitation of Foreign Labour by Germany* (Montreal, 1945), a pioneer work sponsored by the International Labour Office; Edward L. Homze's excellent monograph, *Foreign Labor in Nazi Germany* (Princeton, N.J., 1967); and H. Pfahlmann, *Fremdarbeiter und Kriegsgefangene in der deutschen Kriegswirtschaft, 1939–1945* (Darmstadt, 1968).

8. THE CONTROL OF POWER

75

1. Decree of August 30, 1939, *RGBl* (1939) 1:1539–40; Lammers testimony, *IMT* 11:57; Keitel testimony, *IMT* 10:492.

76

2. Quoted in H. R. Trevor-Roper's introduction to *The Bormann Letters: The Private Correspondence between Martin Bormann and His Wife, from January 1943 to April 1945,* ed. H. R. Trevor-Roper (London, 1954), p. xxviii, from the memoirs of Hitler's secretary (A. Zoller, *Hitler Privat* [Düsseldorf, 1949], p. 221).

3. *Bormann Letters,* p. xvii.

77

4. See the brilliant first chapter, "Hitler and His Court," of H. R. Trevor-Roper's book *The Last Days of Hitler* (New York, 1962).

9. THE PERIOD OF PREPARATION

81

1. Gerhard L. Weinberg, *The Foreign Policy of Hitler's Germany: Diplomatic Revolution in Europe, 1933–1936* (Chicago, 1970), provides an authoritative and readable analysis of the international complications of this period; see also the balanced and lucid work of Raymond J. Sontag, *A Broken World, 1919–1939* (New York, 1971), chap. 12.

82

2. See above, p. 21.

3. The platform of the Democratic party, Roosevelt's campaign speeches, and his inaugural address of March 4, 1933, gave promise of such a change in American policy, but already on July 3, 1933, his repudiation of the World Economic and Monetary Conference meeting in London showed that he too was still primarily concerned with domestic affairs. *The Public Papers and Addresses of Franklin D. Roosevelt,* compiled and collated by Samuel I. Rosenman, vols. 1 and 2 (New York, 1938).

83

4. See Foreign Minister von Neurath's depressing analysis of the situation in his letter to President Hindenburg of June 19, 1933, *IMT* 40:465–68.

5. Karlheinz Niclauss, *Die Sowjetunion und Hitlers Machtergreifung. Eine Studie über die deutsch-russischen Beziehungen der Jahre 1929 bis 1935* (Bonn, 1966); James E. McSherry, *Stalin, Hitler and Europe, 1933–1939. The Origins of World War II* (Cleveland, 1968); W. E. Scott, *Alliance against Hitler. The Origins of the Franco-Soviet Pact* (Durham, N.C., 1962).

6. John A. Lukacs, *The Great Powers and Eastern Europe* (New York, 1953).

7. Roman Debicki, *The Foreign Policy of Poland, 1919–1939: From the Rebirth of the Polish Republic to World War II* (New York, 1962.)

8. The problem of Italy constitutes a major theme in German-Austrian relations during this period. See the monographs of Jürgen Gehl, *Austria, Germany, and the Anschluss, 1931–1938* (London, 1963), and Ulrich Eichstädt, *Von Dollfuss zu Hitler. Geschichte des Anschlusses Österreichs, 1933–1938* (Wiesbaden, 1955).

9. In a speech to leaders of his armed forces of February 3, 1933, Hitler reminded his listeners of the risks involved in a large-scale rearmament program. "The most dangerous period will be that of the building up of the Wehrmacht. We will then see if France has *statesmen;* if yes, then it will not give us time, but will attack us (presumably with its Eastern satellites)." Memorandum of General Liebmann, "Neue Dokumente zur Geschichte der Reichswehr, 1930–1933," *VfZ* 2 (1954):434–35. For other versions of this speech, see K. D. Bracher, W. Sauer, and G. Schulz, *Die Nationalsozialistische Machtergreifung* (Cologne, 1962), p. 748, n. 9; and Weinberg, *Foreign Policy,* pp. 26–27. On the entire problem of rearmament, see Bibliography, 10. The Economy, Rearmament, and Raw Materials.

84

10. Hitler's "peace speech" before the Reichstag of May 17, 1933; his appeal to the German people and radio address on the occasion of Germany's withdrawal from the League of Nations of October 14, 1933; and the explanations

provided by Foreign Minister von Neurath for Germany's withdrawal from the disarmament conference are all printed in the official publication of German documents in a chapter significantly entitled "The Fight for Peace" (*DDP* 1:77 ff.). See also *DGFP, C*, 1 and 2.

11. Weinberg, *Foreign Policy*, pp. 166–73.

12. Hitler's various speeches and proclamations are published in *DDP* (see above, n. 10). The relevant chapter in volume 2 is called "Germany's Policy of Peace"; in volume 3, "Germany's Fight for Peace and Justice (*Gleichberechtigung*)"; in volume 4, "The Fight for Peace and German Honor"; while the chapter in volume 6 becomes "The Establishment of the Greater German Reich." Hitler's most important public statements on foreign policy, including interviews with foreign journalists, are published in translation in volume 2 of *The Speeches of Adolf Hitler, April 1922–August 1939*, ed. Norman H. Baynes (Oxford, 1942).

85

13. Proclamation of the Reich government to the German people, March 16, 1935, *RGBl* (1935) 1:369; Law on the Reconstruction (*Aufbau*) of the Wehrmacht, March 16, 1935, *RGBl* (1935) 1:375.

14. Hitler's negotiation of the naval agreement with Britain through Ribbentrop is a striking example of his method of operating through diverse channels, official and unofficial. On the Dienststelle Ribbentrop, see Hans-Adolf Jacobsen, *Nationalsozialistische Aussenpolitik, 1933–1938* (Frankfurt am Main, 1968), pp. 252 ff.; on Hitler's methods of conducting foreign policy, pp. 347 ff.

15. On the Anglo-German naval agreement, signed June 18, 1935 (the anniversary of the Battle of Waterloo!), see Donald C. Watt, "The Anglo-German Naval Agreement of 1935: An Interim Judgment," *Journal of Modern History* 28 (1956):155–75; Robert Ingrim, *Hitlers glücklichster Tag. London, am 18. Juni 1935* (Stuttgart, 1962); and Weinberg, *Foreign Policy*, pp. 210–16, who provides an able summary of the problem. The text of the treaty is published in *DGFP*, C, 4:319–26.

86

16. George W. Baer, *The Coming of the Italo-Ethiopian War* (Cambridge, Mass., 1967); Mario Toscano, "Eden's Mission to Rome on the Eve of the Italo-Ethiopian Conflict," in *Studies in Diplomatic History and Historiography in Honour of G. P. Gooch*, ed. A. O. Sarkissian (London, 1961), pp. 126–52; D. C. Watt, "The Secret Laval-Mussolini Agreement of 1935 on Ethiopia," *Middle East Journal* 15 (1961):69–78; H. Braddick, "The Hoare-Laval Plan: A Study in International Politics," *Review of Politics* 24 (1962):342–64; F. D. Laurens, *France and the Italo-Ethiopian Crisis, 1935–1936* (The Hague, 1967).

87

17. Hitler's order for the remilitarization of the Rhineland, March 2, 1936, *IMT* 34:644–47; German military orders, March 6, 1936, *IMT* 34:779–82. On the diplomatic background and warnings of military leaders, *DGFP*, C, 4 and 5. See also M. Braubach, *Der Einmarsch deutscher Truppen in die entmilitarisierte Zone am Rhein im März 1936: Ein Beitrag zur Vorgeschichte des Zweiten Weltkrieges* (Cologne, 1956); E. Robertson, ed. "Zur Wiederbesetzung des Rheinlandes, 1936," *VfZ* 10 (1962):178–205; D. C. Watt, "German Plans for the Reoccupation of the Rhineland. A Note," *Journal of Contemporary History* 1 (1966):193–99; and W. F. Knapp, "The Rhineland Crisis of March 1936," in *The Decline of the Third Republic*, ed. James Joll (London, 1959), pp. 67–85. The official Nazi explanations for the reoccupation of the Rhineland are collected in *DDP* 4:92 ff. The entire episode is well analyzed in Weinberg, *Foreign Policy*, chap. 10.

88

18. The importance of the Ethiopian conflict in itself in this connection should not be overemphasized, as M. Funke has convincingly demonstrated (*Sanktionen und Kanonen. Hitler, Mussolini und der internationale Abessinienkonflikt*,

1934–1936 (Düsseldorf, 1970); see also the trenchant comments of Weinberg, *Foreign Policy,* pp. 216–38.

19. See above, p. 9. It is significant that Hitler automatically assumed that Germany had inherited Austria's claims to the South Tyrol, although this region lay on the Austrian, not the German, border. On this whole problem, see Conrad F. Latour, *Südtirol und die Achse Berlin-Rom, 1938–1945* (Stuttgart, 1962); and Dennison I. Rusinow, *Italy's Austrian Heritage, 1919–46* (Oxford, 1969).

20. *DGFP,* C, 5:756–60. On this problem, see below, p. 95.

21. *DGFP,* D, 3; Weinberg, *Foreign Policy,* pp. 284–99; Dante A. Puzzo, *Spain and the Great Powers, 1936–1941* (New York, 1962).

22. *DGFP,* C, 5:1136–8.

89

23. Elizabeth Wiskemann, *The Rome-Berlin Axis: A History of the Relations between Hitler and Mussolini* (New York, 1949); D. C. Watt, "The Rome-Berlin Axis, 1936–1940. Myth and Reality," *Review of Politics* 22 (1960):519–43; Mario Toscano, *The Origins of the Pact of Steel* (Baltimore, 1968); F. Siebert, *Italiens Weg in den zweiten Weltkrieg* (Frankfurt am Main, 1962); and Weinberg, *Foreign Policy,* pp. 331–37.

10. EXPANSION IN THE NAME OF SELF-DETERMINATION

90

1. *Mein Kampf,* p. 3. See also H. Rauschning, *The Voice of Destruction* (New York, 1940), p. 87.

91

2. J. Gehl, *Austria, Germany, and the Anschluss, 1931–1938* (London, 1963), pp. 52–60; G. L. Weinberg, *The Foreign Policy of Hitler's Germany: Diplomatic Revolution in Europe, 1933–1936* (Chicago, 1970), pp. 87–107. See also Gordon Brook-Shepherd, *The Anschluss: The Rape of Austria* (London, 1963) and U. Eichstädt, *Von Dollfuss zu Hitler. Geschichte des Anschlusses Österreichs, 1933–1938* (Wiesbaden, 1955).

92

3. Charles A. Gulick, *Austria: From Habsburg to Hitler,* 2 vols. (Berkeley, Calif., 1948); Andrew G. Whiteside, *Austrian National Socialism before 1918* (The Hague, 1962).

4. R. R. Koerner, *So haben sie es damals gemacht. Die Propagandavorbereitungen zum österreichanschluss durch das Hitlerregime, 1933–1938* (Vienna, 1958).

93

5. Paul R. Sweet, "Mussolini and Dollfuss: An Episode in Fascist Diplomacy," in *The Tragedy of Austria,* ed. Julius Braunthal (London, 1948); Gehl, *Austria,* chap. 3 and pp. 69–87.

6. *DGFP,* C, 2:614–17.

7. Neurath memorandum, June 15, 1934; Hassell to the Foreign Office, July 5, 1934, *DGFP,* C, 3:10–12, 131–32.

94

8. *IMT,* 9:294.

9. There is a good brief summary of the entire episode in Weinberg, *Foreign Policy,* pp. 99–107. For the official Austrian version of the affair, *Beiträge zur Vorgeschichte und Geschichte der Julirevolte* (Vienna, 1934); for the Nazi, *Die Erhebung der österreichischen Nationalsozialisten im Juli 1934. Bericht der historischen Kommission des Reichsführers* SS, ed. H. Steiner and L. Jedlicka (Vienna, 1965). See also Gordon Brook-Shepherd, *Dollfuss* (London, 1961); Dieter Ross, *Hitler und Dollfuss. Die deutsche österreich-Politik, 1933–1934* (Hamburg, 1966); and J. Gehl, *Austria,* pp. 92–100.

10. Notes by State Secretary Bülow, July 27 and 30, 1934; German Foreign Office memorandum, August 7, 1934; Papen to State Secretary Bülow, August 19,

1934; Hess to the Austrian Nazi leader Alfred Frauenfeld, August 21, 1934, *DGFP*, C, 3:251–52, 271–72, 293–94, 336–43, 352–53; report by the Austrian Nazi leader Fritz Rainer on the activities of the Austrian Nazis from 1933 to the Anschluss, July 6, 1939, *IMT* 26:348–58; Papen to Hitler, April 4, 1935, *IMT* 35:378–81. Also J. Gehl, *Austria*, pp. 101–4; Weinberg, *Foreign Policy*, pp. 106, 195–96, 233.

95

11. Papen to Hitler, October 18, 1935; Hassell to the Foreign Office, January 7, 1936. *DGFP*, C, 4:751–53, 974–78.

12. See above, pp. 88, 93; *DGFP*, D, 1:278–81, 283–85; Gehl, *Austria*, pp. 133–43.

13. Rainer report on the activity of the Austrian Nazis, *IMT*, 26:352; Gehl, *Austria*, pp. 147–48.

14. State Secretary Weizsäcker memoranda of July 8 and 13, 1937, *DGFP*, D, 1:439–40, 448; Gehl, *Austria*, 154–56.

96

15. Seyss-Inquart personnel file, Berlin Document Center. Cited in Konrad Kwiet, *Reichskommissariat Niederlande. Versuch und Scheitern nationalsozialistischer Neuordnung* (Stuttgart, 1968), p. 90; Seyss-Inquart testimony and declaration, *IMT* 15: 610 ff.; 32:273–79; Rainer testimony, *IMT* 16:123 ff.

16. Seyss-Inquart memorandum on the Austrian question, 1934–38, *NCA* 5:961–62; *IMT* 32:66–70; Rainer memorandum, *IMT* 26:353; Altenburg memorandum, January 8, 1938, *DGFP*, D, 1:491; Gehl, *Austria*, pp. 156, 161.

97

17. This was the conference recorded in the memorandum of Colonel Hossbach, dated November 10, 1937, *IMT*, 386-PS, 25:402–13. The importance and reliability of this document has frequently been questioned, and with some justification, for it is never possible to know for certain whether Hitler was merely speaking for effect or whether he meant what he said. In this case, however, Hitler opened the conference by informing those present—Blomberg, the minister of war, the commanders in chief of the army, navy, and Luftwaffe (Fritsch, Raeder, and Göring), Foreign Minister von Neurath, and Hossbach himself, Hitler's adjutant—that the subject of the meeting was of such importance that he had decided not to discuss these problems in the larger circle of the Reich cabinet; that his statements were the result of thorough deliberation and the experience of four and a half years of government; that he wanted to explain his fundamental ideas about the opportunities and necessities of Germany's international position; and that in the interests of long-range German policy he wanted his statements to be regarded as his last will and testament in the event of his death. The ideas Hitler expressed at this conference, far from marking a turning point in his policy as some writers (including Hossbach) have maintained, were indeed an analysis of the opportunities open to Germany, a presentation of a series of contingency plans and possibilities, but otherwise they fit completely within the ideological framework of *Mein Kampf.* The most significant change in his point of view at this time was his belief that he could not gain an alliance with Britain in the time available for the realization of his expansionist plans, and that Germany would have to count on Britain's opposition to German expansion into Eastern Europe (see above, p. 9, n. 24).

As for the document itself, the original of Hossbach's memorandum has not been found, but only a copy made by an officer. In an affidavit not submitted in evidence at the Nuremberg trials (at which the Hossbach memorandum served as a critical piece of evidence), Hossbach stated that he could not say for certain whether the existing copy of his memorandum was a verbatim reproduction of the original; even his original memorandum was not written until five days after the conference on the basis of brief notes and his recollection of what Hitler had said. In his memoirs, however, published in 1949, Hossbach did not discredit the significance of the November 5 conference or the reliability of the copy of the re-

287

cord of that conference presented in evidence at Nuremberg. On the contrary, he emphasized the importance of the conference as the point of departure (*Ausgangspunkt*) of the Blomberg-Fritsch crisis (see above, pp. 51–54), and as a decisive point of departure (again he used the word *Ausgangspunkt*) for a change in Hitler's foreign and domestic policy. Hossbach acknowledged that there was no complete and verbatim record of the November 5 conference, but stated that his memorandum of November 10 provided a clear indication of the course and content of the conference. He specifically repeated the statement in the memorandum itself that Hitler wanted the ideas he expressed at this conference to be regarded as his "political testament." Hossbach's only significant criticism of his record of the conference (or the Nuremberg copy thereof) was that it did not deal adequately with the doubts and reservations expressed by Blomberg, Fritsch, and Neurath in response to Hitler's ideas (F. Hossbach, *Zwischen Wehrmacht und Hitler, 1934–1938* [*Wolfenbüttel, 1949*], pp. 137, 186–91). Göring, as is hardly surprising, tried to discredit the validity of the document in his testimony at Nuremberg (*IMT* 9:306). For a more scholarly criticism, see Hans-Günther Seraphim, "Nachkriegsprozesse und zeitgeschichtliche Forschung," in *Mensch und Staat in Recht und Geschichte. Festschrift für Herbert Kraus* (Kitzingen am Main, 1954), p. 445; W. Bussmann, "Zur Entstehung und Überlieferung der 'Hossbach Niederschrift,'" *VfZ* 16 (1968):373–84; H. Gackenholz, "Reichskanzlei, 5. November 1937," *Forschungen zu Staat und Verfassung. Festgabe für Fritz Hartung* (Berlin, 1958).

18. See above, p. 95.

98

19. *DGFP*, D, 1:448–49, 463–64; *Ciano's Diplomatic Papers*, ed. Malcolm Muggeridge (London, 1948), p. 146.

20. Unofficial memorandum of the Hitler-Halifax conversation, November 19, 1937, *DGFP*, D, 1:62; Keith Feiling, *Life of Neville Chamberlain* (London, 1946), pp. 332–33.

21. This statement was made to Friedrich Sieburg, the Paris correspondent of the *Frankfurter Zeitung*, and reported by the German ambassador on November 27, *DGFP*, D, 1:83.

22. *DGFP*, D, 5:38, 203–4, 222–29; *Ciano's Diplomatic Papers*, p. 100.

23. Keppler to Neurath, February 2, 1938; Keppler to Ribbentrop, February 7, 1938; Veesenmayer report on Seyss-Inquart's final negotiations with Schuschnigg, undated, *DGFP*, D, 1:497–98, 500–502, 512–13; Gehl, *Austria*, pp. 166–73.

24. Draft and final protocol and communiqué of the Hitler-Schuschnigg conference of February 12, 1938, *DGFP*, D, 1:513–17. There appears to have been no need whatever for Hitler's bullying and military threats at this conference. Schuschnigg's subsequent claim that Hitler's demands were a complete surprise (*Austrian Requiem* [New York, 1936], chap. 1) would seem to be quite without foundation.

25. Report of the German chargé d'affaires in Vienna on the reorganization of the Austrian government, February 17, 1938; memoranda on Hitler's decisions about Nazi policy in Austria, February 22 and 28, 1938, *DGFP*, D, 1:526–28, 539–41, 548–49; Rainer memorandum, *IMT* 26:354.

99

26. *DGFP*, D, 1:562–63, 566–68; Schuschnigg affidavit, November 19, 1945, *NCA* 5:713; *Austrian Requiem*, pp. 35–36; Gehl, *Austria*, pp. 182–84.

27. Rainer memorandum, *IMT* 26:356; Schuschnigg and Seyss-Inquart affidavits, *NCA* 5:713, 981; Göring testimony, *IMT* 9:103–4.

100

28. Hitler's orders for the invasion of Austria, March 11, 1938, *IMT* 34:335–37, 774; Seyss-Inquart affidavit, *NCA* 5:714–15; Seyss-Inquart statement, *IMT* 32:277–78; German ultimatum, March 11, 1938, *DGFP*, D, 1:578; transcript of Göring's telephone conversations with Vienna, *IMT* 31:354 ff.; Rainer memorandum, *IMT* 26:357; Göring telephone order, March 11, 1938, 6:45 P.M., *DGFP*, D, 1:589–90.

29. Hitler to Mussolini, March 11, 1938, *DGFP*, D, 1:573–76; Mussolini's acceptance of the German action, *NCA* 5:641–42.

30. Seyss-Inquart to Hitler, March 11, 1938, 9:40 P.M., *DGFP*, D, 1:580, 584–85.

31. Brook-Shepherd, *Anschluss*, pp. 189–92.

32. *RGB1* (1938) 1:237; *DDP* 6, part C.

101

33. "Wehrwirtschaftliche Bedeutung der Eingliederung Österreichs," May 3, 1938, T175/657/1857799–816.

34. Winston S. Churchill, *The Gathering Storm* (Boston, 1948), pp. 272–74.

102

35. Dagmar H. Perman, *The Shaping of the Czechoslovak State* (Leyden, 1962). And for the entire problem, the massively detailed treatment of Helmuth Rönnefarth, *Die Sudetenkrise in der internationalen Politik: Entstehung-Verlauf-Auswirkung*, 2 vols. (Wiesbaden, 1961).

36. J. W. Brügel, *Tschechen und Deutsche, 1918–1938* (Munich, 1967); Boris Celovsky, *Das Münchener Abkommen von 1938* (Stuttgart, 1958), pp. 108–11; Weinberg, *Foreign Policy*, pp. 107–10.

37. Koch (the German minister in Prague) to the German Foreign Office, October 5 and 10, 1933, and his report on the history of the most important German nationalist groups, November 8, 1933, *DGFP*, C, 1:892, 904–6; 2:91–95. See Vojtěch Mastny, *The Czechs under Nazi Rule: The Failure of National Resistance, 1939–1942* (New York, 1971), chap. 1; and Radomír Luža, *The Transfer of the Sudeten Germans: A Study of Czech-German Relations, 1933–1962* (London, 1964), chap. 3.

38. *DGFP*, C, 3:908–10, 968–69; 4:186–89, 229–30, 679–80, 742, 821; 5:1011.

39. *DGFP*, C, 5:608–9, 830–31.

104

40. *DGFP*, D, 2:198, 204, 289, 556–57.

41. See above, p. 97 and n. 17.

42. *DGFP*, D, 7:635–36.

105

43. The language of the document leaves unclear whether this was to be a manufactured or accidental incident. The German text is printed in *IMT* 25:415–16.

44. *DGFP*, D, 2:357–62.

45. Ibid., pp. 473–77.

46. *DGFP*, D, 7:640–41; *IMT* 21:48.

47. *DGFP*, D, 1:35. See above, p. 97 and n. 17.

106

48. Ibid., pp. 62–63. See above, p. 98.

49. Feiling, *Life of Chamberlain*, pp. 332–33 (entry for November 26, 1937).

50. March 20, 1938. Feiling, *Chamberlain*, pp. 347–48.

51. Neville Chamberlain, *In Search of Peace* (New York, 1939), pp. 79–91.

107

52. July 10, 1938. *Falsificators of History* (Moscow, 1948), pp. 21–22; *Documents and Materials Relating to the Eve of the Second World War*, Dirksen papers (New York, 1948), 2:34.

53. *DGFP*, D, 2:633–47, 660–61, 711–12. By September 15 Henlein, in accordance with instructions from Berlin, was demanding union with the Reich (pp. 801–2).

54. Ibid., pp. 751–52, 757–58; *DDP* 6:302–4.

55. Text in *DDP* 6:293–302.

56. September 13, 1938, *DGFP*, D, 2:754–55; Feiling, *Chamberlain*, pp. 357–64.

108

57. *DGFP*, D, 2:786–98; *Documents on British Foreign Policy, 1919–1939* (London, 1946–   ), 3d ser., 2:338–41.

58. Feiling, *Chamberlain*, pp. 368–69; *DGFP*, D, 2:870; Hubert Ripka, *Munich: Before and After* (London, 1939), p. 55 ff.

59. *DGFP*, D, 2:831–33, 858–59; Jodl diary, *IMT* 28:383; *Documents and Materials Relating to the Eve of the Second World War* 1:203–4.

60. *DGFP*, D, 2:870–79, 887–91, 898–910.

61. *Documents on British Foreign Policy*, 3d ser., 2:518–19.

109

62. *DGFP*, D, 2:933; Chamberlain, *In Search of Peace*, pp. 173–75.

63. *Documents on British Foreign Policy*, 3d ser., 2:587; *DGFP*, D, 2:985–90, 993–95.

64. H. Celovsky, *Das Münchener Abkommen*, p. 462; *DGFP*, D, 2:1003–8, 1011–14.

65. *DGFP*, D, 2:1014–16.

66. Hitler himself professed to be flabbergasted by his success. "Do you think," he asked the Hungarian foreign minister in January 1939,

> that I myself would have thought it possible half a year ago that Czechoslovakia would be served up to me, so to speak, by her friends? I did not believe that England and France would go to war, but I was convinced that Czechoslovakia would have to be destroyed by a war. The way in which everything happened is historically unique. We can offer each other heartfelt congratulations (*DGFP*, D, 5:364).

67. On the Hungarian annexations, see below, pp. 114, 184.

110

68. Memoranda by the head of the Foreign Office Economics Department, September 20 and 21, 1938, *DGFP*, D, 2:856, 865–69; Christopher Thorne, *The Approach of War, 1938–1939* (London, 1967), p. 86.

11. FROM SELF-DETERMINATION TO LEBENSRAUM

111

1. *DGFP*, D, 4:99–100. A second supplement to this order was issued on December 17, 1938, which stated that plans were to be prepared "on the assumption that no appreciable resistance was to be expected. Outwardly it must be quite clear that it is only a peaceful action and not a warlike undertaking" (pp. 185–86). For the German text, *IMT* 34:477–81, 483–84. See also Vojtěch Mastny, *The Czechs under Nazi Rule: The Failure of National Resistance, 1939–1942* (New York, 1971), chap. 2.

2. *DGFP*, D, 4, chap. 1, especially pp. 60–63, 69–72, 190–202; Hubert Ripka, *Munich: Before and After* (London, 1939), pp. 240 ff.

3. *DGFP*, D, 4: 32, 82–83, 86–93; Jozef Lettrich, *A History of Modern Slovakia* (New York, 1955), pp. 94–95, 111–12, 296–97; Gilbert L. Oddo, *Slovakia and Its People* (New York, 1960), pp. 236–37; Ripka, *Munich*, pp. 241–42.

112

4. *DGFP*, D, 4:173–77.

5. Ibid., p. 32.

6. Ibid., pp. 30, 40, 46–49.

113

7. The Slovak People's party was formed in 1905 by another Roman Catholic priest, Andrej Hlinka, to fight for Slovakia's independence from Hungary and, after 1918, from the Czechs. With the exception of a brief period from 1927 to 1929, when it entered the national government in return for promises of greater regional autonomy for Slovakia, the Hlinka party consistently opposed the Prague

regime. Upon his death on August 16, 1938, Hlinka was succeeded as acting head of the party by Tiso, who had served as minister of health in the central government in 1927. At the time Tiso took over its leadership, the SPP was the largest single party in Slovakia with about 40 per cent of the popular vote, drawn largely from the rural, Roman Catholic, population. See J. K. Hoensch, *Die Slowakei und Hitlers Ostpolitik. Hlinkas Slowakische Volkspartei zwischen Autonomie und Separation, 1938/39* (Cologne, 1965); Lettrich, *History of Modern Slovakia;* and Oddo, *Slovakia and Its People.*

8. Lettrich, *History,* pp. 111–12, 175, 296–97; Oddo, *Slovakia,* pp. 236–37; *DGFP,* D, 4:40.

9. *DGFP,* D, 4:49, 52.

114

10. Ibid., pp. 82–83, 86–93.

11. Ibid., pp. 110–11, 125–27.

12. Conference of January 16, 1939, *DGFP,* D, 5:361–66; also Hitler's speech to his officers, January 25, 1939, Andreas Hillgruber, *Hitlers Strategie. Politik und Kriegsführung, 1940–1941* (Frankfurt am Main, 1965), p. 14, n. 4.

13. Fritzsche affidavit, *IMT* 6:62; *DGFP,* D, 4:235, 239–40.

115

14. *DGFP,* D, 4:240.

15. Ibid., pp. 209–13.

16. Ibid., pp. 229–30.

17. Ibid., pp. 233–34, 236–37; Lettrich, *History,* pp. 123–30.

116

18. *DGFP,* D, 4:234–35, 239, 241, 243–45, 250, 252–53, 259–60, 266, and n. 1; Lettrich, *History,* pp. 130–31, 135.

19. *DGFP,* D, 4:249.

20. Ibid., pp. 260, 263–69; *Hitler's Secret Conversations, 1941–1944* (paperback, New York, 1961), p. 211.

21. *TWC* 12:877.

22. *DGFP,* D, 4:251, 254–56, 276; 6:10–11; Lettrich, *History,* p. 298.

23. Martin Broszat, "Die Reaktion der Mächte auf den 15. März 1939," *Bohemia: Jahrbuch des Collegium Carolinum* 8 (1967):253–80.

117

24. See the Hossbach memorandum, *DGFP,* D, 1:34–35: "If the Führer was still living, it was his unalterable resolve to solve Germany's problem of space at the latest by 1943–45." Hitler immediately went on to describe situations which might make action desirable before 1943–45.

118

25. This line of reasoning may be found not only in Hossbach's record of Hitler's conference of November 5, 1937, but in a series of conferences and policy directives of 1939. See *IMT* 26:327–36, 338–41; 37:466–86; etc. It is significant that in his various analyses of the overall international situation, Hitler paid so little attention to Russia, although he might have cited the recent purges in that country as further evidence of the weakness of his opponents.

26. German Office of Military Economy report, *NCA* 7:264–65; W. Churchill, *The Gathering Storm* (Boston, 1948), pp. 280–81, 336–37; Göring testimony, *IMT* 9:301 ff.; Mastny, *Czechs under Nazi Rule,* p. 66.

27. On the treaty status of Memel, *DGFP,* D, 5:421, n. 3.

119

28. Martin Broszat, "Die Memeldeutschen Organisationen und der Nationalsozialismus," *VfZ* 5 (1957): 273–78; G. Weinberg, *The Foreign Policy of Hitler's Germany: Diplomatic Revolution in Europe, 1933–1936* (Chicago, 1970), pp. 82–85, 300–302.

29. *DGFP*, D, 5:462–63, 491–92, 515–16; Christopher Thorne, *Approach of War, 1938–1939* (London, 1968), pp. 106–7.

30. *IMT* 34:481.

31. *DGFP*, D, 5, chap. 3.

120

32. *DGFP*, D, 5:524–26.

33. *RGBl* (1939) 2:608; *DGFP*, D, 5:528–30.

34. *RGBl* (1939) 2:559.

12. THE WAR FOR LEBENSRAUM: THE ATTACK ON POLAND

122

1. *Hitler's Secret Book* (paperback, New York, 1961), p. 45.

123

2. G. L. Weinberg, *The Foreign Policy of Hitler's Germany: Diplomatic Revolution in Europe, 1933–1936* (Chicago, 1970), pp. 57–75, 184–94, 302–10.

3. *DGFP*, D, 6:345–55.

4. Instructions of March 25, 1939, *DGFP*, D, 6:117–18; of April 3, 1939, pp. 186–87.

5. The directive of March 25, 1939 (see n. 4) stated, "The Führer *does not* wish to solve the Danzig question by force, however. He does not wish to drive Poland into the arms of Britain by this."

124

6. *DGFP*, D, 6:223–28.

7. Ibid., pp. 70–72, 121–24, etc.

8. Franz Halder, *Kriegstagebuch. Tägliche Aufzeichnungen des Chefs des Generalstabes des Heeres, 1939–1942*, ed. Hans-Adolf Jacobsen, 3 vols. (Stuttgart, 1962–64), 1:9, 11, 13, 23, 25.

9. A document introduced in evidence at Nuremberg purporting to be a record of a Hitler conference of May 23, 1939 (*IMT*, 79-L, 37:546–56) makes it appear as though Hitler had definitely decided on war by this time—against Poland, if he could be sure Britain and France would remain neutral; otherwise in the first instance against the West. The authenticity of this document is suspect, however, in particular its date, which was written on a covering note listing the names of the participants at the conference, some of whom, as was proved later, were not present. The document is typewritten and unsigned; it is not entered in the government document record, as was customary; and Hitler's statements recorded therein are at variance with other expressions of his opinions at this time found in documents of proven authenticity. See Hans-Günther Seraphim, "Nachkriegsprozesse und zeitgeschichtliche Forschung," in *Mensch und Staat in Recht und Geschichte. Festschrift für Herbert Kraus* (Kitzingen am Main, 1954), pp. 446–50. Admiral Raeder, General Milch, Captain von Below (Hitler's adjutant), who admitted being present at this May 23 conference, all testified after the war that the existing record of the conference was spurious. Their testimony does not mean much in itself, but it helps substantiate suspicions raised by the nature of the document. *IMT* 14:38–39, 134; NOKW 3516.

10. Martin Broszat, *Nationalsozialistische Polenpolitik, 1939–1945* (Stuttgart, 1961), pp. 9 ff. The strongest support for this interpretation is the dubious record of the Führer conference of May 23, 1939 (see n. 9). According to this document Hitler said, "The problem 'Poland' cannot be dissociated from the showdown with the West. . . . We cannot expect a repetition of the Czech situation. There will be war. Our task is to isolate Poland."

11. *DGFP*, D, 6:224.

125

12. Ibid., pp. 172–73; Halder, *Kriegstagebuch,* 1:12.

13. See below, pp. 129–30.

14. Chamberlain, for example, wrote in his journal on March 26, 1939; "I must confess to the most profound distrust of Russia. I have no belief whatever in her ability to maintain an effective offensive, even if she wanted to" (Keith Feiling, *The Life of Neville Chamberlain* [London, 1946], p. 403). In a memorandum of May 1939 a British Foreign Office official expressed the fear that the Russians hoped to get Britain and France involved in a war with Germany while staying out of it themselves. But even if the Russians did participate, he believed it to be "unlikely that on land their [the Russian] military effort could be of very much effect" (*Documents on British Foreign Policy, 1919–1939* [London, 1946–], 3d ser., 5:639–47). In the German Foreign Office files (Inland II geheim 69/2) there is a folder containing documents on the British and French negotiations with Russia, March to July 1939 (intercepted by German intelligence agents or captured after the fall of France), with two annexes containing analyses by British and French military experts of the Russian army and air force, both of which were considered to be very weak indeed.

126

15. Carl J. Burckhardt, *Meine Danziger Mission, 1937–1939* (Munich, 1960), p. 348. These ideas were duly passed on to the British and French. *Documents on British Foreign Policy*, 3d ser., 6:688–98.

127

16. *The Ciano Diaries, 1939–1943* (New York, 1946), entry for August 11, 1939, p. 119; *DGFP*, D, 6:39–49, 53–56; *Documenti diplomatici italiani, 1861–1943* (Rome, 1952–), 8th ser., 13:1–7, 19–20; *Ciano's Diplomatic Papers*, ed. Malcolm Muggeridge (London, 1948), pp. 297–304; Halder, *Kriegstagebuch*, 1: 15.

17. Halder, *Kriegstagebuch*, 1:8–14; *DGFP*, D, 7:551–56.

18. Halder, *Kriegstagebuch*, 1:25.

128

19. *DGFP*, D, 7:142–48. The schedule of Soviet deliveries has unfortunately not been printed but is available on film in the National Archives (8379/E591215–21.) The advantages of the treaty to Germany were summarized by Hitler in a conference with his military commanders of August 22 and in a memorandum by an official of the Economic Policy Department of the Foreign Office of August 29. *DGFP*, D, 7:204, 428. Considering Hitler's emphasis on a Blitzkrieg, however, even the economic agreement with Russia cannot have played a major role in his calculations.

129

20. Doubts have been cast on the reliability of an unsigned record of Hitler's August 22 conference introduced in evidence at Nuremberg (*IMT*, 798-PS, 26:338–44), but the notes on this conference in General Halder's diary under the date of August 22 (*Kriegstagebuch*, 1:23–26) and the record prepared by Admiral Böhm that same evening on the basis of notes made at the conference (Raeder document 27, *IMT* 41:16–25) are so similar in all essential details that in my opinion the Nuremberg document can be considered a reliable version of Hitler's remarks. My summary makes use of all three versions. Winfried Baumgart ("Zur Ansprache Hitlers vor den Führern der Wehrmacht am 22. August 1939. Eine quellenkritische Untersuchung," *VfZ* 16 [1968]:120–49) makes a convincing case that Nuremberg document 798-PS is a copy of the notes made at the August 22 conference by Admiral Canaris, and that these notes were the basis for the record of the conference in the OKW war diary prepared by General Greiner (*Kriegstagebuch des Oberkommandos der Wehrmacht* [*Wehrmachtführungsstab*], vol. 1, ed. Hans-Adolf Jacobsen [Frankfurt am Main, 1965], pp. 947–49; Helmuth Greiner, *Die oberste Wehrmachtführung, 1939–1943* [Wiesbaden, 1951], pp. 38–39).

21. Halder, *Kriegstagebuch*, 1:26–27.

22. Ibid., 1:19 (entry for August 17, 1939); unsigned memorandum of Canaris's

talk with Keitel, *IMT*, 795-PS, 26:336–38; Keitel testimony, *IMT* 10:515; Lahousen testimony, *IMT* 2:449–51; Naujocks affidavit, *IMT* 31:90–92.

23. *DGFP*, D, 7:129–30, 155, 164–65, etc.

24. Halder, *Kriegstagebuch*, 1:31; Göring interrogation, *IMT* 39:107.

130

25. *DGFP*, D, 7:279–81; *Documents on British Foreign Policy*, 3d ser., 7:227–31; Birger Dahlerus, *The Last Attempt* (London, 1948), pp. 56–59; Dahlerus testimony, *IMT* 9:452 ff.

26. Halder, *Kriegstagebuch*, 1:34:41.

27. Ibid., 1:38. In this same diary entry, however, Halder noted that, according to the commander in chief of the army, the Führer was "very calm and clear-headed."

28. *DGFP*, D, 7:381–84, 413–15, 451–52, 459–60, 468–70, 480.

29. Halder, *Kriegstagebuch*, 1:47–8; *DGFP*, D, 7:477–79, 548–49 (Directives 1 and 2 for the conduct of the war).

30. *DGFP*, D, 7:491. These were, of course, the attacks arranged by Heydrich by Germans dressed in Polish uniforms on the Gleiwitz frontier station (see above, p. 129).

131

31. *DGFP*, D, 7:492–93, 529–38, 542.

32. *DGFP*, D, 8:164–65, 208–12.

13. SECURITY IN THE NORTH: THE ATTACK ON DENMARK AND NORWAY

132

1. German General Staff analysis, August 25, 1938, *IMT*, 375-PS, 25:383; Hans-Adolf Jacobsen, *Fall "Gelb." Der Kampf um den deutschen Operationsplan zur Westoffensive, 1940* (Wiesbaden, 1957), pp. 1–8, 266–68.

2. Winston Churchill, *The Gathering Storm* (Boston, 1948), pp. 475–80; M. Gamelin, *Servir*, 3 vols. (Paris, 1946–47), 3:34 ff.

133

3. Directives 1 and 2 for the conduct of the war, *DGFP*, D, 7:477–79, 548–49; notes to the war diary of Major Deyhle of the OKW General Staff, *NCA*, 1796-PS, 4:371–72. At his conferences with the navy Hitler brought up the same problem, and also mentioned the possibility of driving a wedge between Britain and France. *Fuehrer Conferences on Matters Dealing with the German Navy, 1939–1945*, 8 vols. (Washington, 1946–47), 1939, pp. 3, 9.

4. See below, pp. 149–50.

5. In his memorandum and guidelines for waging the war in the west of October 9, 1939, Hitler assumed the neutrality of the Nordic states even in the event of a long war "provided no completely unforeseen factors appear" (*IMT*, 052-L, 37:471). At the Nuremberg trials Jodl described this unsigned document as a personal memorandum of Hitler's which he had dictated word for word (*IMT*, 15:376).

6. Secret additional protocol, signed August 23, 1939, *DGFP*, D, 7:246–47. It should be recalled that these territories had been part of the Russian Empire before the First World War. See August Rei, ed., *The Nazi-Soviet Conspiracy and the Baltic States: Diplomatic Documents and Other Evidence* (London, 1948); and W. F. Reddaway, *Problems of the Baltic* (Cambridge, Eng., 1940), an excellent background survey.

7. Max Jakobson, *The Diplomacy of the Winter War: An Account of the Russo-Finnish War, 1939–1940* (Cambridge, Mass., 1961); Anatole G. Mazour, *Finland between East and West* (Princeton, N.J., 1956); C. Leonard Lundin, *Finland in the Second World War* (Bloomington, Ind., 1956); John H. Wuorinen, ed., *Finland and World War II, 1939–1944* (New York, 1948).

8. For a brief summary of the plans the Allies actually did make with regard to Scandinavia, see Olaf Riste, ed., *Norway and the Second World War* (Oslo, 1966), pp. 14–28.

134

9. Walther Hubatsch, "*Weserübung.*" *Die deutsche Besetzung von Dänemark und Norwegen, 1940* (Göttingen, 1960), describes the background and course of Hitler's decision to launch a campaign in Scandinavia, with an appendix of important documents and a full bibliography. Hubatsch's work has now been supplemented by the excellent monograph of Hans-Dietrich Loock, *Quisling, Rosenberg und Terboven. Zur Vorgeschichte und Geschichte der nationalsozialistischen Revolution in Norwegen* (Stuttgart, 1970), which de-emphasizes (too much, in my opinion) the defensive nature of Hitler's Scandinavian operation.

10. German figures as of February 22, 1940, *Fuehrer Conferences,* 1940, 1:18–19; Jodl analysis, November 7, 1943, *IMT,* 172-L, 37:636, 646–49; Sohl affidavit, October 6, 1947, NI 11,724; Rolf Karlbom, "Sweden's Iron Ore Exports to Germany, 1933–1944," *Scandinavian Economic History Review* 13 (1965): 65–93; A. F. Rickman, *Swedish Iron Ore* (London, 1939); *Annuaire Statistique de la Norvège* (Christiania, 1938–40).

11. Churchill, *Gathering Storm,* pp. 461–62, 531–36, 544–48, 579, n. 1.

136

12. Raeder note on discussion with Hitler, November 2, 1934, *IMT,* 190-C, 34:775–76; Hermann Rauschning, *The Voice of Destruction* (New York, 1940), pp. 140–41.

13. Battle instructions for the navy, May 1939, *Fuehrer Directives and Other Top-Level Directives of the German Armed Forces, 1939–1941,* vol. 1 (Washington, 1948), p. 25; Jodl testimony, *IMT,* 15:375.

14. Navy war diary, *IMT,* 879-D, 35:628–30; also 005-C, 122-C, 34:159–61, 422–25; *Fuehrer Conferences,* 1939, p. 14; 1940, 1:41; Raeder testimony, *IMT* 14:85–86, 92–93. On the entire problem of German naval strategy, see the work of Carl-Axel Gemzell, *Raeder, Hitler und Skandinavien. Der Kampf für einen maritimen Operationsplan* (Lund, 1965); and Admiral Kurt Assmann, *The German Campaign in Norway: Origin of the Plan, Execution of the Operation, and Measures against Allied Counter-Attack* (London, 1949).

15. Raeder to Assmann, January 1, 1944, *IMT,* 066-C, 34:281.

16. Memorandum and guidelines for waging the war in the west, October 9, 1939. *IMT,* 052-L, 37:471.

137

17. The question of the responsibility for Quisling's invitation to Berlin at this time is discussed by H.-D. Loock, *Quisling,* pp. 217–22, who also provides a detailed account of his career and the development of his ideas. See also Paul M. Hayes, "Quislings politische Ideen," in *Internationaler Faschismus, 1920–1945* (Munich, 1966), pp. 201 ff., and Ralph Hewins, *Quisling: Prophet without Honour* (London, 1965), an apologia which contains much interesting and, on the whole, accurate information.

138

18. Hewins, *Quisling,* p. 138.

19. On Rosenberg's conception of foreign policy, his Foreign Political Office (Aussenpolitisches Amt), and the feuds within the Nazi party over the control of "Germanic work," see Loock, *Quisling,* pp. 158–204; and Hans-Adolf Jacobsen, *Nationalsozialistische Aussenpolitik, 1933–1938* (Frankfurt am Main, 1968), pp. 45 ff.

20. Rosenberg's report on the political preparation of the Norway action, submitted to the Führer's deputy, June 17, 1940, *IMT,* 25:26–35, 40–43.

139

21. Loock, *Quisling,* pp. 199–200.
22. *DGFP,* D, 8:133, n. 3; Loock, *Quisling,* pp. 200 ff.
23. See Loock, *Quisling,* pp. 217–22.

140

24. Raeder's notes on his report to Hitler, December 12, 1939, *IMT*, 064-C, 34:271–73; Raeder to Assmann, January 30, 1944, *IMT*, 066-C, 34:281.

25. Jodl diary, December 13 and 18, 1939; Halder diary, December 14, 1939; Rosenberg diary, December 19 and 20, 1939; relevant excerpts published in Hubatsch, *Weserübung*, pp. 355–56, 482. In a memorandum of June 17, 1940, Rosenberg said that after his first reception by Hitler, Quisling was received again on December 16 and 18. *IMT*, 004-PS, 25:28; also 007-PS, 25:41. On the problem of the dates of Quisling's reception by Hitler, see Loock, *Quisling*, p. 223, n. 78.

26. Halder diary, January 1, 1940; Navy war diary, January 13, 1940; Keitel transmission of Hitler order, January 27, 1940; Hubatsch, *Weserübung*, pp. 356, 391–93, 435–36.

27. *Fuehrer Conferences*, 1940, 1:4; Jodl testimony, *IMT*, 15:376.

28. Rosenberg memorandum, June 17, 1940, *IMT*, 004-PS, 25:28–30. Quisling's reports attached to this document have not been printed. See also Raeder's testimony, *IMT*, 14:95, 98.

29. For example the German minister's report of March 28, 1940, *DGFP*, D, 9:35–36; also 8:695, 702, 846, 932, etc.

141

30. Churchill, *Gathering Storm*, p. 579, n. 1. For a summary of Allied plans for Norway, see Riste, *Norway*, pp. 14–27.

31. Jodl diary, February 19 and 21, 1940; Keitel order, February 21, 1940; Hubatsch, *Weserübung*, pp. 357, 393; Franz Halder, *Kriegstagebuch. Tägliche Aufzeichnungen des Chefs des Generalstabes des Heeres, 1939–1942*, ed. Hans-Adolf Jacobsen, 3 vols. (Stuttgart, 1962–64), 1:218, 221; Loock, *Quisling*, p. 251; *Trial of Nikolaus von Falkenhorst*, ed. E. H. Stevens (London, 1949), p. xxix.

32. Jodl diary, February 28, 1940; Rosenberg diary, February 29, 1940. Hubatsch, *Weserübung*, pp. 358–59, 484; Halder, *Kriegstagebuch*, 1:237.

142

33. *DGFP*, D, 8:831–33.

34. Navy war diary, March 3 and 7, 1940; Halder diary, March 3 and 6, 1940. Hubatsch, *Weserübung*, pp. 360–63; Goes (a military archivist) memorandum and conversation with Himer, August 12, 1940. Nuremberg document PS 3596.

35. Orders of March 3, 12, 13, 21, and April 4, 1940. Hubatsch, *Weserübung*, pp. 441–55, 464–69; *IMT*, 119-C, 34:365–80.

36. The following account is based on Loock, *Quisling*, pp. 271–77.

144

37. Navy war diary, March 15, 1940; Loock, *Quisling*, p. 255.

38. Navy war diary, March 13, 15, 22–29; Jodl diary, March 14, 26, 1940; Loock, *Quisling*, pp. 255–56.

39. Halder, *Kriegstagebuch*, 1:237.

40. Jodl diary, April 2, 1940, Hubatsch, *Weserübung*, p. 367; *DGFP*, D, 9:66–73.

41. On the military campaigns in Scandinavia, see Earl F. Ziemke, *The German Northern Theater of Operations, 1940–1945* (Washington, D.C., 1959), a U.S. Department of the Army pamphlet; T. K. Derry, *The Campaign in Norway* (London, 1952), an official British history; and the more recent work of J. L. Moulton, *The Norwegian Campaign of 1940* (London, 1966).

145

42. The last of the British forces sent to Norway were not withdrawn until June 7; the final official surrender of all Norwegian forces did not take place until June 10.

14. SECURITY IN THE WEST: THE ATTACK ON FRANCE AND THE LOW COUNTRIES

146

1. *DGFP*, D, 1:32.

147

2. Memorandum and guidelines for waging the war in the west, October 9, 1939, *IMT*, 052-L, 37:466–86. See above, p. 133, n. 5, and Hans-Adolf Jacobsen, *Fall "Gelb." Der Kampf um den deutschen Operationsplan zur Westoffensive, 1940* (Wiesbaden, 1957), pp. 12–24.

3. *DGFP*, D, 8:227–28, 275–76.

4. Hitler made this point in conferences with his naval leadership, *Fuehrer Conferences on Matters Dealing with the German Navy, 1939–1945*, 8 vols. (Washington, D.C., 1946–47), 1939, pp. 3, 9.

149

5. Memorandum and guidelines of October 9, 1939, *IMT*, 052-L, 37:466–86. This memorandum spells out many of the points made in Directive 6 for the conduct of the war of the same day. *DGFP*, D, 8:248–50.

6. Hans-Adolf Jacobsen, ed., *Dokumente zur Vorgeschichte des Westfeldzuges, 1939–1940* (Göttingen, 1956), p. 29. The Schlieffen plan was the pre-1914 German military plan for a campaign in the west, which was used, with modifications, in the First World War. See Gerhard Ritter, *The Schlieffen Plan: Critique of a Myth* (New York, 1958).

7. Directive 6 for the conduct of the war. See above, n. 5. Also Jacobsen, *Fall "Gelb,"* pp. 25–36.

8. *IMT*, 062-C, 34:268–69.

150

9. Deyhle diary, October 6, 1939, ff.; Jacobsen, *Dokumente*, pp. 29–30; Directive 8 for the conduct of the war, November 20, 1939, *DGFP*, D, 8:430–34; *Hitler's Secret Conversations, 1941–1944* (paperback, New York, 1961), p. 182; Jacobsen, *Fall "Gelb,"* p. 44 ff.

10. The sequence of orders postponing the attack is published under document 072-C, *IMT*, 34:284–97; Jacobsen, *Dokumente*, pp. 25–26, 41–46; *Fall "Gelb,"* pp. 65 ff.

11. Jacobsen, *Dokumente*, pp. 26–28, 161–86; *Fall "Gelb,"* pp. 93 ff.

12. Jodl diary, *IMT*, 1809-PS, 28:408–16.

151

13. For samples of the vast literature on this subject, see Max DuPrel and Willi Janke, eds., *Die Niederlande im Umbruch der Zeiten. Alte und neue Beziehungen zum Reich* (Würzburg, 1942); Gerda Merschberger, "Geschichtsbildende Kräfte in der Vor-und Frühzeit der Niederlande," *Deutsche Zeitung in den Niederlanden*, February 13, March 11 and 31, 1941; Walter Söchting, *Das Niederlandbuch. Sammlung deutscher und niederländischer Arbeiten* (Frankfurt am Main, 1942); Hans Zech, *Die flämische Frage. Ein Germanisches Volk kämpft um sein Lebensrecht* (Leipzig, 1938); and above all the periodical *Westland*, whose principal themes are reviewed by K. Rabl in the journal *Reich, Volksordnung, Lebensraum*, 5:366–72.

14. Seyss-Inquart speech of May 22, 1940, recorded in Hans Frank's diary, *IMT*, 2233-PS, 29:402.

152

15. NOKW 485; NG 5347, *TWC* 12:1211.

16. *DGFP*, D, 9:300–301.

17. Ibid., pp. 301–6.

18. Ibid., pp. 306–7.

156

19. Hans-Adolf Jacobsen, ed., *Dokumente zum Westfeldzug, 1940* (Göttingen, 1960), is an excellent collection of documents on the German conduct of the campaign. For an official British view, see L. F. Ellis, *The War in France and Flanders, 1939–1940* (London, 1953), a detailed and highly technical analysis of the Allied defeat. On the conflict over and responsibility for German campaign plans, see above all Jacobsen, *Fall "Gelb."*

15. THE PROBLEM OF BRITAIN

157

1. Alfred Rosenberg, *Das politische Tagebuch Alfred Rosenbergs aus den Jahren 1934/35 und 1939/40*, ed. Hans-Günther Seraphim (Göttingen, 1956), p. 85.
2. Karl Klee, *Das Unternehmen "Seelöwe." Die geplante deutsche Landung in England, 1940* (Göttingen, 1958), p. 189.

158

3. *New York Journal American*, June 14, 1940; Andreas Hillgruber, *Hitlers Strategie. Politik und Kriegsführung, 1940–1941* (Frankfurt am Main, 1965), p. 146.
4. Franz Halder, *Kriegstagebuch. Tägliche Aufzeichnungen des Chefs des Generalstabes des Heeres, 1939–1942*, ed. Hans-Adolf Jacobsen, 3 vols. (Stuttgart, 1962–64), June 30, 1940, 1:375 (on the basis of information about Hitler's views from State Secretary Weizsäcker); July 13, 1940, 2:21.
5. *Schulthess' Europäischer Geschichtskalender*, pp. 141–58; Winston Churchill, *Their Finest Hour* (Boston, 1949), pp. 259–62, 320–21.
6. *DGFP*, D, 10:287. Halifax's speech is printed in the London *Times*, July 23, 1940.

159

7. The most important documents of Hitler's plans for an invasion of Britain are collected in Karl Klee, ed., *Dokumente zum Unternehmen "Seelöwe." Die geplante deutsche Landung in England 1940* (Göttingen, 1959). In addition to Klee's own study of the subject (see above, n. 2), there is an excellent monograph by Ronald Wheatley, *Operation Sea Lion: German Plans for the Invasion of England, 1939–1942* (Oxford, 1958). See also Walter Ansel, *Hitler Confronts England* (Durham, N.C., 1960); and Peter Fleming, *Operation Sea Lion* (London, 1956). The brief entry in the German naval war staff diary of November 15, 1939, about examining the possibilities for an invasion of England is cited in Wheatley, p. 4. See also *Fuehrer Conferences on Matters Dealing with the German Navy, 1939–1945*, 8 vols. (Washington, D.C., 1946–47), 1940, 1:51.
8. Klee, *Dokumente*, pp. 238–39, 301–2; Wheatley, *Operation Sea Lion*, pp. 15–16.
9. Directive 16 for the conduct of the war, Klee, *Dokumente*, pp. 310–14.
10. *Fuehrer Conferences*, 1940, 1:81; Klee, *Dokumente*, pp. 245–46.

160

11. Halder, *Kriegstagebuch*, July 22, 1940, 2:30–34.
12. See Hillgruber, *Hitlers Strategie*, p. 170.
13. *Fuehrer Conferences*, 1940, 2:1–3, 8–14; Klee, *Dokumente*, pp. 186, 247–60, 315–24, 333–36, 356–57; affidavit of Walter Giese, former clerk in the Naval High Command, *IMT*, 722-D, 35:404–5.

161

14. *Fuehrer Conferences*, 1940, 2:9–10, 13–14.
15. Ibid., pp. 11–12.
16. National Archives documents, T77/545/1702426–27; T77/564/1741766–67.
17. Klee, *Dokumente*, pp. 53, 196–98, 263–64, 369; Halder, *Kriegstagebuch*, 2:98–100.

162

18. Klee, *Dokumente*, pp. 441–42.
19. OKW war diary, January 22, 1941, Klee, *Dokumente*, p. 86.
20. See below, Chap. 16.
21. See below, pp. 174–76.

163

22. See below, pp. 210–11.

23. Reports on talks with Hess, *IMT*, 116–19 M, 38:174–76; Ribbentrop-Mussolini conference, May 13, 1941, *DGFP*, D, 13:797–806; Halder, *Kriegstagebuch*, May 14 and 15, 1941, 2:412–14; see also the book of the Duke of Hamilton's son, James Douglas-Hamilton, *Motive for a Mission: The Story behind Hess's Flight to Britain* (New York, 1971).

24. Hitler had already used this argument in July 1940 when he issued his first instructions to prepare for an invasion of Russia, and he ·was to repeat it frequently until the invasion itself took place. Halder, *Kriegstagebuch*, July 22, 1940, 2:30–31; Hitler speeches of January 8 and 9, 1941, p. 244; March 30, 1941, p. 335.

25. *DGFP*, D, 12:1066–69.

26. Orders for camouflage operations *Seebär, Haifisch,* and *Harpune,* April 23 and 24, May 2, June 22 and 29, 1941, T78/346/6303780–98, 6303805–27, 6303840; T77/777/5503697–98; *Fuehrer Conferences,* 1941, 2:15.

27. Hillgruber, *Hitlers Strategie,* p. 269. See also *DGFP*, D, 12:1012–16. For the order of August 5, T77/16/727722. The files filmed in this series, and in T77/17, show how much effort was still expended on the invasion project and that invasion plans were certainly not intended for camouflage purposes only.

164

28. Order of August 31, 1941, T78/346/6303800, 6303841–44; See also *DGFP*, D, 13:422–33.

29. Wheatley, *Operation Sea Lion,* p. 98.

16. SECURITY IN THE SOUTHWEST: SPAIN AND NORTH AFRICA

166

1. On this problem, see Donald S. Detwiler, *Hitler, Franco und Gibraltar. Die Frage des spanischen Eintritts in den zweiten Weltkrieg* (Wiesbaden, 1962); Charles B. Burdick, *Germany's Military Strategy and Spain in World War II* (Syracuse, N.Y., 1968); and, especially for the economic factors, the brilliant work of Herbert Feis, *The Spanish Story: Franco and the Nations at War* (New York, 1948).

2. See Gerhard L. Weinberg, *The Foreign Policy of Hitler's Germany: Diplomatic Revolution in Europe, 1933–1936* (Chicago, 1970), pp. 284–99 ·and footnotes; *DGFP*, D, 3; Manfred Merkes, *Die deutsche Politik gegenüber dem spanischen Bürgerkrieg, 1936–1939* (Bonn, 1961).

3. Hossbach memorandum of Hitler conference of November 5, 1937, *DGFP*, D, 1:36–37.

4. Treaties of 1937: *DGFP*, D, 3:256–57, 413–14, 417, 421–22; treaties of 1939: 3:884–86; 8:568–69. See Glenn T. Harper, *German Economic Policy in Spain during the Spanish Civil War, 1936–1939* (The Hague, 1967); and Feis, *Spanish Story,* pp. 19–27.

167

5. *DGFP*, D, 9:509–10.

6. Ibid., pp. 560, 565.

7. *DGFP*, D, 9:620–21; see also pp. 511, 585–88.

8. *DGFP*, D, 10:15–16. See the record of Hitler's conference with Mussolini and Ciano of October 4, 1940, *DGFP*, D, 11:252.

168

9. Franz Halder, *Kriegstagebuch. Tägliche Aufzeichnungen des Chefs des Generalstabes des Heeres, 1939–1942,* ed. Hans-Adolf Jacobsen, 3 vols. (Stuttgart, 1962–64), 2:20, 47; *DGFP*, D, 10:396 ff.

10. *Kriegstagebuch,* 2:100.

11. *DGFP*, D, 11:102–5.

12. Hitler conference with Serrano Suñer, *DGFP*, D, 11:93–98; Hitler to Franco, September 19, 1940, pp. 106–8; Franco to Hitler, September 22, 1940, pp. 153–55.

169

13. The Tripartite Pact between Germany, Italy, and Japan, signed September 27, 1940. See below, p. 227.

14. *Fuehrer Conferences on Matters Dealing with the German Navy, 1939–1945*, 8 vols. (Washington, D.C., 1946–47), 1940, 2:24–25.

15. *DGFP*, D, 11:211–14, 245–59; *The Ciano Diaries, 1939–1943* (New York, 1946), pp. 296–99.

170

16. *DGFP*, D, 11:371–76.

17. Ribbentrop's conversation with Serrano Suñer, also on October 23, 1940, *DGFP*, D, 11:376–79.

18. Ibid., pp. 377, n. 4, 380 ff., 466–67, 478–79.

171

19. Hitler-Mussolini conversation in Florence, October 28, 1940, *DGFP*, D, 11:411–22.

20. See below, pp. 195–97.

21. *Kriegstagebuch*, 2:164; *Fuehrer Conferences*, 1940, 2:32–34, 40–41.

172

22. Directive 18 for the conduct of the war, *DGFP*, D, 11:527–31.

23. *DGFP*, D, 11:598–610, 639–43.

24. Molotov had conversations with Hitler, Ribbentrop, and Göring in Berlin on November 12 and 13, 1940, *DGFP*, D, 11:533 ff.

173

25. Hitler to Mussolini, November 20, 1940, *DGFP*, D, 11:639–43.

26. Mussolini to Hitler, November 22, 1940, *DGFP*, D, 11:671–72; the German ambassador in Spain to the German Foreign Office, November 28 and 29, 1940, pp. 725, 739–41.

174

27. *DGFP*, D, 11:782, 812. On Canaris, see Karl Heinz Abshagen, *Canaris. Patriot und Weltbürger* (Stuttgart, 1949); and Ian Colvin, *Chief of Intelligence* (London, 1951); also Burdick, *Germany's Military Strategy*, pp. 24–30, 80, 102–9.

28. *DGFP*, D, 11:816–17, 852–53.

29. Order of December 11, *Fuehrer Directives, and Other Top-Level Directives of the German Armed Forces*, vol. 1, 1939–1941 (Washington, D.C., 1948), p. 125; T77/781/5508325; of December 18, DGFP, D, 11:899–902.

30. *DGFP*, D, 11:990–94.

175

31. Ibid., pp. 1056–60.

32. Hitler-Mussolini conversations, January 19 and 20, 1941, *DGFP*, D, 11:1127–33, 1145–51; *Ciano's Diplomatic Papers*, ed. Malcolm Muggeridge (London, 1948), p. 419–20.

33. *DGFP*, D, 11:1140–43, 1157–58, 1173–75, 1217–18, 1222–23.

34. *DGFP*, D, 12:37–42, 96–98, 112–13; *Ciano's Diplomatic Papers*, pp. 421–30.

35. *DGFP*, D, 12:131–32.

36. February 28, 1941, *DGFP*, D, 12:197–99.

176

37. Halder, *Kriegstagebuch*, 2:292; Burdick, *Germany's Military Strategy*, p. 122.

38. T77/781/5508323–24.

39. Halder order of May 7, 1941, *DGFP*, D, 12:731–33.

40. Burdick, *Germany's Military Strategy*, pp. 153–54, 157, 164, 187. A collection of what appear to have been the most important orders and military plans relating to Spain and the Mediterranean are on microfilm in the National Ar-

chives under code numbers T77/781 and T78/319. For the directive for Operation Ilona, T78/319/6273407–11; the change to Gisela, T78/319/6273413–15; to Nürnberg, T78/319/6273519–20.

177

41. *Fuerher Directives*, p. 126; T77/781/5508325.
42. Directive 22 for the conduct of the war, *DGFP*, D, 11:1073–75, 1158–59.
43. *DGFP*, 11:1127–33, 1145–51, 1158–59.
44. *The Rommel Papers*, ed. B. H. Liddell Hart (New York, 1953), pp. 91 ff.
45. *DGFP*, D, 12:26–30.

178

46. *DGFP*, D, 12:62–63; Mussolini to Hitler, February 22, 1941, pp. 135–38.
47. *Fuehrer Directives*, p. 142; *Rommel Papers*, pp. 98 ff.
48. *Rommel Papers*, chaps. 10 and 11; F. W. Deakin, *The Brutal Friendship: Mussolini, Hitler, and the Fall of Italian Fascism* (New York, 1966), p. 22.
49. *Hitler's Secret Conversations, 1941–1944* (paperback, New York, 1961), pp. 515, 536–38.

17. SECURITY IN THE SOUTHEAST: HUNGARY AND THE BALKANS

180

1. A term used by Rosenberg in a report on the activities of the Aussenpolitisches Amt of the NSDAP, *IMT*, 007-PS, 25:35. For Nazi attitudes to Southeastern Europe, see Walther Pahl, *Das politische Antlitz der Erde. Ein weltpolitischer Atlas* (Leipzig, 1938), pp. 47–49; J. Kühn, "Über den Sinn des gegenwärtigen Krieges," *Zeitschrift für Geopolitik* 17 (1940):60–61; Walther Schneefuss, *Donauräume und Donaureiche* (Vienna, 1944). On Southeastern Europe in general, see Bibliography, 19. Hungary and the Balkans.

181

2. France's actual ability to protect the new states of Eastern Europe had already been badly weakened through Germany's remilitarization of the Rhineland. See above, p. 86.

182

3. Hitler's belief in the need for a large measure of political control was very evident in his attitude toward Yugoslavia after the coup d'état in that country in March 1941. See below, pp. 201–2.
4. Ferdinand Friedensburg, *Die mineralischen Bodenschätze als weltpolitische und militärische Machtfaktoren* (Stuttgart, 1939); "Kann der Treibstoffbedarf der heutigen Kriegsführung überhaupt befriedigt werden?" *Deutsche Wirtschaft*, April 16, 1937; *Das Erdoel im Weltkrieg* (Stuttgart, 1939), p. 185; see also the important article by H. Steinberger, "Der Treibstoffverbrauch im Kriege," *Deutsche Wehr* 1 (1939):3 ff. Prewar estimates of German oil needs were not unduly pessimistic, as official statistics compiled during the war were to show. Detailed statistics on German oil production and consumption during wartime are on microfilm in the National Archives, code numbers T77/84 and T77/594. See especially the report prepared by the German army's economic office (Wi-Rü Amt) of August 31, 1941, "Mineralöle und die Versorgungslage im Kriege," T77/438/1301640–832.
5. *World Production of Raw Materials* (London, 1941) and *Southeastern Europe: A Political and Economic Survey* (London, 1939), both published by the Royal Institute of International Affairs; *Statistisches Jahrbuch für das Deutsche Reich; Vierteljahrshefte zur Statistik des deutschen Reiches*.

183

6. Antonin Basch, *Conquest by Planned Trade: Foreign Trade between Free Countries vs. Controlled Economy* (New York, 1941); and *The Danube Basin and the German Economic Sphere* (New York, 1943); Paul Einzig, *Bloodless Invasion: German Economic Penetration into the Danubian States and the Balkans* (London, 1939).

7. Martin Broszat, "Deutschland-Ungarn-Rumänien. Entwicklung and Grund-faktoren nationalsozialistischer Hegemonial-and Bündnispolitik, 1938–1941," *Historische Zeitschrift* 206 (1968):45–96; *Southeastern Europe: A Brief Survey* (London, 1940), published by the Royal Institute of International Affairs, pp. 61–62, 116–18.

8. Typical of Hungarian revisionist literature is the pamphlet *Justice for Hungary! The Cruel Errors of Trianon,* published by the journal *Pesti Hirlap* (Budapest, 1931). For a more balanced account, R. W. Seton-Watson, *Treaty Revision and the Hungarian Frontiers* (London, 1934). The most detailed work on Hungary before and during the Second World War is C. A. Macartney, *October Fifteenth: A History of Modern Hungary, 1929–1945,* 2 vols. (Edinburgh, 1956–57).

9. Gerhard L. Weinberg, *The Foreign Policy of Hitler's Germany: Diplomatic Revolution in Europe, 1933–1936* (Chicago, 1970), pp. 110–16.

184

10. *DGFP,* D, especially the documents in volumes 2 and 5.

11. *DGFP,* D, 4:118–27; 5:78. See above, p. 109.

12. Ibid., p. 241.

13. The German-Japanese agreement of November 25, 1936, ostensibly directed against Communism and the Third International. See below, p. 224.

14. *DGFP,* D, 6:1093–1100, etc. Macartney, *October Fifteenth,* 1, chaps. 14, 16, and 17.

186

15. *DGFP,* D, 10:37 ff.

16. Ibid., pp. 581–87; 11:7–8; Grigoire Gafencu, *Prelude to the Russian Campaign: From the Moscow Pact (August 21st 1939) to the Opening of Hostilities in Russia (June 22nd 1941)* (London, 1945), by the former Rumanian minister for foreign affairs and minister to Moscow, pp. 55 ff.

17. *DGFP,* D, 11:226; see below, pp. 189–90.

18. See below, pp. 201–2.

19. March 17, 1941, *DGFP,* D, 12:302.

20. *DGFP,* D, 12:369–71; Paulus testimony, *IMT* 7:257.

21. *DGFP,* D, 12:400 ff., especially p. 509.

187

22. Ibid., pp. 548, 551, 581–86, 842–44.

23. Ibid., pp. 341, 685, 1030.

24. Ibid., pp. 1070–71; 13:24–25, 63–64.

25. The Balkan Entente, formed February 9, 1934, included Yugoslavia, Rumania, Greece, and Turkey, and was largely the work of Rumanian Foreign Minister N. Titulescu.

188

26. See Broszat, "Deutschland-Ungarn-Rumänien," pp. 45–96; Gafencu, *Prelude to the Russian Campaign;* and especially Andreas Hillgruber, *Hitler, König Carol und Marschall Antonescu. Die deutsch-rumänischen Beziehungen, 1938–1944* (Wiesbaden, 1954).

27. *DGFP,* D, 6:91–96; Gafencu, *Prelude,* p. 231.

189

28. Gafencu, pp. 233–34, 274–75.

29. *DGFP,* D, 8:172–73, 530–32, 868–69, 925–26; 9:459–60, 466–67.

30. *DGFP,* D, 10:74–75, 91.

31. By the Vienna Award of August 30, 1940, Rumania ceded Northern Transylvania to Hungary; by the Treaty of Craiova, September 7, 1940, it ceded Southern Dobruja to Bulgaria.

32. David Dallin, *Soviet Russia's Foreign Policy, 1939–1942* (New Haven, 1942), p. 263.

33. *DGFP,* D, 11:22–25, 28.

190

34. Ibid., pp. 126–28.
35. Ibid., pp. 136–37, 144–46.
36. Ibid., pp. 662–70, 689–90; I. Antonescu affidavit, *IMT* 7:304 ff.; M. Antonescu affidavit, *IMT* 7:308.

191

37. *DGFP*, D, 11:867–69, 899–902, 921–22, 937–41; *Fuehrer Conferences on Matters Dealing with the German Navy, 1939–1945*, 8 vols. (Washington, D.C., 1946–47), 1941, 1:4; *Fuehrer Directives and Other Top-Level Directives of the German Armed Forces*, vol. 1, *1939–1941* (Washington, D.C., 1948), p. 131.

38. *DGFP*, D, 11:1087–95, 1145–51, 1169–70, 1204–6; record of Hitler's conversation with Mussolini and senior German and Italian military and political leaders, January 20, 1941, *NCA*, 6:945. Killinger, German minister in Rumania since January 24, 1941, and one of the SA men appointed by Ribbentrop to diplomatic posts to offset the influence of Himmler's SS, did his best to produce evidence of the connection between Himmler's organizations and the Iron Guard. *DGFP*, D, 12:230.

39. Ibid., pp. 338–43, 440–42, 467–69, 534–35, 592, 616–17, 876.
40. Ibid., pp. 864–65.

192

41. Ibid., pp. 996–1006.
42. Ibid., pp. 1047–49.

193

43. *DGFP*, D, 9:606–7; 10:332–41; 11:37. See above, n. 31.
44. King Boris to Hitler, October 22, 1940, *DGFP*, D, 11:364–66.
45. *DGFP*, D, 11:479–80, 591–92, 652, n. 2, 867–69, 937–41, 1056–60; *Fuehrer Conferences*, 1940, 2:59; 1941, 1:2.

194

46. *DGFP*, D, 11:1081–85, 1101–9; 12:203; *DDP* 9:406–9; G. Stefanov, "Sur la Bulgarie en Guerre. La Politique Extérieure," *RHDGM* 72 (1968):6.
47. *DGFP*, D, 11:937–41, 1216–17; 12:99–100, 160, 182–83; record of staff talks, *NCA*, 1746-PS, 4:272–75; *DDP* 9:409–10; David B. Cohen, "Le Pillage de l'Économie Bulgare par les Allemands," *RHDGM* 72 (1968):49.
48. *DGFP*, D, 12:371–72, 395–96, 440–42.
49. Ibid., pp. 566–67, 577, 623–24, 842–44; 13:135–36; *DDP* 9:127.

195

50. *IMT*, 039-C, 34:230; Cohen, "Pillage," pp. 49–51; N. Gornenski and E. Kamenov, "Sur la Bulgarie en Guerre. La Politique Intérieure," *RHDGM* 72 (1968): 26.
51. *DGFP*, D, 6:248–53; 7:39–49; *The Ciano Diaries 1939–1943* (New York, 1946), pp. 46, 60, 85, 119–20.
52. *Ciano Diaries*, p. 121.

196

53. On this entire problem, see the monograph of Ehrengard Schramm-von Thadden, *Griechenland und die Grossmächte im zweiten Weltkrieg* (Wiesbaden, 1955), which unfortunately stops with the German invasion.
54. See above, pp. 189–90.
55. *Ciano Diaries*, pp. 299–301; *DGFP*, D, 11:408, 422–23.
56. Mussolini to Hitler, August 24, 1940, *DGFP*, D, 10:538–39.
57. *Fuehrer Conferences*, 1940, 2:32–33; *DGFP*, D, 11:411, 530–31, 606–10; Göring testimony, *IMT* 9:334; Keitel testimony, *IMT* 10:522; Jodl testimony, *IMT* 15:287–88.

197

58. *DGFP*, D, 11:639–43.

59. Ibid., pp. 527–31, 789–91, 867–69, 990–94, 1073–75.

198

60. The excellent monograph of J. B. Hoptner, *Yugoslavia in Crisis, 1934–1941* (New York, 1962), contains a good bibliography on the entire Yugoslav problem.

61. Commercial agreements of May 1, 1934, *RGB1* (1934) 2:301; *DGFP*, C, 2:592–96; situation in 1938, *DGFP*, D, 5:217–19; Hoptner, *Yugoslavia*, chap. 4.

62. *DGFP*, C, 4:407–9, 888; Weinberg, *Foreign Policy*, pp. 117, 228–29.

199

63. *DGFP*, D, 1:573; 5:215–17, 221–29, 242.

64. *DGFP*, D, 5:266–67, 274.

65. Ibid., pp. 385–86, 390–91, 411–13.

66. *Ciano Diaries*, pp. 39, 46–50, 58, 87–88.

200

67. *DGFP*, D, 6:255–56, 325–30, 339–43, 635–38, 860–62.

68. Hoptner, *Yugoslavia*, pp. 134 ff. German analysis of Yugoslav foreign policy since the formation of the Cvetković government, July 5, 1940, *DGFP*, D, 10:133–36.

69. *DGFP*, D, 11:728–35.

201

70. *DGFP*, D, 12:34–35, 79–96, 230–33, 247, 255–56, 281–82, 312–15, 353–61; *Ciano's Diplomatic Papers*, ed. Malcolm Muggeridge (London, 1948), p. 432.

71. Hoptner, *Yugoslavia*, chap. 10.

72. *DGFP*, D, 12:383–85, 398–99, 421–22, 451–52.

73. Ibid., pp. 421 ff.; Jodl testimony, *IMT* 15:422; Göring testimony, *IMT* 9:333 ff.

202

74. *DGFP*, D, 12:372–75, 395–98, 440–42, 475–78.

203

75. *Dokumente zum Konflikt mit Jugoslawien und Griechenland* (Berlin, 1941), p. 2.

18. THE FINAL DRIVE FOR LEBENSRAUM

204

1. Memorandum of October 9, 1939, *IMT*, 052-L, 37:469–70.

205

2. November 23, 1939, *DGFP*, D, 8:442.

3. These concessions were made in a secret additional protocol to the German-Russian Nonaggression Pact of August 23, 1939, and the German-Soviet Boundary and Friendship Treaty of September 28, 1939, with its additional protocols, *DGFP*, D, 7:246–47; 8:164–66, 208–12. See also Ribbentrop's explanation for Hitler of the August 23 protocol, June 24, 1940, *DGFP*, D, 10:10.

4. Russian treaty with Estonia, September 29, 1939; with Latvia, October 5; with Lithuania, October 10. See *The Nazi-Soviet Conspiracy and the Baltic States: Diplomatic Documents and Other Evidence*, ed. August Rei (London, 1948); and K. R. Pusta, *The Soviet Union and the Baltic States* (New York, 1942).

5. June 18, 1940, *DGFP*, D, 9:599–600.

6. The Russians demanded the Hanko naval base and Finnish territory around Leningrad. See *The Finnish Blue Book: The Development of Finnish-Soviet Relations during the Autumn of 1939, Including the Official Documents and the Peace Treaty of March 12, 1940* (Philadelphia, 1940); Max Jakobson, *The Diplomacy of the Winter War: An Account of the Russo-Finnish War, 1939–1940* (Cambridge, Mass., 1961); and Anatole G. Mazour, *Finland between East and West* (Princeton, N.J., 1956).

7. *Soviet Documents on Foreign Policy,* ed. Jane Degras (London, 1953), 3:421–24; *Finland Reveals her Secret Documents on Soviet Policy, March 1940–June 1941: The Attitude of the USSR to Finland after the Peace of Moscow* (New York, 1941), pp. 35–38. For a German analysis of these concessions and their effect on the German position in the Baltic, see *DGFP,* D, 8:914–15.

8. *DGFP,* D, 8:200, 236, 277, 280, 484, etc.

206

9. *DGFP,* D, 10:3; on the Bukovina question, pp. 10–13; Navy war diary, *IMT,* 170-C, 34:687.

10. Ibid., pp. 685–98; Jodl diary, *IMT,* 1809-PS, 15:389 ff.; *DGFP,* D, 9:396, 415, 419, 442, 636; 10:50–51, 539 ff.

11. See above, p. 190.

12. *DGFP,* D, 9:712, 767, 806, 833, 1018, etc.; and especially 11:533–49 (Molotov's conversations with Hitler and Ribbentrop in November 1940). Navy war diary, *IMT,* 170-C, 34:693–98; Göring testimony, *IMT,* 9:342.

13. Andreas Hillgruber, *Hitlers Strategie. Politik und Kriegsführung, 1940–1941* (Frankfurt am Main, 1965), pp. 255 ff.; G. Thomas diary, *IMT,* 30:271 ff.; *DGFP,* D, 9:59.

14. January 20, 1941, *IMT,* 134-C, 34:467.

15. German trade treaty with Lithuania, May 20, 1939; with Estonia, October 7, 1939; with Latvia, December 21, 1939, *RGBl* (1939) 2:789, 992; (1940) 2:13. See *DGFP,* D, 9:593–95, for a summary of the problem and references to the secret treaties concluded between Germany and the Baltic States.

207

16. See Schnurre's analysis of September 28, 1940, *DGFP,* D, 11:221–23.

17. See above, p. 182.

18. January 20, 1941, *IMT* 34:469; Navy war diary, *IMT,* 170-C, 34:697–98.

19. German-Soviet trade treaties of August 19 and September 28, 1939; February 11, 1940; January 10, 1941. *DGFP,* D, 7:142–48, 152; 8:167–69, 762–69; 11:1066–69.

20. Schnurre memorandum of February 26, 1940, on the importance of the German-Soviet commercial agreement of February 11, 1940; also memoranda of September 26 and 28, 1940, *DGFP,* D, 8:814–17; 11:189–90, 221–23; Georg Thomas, *Geschichte der deutschen Wehr-und Rüstungswirtschaft* (1918–1943/45), ed. Wolfgang Birkenfeld (Boppard am Rhein, 1966), pp. 228–29, 280–81; memorandum of the Economic Staff East of May 23, 1941, on the importance of Russia's economic resources, *IMT,* 126-EC, 36:135–57.

21. *DGFP,* D, 8:168, 814–17; 11:223.

208

22. Ibid., 8:483, 588–96, 672–73, 762–69; 11:189–90, 221–23, etc.; Navy war diary, *IMT,* 170-C, 34:682–84.

23. Thomas, *Geschichte der deutschen Wehr-und Rüstungswirtschaft,* p. 229.

24. See Schnurre's memorandum of July 22, 1940, *DGFP,* D, 10:270–71.

25. The order to initiate military preparations against Russia was given July 22, 1940. Franz Halder, *Kriegstagebuch. Tägliche Aufzeichnungen des Chefs des Generalstabes des Heeres, 1939–1942,* ed. Hans-Adolf Jacobsen, 3 vols. (Stuttgart, 1962–64), 2:32. Orders to give Germany's armament orders priority were evidently issued early in August, for in a memorandum of September 26, 1940, Schnurre wrote, "The directives issued during the last few weeks by the Reichsmarschall [Göring] concerning the absolute priority of all [German] armaments contracts and the further augmentation of these armaments contracts make it impossible for German industry to execute, in addition to these contracts, the scheduled deliveries to Russia." Two days later Schnurre wrote that if the armament program ordered by the Führer were carried out, Germany could not balance its existing deficit with Russia of seventy-three million Reichsmarks nor deliver on schedule the remainder of the German commitment. In addition there was a directive issued by Göring "to avoid shipments to Russia which would directly or

indirectly strengthen Russia's war potential," *DGFP*, D, 10:374, n. 1; 11:189–90, 222.

26. Thomas, *Geschichte der deutschen Wehr-und Rüstungswirtschaft*, p. 229.

27. *DGFP*, D, 11:971–72 ff., 1066–69.

28. Thomas memorandum of June 20, 1941, on the basis of information received from Todt and later confirmed by Keitel, *IMT*, 1456-PS, 27:220–21.

29. See the long memorandum, "Guiding Principles for the Conduct of Economic Policy," dated June 1941, *IMT*, 1743-PS, 27:3 ff.

209

30. See above, p. 158.

31. Halder, *Kriegstagebuch*, 2:30–34, 46–50 (entries for July 22 and 31, emphasis in original document). See also Navy war diary, *IMT*, 170-C, 34:688 (entry for July 21).

210

32. Navy war diary, *IMT*, 170-C, 34:696 (entry for January 8, 1941). Halder, *Kriegstagebuch*, 2:243–46, 283, 335–38 (entries for January 16, February 17, and March 30, 1941).

33. Hitler conference of November 23, 1939, *IMT*, 789-PS, 26:327–36; Engel diary, cited in Hillgruber, *Hitlers Strategie*, pp. 226–27 (entry for August 10, 1940); Thomas memorandum on a conference with Göring, February 26, 1941, Nuremberg document NI 7291.

34. "Der völkischen Rassentheorie," *Mein Kampf*, p. 952; (1934 German edition, 2:743).

211

35. Navy war diary, *IMT*, 170-C, 34:683 (entry for December 31, 1940, on the basis of observations during the Russo-Finnish war); army intelligence reports on the condition of the Russian army as of January 31, 1941, T78/335/6291300–17; chief of the Army General Staff analysis, February 3, 1941, *IMT*, 872-PS, 26:391–99; Walter Warlimont, *Inside Hitler's Headquarters, 1939–45* (New York, 1964), p. 145.

36. April 30, 1941, *IMT*, 873-PS, 26:400.

37. See Hitler's Directive 32, "Preparations for the Period after *Barbarossa*," June 11, 1941, *DGFP*, D, 12:1012–16.

38. Hitler Directive 21, December 18, 1940, *DGFP*, D, 11:899–902.

39. Diary of General Greiner of the Wehrmacht Operations Staff, quoted in *DGFP*, D, 11:1056–60.

40. Hitler to Mussolini, June 21, 1941, in which Hitler once again marshaled his arguments for the attack on Russia. *DGFP*, D, 11:1066–69.

41. Already on July 3 General Halder, on the basis of a talk on June 30, 1940, with State Secretary Weizsäcker of the Foreign Office who informed him about Hitler's view of the need to pay close attention to the problem of the east, had decided that it would be necessary to consider the military operational problem of a campaign against Russia. On July 22 Hitler himself gave orders to "take up the Russian problem" and "to prepare draft plans," whereupon Halder informed him of the plans already prepared (Halder, *Kriegstagebuch*, 1:374–75; 2:6, 32–33).

212

42. Ibid., 2:49–50.

43. Ibid., pp. 155, 178, 210–11 (entries for October 29, November 13, December 12); OKW Operational Staff diary, December 5, 1940, *IMT*, 1799-PS, 28:393–95; Jodl testimony, *IMT* 15:391–92; Hillgruber, *Hitlers Strategie*, pp. 353–62; Helmuth Greiner, *Die oberste Wehrmachtführung, 1939–1943* (Wiesbaden, 1951), pp. 237, 321–31. Warlimont says that although Hitler approved the army's plans for Russia on December 12, he later altered them significantly—and for the worse. *Inside Hitler's Headquarters*, pp. 137–43.

44. Hitler Directive 21, *DGFP*, D, 11:899–902; Brauchitsch order of January 31, 1941, T78/335/6291236.

45. Conference of February 3, 1941, *IMT*, 872-PS, 26:391–99.

46. Conference of April 30, 1941, *IMT*, 873-PS, 26:399–401.

214

47. Halder, *Kriegstagebuch*, 2:336–37 (entry for March 30, 1941).

48. *IMT* 26:401–8; 34:249–58; appendix 3 of special order 1 for the conduct of German troops in Russia, May 19, 1941, Nuremberg document NOKW 3485; Warlimont, *Inside Hitler's Headquarters*, pp. 160–67; Greiner, *Die oberste Wehrmachtführung*, pp. 370–71.

49. Keitel order of March 13, 1941, *IMT*, 447-PS, 26:53–58; Otto Bräutigam, *Überblick über die besetzten Ostgebiete während des 2. Weltkrieges* (Tübingen, 1954), pp. 5–7; Warlimont, *Inside Hitler's Headquarters*, pp. 150–56; Greiner, *Die oberste Wehrmachtführung*, pp. 369–70.

215

50. Thomas, *Geschichte der deutschen Wehr-und Rüstungswirtschaft*, pp. 261–62, 266–74, 514–32.

51. Thomas memorandum of conference with Göring, February 26, 1941, NI 7291.

52. Economic conference of April 29, 1941, *IMT*, 1157-PS, 27:32–37; the results of the conference summarized in a memorandum of May 5, 1941, NOKW 3485.

216

53. Memorandum of conference with General Thomas, February 28, 1941, *IMT*, 1317-PS, 28:169–71; Thomas memorandum, March 19, 1941, *TWC* 12:1266. The relationship between the military and economic staffs was worked out in great detail in a memorandum of May 14, 1941, NOKW 3335; Keitel testimony, *IMT* 10:571–72.

54. Göring directives for the conduct of German economic policy in the east, June 1941 (Green folder), published in part under 1743-PS, *IMT* 28:3–15. The full text is on film, T77/5/717851–78. See also the guidelines for German agricultural policy in the east, *IMT*, 126-EC, 36:135–57.

217

55. Memorandum on conference of May 2, 1941, *IMT* 31:84.

56. Halder, *Kriegstagebuch*, 2:46–50, 335–38.

57. July 31, 1940. Ibid., p. 50.

58. March 3, 1941. Warlimont, *Inside Hitler's Headquarters*, pp. 150–52; Greiner, *Die oberste Wehrmachtführung*, pp. 369–70.

59. Order of March 13, 1941, *IMT*, 447-PS, 26:53–58; Warlimont, *Inside Hitler's Headquarters*, pp. 152–56.

60. See above, pp. 212–14.

218

61. Special tasks and powers, assigned to the police and SS in the Keitel order of March 13, 1941 (see n. 59), were defined in subsequent negotiations with the OKW (Warlimont, *Inside Hitler's Headquarters*, pp. 157–58; Halder, *Kriegstagebuch*, 2:311, 328, entries for March 13 and 25, 1941) and embodied in an OKW order of March 26, 1941 (Warlimont, pp. 158–60). The negotiations and final orders were summarized in an unsigned memorandum of a Himmler-Rosenberg conference of May 1, 1941 (NOKW 2504, 866-PS and 1188-PS) and in the official diary of the Reichsführer SS, entry for May 1, 1941 (NOKW 2147).

62. NOKW 2504; Greiner, *Die oberste Wehrmachtführung*, p. 370; and Alexander Dallin, *German Rule in Russia, 1941–1945: A Study in Occupation Policies* (London, 1957), p. 29.

219

63. The date of April 2 is given in an unsigned Rosenberg memorandum of April 7, 1941, *IMT*, 1019-PS, 26:557.

64. *Hitler's Secret Conversations, 1941–1944* (paperback, New York, 1961), p. 400; *Goebbels Diaries, 1942–1943* (New York, 1948), entry for March 21, 1942. There is a brief sketch of Rosenberg in Joachim C. Fest, *The Face of the Third Reich: Portraits of the Nazi Leadership* (New York, 1970), pp. 163–74.

65. *IMT*, 447-PS, 26:54–55; Halder, *Kriegstagebuch*, 2:337; Rosenberg memoranda of April 2, 7, 25, etc., in his "Russia" file, Nuremberg documents 1017-PS ff.

220

66. April 2, 1941, *IMT*, 1017-PS, 26:547–54; also 1018-PS, an unsigned forty-six-page memorandum, dated April 7, 1941.

67. *IMT*, 865-PS, 26:383–86.

68. Unsigned Rosenberg report, June 28, 1941, *IMT*, 1039-PS, 26:590.

69. Rosenberg speech of June 20, 1941, to "those most closely concerned with the eastern problem," *IMT*, 1058-PS, 26:610–27.

221

70. *DGFP*, D, 12:341, 685.

71. For example during the visit of Molotov to Berlin in November 1940, *DGFP*, D, 11:533 ff.

72. See above, pp. 205–6.

73. *DGFP*, D, 11:149; testimony of General Erich Buschenhagen and affidavit of Colonel Kitschmann, former German military attaché in Helsinki, *IMT*, 7:310 ff., 327–28; Hitler Directive 21, December 18, 1940, *DGFP*, D, 11:900; Warlimont, *Inside Hitler's Headquarters*, p. 143; Gerhard L. Weinberg, *Germany and the Soviet Union, 1939–1941* (Leyden, 1954), pp. 127–28.

74. See above, pp. 189–90.

222

75. *DGFP*, D, 12:685, 864.

76. Ibid., 1059, 1081; 13:13–14, 25; see above, pp. 187, 191–92.

77. Ibid., 12:1051; 13:3.

78. Ibid., 12:1040; 13:20.

79. Ibid., 12:219–20.

19. THE JAPANESE ALLIANCE

224

1. *Mein Kampf*, pp. 205, 399.

2. On the general literature of German-Japanese relations, see Bibliography, 21. Japan.

3. Gerhard L. Weinberg, ed., "Die geheimen Abkommen zum Antikominternpakt," *VfZ* 2 (1954):193–201; *DGFP*, D, 1:734, n. 2a; *Documents on International Affairs* (London, 1937), 297–300.

225

4. *DGFP*, D, 1, chap. 4.

5. Ribbentrop memorandum, January 2, 1938, *DGFP*, D, 1:162–68; Theo Sommer, *Deutschland und Japan zwischen den Mächten, 1935–1940. Vom Antikominternpakt zum Dreimächtepakt* (Tübingen, 1962), pp. 96–116.

6. See above, pp. 127–28.

7. Sommer, *Deutschland und Japan*, pp. 275–323; Hubertus Lupke, *Japans Russlandpolitik von 1939 bis 1941* (Frankfurt am Main, 1962), pp. 5–10.

8. Ambassador Ott to the Foreign Office, June 24, 1940, *DGFP*, D, 10:5; Sommer, *Deutschland und Japan*, pp. 324 ff.

226

9. Franz Halder, *Kriegstagebuch. Tägliche Aufzeichnungen des Chefs des Generalstabes des Heeres, 1939–1942*, ed. Hans-Adolf Jacobsen, 3 vols. (Stuttgart, 1962–64), 2:21.

10. See Jodl's memorandum, "The Continuation of the War against England,"

dated June 30, 1940, in which he says, "The fight against the English empire can only be carried on with or through those countries that have an interest in the collapse of the English world empire and hope for a lucrative inheritance. These are, in the first instance, Italy, Spain, Russia, and Japan" (*IMT*, 1776-PS, 28:303).

11. Halder, *Kriegstagebuch*, 2:49.

227

12. Sommer, *Deutschland und Japan*, pp. 349 ff.; Nobutaka Ike, ed., *Japan's Decision for War: Records of the 1941 Policy Conferences* (Stanford, Calif., 1967), pp. 3–4; Herbert Feis, *The Road to Pearl Harbor: The Coming of the War between the United States and Japan* (paperback, New York, 1964) pp. 76–83; On General Tojo see Robert J. C. Butow, *Tojo and the Coming of the War* (Princeton, N.J., 1961).

13. These proposals were presented to Matsuoka in the course of conferences on September 9 and 10, *DGFP*, D, 11:57–58.

14. Letter of September 17, 1940, *DGFP*, D, 11:102–5.

15. *DGFP*, D, 11:204–5.

228

16. Ott-Matsuoka letter of September 27, 1940, *DGFP*, D, 11:205–7; Johanna M. Menzell, "Der geheime deutsch-japanische Notenaustausch zum Dreimächtepakt," *VfZ* 5 (1957):182–93.

17. *Kriegstagebuch*, 2:116.

18. Feis, *Road to Pearl Harbor*, chaps. 14, 20, 22; Saul Friedländer, *Prelude to Downfall: Hitler and the United States, 1939–1941* (New York, 1967), pp. 200–202, 233.

19. Ribbentrop-Oshima talk of February 23; Ribbentrop to Ott, February 27; Ribbentrop-Matsuoka talk (in Berlin), March 27, 1941, *DGFP*, D, 12: 139–51, 183, 376–83, 386–94; *Fuehrer Conferences on Matters Dealing with the German Navy, 1939–1945*, 8 vols. (Washington, D.C., 1946–47), 1941, 1:12–19.

20. *IMT*, 075-C, 34:302–5; *DGFP*, D, 12:219–20.

229

21. Lupke, *Japans Russlandpolitik*, pp. 71 ff.; Feis, *Road to Pearl Harbor*, chap. 23; Weizsäcker to Ott, April 16, 1941, *DGFP*, D, 12:570.

230

22. *DGFP*, D, 13:40–41, 61–63, 110–13, 131–34, 141, 375–79, 466–67; *Fuehrer Conferences*, 1941, 2:27.

23. Ike, *Japan's Decision for War*, pp. 56 ff.; Feis, *Road to Pearl Harbor*, pp. 209–26; *DGFP*, D, 13:73–77, 158–60, 367–68, 798–800.

231

24. September 4, 1941. Cited in James V. Compton, *The Swastika and the Eagle: Hitler, the United States, and the Origins of World War II* (Boston, 1967), p. 212.

25. Ribbentrop's arguments were presented either to the Japanese ambassador to Berlin (Oshima) or through the German ambassador to Tokyo (Ott). *DGFP*, D, 13:375–79, 608–11, 798–800.

232

26. *DGFP*, D, 13:108–13, 121, 179–81.

27. Ribbentrop's instruction to the German embassy in Japan of November 9, 1941, *DGFP*, D, 13:760–62. In the original draft of this document, the key sentence quoted above reads as follows: "as long as American territories (the Philippines) or American basis for raw materials (Netherlands Indies) are not affected by such an action." The passage about the Netherlands Indies was deleted before the instruction was sent to Tokyo.

28. Feis, *Road to Pearl Harbor*, chaps. 29–31; Joseph C. Grew, *My Ten Years in Japan: A Contemporary Record Drawn from the Diaries and Private and Official*

Papers of Joseph C. Grew, United States Ambassador to Japan, 1932–1942 (New York, 1944), pp. 408–9, 422–25.

233

29. Feis, *Road to Pearl Harbor*, p. 265 and n. 11; Ike, *Japan's Decision for War*, p. 135.

30. Ike, *Japan's Decision*, pp. 167 ff.; Feis, *Road*, pp. 282–97; Butow, *Tojo and the Coming of the War*, chap. 11; Ott to the Foreign Office, November 18, 1941, *DGFP*, D, 13:798–800.

31. Ike, *Japan's Decision*, pp. 208–39; Feis, *Road*, chap. 37; Butow, *Tojo*, pp. 325 ff.

234

32. Ott to the Foreign Office, November 18; Ribbentrop to the German Embassy in Japan, November 21; Ott to Ribbentrop, November 23; Oshima-Ribbentrop conversation, November 28; Oshima to Tokyo, November 29, 1941. *DGFP*, D 13:798–800, 806–7, 813–14, 868–70.

33. *DGFP*, D, 13:958–59, 982–84.

34. Oshima to Tokyo, December 8, 1941, quoted in *DGFP*, D, 13:991, n. 4.

235

35. PS-3776; WF 2871/564945-59; published in *RGB1*, February 13, 1942.

36. *ADAP, E, 1*:23–26.

37. *ADAP*, E, 1:97–98, 133–34, 257, 260–62; Johanna M. Meskill, *Hitler and Japan: The Hollow Alliance* (New York, 1967), pp. 89–123.

236

38. See John Erickson, *The Soviet High Command: A Military-Political History, 1918–1941* (London, 1962), pp. 631–32.

20. HITLER'S DECLARATION OF WAR ON THE UNITED STATES

238

1. See, for example, the articles of G. L. Weinberg, "Hitler's Image of the United States," *American Historical Review* 49 (1964):1006–21; and Joachim Remak, "Hitlers Amerikapolitik," *Aussenpolitik* 6 (1955):706–14. On German-American relations in general, see Bibliography, 22. The United States.

2. *Mein Kampf*, pp. 180–81, 658, 929; *Hitler's Secret Book* (paperback, New York, 1961), pp. 83, 91, 100 ff., 156–57, 209.

239

3. See the articles cited in n. 1, above; Saul Friedländer, *Prelude to Downfall: Hitler and the United States, 1939–1941* (New York, 1967), chap. 1; J. Compton, *The Swastika and the Eagle: Hitler, the United States and the Origins of World War II* (New York, 1965), chaps. 1 and 2.

4. Before the Munich treaty, for example, Hitler had rejected Japanese overtures to conclude a defensive alliance "for fear of repercussions in America" (*DGFP*, D, 4:516) and because it might promote an alliance between the United States and Britain (*Ciano's Diplomatic Papers*, ed. Malcolm Muggeridge [London, 1948], p. 243). Hitler was emboldened by his success at Munich to consider anew a defensive alliance between Germany, Italy, and Japan; but for the time being nothing came of this idea (*DGFP*, D, 4, chap. 8).

5. Friedländer, *Prelude to Downfall*, pp. 15–18, 21–22, 26, 42–43, 49–65.

6. *Fuehrer Conferences on Matters Dealing with the German Navy, 1939–1945*, 8 vols. (Washington, D.C., 1946–47), 1939, pp. 3, 5; *DGFP*, D, 8:148–50; Hitler memorandum of October 9, 1939, *IMT*, 052-L, 37:472; Jodl testimony, *IMT* 15:376.

240

7. *Fuehrer Conferences*, 1939, pp. 12 ff.; Navy war diary, January 1940 and March 5, 1940, *IMT* 34:177–80; 40:99; Hitler order of May 24, 1940, *DGFP*, D, 9:427–29, 524–25; 11:505–6, 514; Friedländer, *Prelude to Downfall*, p. 65.

8. Hitler estimate, November 23, 1939, *DGFP*, D, 8:439; of September 14, 1940, Franz Halder, *Kriegstagebuch. Tägliche Aufzeichnungen des Chefs des Generalstabes des Heeres, 1939–1942*, ed. Hans-Adolf Jacobsen, 3 vols. (Stuttgart, 1962–64), 2:98; Naval staff estimate, December 27, 1940, *Fuehrer Conferences*, 1940, 2:70; Friedländer, *Prelude to Downfall*, pp. 119, n. 5, 171, 246–51, 310.

9. See above, pp. 227–28.

10. See above, pp. 229–30.

241

11. See above, pp. 234–35.

12. Orders in force in May 1941; of June 21, 1941, *Fuehrer Conferences*, 1941, 1:68–73; 2:1–2; German Foreign Office memorandum, June 9, 1941, *IMT*, 850-D, 35:546.

13. Friedländer, *Prelude to Downfall*, pp. 49–55, 167 ff., 242–46.

14. Friedländer, *Prelude*, p. 95.

242

15. Halder, *Kriegstagebuch*, 2:30–31, 49; *Fuehrer Conferences*, 1941, 2:12–19; Friedländer, *Prelude*, pp. 170–71.

16. *Fuehrer Conferences*, 1941, 1:68–73; 2:1–2; Naval war staff teletype of July 10, 1941, Nuremberg document C-192; Friedländer, *Prelude*, pp. 255–57.

243

17. See above, p. 240. On the subject of American attitudes and policies, the most authoritative and comprehensive treatment is William L. Langer and S. Everett Gleason, *The Challenge to Isolation: The World Crisis of 1937–1940 and American Foreign Policy*, 2 vols. (New York, 1952).

18. Langer and Gleason, *Challenge to Isolation*, 2, chap. 22.

19. William L. Langer and S. Everett Gleason, *The Undeclared War, 1940–1941* (New York, 1953), chaps. 7–9.

20. This was done in response to information from the German consulate general in New York that a convoy of 120 ships was being assembled to be sent under American protection to Iceland. Memorandum of March 14, 1941, and OKW directive of March 25, *DGFP*, D, 12: 295, 363.

244

21. Langer and Gleason, *Undeclared War*, chaps. 14 and 18.

22. Friedländer, *Prelude to Downfall*, pp. 205–7; *Fuehrer Conferences*, 1941, 1:68–73.

23. Langer and Gleason, *Undeclared War*, chaps. 14, 18, 21.

24. The *Greer* incident occurred 175 miles southwest of Iceland within the area proclaimed by the Germans as a war zone. The *Greer*, which had been notified of the presence of the submarine by a British plane, had been trailing the submarine for three hours, probably in order to give British planes an opportunity to attack. According to German naval records, the *Greer* was the first to fire on the German submarine, whereupon the submarine replied by firing two torpedoes at the destroyer, both of which missed their mark. According to American records it was the submarine which fired first. Friedländer, *Prelude to Downfall*, p. 290; Langer and Gleason, *Undeclared War*, pp. 743–44; Samuel Eliot Morison, *The Battle of the Atlantic* (Boston, 1947), pp. 79–81.

245

25. Langer and Gleason, *Undeclared War*, chap. 23; Friedländer, *Prelude*, pp. 290–91.

26. *Fuehrer Conferences*, 1941, 2:1–2, 94, 109, 119–20; Friedländer, *Prelude*, pp. 255–58, 292–96; Compton, *Swastika and Eagle*, pp. 169–70.

27. See above, pp. 231–35.

28. *New York Times*, December 10, 1941.

29. *DGFP*, D, 13:999–1000, 1004–5.

30. *Hitler's Secret Conversations, 1941–1944* (paperback, New York, 1961), pp.

190, 293, 460; Henry Picker, *Hitlers Tischgespräche im Führerhauptquartier, 1941–1942*, ed. Percy Ernst Schramm, Andreas Hillgruber, and Martin Vogt (Stuttgart, 1963), p. 88; Friedländer, *Prelude*, pp. 308–9; Compton, *Swastika*, pp. 236–37.

Bibliography

A NOTE ON THE SOURCES.

The documentary materials available for the study of Nazi Germany, Nazi occupation policies, and the Second World War are intimidatingly massive. There are literally tons of such documents, most of them still unpublished.

In going through this unwieldy body of evidence I enjoyed the unusual privilege of being for five years a member of the board of editors of the captured German documents deposited at Whaddon Hall, Buckinghamshire, England. Although this collection consisted primarily of German Foreign Office files, it included records of some of Hitler's most important conferences, a substantial number of files from the Reich Chancellery (the clearing house for many of Hitler's most important decisions), as well as files from numerous other state and party offices. All these documents have long since been returned to Germany and are available to scholars in the Foreign Office archives in Bonn and the Bundesarchiv in Koblenz.

The Foreign Office and Reich Chancellery, however, were only a part, and in the case of the Foreign Office often a very peripheral part, of the Nazi government. Far more representative of the entire spectrum of the Nazi administration are the collections of published and unpublished documents assembled for the various postwar trials of Nazi officials and their collaborators. Because these documents were collected primarily for purposes of prosecution, they must be used with appropriate caution and reserve. They were amassed in such profusion, however, that they include an enormous range of material and constitute an invaluable source for the study of the Nazi era.

Also invaluable are the microfilms of another immense body of captured documents assembled after the war in Alexandria, Virginia, a collection so vast that it can only be approached with the aid of fifty-odd volumes of catalogues prepared under the auspices of the American Historical Association. The originals of most of these documents have also been returned to Germany and are deposited in German archives.

For the study of Nazi occupation policies, collaborationists, and the resistance, there are large collections of documents in the archives of all the states that came under German occupation during the Second World War. So far as the main course of German occupation policy is concerned, I found that these documents largely duplicate what is available in other collections. For this reason, and because I was already overwhelmed with material, I was not unhappy to be denied access to the archives of the countries of Eastern Europe and East Germany.

Almost as intimidating as the mass of unpublished documents on the Nazi era

313

are the volumes of published materials. The records of the multitude of Nazi state and party agencies, the notes of secret conferences and conversations, high-level directives, speeches, diaries, letters, and memoirs continue to flow inexorably from the presses of the world, their number compounded by the publication of similar records of every other country involved, directly or indirectly, in the Second World War. Many of these publications are of great value, superbly produced and edited by expert scholars. But even those published for propaganda purposes, whether as apologias or denunciations, frequently contain important material. The publications of the Nazis themselves, their ideological tracts, official pronouncements, or explanations of policy, can be remarkably self-revealing. Of these the most important for my purposes were the publications of Nazi laws for Germany and the occupied territories which perforce contain clear and unequivocal statements of policy.

Although I have tried to base this book on contemporary sources to the greatest possible extent, so voluminous is the literature on the Nazi era that a single person cannot hope to read it all, much less digest and master it. I have, therefore, often depended heavily on the work of other writers and scholars, a debt which I hope has been properly acknowledged in my footnotes. Further evidence of this debt is provided in this bibliography. An additional bibliography dealing primarily with Nazi occupation policies will appear at the end of the second volume.

ORGANIZATION OF THE BIBLIOGRAPHY

1. Bibliographies, Guides, Reference Works
2. Published Documents
3. Nazi Newspapers and Journals
4. Diaries, Letters, and Memoirs
5. Biographies
6. Ideology
7. General Works, the Nazi Party and Government
8. The Himmler Organizations
9. The Armed Forces
10. The Economy, Rearmament, and Raw Materials
11. Society and Culture, the Churches, and the Resistance
12. Expansionism, Foreign Policy, and the Origins of the Second World War
13. Austria and the Anschluss
14. Czechoslovakia and the Sudetenland
15. Poland, Danzig, and Memel
16. Scandinavia
17. The West: The Low Countries, France, and Britain
18. Italy, Spain, and North Africa
19. Hungary and the Balkans
20. Russia and the Baltic States
21. Japan
22. The United States

1. BIBLIOGRAPHIES, GUIDES, AND REFERENCE WORKS

American Historical Association, Committee for the Study of War Documents, and National Archives and Records Service, *Guides to German Documents Microfilmed at Alexandria, Virginia*. Washington, D.C., 1958–.)

Facius, Friedrich; Boom, Hans; Boberach, Heinz. *Das Bundesarchiv und seine Bestände*, Boppard am Rhein, 1961.

Kent, George O. *A Catalog of the Files and Microfilms of the German Foreign Ministry Archives 1920–1945*. 3 vols. Stanford, Calif., 1962–66.

Lötzke, Helmut. *Übersicht über die Bestände des deutschen Zentralarchivs Potsdam*. East Berlin, 1957.

Schulthess' Europäischer Geschichtskalender. Munich, published annually.

314

BIBLIOGRAPHY

Statesman's Year-Book: Statistical and Historical Annual of the States of the World. London, published annually.
Statistisches Jahrbuch für das Deutsche Reich. Berlin, published annually.
Weinberg, Gerhard L., and staff. *Guide to Captured German Documents.* Montgomery, Ala., 1952; suppl., Washington, 1959.
Who's Who in Nazi Germany. London, 1944.

Of the many periodicals containing bibliographies and important articles on the Nazi era, I relied chiefly on *Foreign Affairs,* and its periodic cumulative bibliographies; *Geschichte in Wissenschaft und Unterricht,* which contains useful review articles; *Revue d'Histoire de la Deuxième Guerre Mondiale; Vierteljahrshefte für Zeitgeschichte;* and, for East Germany, *Zeitschrift für Geschichtswissenschaft.*

2. PUBLISHED DOCUMENTS

Akten zur deutschen auswärtigen Politik, 1918–1945. Baden Baden and Göttingen. The German text of *Documents on German Foreign Policy* (see below). Series E, covering the years 1941–45, has so far been published only in German. Indispensable for the study of German foreign policy, although the peripheral character of the German Foreign Office during the Nazi era must be borne in mind.
Documenta Occupationis Teutonicae, 7 vols., Poznań, 1945–59. A very important source, especially for Nazi occupation policies.
Dokumente der deutschen Politik. Berlin, 1937–44. Only nine volumes covering the years 1933–41 were published. A valuable collection of official Nazi documents with commentaries reflecting the official Nazi point of view.
Documenti diplomatici italiani, 1861–1943. Rome, 1952–. The seventh series covers the years 1922–35, the eighth, 1935–39. Publication is proceeding at a very slow pace.
Documents and Materials Relating to the Eve of the Second World War. 2 vols. New York, 1948. A selection from the files of the German Foreign Office captured by the Russians.
Documents diplomatiques belges, 1920–1940. Brussels, 1964–. Volumes 3 and 4 cover the period from 1931–37.
Documents diplomatiques français, 1932–1939. Paris, 1963–. The first series covers the years 1932–35; the second, 1936–39. The pace of publication is slow.
Documents on British Foreign Policy, 1919–1939. London, 1946–. The second series covers the years 1930–38: the third, 1938–39.
Documents on German Foreign Policy, 1918–1945. Washington, 1949–. Series C covers the years 1933–36; Series D, 1936–41. For Series E, see *Akten zur deutschen auswärtigen Politik.*
Documents on International Affairs. London: Royal Institute of International Affairs, 1929–.
Falsificators of History. Moscow, 1948. A Russian document collection replying to *Nazi-Soviet Relations* (below).
Feder, Gottfried. *Das Programm der NSDAP.* Munich, 1927. Translated as *Hitler's Official Programme and Its Fundamental Ideas.* London, 1934.
Foreign Relations of the United States. Washington, 1861–.
Fuehrer Conferences on Matters Dealing with the German Navy, 1939–1945. 8 vols. Washington, D.C., 1946–47. Enormously valuable source.
Fuehrer Directives and Other Top-Level Directives of the German Armed Forces. Vol. 1, *1939–1941.* Washington, D.C., 1948. So far as I can ascertain, only one volume was ever published.
Hitler, Adolf. *Blitzkrieg to Defeat: Hitler's War Directives, 1939–1945.* Edited by H. R. Trevor-Roper. New York, 1965.
————. *Deutschlands Rüstung im zweiten Weltkrieg. Hitlers Konferenzen mit Albert Speer, 1942–1945.* Edited by Willi A. Boeleke. Frankfurt am Main, 1969.

——. *Hitler Directs His War: The Secret Records of his Daily Military Confer-ences.* Edited by Felix Gilbert. New York, 1950. Fragments.

——. *Hitler. Reden und Proklamationen, 1932–1945.* Edited by M. Domarus. 2 vols. Würzburg, 1962–63.

——. "Hitlers Denkschrift zum Vierjahresplan, 1936." Edited by Wilhelm Treue. *VfZ*3 (1955); 184–210. A very important document.

——. *Hitlers Lagebesprechungen. Die Protokollfragmente seiner militärischen Konferenzen, 1942–1945.* Edited by H. Heiber. Stuttgart, 1962.

——. "Hitler's Private Testament of May 2, 1938." Edited by G. L. Weinberg. *Journal of Modern History* 27 (1955): 415–19.

——. *Hitler's Secret Conversations, 1941–1944.* New York, 1953; paperback, 1961. Martin Bormann's notes of Hitler's table talk. Available only in English and French translations.

——. *Hitlers Tischgespräche im Führerhauptquartier, 1941–1942.* Edited Percy Ernst Schramm, Andreas Hillgruber, and Martin Vogt. Stuttgart, 1963. The notes of Dr. Henry Picker, an official assigned to Hitler's headquarters. Compa-rable to the notes of Bormann, who probably drew on them for his own rec-ords.

——. *Hitlers Weisungen für die Kriegsführung, 1939–1945. Dokumente des Oberkommandos der Wehrmacht.* Edited by W. Hubatsch. Frankfurt am Main, 1962.

——. *Hitlers zweites Buch. Ein Dokument aus dem Jahre 1928.* Edited by G. L. Weinberg. Stuttgart, 1961. English translation, *Hitler's Secret Book.* Paperback, New York, 1961. A valuable supplement to *Mein Kampf.*

——. *Mein Kampf,* 2 vols. Munich, 1925–27; English translation. New York, 1939. A memoir which is at the same time an invaluable document of Hitler's ideas and program.

——. *The Speeches of Adolf Hitler, April 1922–August 1939.* Edited by Norman H. Baynes. 2 vols., Oxford, 1942.

——. *Staatsmänner und Diplomaten bei Hitler. Vertrauliche Aufzeichnungen über Unterredungen mit Vertretern des Auslandes, 1939–1941.* Edited by A. Hillgruber. Frankfurt am Main, 1967.

——. *The Testament of Adolf Hitler: The Hitler-Bormann Documents, February–April, 1945.* Edited by F. Genoud. London, 1961. Unfortunately only available in English and French translations.

International Military Tribunal. *Trial of the Major War Criminals before the In-ternational Military Tribunal: Proceedings and Documents.* 42 vols. Nurem-berg, 1947–49. Enormously important records of the trials. Unfortunately only a small number of the documents assembled at Nuremberg is published in this collection. Microfilms and mimeographed copies of the unpublished documents are available in major libraries in the United States and Europe.

Kriegstagebuch des Oberkommandos der Wehrmacht (Wehrmachtführungsstab), 1940–1945. Edited by P. E. Schramm, A. Hillgruber, W. Hubatsch, and H. A. Jacobsen. 4 vols. in 7. Frankfurt am Main, 1961–65. An important source for military decisions.

Meldungen aus dem Reich. Auswahl aus den geheimen Lageberichten des Sicher-heitsdienstes der SS, *1939 bis 1944.* Edited by H. Boberach. Berlin, 1965.

Ministerialblatt des Reichs-und Preussischen Ministeriums des Innern. Berlin, published annually. Valuable collection of laws and decrees.

Nazi Conspiracy and Aggression. 8 vols. and 2 suppls. Washington, 1946–48. A selection in English translation of documents and affidavits presented in evi-dence at the Nuremberg trials, some of them not published in the *IMT* collec-tion.

Nazi-Soviet Relations, 1939–1941. Edited by R. J. Sontag and J. S. Beddie. Washington, 1948. Superseded by the relevant volumes of *Documents on Ger-man Foreign Policy.*

New Documents on the History of Munich: A Selection from the Soviet and Czech Archives. Prague, 1958.

316

BIBLIOGRAPHY

Preussische Gesetzsammlung. Berlin, published annually.
Reichsgesetzblatt. Published annually in two volumes in Berlin. Contains laws
and treaties pertaining not only to Germany, but also to all the occupied countries.
*Trials of the War Criminals before the Nuernberg Military Tribunals under Con-
trol Council Law N-10.* 15 vols. Nuremberg, 1946–49. Includes trial records
and documents in evidence of Nazi doctors, industrialists, diplomats. Unfortunately only excerpts of many important testimonies and documents are printed.

3. NAZI NEWSPAPERS AND JOURNALS

Der Angriff (Goebbels).
Essener Zeitung (Göring).
Jahrbuch der Auslands-Organisation der NSDAP.
Nationalsozialistisches Jahrbuch.
Reich, Volksordnung, Lebensraum. Enormously valuable journal for Nazi occupa-
tion policies, for it contains articles by officials of Nazi occupation governments
which are often astonishingly frank and revealing.
Der SA Mann. The journal of the SA (Brown Shirts).
Das Schwarze Korps. The journal of the SS (Black Shirts).
Der Vierjahresplan. The journal of the Four-Year Plan (Göring).
Völkischer Beobachter. The official Nazi party newspaper; a valuable source for
the official party line.

4. DIARIES, LETTERS, AND MEMOIRS
Chiefly German. For works of non-Germans, see under the individual countries.

Abetz, Otto. *Das offene Problem. Ein Rückblick auf zwei Jahrzehnte deutscher
Frankreichpolitik.* Cologne, 1951. A valuable, if not always reliable, memoir by
a leader of the German occupation administration in France.
Assmann, Kurt. *Deutsche Schicksalsjahre. Historische Bilder aus dem zweiten
Weltkrieg und seiner Vorgeschichte.* Wiesbaden, 1950. Memoirs of a German
admiral.
Blücher, Wipert von. *Gesandter zwischen Diktatur und Demokratie. Erinnerun-
gen aus den Jahren 1935–1944 von Wipert von Blücher, letztem deutschen
Gesandten in Finnland.* Wiesbaden, 1951.
Bormann, Martin. *The Bormann Letters: The Private Correspondence between
Martin Bormann and His Wife, from January 1943 to April 1945.* Edited by
H. R. Trevor-Roper. London, 1954. An important source for understanding this
sinister figure.
Diels, Rudolf. *Lucifer ante Portas. Es spricht der erste Chef der Gestapo.* Stutt-
gart, 1950.
Dietrich, Otto. *Mit Hitler an die Macht.* Munich, 1934.
——. *Zwölf Jahre mit Hitler.* Munich, 1955. Translated as *Hitler.* Chicago, 1955.
Dirksen, Herbert von. *Moskau, Tokio, London. Erinnerungen und Betrachtungen
zu 20 Jahre deutscher Aussenpolitik, 1919–1939.* Stuttgart, 1949. Translated as
Moscow, Tokyo, London: Twenty Years of German Foreign Policy. Norman,
Okla., 1952.
Doenitz, Karl. *Memoirs: Ten Years and Twenty Days.* Cleveland, 1959. By the
German admiral and head of the government at the time of the German sur-
render.
Frank, Hans. *Im Angesicht des Galgens. Deutung Hitlers und seiner Zeit auf
Grund eigener Erlebnisse und Erkenntnisse,* Munich, 1953. The interesting but
unreliable memoirs of Hitler's legal expert and governor general of occupied
Poland.
Geyr von Schweppenberg, L. *Erinnerungen eines Militärattaches. London,
1933–1937.* Stuttgart, 1949. Translated as *The Critical Years.* London, 1952.
Gilbert, G. M. *Nuremberg Diary.* New York, 1947. Interesting records of conver-
sations with the Nazi defendants, recorded by the prison psychologist.

317

BIBLIOGRAPHY

Gisevius, Hans. *Bis zum bittern Ende.* 2 vols. Zürich, 1946. Translated in slightly abridged form as *To the Bitter End.* Boston, 1947. The memoirs of a former member of the Gestapo who joined the anti-Nazi resistance. Often the sole source on the infighting within the secret police, so that it is difficult to check the author's reliability.

Goebbels, Joseph. *Dr. Goebbels. Nach Aufzeichnungen aus seiner Umgebung.* Edited by B. von Borresholm. Berlin, 1949.

———. *Goebbels Tagebücher aus den Jahren 1942–1943, mit anderen Dokumenten.* Edited by Louis P. Lochner. Zürich, 1948. English translation, *The Goebbels Diaries, 1942–1943.* New York, 1948.

———. *Das Tagebuch von Joseph Goebbels, 1925–26.* Edited by H. Heiber. Stuttgart, 1960. Translated as *The Early Goebbels Diaries, 1925–1926.* New York, 1963.

———. *Vom Kaiserhof zum Reichskanzlei.* Munich, 1934. Translated as *My Part in Germany's Fight.* London, 1938. Goebbels's own edition of his diaries.

———. *Wesen und Gestalt des Nationalsozialismus.* Berlin, 1934. Goebbels's version of the meaning of the Nazi movement.

Göring, Hermann. *Aus Görings Schreibtisch. Ein Dokumentenfund.* Edited by T. R. Emessen. Berlin, 1947.

———. *Gespräche mit Hermann Göring während des Nürnberger-Prozesses.* Edited by W. Bross. Flensburg-Hamburg, 1950.

Greiner, Helmuth. *Die oberste Wehrmachtführung, 1939–1943.* Wiesbaden. 1951. Based on Greiner's war diary of the German high command.

Grobba, Fritz. *Männer und Mächte im Orient. 25. Jahre diplomatischer Tätigkeit im Orient.* Göttingen, 1967. Memoirs of a prominent German diplomatic agent in the Near and Middle East.

Guderian, Heinz. *Erinnerungen eines Soldaten.* Heidelberg, 1951.

Hagen, Walter [Wilhelm Hoettl]. *Die geheime Front.* Linz, 1950. Translated as *The Secret Front: The Story of Nazi Political Espionage.* London, 1955. Hoettl was the head of the southeastern department of the political secret service of the Nazi Security Service (Sicherheitsdienst). Amusing anecdotes, of doubtful accuracy.

Halder, Franz. *Kriegstagebuch. Tägliche Aufzeichnungen des Chefs des Generalstabes des Heeres, 1939–1942.* Edited by Hans-Adolf Jacobsen. 3 vols. Stuttgart, 1962–64. Invaluable source.

———. *Hitler als Feldherr.* Munich, 1949.

Hanfstaengl, Ernst. *Unheard Witness.* Philadelphia, 1957. English ed., *Hitler: The Missing Years.* London, 1957. By an early supporter of Hitler and a major source for his information about the United States.

Hassell, Ulrich von. *Vom andern Deutschland. Aus den nachgelassenen Tagebüchern, 1938–1944.* Zürich, 1946. Translated in abridged form as *The Von Hassell Diaries, 1938–44: The Story of the Forces against Hitler inside Germany as Recorded by Ambassador Ulrich von Hassell, a Leader of the Movement.* New York, 1947.

Hess, Rudolf. *England-Nürnberg-Spandau. Ein Schicksal in Briefen.* Leoni am Starnberger See, 1961. A pathetic personal chronicle assembled by his wife, Ilse, which does not even shed much light on Hess's personality.

Hesse, Fritz. *Hitler and the English.* London, 1954. The memoirs of the representative of the German government news agency in London from 1933 to 1939 and adviser on British affairs at Hitler's headquarters from 1939 to 1945.

Hensinger, Adolf. *Befehl im Widerstreit. Schicksalsstunden der deutschen Armee, 1923–1945.* Tübingen, 1957. Fascinating series of scenes, based on memoranda and recollections of the author, including speeches and conversations of Hitler. Unfortunately of dubious reliability.

Hilger, Gustav, and Meyer, A. G. *The Incompatible Allies: A Memoir-History of German-Soviet Relations, 1918–1941.* New York, 1953. By an official of the German Embassy in Moscow, 1926–41, written in collaboration with an American historian.

318

Himmler, Heinrich. "Denkschrift Himmlers über die Behandlung der Fremdvölk-
ischen im Osten (May 1940)." Edited by H. Krausnick. VfZ 5 (1957): 194–98.
———. "Diaries of Heinrich Himmler's Early Years." Edited by W. T. Angress and
B. F. Smith. *Journal of Modern History* 31 (1959): 206 ff.
———. *Reichsführer! Briefe an und von Himmler.* Edited by H. Heiber. Stuttgart,
1968.
Hindenburg, Paul von. *Hindenburg und der Staat. Aus den Papieren des Gener-
alfeldmarschalls und Reichspräsidenten von 1878 bis 1934.* Edited by W. Hu-
batsch. Göttingen, 1966.
Hitler, Adolf. *Hitler e Mussolini: Lettere e documenti.* Milan, 1946. Unfortu-
nately only otherwise available in French translation, *Les Lettres Secrètes
Échangées par Hitler et Mussolini.* Paris, 1946.
———. *Mein Kampf* (see Published Documents).
Hoess, Rudolf. *Kommandant in Auschwitz. Autobiographische Aufzeichnungen.*
Edited by M. Broszat. Stuttgart, 1958. Memoirs of the master exterminator.
Hossbach, Friedrich. *Zwischen Wehrmacht und Hitler, 1934–1938.* Wolfenbüttel,
1949. Memoirs of an adjutant to Hitler in 1937 and author of the famous Hoss-
bach memorandum; later on active military service.
Jodl, Alfred. "Das dienstliche Tagebuch des Chefs des Wehrmachtführungsstabes
im OKW, Generalmajor Jodl, für die Zeit vom 13.10. 1939 bis 30. 1. 1940."
Edited by W. Hubatsch. *Die Welt als Geschichte*, 1952, pp. 274 ff., 1953,
pp. 58 ff.; the diary from February 1 to May 26, 1940, is printed in *IMT*,
1809-PS, 28: 397 ff.
Keitel, Wilhelm. *Generalfeldmarschall Keitel. Verbrecher oder Offizier. Erinnerungen, Briefe und Dokumente des Chef OKW.* edited by Walter Görlitz. Göttingen, 1961. Translated as *The Memoirs of Field Marshal Keitel* London,
1965.
Kelley, Douglas M. *22 Cells in Nuremberg.* New York, 1947. Similar to the work
of G. M. Gilbert; interviews with Nazi leaders by a prison psychologist.
Kersten, Felix. *The Kersten Memoirs, 1940–1945.* London, 1956. The remarkable
memoirs of Himmler's physician. This edition is far preferable to the American
version, *The Memoirs of Doctor Felix Kersten*, edited by Herma Briffault (New
York, 1947), which is so much edited that it is impossible to see what Kersten
himself wrote.
Kesselring, Albert. *Gedanken zum zweiten Weltkrieg.* Bonn, 1955.
———. *Soldat bis zum letzten Tag.* Bonn, 1953. Translated as *Kesselring: A Soldier's Record.* New York, 1953.
Kleist, Peter. *Zwischen Hitler und Stalin (1939–1945). Aufzeichnungen.* Bonn,
1950. The memoirs of a member of the Dienststelle Ribbentrop, 1936–43; in
July 1941 Kleist was assigned to Rosenberg's Ministry for the Occupied East-
ern Territories.
Kordt, Erich. *Nicht aus den Akten. Die Wilhelmstrasse in Frieden und Krieg. Er-
lebnisse, Begegnungen, Eindrücke, 1928–1945.* Stuttgart, 1950.
———. *Wahn und Wirklichkeit. Die Aussenpolitik des dritten Reiches: Versuch
einer Darstellung.* Stuttgart, 1948. Two volumes of memoirs by a senior coun-
selor in the German Foreign Office and head of the special bureau of the
Reich foreign minister (*Büro RAM*.)
Kubizek, August. *Adolf Hitler, Mein Jugendfreund.* Graz, 1953. Translated as
The Young Hitler I Knew. Boston, 1955. Recollections of a boyhood friend. To
be used with caution.
Ludecke, Kurt. *I Knew Hitler: The Story of a Nazi Who Escaped the Blood
Purge.* New York, 1937. Also to be used with caution.
Manstein, Erich von, *Aus einem Soldatenleben, 1887–1939.* Bonn, 1958.
———. *Verlorene Siege.* Bonn, 1955. Translated as *Lost Victories.* Chicago, 1958.
Especially valuable for the German campaigns in the east.
Meissner, Hans Otto. *Staatssekretär unter Ebert-Hindenburg-Hitler. Das Schick-
salsweg des deutschen Volkes von 1918–1945, wie ich ihn erlebte.* Hamburg,
1950. Disappointingly few insights, despite the strategic position of the author.

Nadolny, Rudolf. *Mein Beitrag.* Wiesbaden, 1955. The memoirs of one of the shrewder German diplomats.

Neubacher, Hermann. *Sonderauftrag Südost, 1940–1945. Bericht eines fliegenden Diplomaten.* Göttingen, 1956. Valuable memoirs of the chief German civil representative in the Balkans.

Papen, Franz von. *Der Wahrheit eine Gasse.* Munich, 1952; Translated as *Memoirs.* New York, 1953. Papen's *Gasse* proves to be something of a dead end.

Prittwitz und Gaffron, Friedrich von. *Zwischen Petersburg und Washington. Ein Diplomatenleben.* Munich, 1952.

Raeder, Erich. *Mein Leben.* 2 vols. Tübingen, 1957. Translated as *My Life.* Annapolis, 1960. By the head of Hitler's navy.

Rahn, Rudolf. *Ruheloses Leben. Aufzeichnungen und Erinnerungen eines deutschen Diplomaten.* Düsseldorf, 1949. Fascinating memoirs of a diplomat who represented German interests in the Near and Middle East, and was ambassador to Mussolini's Italy from 1943 to 1945.

Rauschning, Hermann. *Gespräche mit Hitler.* Vienna and New York, 1940. Translated as *Hitler Speaks.* London, 1939, and *The Voice of Destruction.* New York, 1940. Conversations with Hitler between 1932 and 1934 by the former president of the Danzig Senate. It is probable that the author retouched his records of these conversations before their publication.

———. *Mem of Chaos.* New York, 1942. A remarkable analysis of Hitler's subordinates and the reasons for the success of the Nazi movement.

Ribbentrop, Joachim von. *Zwischen London und Moskau. Erinnerungen und letzte Aufzeichnungen. Aus dem Nachlass.* Edited by Annelies von Ribbentrop. Leoni am Starnberger See, 1953. Translated as *The Ribbentrop Memoirs.* London, 1954. Of little value.

Rintelen, Enno von. *Mussolini als Bundesgenosse. Erinnerungen des deutschen Militärattaches in Rom, 1936–1943.* Tübingen, 1951.

Rommel, Erwin. *The Rommel Papers.* Edited by B. H. Liddell Hart, assisted by L. M. Rommel and F. Bayerlein. New York, 1953. Of great interest.

Rosenberg, Alfred. *An die Dunkelmänner unserer Zeit: eine Antwort auf die Angriffe gegen den "Mythos des 20 Jahrhunderts."* Munich, 1935.

———. *Krisis und Neubau Europas.* Berlin, 1934.

———. *Letzte Aufzeichnungen. Ideale und Idole der nationalsozialistischen Revolution.* Göttingen, 1955. Chiefly personal memoirs, with very little about his political role.

———. *Der Mythus des 20. Jahrhunderts.* Munich, 1930. Rosenberg's major contribution to the philosophy of National Socialism; dismissed by Hitler as unreadable rubbish, a sound evaluation.

———. *Das politische Tagebuch Alfred Rosenbergs aus den Jahren 1934/35 und 1939/40.* Edited by Hans-Günther Seraphim. Göttingen, 1956. Gossipy, with only occasional bits of historical interest.

———. *Portrait eines Menschheitsverbrechers, nach den hinterlassenen Memoiren des ehemaligen Reichsministers Alfred Rosenberg.* Edited by S. Lang and E. von Schenck. St. Gallen, 1947. Translated as *Memoirs of Alfred Rosenberg.* Chicago, 1949. Tendentiously distorted, and in any case of little historical interest.

———. *Wesen, Grundsätze und Ziele der NSDAP. Das Programm der Bewegung.* Munich, 1937.

———. *Der Zukunftsweg einer deutschen Aussenpolitik.* Munich, 1927. Of considerable interest for the development of Rosenberg's ideas about Eastern Europe.

Schacht, Hjalmar. *Abrechnung mit Hitler.* Stuttgart, 1948. Translated as *Account Settled.* London, 1949.

———. *76 Jahre meines Lebens.* Bad Wörishofen, 1953. Translated as *Confessions of the Old Wizard.* Boston, 1956. The memoirs of one of Hitler's foremost economic experts.

Schlabrendorff, Fabian von. *Offiziere gegen Hitler.* Zürich, 1946. Translated as *They Almost Killed Hitler.* New York, 1947. A firsthand account of the German army plots against the Hitler regime.

320

BIBLIOGRAPHY

Schellenberg, Walter. *Memoiren.* Cologne, 1959. Translated as *The Labyrinth: Memoirs of Walter Schellenberg.* New York, 1956. By a leading official of the Nazi intelligence service.

Schmidt, Paul. *Statist auf diplomatischer Bühne, 1923–45. Erlebnisse des Chefdolmetschers im Auswärtigen Amt mit den Staatsmännern Europas.* Bonn, 1949. Translated in abbreviated form as *Hitler's Interpreter.* London, 1951. Valuable comments on some of Hitler's major diplomatic conversations.

Schwerin von Krosigk, Lutz. *Es geschah in Deutschland. Menschenbilder unseres Jahrhunderts.* Tübingen, 1951. By Hitler's finance minister.

Schirach, Baldur von. *Die Hitler Jugend. Idee und Gestalt.* Berlin, 1934. By the leader of the Hitler Youth.

Skorzeny, Otto. *Geheimkommando Skorzeny.* Hamburg, 1950. Translated as *Skorzeny's Secret Missions: War Memoirs of the Most Dangerous Man in Europe.* New York, 1950. By the man who, among other things, "rescued" Mussolini in 1943.

Speer, Albert. *Inside the Third Reich.* New York, 1970. The memoirs of Hitler's architect and minister of armaments and munitions. Although Speer may overplay his own abilities and importance, the insights he offers into the personality of Hitler and his working methods are of enormous historical interest.

Starhemberg, Prince. *Between Hitler and Mussolini: Memoirs of Ernst Rüdiger, Prince Starhemberg.* London, 1942.

Strasser, Otto, *Hitler and I.* Boston, 1940. By a leader of the left wing of the Nazi party whose brother, Gregor, was killed in the purge of 1934.

Thomas, Georg. *Geschichte der deutschen Wehr-und Rüstungswirtschaft (1918–1943/45).* Edited by Wolfgang Birkenfeld. Boppard am Rhein, 1966. By the head of the army's armaments office, based on contemporary notes. Invaluable for the study of the Nazi economy, although not always completely accurate.

Thyssen, Fritz. *I Paid Hitler.* New York, 1941. By a disillusioned German industrialist who contributed to Hitler's campaign funds.

Warlimont, Walter. *Im Hauptquartier der deutschen Wehrmacht, 1939–1945. Grundlagen-Formen-Gestalten.* Frankfurt am Main, 1962. Translated as *Inside Hitler's Headquarters, 1939–45.* New York, 1964. Valuable, although like most military memoirs it attempts to blame Hitler for military errors and exonerate the army with respect to military atrocities.

Weizsäcker, Ernst von. *Erinnerungen.* Edited by Richard von Weizsäcker. Munich, 1950. Translated as *Memoirs.* Chicago, 1951. By the state secretary in the German Foreign Office.

Westphal, Siegfried. *Heer in Fesseln. Aus den Papieren des Stabschefs von Rommel, Kesselring und Rundstedt.* Bonn, 1950.

5. BIOGRAPHIES
For biographies of non-Germans, see under individual countries.

Abshagen, Karl Heinz. *Canaris. Patriot und Weltbürger.* Stuttgart, 1949.

Besgen, Achim. *Der stille Befehl. Medizinalrat Kersten, Himmler und das dritte Reich.* Munich, 1960. On the remarkable career of Felix Kersten, Himmler's doctor.

Bewley, Charles. *Hermann Göring and the Third Reich: A Biography based on Family and Official Records.* New York, 1962. An apologia by the former Irish minister to the Holy See, 1929–33, and to Berlin, 1933–39.

Bullock, Alan. *Hitler: A Study in Tyranny.* Paperback New York, 1964. A masterful work, balanced and supremely readable.

Colvin, Ian. *Chief of Intelligence.* London, 1951. A useful study on Canaris.

Dorpalen, Andreas. *Hindenburg and the Weimar Republic.* Princeton, 1964.

Douglas-Hamilton, James. *Motive for a Mission: The Story behind Hess's Flight to Britain.* New York, 1971. By the son of the Duke of Hamilton, the man Hess approached about a peace settlement with Britain.

Fest, Joachim C. *Das Gesicht des dritten Reiches. Profile einer totalitären Herr-*

schaft. Munich, 1963. Translated as *The Face of the Third Reich: Portraits of the Nazi Leadership*. New York, 1970. Excellent brief biographical and character sketches of the principal Nazi leaders.

Heiber, Helmut. *Adolf Hitler. Eine Biographie*. Berlin, 1960.

———. *Joseph Goebbels*. Berlin, 1962.

———. *Walter Frank und sein Reichsinstitut für Geschichte des neuen Deutschlands*. Stuttgart, 1966.

Heiden, Konrad. *Der Fuehrer: Hitler's Rise to Power*. Boston, 1944. One of many editions of this still valuable work.

Hutton, J. Bernard. *Hess: The Man and His Mission*. New York, 1971.

Jenks, William A. *Vienna and the Young Hitler*. New York, 1960.

Jetzinger, Franz. *Hitlers Jugend. Phantasien, Lügen—und die Wahrheit*. Vienna, 1956. Translated as *Hitler's Youth*. London, 1958. Full of valuable material, but creates some new myths, notably the story about Hitler's Jewish grandfather.

Kessel, Joseph. *The Man with the Miraculous Hands*. New York, 1961. Translated from the French. Another biography of Himmler's doctor, Felix Kersten.

Lesor, James. *The Uninvited Envoy*. New York, 1962. Another account of Hess's flight to Scotland.

Manvell, Roger, and Fraenkel, Heinrich. *Doctor Goebbels: His Life and Death*. London, 1960.

———. *Göring*. New York, 1962.

———. *Heinrich Himmler*. London, 1965. Three competent biographies, based on documentary materials and interviews.

Paget, R. T. *Manstein: His Campaigns and His Trial*. London, 1951.

Peterson, Edward N. *Hjalmar Schacht: For and Against: A Political-Economic Study of Germany, 1923–1945*. Boston, 1954.

Schramm, Percy Ernst. *Hitler als militärischer Führer. Erkenntnisse und Erfahrungen aus dem Kriegsstagebuch des Oberkommandos der Wehrmacht*. Frankfurt am Main, 1962.

Smith, Bradley F. *Adolf Hitler: His Family, Childhood, and Youth*. Stanford, Calif., 1967. Corrects and amplifies Jetzinger.

Wighton, Charles. *Heydrich: Hitler's Most Evil Henchman*. Philadelphia, 1962. Undocumented and impressionistic, but full of interesting information.

Wulf, Joseph. *Martin Bormann. Hitlers Schatten*. Gütersloh, 1962. A competent biography, based on the obvious sources.

6. IDEOLOGY

Arendt, Hannah. *The Origins of Totalitarianism*. New York, 1958.

Bullock, Alan. "The Political Ideas of Adolf Hitler." In *The Third Reich*, edited by M. Baumont. London, 1955.

Butler, Rohan. *The Roots of National Socialism*. New York, 1942.

Carsten, F. L. *The Rise of Fascism*. Berkeley, Calif., 1968.

Chandler, Albert R. *Rosenberg's Nazi Myth*. Ithaca, N.Y., 1945.

Conrad-Martius, Hedwig. *Utopien der Menschenzüchtung—der Sozialdarwinismus und seine Folgen*. Munich, 1955.

Daim, Wilfried. *Der Mann, der Hitler die Ideen gab. Von den religiösen Verirrungen eines Sektierers zum Rassenwahn des Diktators*. Munich, 1958. On the ideas of Jörg Lanz von Liebenfels.

Dickmann, F. "Machtwille und Ideologie in Hitlers aussenpolitischer Zielsetzung vor 1933." In *Spiegel der Geschichte. Festschrift für M. Braubach*, edited by K. Repken and St. Skalweit. Münster, 1964.

Glaser, Hermann. *Spiesser-Ideologie. Von der Zerstörung des deutschen Geistes im 19. und 20. Jahrhunderts*. Freiburg, 1964.

Greiner, Joseph. *Das Ende des Hitler-Mythos*. Zürich, 1947.

Hammer, Hermann. "Die deutschen Ausgaben von Hitlers 'Mein Kampf.'" *VfZ* 4 (1956):161–78.

Holborn, Hajo. "Ursprünge und politischer Charakter der NS-Ideologie." *Das Parlament*, 11 (1964):16–22.

BIBLIOGRAPHY

Jäckel, Eberhard. *Hitlers Weltanschauung. Entwurf einer Herrschaft.* Tübingen, 1969. An intelligent analysis based on a chronological examination of the development of Hitler's ideas.

Klee, Paul. "Nationalsozialistische Europaideologie." *VfZ* 3 (1955):240–75.

Kruck, Alfred. *Geschichte des Alldeutschen Verbandes, 1890–1939.* Wiesbaden, 1954. A history of the society from which Hitler drew much of his inspiration.

Lange, Karl. *Hitler's unbeachtete Maximen. "Mein Kampf" und die Öffentlichkeit.* Stuttgart, 1968. An examination of the significance of *Mein Kampf* as a guide to Hitler's actions, and its neglect by both German and foreign political observers.

——. "Der Terminus 'Lebensraum' in Hitlers 'Mein Kampf.'" *VfZ* 13 (1965):426–37.

Loock, Hans-Dietrich. "Zur 'grossgermanischen Politik' des Dritten Reiches." *VfZ* 8(1960):37–63.

Maser, Werner. *Hitlers Mein Kampf. Entstehung, Aufbau, Stil, Änderungen, Quellen, Quellenwert, kommentierte Auszüge.* Munich, 1966. Reaches same conclusions as Hammer, that no substantive changes were made in the text of the book between its first publication and 1945.

Moltmann, Günther. "Weltherrschaftsideen Hitlers." *In Europa und Übersee, Festschrift für Egmont Zechlin,* pp. 197–240, edited by O. Brunner and D. Gerhard. Hamburg, 1961.

Mosse, George L. *The Crisis of German Ideology: Intellectual Origins of the Third Reich.* New York, 1964.

Murphy, Raymond E.; Stevens, Francis B.; Trivers, Howard; and Roland, Joseph M. *National Socialism. Basic Principles: Their Application by the Nazi Party's Foreign Organization and the Use of Germans Abroad for Nazi Aims.* Washington, 1943.

Nolte, Ernst. *Die Krise des liberalen Systems und die faschistischen Bewegungen.* Munich, 1968.

——. *Three Faces of Fascism: Action Française, Italian Fascism, National Socialism.* New York, 1966. Translation of *Der Faschismus in seiner Epoche.* Munich, 1963.

Parrella, Frank. *Lebensraum and Manifest Destiny: A Comparative Study in the Justification of Expansionism.* Washington, 1950.

Pese, Walter Werner. "Hitler und Italien, 1920–1926." *VfZ* 3 (1955):113–26.

Saller, Karl. *Die Rassenlehre des Nationalsozialismus in Wissenschaft und Propaganda.* Darmstadt, 1961.

Skalnik, Kurt. *Dr. Karl Lueger—der Mann zwischen den Zeiten.* Vienna, 1954. On the mayor of Vienna who can be regarded as a precursor of Hitler in his political use of nationalism, socialism, and racism.

Stern, Fritz. *The Politics of Cultural Despair: A Study in the Rise of German Ideology.* New York, 1965.

Trevor-Roper, Hugh R. "Hitlers Kriegsziele." *VfZ* 8 (1960): 121–33. An excellent and convincing interpretation.

Whiteside, Andrew G. "The Nature and Origins of National Socialism." *Journal of Central European Affairs* 17 (1957): 48–73. A bibliographical essay evaluating various interpretations.

Woerden, A. V. N. van. "Hitler Faces England: Theories, Images and Policies." *Acta Historiae Nederlandica* 3 (1968): 141 ff.

7. GENERAL WORKS, THE NAZI PARTY AND GOVERNMENT

Abel, Theodore. *The Nazi Movement.* New York, 1967.

Allen, William Sheridan. *The Nazi Seizure of Power: The Experience of a Single German Town, 1930–1935.* Chicago, 1965.

Baumont, Maurice. *La faillité de la paix (1918–1938).* 2 vols. Paris, 1967–68. With a splendid bibliography.

——; Fried, J.; and Vermeil, E.; eds. *The Third Reich.* New York, 1955. A valuable collection of essays.

BIBLIOGRAPHY

Bennecke, Heinrich. *Hitler und die SA.* Munich, 1962. An analysis by an early member of the SA which emphasizes the confusion as to tactics, policies, and goals among party members and local leaders.

Boelcke, Willi A. ed. *Kriegspropaganda, 1939–1941. Geheime Ministerkonferenzen im Reichspropagandaministerium.* Stuttgart, 1966.

Bonnin, Georges. *Le Putsch de Hitler à Munich en 1923.* Les Sables d'Olonne, 1966. Essentially a collection of documents.

Bracher, Karl Dietrich. *Die Auflösung der Weimarer Republik. Eine Studie zum Problem des Machtverfalls in der Demokratie.* Villingen, 1960. An encyclopedic work, covering all aspects of the problem, with a magnificent bibliography.

———. *The German Dictatorship: The Origins, Structure, and Effects of National Socialism.* New York, 1970. Translated from *Die deutsche Diktatur.* Cologne, 1969. A superb scholarly synthesis.

———; Sauer, Wolfgang and Schulz, Gerhard. *Die nationalsozialistische Machtergreifung. Studien zur Errichtung des totalitären Herrschaftssystems in Deutschland, 1933/34.* Cologne, 1962. A detailed analysis of every step in Hitler's consolidation of power.

Bramsted, E. K. *Goebbels and National Socialist Propaganda 1925–1945.* East Lansing, Mich., 1965. One of the best and fullest studies of Goebbels.

Burden, H. T. *The Nuremberg Party Rallies, 1923–1939.* London, 1967.

Deuerlein, Ernst, ed. *Der Hitler-Putsch.* Stuttgart, 1962. A well-edited collection of documents.

———. "Hitlers Eintritt in die Politik und die Reichswehr." *VfZ* 7 (1959): 177–227.

Ehrich, Emil. *Die Auslands-Organisation der NSDAP.* Berlin, 1937. An official tract.

Eilers, R. *Die nationalsozialistische Schulpolitik. Eine Studie zur Funktion der Erziehung im totalitären Staat.* Cologne, 1963.

Epstein, Klaus. "Nazi Consolidation of Power." *Journal of Modern History* 34 (1962): 74–80. An excellent review article.

Ermarth, Fritz. *The New Germany: National Socialist Government in Theory and Practice.* Washington, D.C., 1936. Still valuable, especially for economic policies.

Fraenkel, Ernst. *The Dual State: A Contribution to the Theory of Dictatorship.* New York, 1941. Brilliant work, with emphasis on legal problems.

Frank, Hans. *Deutsche Verwaltungsrecht.* Munich, 1937.

———. *Heroisches und geordnetes Recht.* Berlin, 1938.

———. *Rechtsgrundlegung des nationalsozialistischen Führerstaates.* Munich, 1938. By the president of the Academy of German Law and later governor general of occupied Poland.

Franz-Willing, Georg. *Die Hitlerbewegung. Der Ursprung, 1919–22.* Hamburg, 1962. The first of a multivolume work, examining the driving impulses of the movement and its capacity to attract supporters.

Gauweiler, Otto. *Rechtseinrichtungen und Rechtsaufgaben der Bewegung.* Munich, 1939. Official explanation of the party's legal status and functions.

Gerth, Hans. "The Nazi Party: Its Leadership and Composition." *American Journal of Sociology* 45 (1940): 517–41.

Hagemann, Walter. *Publizistik im Dritten Reich.* Hamburg, 1948.

Hale, Oron J. *The Captive Press in the Third Reich.* Princeton, 1964.

Hegner, H. S. *Die Reichskanzlei, 1933–1945.* Frankfurt am Main, 1960. On one of the most important offices in the Nazi government.

Heiden, Konrad. *A History of National Socialism.* New York, 1935. Full of important information, although outdated.

Huber, Ernst Rudolf. *Verfassungsrecht des grossdeutschen Reiches.* Hamburg, 1939. An important Nazi interpretation.

Huber, Heinz, and Müller, Arthur, eds. *Das Dritte Reich; seine Geschichte in Texten, Bildern und Dokumente.* 2 vols. Munich, 1965. Comprehensive record, with fine illustrations.

Hüttenberger, Peter. *Die Gauleiter*. Stuttgart, 1969.
Jacobsen, Hans-Adolf. *Nationalsozialistische Aussenpolitik, 1933–1938* (Frankfurt am Main, 1968.) Primarily a study of the machinery and decision-making process, with important sections on ideology and efforts to spread Nazism in other parts of the world.
——, and Dollinger, Hans, eds. *Der zweite Weltkrieg in Bildern und Dokumenten*. 3 vols. Munich, 1962–63. Similar to the work of Huber and Müller, also with fine illustrations.
Kienast, F. *Der grossdeutsche Reichstag*. Berlin, 1943.
Klönne, A. *Hitlerjugend. Die Jugend und ihre Organisation im Dritten Reich*. Hanover, 1955.
Kneller, George F. *The Educational Philosophy of National Socialism*. New Haven, 1941.
Krebs, Albert. *Tendenzen und Gestalten der NSDAP*. Stuttgart, 1959. On the early years of the movement. The author was the former Gauleiter of Hamburg.
Lacqueur, Walter. *Young Germany: A History of the German Youth Movement*. London, 1962.
Lerner, Daniel, *The Nazi Elite*. Stanford, Calif., 1951. A shallow sociological-psychological analysis which deals with general characteristics rather than specific personalities. Fails to consider basic problems or to ask the right questions.
Lilge, Fredric. *The Abuse of Learning: The Failure of the German University*. New York, 1948.
Loewenstein, Karl. *Hitler's Germany: The Nazi Background to War*. New York, 1939. Excellent brief analysis of the Nazi government, based on the sources available at that time.
Maser, Werner. *Die Frühgeschichte der NSDAP. Hitlers Weg bis 1924*. Frankfurt am Main, 1965.
Matthias, Erich, and Morsey, Rudolf, eds. *Das Ende der Parteien, 1933*. Düsseldorf, 1960. Documentary history of the destruction of rival political parties during the early months of the Hitler regime.
Mau, Hermann. "Die 'Zweite Revolution.' Der 30. Juni 1934," *VfZ* 1 (1953): 119–37.
Mommsen, Hans. *Beamtentum im Dritten Reich. Mit ausgewählten Quellen zur nationalsozialistischen Beamtenpolitik*. Stuttgart, 1966. Valuable analysis of an important problem.
——. "Der Reichstagsbrand und seine politischen Folgen." *Das Parlament*, 46 (1964): 3–46.
Nationalsozialistisches Handbuch für Recht und Gesetzgebung. Edited by H. Frank. Munich, 1935–.
Nationalsozialistisches Jahrbuch. Published annually by the party.
Neesse, Gottfried. *Die Nationalsozialistische Deutsche Arbeiterpartei. Versuch einer Rechtsdeutung*. Stuttgart, 1935. An official tract.
Neumann, Franz. *Behemoth: The Structure and Practice of National Socialism, 1933–1944*, New York, 1944. An important pioneering work, but awkwardly written and now somewhat out of date.
Nova, Fritz. *The National Socialist Führerprinzip and Its Background in German Thought*. Philadelphia, 1943.
Nyomarkay, Joseph. *Charisma and Factionalism in the Nazi Party*. Minneapolis, 1967.
Office of Strategic Services, Research and Analysis Branch, *Civil Affairs Handbook. Germany*, section 2, *Government and Administration*, section 2A, *The National Socialist Party*, section 3, *Legal Affairs*, Army Service Forces Manual M356. Washington, D.C., 1944.
Organisationsbuch der NSDAP. Published annually by the party.
Orlow, Dietrich. *History of the Nazi Party, 1919–1933*. Pittsburgh, 1969. Based on documents made available after the Second World War. Takes the story to Hitler's appointment as chancellor.

BIBLIOGRAPHY

Peterson, E. N. "The Bureaucracy of the Nazi Party." *Review of Politics* 28 (1966): 172–92.
——. *The Limits of Hitler's Power*. Princeton, 1969. An important monograph on the workings of the Nazi government which, however, fails to take adequate account of how great Hitler's power actually was.
Petzina, D. "Germany and the Great Depression." *Journal of Contemporary History* 4 (1969): 59 ff.
Phelps, Reginald H. "Hitler and the Deutsche Arbeiterpartei." *American Historical Review* 68 (1963): 974–86.
Sauberzweig, Dieter. "Die Hochschulen im Dritten Reich." *Die Zeit*. March 10, 1961.
Schäfer, Wolfgang, *NSDAP. Entwicklung und Struktur der Staatspartei des Dritten Reiches*. Hanover, 1956. Valuable for details on organization and statistics.
Schmitt, Carl. *Das Reichsstatthaltergesetz*. Berlin, 1934.
Schneider, Hans. *Das Ermächtigungsgesetz vom 24. März, 1933*. Bonn, 1961.
Schorn, Hubert. *Die Gesetzgebung des Nationalsozialismus als Mittel der Machtpolitik*. Frankfurt am Main, 1963.
——. *Die Richter im Dritten Reich. Geschichte und Dokumente*. Frankfurt am Main, 1959.
Scurla, Herbert. *Die Grundgedanken des Nationalsozialismus und das Ausland*. Berlin, 1938. An official tract.
Schweitzer, Arthur. "The Nazification of the Lower Middle Class and Peasants." In *The Third Reich*, edited by M. Baumont. London, 1955.
Seraphim, Hans-Günther. "Nachkriegsprozesse und zeitgeschichtliche Forschung." In *Mensch und Staat in Recht und Geschichte. Festschrift für Herbert Kraus*, pp. 436–55. Kitzingen am Main, 1954. A critical examination of key documents used by the Nuremberg prosecution.
Shirer, William L. *The Rise and Fall of the Third Reich: A History of Nazi Germany*. New York, 1960. Readable, but shallow and disconcertingly smug.
Seabury, Paul, "Ribbentrop and the German Foreign Office," *Political Science Quarterly*, 66 (1951): 532 ff.
——. *The Wilhelmstrasse: A Study of German Diplomats under the Nazi Regime* (Berkeley, Calif., 1954.) An analysis of the machinery of government in operation, "the behavior and moral responsibility of the bureaucratic technician in modern society."
Sontag, Raymond J. *A Broken World, 1919–1939*. New York, 1971. Scholarly, balanced, readable, with an excellent bibliography.
Staff, Ilse, *Justiz im Dritten Reich. Eine Dokumentation*. Frankfurt am Main, 1964.
Stuckart, Wilhelm. *Führung und Verwaltung im Kriege*. Berlin, 1941. By the state secretary in the Reich Ministry of the Interior.
Taylor, A. J. P. "The Seizure of Power." In *The Third Reich*, pp. 523–36, edited by M. Baumont. London, 1955. An excellent analysis.
Tobias, Fritz. *The Reichstag Fire*. New York, 1964. Translated from *Der Reichstagsbrand*. Rastatt, 1962. Makes the case that Marinus van der Lubbe set fire to the Reichstag as an act of protest against the Nazis and as a signal for the German people to rise against Hitler, that he acted alone, without either Nazi or Communist accomplices.
Toynbee, Arnold, and Toynbee, Veronica, eds. *Hitler's Europe*. London, 1954. The only comprehensive survey of the government of Nazi Germany and the occupied territories.
Trevor-Roper, Hugh R. *The Last Days of Hitler*. New York, 1962. A brilliant analysis of the Nazi government and leadership.
Watt, D. C. "Hitler Comes to Power." *History Today* 13 (1963): 152–59.
Wheaton, Eliot Barculo. *The Nazi Revolution, 1933–1935: Prelude to Calamity*. Paperback, New York, 1969. Intelligent analysis, with valuable chronologies, statistics, reviews of the evidence and the historical literature. Magnificent bibliography.

BIBLIOGRAPHY

Wolf, A. *Higher Education in German-Occupied Countries.* London, 1945.
Wright, Gordon. *The Ordeal of Total War, 1939–1945.* New York, 1968. With a splendid bibliography.
Zeman, Z. A. B. *Nazi Propaganda.* New York, 1964.
Ziemer, G. *Education for Death: The Making of the Nazi.* London, 1941.

8. THE HIMMLER ORGANIZATIONS

Akerman, Josef. *Himmler als Ideologe.* Göttingen, 1970.
Alquen, Gunter d'. *Die SS. Geschichte, Aufgabe und Organisation der Schutzstaffeln der NSDAP.* Berlin, 1939. The official tract.
Aronson, Shlomo. *Heydrich und die Anfänge des SD und der Gestapo.* Doctoral dissertation, University of Berlin, 1966.
Best, Werner. *Die deutsche Polizei.* Darmstadt, 1941. By a high official in the Nazi security services and later Reich plenipotentiary in Denmark.
Bramstedt, E. K. *Dictatorship and Political Police: The Technique of Control by Fear.* New York, 1945.
Buchheim, Hans. "Die Höheren SS-und Polizeiführer." *VfZ* 11 (1963): 362–91.
———. "Die organisatorische Entwicklung der politischen Polizei in Deutschland in den Jahren 1933 und 1934." In *Gutachten des Instituts für Zeitgeschichte.* Munich, 1958.
———. "Rechtsstellung und Organisation des RKF des deutschen Volkstums." *Gutachten des Instituts für Zeitgeschichte.* Munich, 1958.
———. "Die SS in der Verfassung des Dritten Reiches." *VfZ* 3 (1955):127–57.
———. *SS und Polizei im NS-Staat.* Boppard am Rhein, 1964. All scholarly and intelligent studies on vitally important subjects.
Delarue, Jacques. *Histoire de la Gestapo.* Paris, 1962. Full of important information, but undocumented so that it is impossible to check the book's accuracy on many points.
Festgabe für Heinrich Himmler. Darmstadt, 1941. With revealing essays by Nazi leaders.
Georg, Enno. *Die wirtschaftlichen Unternehmungen der SS.* Stuttgart, 1963. Scholarly monograph on a difficult but important subject.
Görlitz, Walter. *Die Waffen-SS.* Berlin, 1960.
Greifelt, Ulrich. "Das Reichskommissariat für die Festigung des deutschen Volkstums." *Deutsche Verwaltung* January 2, 1940. By the head of the central office of the RKFDV.
Koehl, Robert L. "The Character of the Nazi SS." *Journal of Modern History* 34 (1962): 275–83.
———. *RKFDV: German Resettlement and Population Policy, 1939–1945: A History of the Reich Commission for the Strengthening of Germandom.* Cambridge, Mass., 1957. Full of important information.
Kogon, Eugen. *Der SS-Staat. Das System der deutschen Konzentrationslager.* Frankfurt am Main, 1959. Translated as *The Theory and Practice of Hell: The German Concentration Camps and the System behind Them.* New York, 1951. A moving study based on firsthand experience.
Krausnick, Helmut; Buchheim, Hans; Broszat, Martin; and Jacobsen, Hans-Adolf. *Anatomy of the SS State.* New York, 1968. Translated from *Anatomie des SS-Staates,* 2 vols. Freiburg im Breisgau, 1965. Scholarly and valuable set of essays, dealing with the persecution of the Jews, the SS and police, the concentration camps, and the mass execution of Russian prisoners of war.
Neufeldt, H. J.; Huck, J.; and Tessin, G. *Zur Geschichte der Ordnungspolizei, 1936–1945.* Koblenz, 1957.
Paetel, Karl. "Die SS. Ein Beitrag zur Soziologie des Nationalsozialismus." *VfZ* 2 (1954): 1–33.
Reitlinger, Gerald. *The SS: Alibi of a Nation, 1922–1945.* London, 1956. Readable.
Schnabel, Reimund. *Macht ohne Moral. Eine Dokumentation über die SS.* Frank-

327

furt am Main, 1957. A collection of documents and pictures. Deals almost entirely with atrocities. Very brief sections on organization and principles.
Stein, George H. *The Waffen SS: Hitler's Elite Guard at War, 1939–45.* Ithaca, N.Y., 1966. Deals with the relationship of the Waffen-SS and the regular army and the recruiting in occupied territories.
Vollmer, Bernard, ed. *Volksopposition im Polizeistaat. Gestapo und Regierungsberichte, 1934–1936.* Stuttgart, 1957. An important collection on an elusive subject.
Zipfel, Friedrich. *Gestapo und Sicherheitsdienst.* Berlin, 1960.

9. THE ARMED FORCES

Absolon, Rudolf. *Die Wehrmacht im Dritten Reich, 30. January 1933 bis 2. August 1934.* Boppard am Rhein, 1969.
——. *Wehrgesetz und Wehrdienst, 1935–1945. Das Personalwesen der Wehrmacht.* Boppard am Rhein, 1960.
Bennecke, Heinrich. *Die Reichswehr und der "Röhm-Putsch."* Munich, 1964. Argues that the army's co-operation in the events of June 30, 1934, was the real turning point in the army's relationship to Hitler. Henceforth they were partners in crime. By a former SA member.
Bensel, Rolf. *Die deutsche Flottenpolitik von 1933 bis 1939. Eine Studie über die Rolle des Flottenbaus in Hitlers Aussenpolitik.* Berlin, 1958.
Berghahn, Volker R. *Der Stahlhelm: Bund der Frontsoldaten, 1918–1935.* Düsseldorf, 1966.
Buchheit, Gert. *Der deutsche Geheimdienst. Geschichte der militärischen Abwehr.* Munich, 1966.
——. *Soldatentum und Rebellion.* Rastatt, 1961.
Craig, Gordon A. *The Politics of the Prussian Army, 1640–1945.* New York, 1955.
Erfurth, Waldemar. *Die Geschichte des deutschen Generalstabes von 1918 bis 1945.* Göttingen, 1957.
Foertsch, Hermann. *Schuld und Verhängnis. Die Fritsch-Krise im Frühjahr 1938 als Wendepunkt in der Geschichte der nationalsozialistischen Zeit.* Stuttgart, 1951.
Giese, Friedrich. *Die deutsche Marine, 1920 bis 1945. Aufbau und Untergang.* Frankfurt am Main, 1956.
Görlitz, Walter. *The German General Staff: Its History and Structure.* London, 1953.
Hahn, F. *Deutsche Geheimwaffen, 1939–1945.* Heidenheim, 1963.
Hubatsch, Walther. *Der Admiralstab und die obersten Marinebehörden in Deutschland, 1848–1945.* Frankfurt am Main, 1958.
Kielmansegg, Johann Adolf Graf. *Der Fritschprozess, 1938. Ablauf und Hintergründe.* Hamburg, 1949.
Leverkuehn, Paul. *German Military Intelligence.* New York, 1954.
Lusar, R. *Die deutschen Waffen und Geheimwaffen im Zweiten Weltkrieg.* Munich, 1962.
Martienssen, Anthony. *Hitler and His Admirals.* London, 1948.
Müller, Klaus-Jürgen. *Das Heer und Hitler. Armee und nationalsozialistische Regime, 1933–1940.* Stuttgart, 1969.
Müller-Hillebrand, Burkhart. *Das Heer, 1933–1945. Entwicklung des organisatorischen Aufbaues.* Darmstadt, 1954.
O'Neill, Robert J. *The German Army and the Nazi Party.* London, 1966. Authoritative and perceptive treatment of this difficult subject.
Schüddekopf, Otto-Ernst. *Die Wehrmacht im Dritten Reich, 1934–1945.* Hanover, 1961.
Siegler, Fritz von. *Die höheren Dienststellen der deutschen Wehrmacht, 1933–1945.* Munich, 1953.
Taylor, Telford. *Sword and Swastika: Generals and Nazis in the Third Reich.* New York, 1952.

Vogelsang, Thilo. *Reichswehr, Staat und NSDAP. Beiträge zur deutschen Geschichte, 1930–1932.* Stuttgart, 1962.

Wheeler-Bennett, John W. *The Nemesis of Power: The German Army in Politics, 1918–1945.* Paperback, New York, 1964.

10. THE ECONOMY, REARMAMENT, AND RAW MATERIALS

Backe, Herbert. *Das Ende des Liberalismus in der Wirtschaft.* Berlin, 1936. By the state secretary of the Reich Ministry for Food and Agriculture.

Barth, Eberhard. *Wesen und Aufgaben der Organisation der gewerblichen Wirtschaft.* Hamburg, 1939.

Barthel, Johannes. *Tätigkeit und Wirkung der Überwachungsstellen.* Berlin, 1939.

Baumgarten, H. "Die neue Waffe." *Der deutsche Volkswirt,* October 18, 1940. The new weapon was economic warfare.

Becker, Theodor. "Die Kartellpolitik der Reichsregierung." *Rechtsfragen der Wirtschaft,* vol. 2. Berlin, 1935.

Bernhardt, Walter. *Die deutsche Aufrüstung, 1934–1939. Militärische und politische Konzeptionen und ihre Einschätzung durch die Alliierten.* Frankfurt am Main, 1969.

Birkenfeld, Wolfgang. *Der synthetische Treibstoff, 1943–1945. Ein Beitrag zur nationalsozialistischen Wirtschaft-und Rüstungspolitik.* Göttingen, 1964.

Brandt, Karl; Schiller, Otto; and Ahlgrimm, Franz. *Management of Agriculture and Food in the German-Occupied and Other Areas of Fortress Europe.* Stanford, Calif., 1953. A work of fundamental importance.

Bühring, Otto. *Wesen und Aufgaben der industriellen Wirtschaftsgruppen.* Berlin, 1940.

Carroll, Berenice. *Design for Total War: Arms and Economics in the Third Reich.* The Hague, 1968. An important and convincing monograph which argues that the German economy was directed toward war even if it was not fully geared to war.

Darré, R. Walther. *Das Bauerntum als Lebensquell der nordischen Rasse.* Munich, 1929.

———. *Neuadel aus Blut und Boden.* Munich, 1930.

———. *Um Blut und Boden.* Munich, 1942. Works by the foremost Nazi theorist on race, soil, and agriculture.

Decker, Will. *Die deutsche Arbeitsfront.* Berlin, 1941.

Didier, Friedrich, ed. *Handbuch für die Dienststellen des G.B.A. und die interessierten Reichsstellen im grossdeutschen Reich und in den besetzten Gebieten.* Berlin, 1944. A collection of the most important government decrees relating to labor, particularly the use of foreign labor.

Eichholtz, D. *Geschichte der deutschen Kriegswirtschaft, 1939–1945.* Berlin, 1969.

Erbe, René. *Die nationalsozialistische Wirtschaftspolitik, 1933–1939, im Lichte der modernen Theorie.* Zürich, 1958.

Fischer, Wolfram. *Die Wirtschaftspolitik Deutschlands, 1918–1945.* Lüneburg, 1961. By one of Germany's most perceptive economic historians.

Fried, J. H. E. *The Exploitation of Foreign Labour by Germany.* Montreal, 1945. Sponsored by the International Labor Office.

Friedensburg, Ferdinand. *Das Erdoel im Weltkrieg.* Stuttgart, 1939.

———. *Die mineralischen Bodenschätze als weltpolitische und militärische Machtfaktoren.* Stuttgart, 1939.

———. *Die Rohstoffe und Energiequellen in meuen Europa.* Oldenburg, 1943.

Gunther, A. E. *The German War for Crude Oil in Europe, 1934–1945.* Celle, 1947.

Guth, Karl. *Die Reichsgruppe Industrie.* Berlin, 1941.

Hallgarten, George W. F. *Hitler, Reichswehr und Industrie: zur Geschichte der Jahre 1918–1933.* Frankfurt am Main, 1962.

Homze, Edward L. *Foreign Labor in Nazi Germany.* Princeton, N.J., 1967. A

BIBLIOGRAPHY

study of the organization and administration of the Nazi foreign labor program and its relationship to the war economy. With an excellent bibliography.

Klein, Burton. *Germany's Economic Preparations for War.* Cambridge, Mass., 1959. Minimizes extent of German rearmament. Less convincing than the theses of Carroll and Milward.

Kreutz, Werner. *Die Zwangskartellierung in der gewerblichen Wirtschaft der Gegenwart.* Berlin, 1936.

Kumpf, W. *Die Organisation Todt im Kriege.* Oldenburg, 1953.

Leeb, Emil. *Aus der Rüstung des Dritten Reiches: Das Heereswaffenamt, 1938–1945.* Berlin, 1958.

Lévêque, M. *Le pétrole et la guerre.* Paris, 1958.

Liesbach, Ingolf. *Der Wandel der politischen Führungsschicht der deutschen Industrie von 1918 bis 1945.* Hanover, 1957.

Lochner, Louis P. *Tycoons and Tyrant.* Chicago, 1954. The relationship of Germany's industrial magnates with Hitler.

Mason, T. W. "Labour in the Third Reich." *Past and Present* 30 (1966):112–41.

Meinck, G. *Hitler und die deutsche Aufrüstung, 1933–1937.* Wiesbaden, 1959.

Milward, Alan S. "Fritz Todt als Minister für Bewaffnung und Munition." *VfZ* 14 (1966):40–58.

——. *The German Economy at War.* London, 1965. Argues that Hitler's economic policies were based on the concept of a Blitzkrieg. An intelligent and convincing monograph.

Pfahlmann, H. *Fremdarbeiter und Kriegsgefangene in der deutschen Kriegswirtschaft, 1939–1945.* Darmstadt, 1968.

Pottgiesser, H. *Die deutsche Reichsbahn im Ostfeldzug, 1939–1944.* Neckargemünd, 1961.

Schumann, Hans-Gerd. *Nationalsozialismus und Gewerkschaftsbewegung. Die Vernichtung der deutschen Gewerkschaften und der Aufbau der "Deutschen Arbeitsfront."* Hanover, 1958.

Schweitzer, Arthur. *Big Business in the Third Reich.* Bloomington, Ind., 1964. An important interpretation, with emphasis on the early years of the regime.

Simon, Leslie E. *German Research in World War II.* New York, 1947. By the director of the U.S. Ballistic Research Laboratories.

Steinberger, II. "Der Treibstoffverbrauch im Kriege," *Deutsche Wehr,* 1 (1939):3 ff.

Stuebel, Heinrich. "Die Finanzierung der Aufrüstung im Dritten Reich." *Europa-Archiv* 6 (1951):4128–36.

Treue, W. *Gummi in Deutschland. Die deutsche Kautschukversorgung und die Gummi-Industrie im Rahmen weltwirtschaftlicher Entwicklungen.* Munich, 1955.

Wagenführ, Rolf. *Die deutsche Industrie im Kriege, 1939–1945.* Berlin, 1963. By the head of the planning department of the Speer ministry.

11. SOCIETY AND CULTURE, THE CHURCHES, AND THE RESISTANCE

Brenner, Hildegard. *Die Kunstpolitik des Nationalsozialismus.* Hamburg, 1963.

Bussmann, Walter. *Die innere Entwicklung des deutschen Widerstandes gegen Hitler.* Berlin, 1964.

Conway, J. W. *The Nazi Persecution of the Churches, 1933–1945.* New York, 1968.

Deutsch, Harold C. *The Conspiracy against Hitler in the Twilight War.* Minneapolis, 1968.

Donohoe, James. *Hitler's Conservative Opponents in Bavaria, 1930–1945: A Study of Catholic, Monarchist, and Separatist Anti-Nazi Activists.* Leiden, 1961.

Dulles, A. W. *Germany's Underground.* New York, 1947. By one of America's leading intelligence officers.

Friedländer, Saul. *Pius XII and the Third Reich: A Documentation.* New York, 1966.

Glaser, Hermann, *Spiesser-Ideologie. Von der Zerstörung des deutschen Geistes im 19. und 20. Jahrhundert* (Freiburg, 1964).

Grunberger, Richard. *The 12-Year Reich: A Social History of Nazi Germany, 1933–1945*. New York, 1971.

Guillebaud, C. W. *The Social Policy of Nazi Germany*. Cambridge, Eng., 1941.

Hoffman, Peter. *Widerstand, Staatsstreich, Attentat*. Munich, 1969. The most scholarly, detailed, and lucid work on the subject.

Lane, Barbara Miller. *Architecture and Politics in Germany, 1918–1945*. Cambridge, Mass., 1968. An interesting study.

Levai, Jenö, ed. *Geheime Reichssache. Papst Pius XII hat nicht geschwiegen. Berichte, Dokumente, Akten.* Cologne, 1966. A reply to critics of the Pope.

Lewy, Guenter. *The Catholic Church and Nazi Germany* (New York 1964).

Manvell, Roger, and Fraenkel, Heinrich. *The Men Who Tried to Kill Hitler*. New York, 1964. Reliable and readable.

Mosse, George L., ed. *Nazi Culture: Intellectual, Cultural and Social Life in the Third Reich*. New York, 1966.

Poliakov, L., and Wulf, J. *Das Dritte Reich und seine Denker. Dokumente.* Berlin, 1959.

Ritter, G. *Carl Goerdeler und die deutsche Widerstandsbewegung.* Stuttgart, 1954.

Rothfels, Hans. *The German Opposition to Hitler*. Chicago, 1964.

Saller, Karl. *Die Rassenlehre des Nationalsozialismus in Wissenschaft und Propaganda.* Darmstadt, 1961.

Schlabrendorff, Fabian von. *The Secret War against Hitler*. New York, 1965. Personal recollections of one of the leaders of the movement.

Schoenbaum, David. *Hitler's Social Revolution: Class and Status in Nazi Germany, 1933–1939*. Garden City, N.Y., 1966.

Vollmer, Bernard, ed. *Volksopposition im Polizeistaat. Gestapo und Regierungsberichte, 1934–1936.* Stuttgart, 1957.

Wulf, Joseph. *Die bildenden Künste im Dritten Reich. Eine Dokumentation.* Gütersloh, 1963.

———. *Literatur und Dichtung im Dritten Reich. Eine Dokumentation.* Gütersloh, 1966.

———. *Musik im Dritten Reich. Eine Dokumentation.* Gütersloh, 1963.

Zahn, Gordon C. *German Catholics and Hitler's Wars: A Study in Social Control.* New York, 1962.

Zipfel, Friedrich. *Kirchenkampf in Deutschland, 1933–1945*. Berlin, 1965.

12. EXPANSIONISM, FOREIGN POLICY, AND THE ORIGINS OF THE SECOND WORLD WAR

Baer, George W. *The Coming of the Italo-Ethiopian War*. Cambridge, Mass., 1967.

Baumgart, Winfried. "Zur Ansprache Hitlers vor den Führern der Wehrmacht am 22. August 1939. Eine quellenkritsche Untersuchung." *VfZ* 16 (1968):120–49. An intelligent critical analysis of a key document.

Braddick, H. "The Hoare-Laval Plan: A Study in International Politics," *Review of Politics* 24 (1962):342–64.

Braubach, M. *Der Einmarsch deutscher Truppen in die entmilitarisierte Zone am Rhein im März 1936. Ein Beitrag zur Vorgeschichte des zweiten Weltkrieges.* Cologne, 1956.

———. *Hitlers Weg zur Verständigung mit Russland im Jahre 1939.* Bonn, 1960.

Bullock, Alan. "Hitler and the Origins of the Second World War." *Proceedings of the British Academy* 53 (1967):259–87. A masterful analysis.

Bussmann, W. "Zur Entstehung und Überlieferung der 'Hossbach Niederschrift.'" *VfZ* 16 (1968):373–84. Critical analysis of a key document.

Dahlerus, Birger. *Der letzte Versuch. London-Berlin, Sommer 1939.* Munich, 1948. Memoirs of the Swedish businessman whom the Germans tried to use as a negotiator in a last-minute effort to stave off British intervention.

BIBLIOGRAPHY

Dickmann, F., "Machtwille und Ideologie in Hitlers aussenpolitischer Zielsetzung vor 1933." In *Spiegel der Geschichte. Festschrift für M. Braubach*, edited by K. Repken and St. Skalweit (Münster, 1964.)

Esch, P. A. M. *Prelude to War: The International Repercussions of the Spanish Civil War*. The Hague, 1951.

Eubank, Keith. *The Origins of World War II*. New York, 1969. Intelligent brief analysis. Excellent bibliography.

Funke, M. *Sanktionen und Kanonen. Hitler, Mussolini und der internationale Abessinienkonflikt, 1934–1936*. Düsseldorf, 1970. Challenges theory that the foundation of the Rome-Berlin Axis was laid during the Abyssinian war.

Gackenholz, H. "Reichskanzlei, 5. November 1937," *Forschungen zu Staat und Verfassung. Festgabe für Fritz Hartung*. Berlin, 1958.

Gasiorowski, Z. J. "The German-Polish Non-Aggression Pact of 1934." *Journal of Central European Affairs* 15 (1955):3 ff.

Hildebrand, Klaus. *Deutsche Aussenpolitik, 1933–1945. Kalkül oder Dogma?* Stuttgart, 1971. An admirable brief analysis.

———. *Vom Reich zum Weltreich*. Munich, 1969.

Hillgruber, Andreas. *Deutschlands Rolle in der Vorgeschichte der beiden Weltkriege*. Göttingen, 1967.

———. *Kontinuität und Diskontinuität in der deutschen Aussenpolitik von Bismarck bis Hitler*. Düsseldorf, 1969.

———. *Hitlers Strategie. Politik und Kriegsführung, 1940–1941*. Frankfurt am Main, 1965. A magnificent piece of scholarship, covering far more than the title implies.

———. ed. *Probleme des zweiten Weltkrieges*. Cologne, 1967. Valuable collection of essays.

Hofer, W. *Die Entfesselung des zweiten Weltkrieges. Eine Studie über die internationalen Beziehungen im Sommer 1939. Mit Dokumenten*. Frankfurt am Main, 1964.

Ingrim, Robert. *Hitlers glücklichster Tag. London, am 18. Juni 1935*. Stuttgart, 1962.

Jacobsen, Hans-Adolf. *Misstrauische Nachbarn. Deutsche Ostpolitik, 1919/1970. Analysen und Dokumente*. Düsseldorf, 1971.

———. *Nationalsozialistische Aussenpolitik, 1933–1938*. Frankfurt am Main, 1968. Primarily a study of the machinery and decision-making process, with important sections on ideology and efforts to spread Nazism in other parts of the world.

Jong, Louis de. *The German Fifth Column in the Second World War*. Chicago, 1956.

Klee, Paul. "Nationalsozialistische Europaideologie," *VfZ*, 3 (1955):240–75.

Knapp, W. F. "The Rhineland Crisis of March 1936." In *The Decline of the Third Republic*, pp. 67–85, edited by James Joll. London, 1959.

Kruck, Alfred, *Geschichte des Alldeutschen Verbandes, 1890–1939*. Wiesbaden, 1954. A history of the society from which Hitler drew much of his inspiration.

Latour, Conrad F. *Südtirol und die Achse Berlin-Rom, 1938–1945*. Stuttgart, 1962. Excellent monograph on one of the most important problems affecting German-Italian relations.

Laurens, F. D. *France and the Italo-Ethiopian Crisis, 1935–1936*. The Hague, 1967.

Loock, Hans-Dietrich, "Zur 'grossgermanischen Politik' des Dritten Reiches," *VfZ* 8 (1960): 37–63.

Lukacs, John A. *The Great Powers and Eastern Europe*. New York, 1953.

Mason, T. W. "Some Origins of the Second World War." *Past and Present*, no. 29 (1964), pp. 67–87. An able review of the literature, above all on Germany's economic preparations for war.

McSherry, James E. *Stalin, Hitler and Europe, 1933–1939: The Origin of World War II*. Cleveland, 1968.

BIBLIOGRAPHY

Merkes, Manfred. *Die deutsche Politik gegenüber dem spanischen Bürgerkrieg, 1936–1939.* Bonn, 1969.

Moltmann, Günther, "Weltherrschaftsideen Hitlers." In *Europa und Übersee, Festschrift für Egmont Zechlin,* pp. 197–240, edited by O. Brunner and D. Gerhard. Hamburg, 1961.

Niclauss, Karlheinz. *Die Sowjetunion und Hitlers Machtergreifung. Eine Studie über die deutsch-russischen Beziehungen der Jahre 1929 bis 1935.* Bonn, 1966.

Nikonov, A. D. *The Origin of World War II and the Prewar European Political Crisis of 1939.* Moscow, 1955. Soviet point of view. In Russian.

Parrella, Frank. *Lebensraum and Manifest Destiny: A Comparative Study in the Justification of Expansionism.* Washington, D.C. 1950.

Pese, Walter Werner. "Hitler und Italien, 1920–1926," *VfZ* 3 (1955): 113–26.

Puzzo, Dante A. *Spain and the Great Powers, 1936–1941.* New York, 1962.

Ritschel, Karl-Heinz. *Diplomatie um Südtirol. Politische Hintergründe eines europäischen Versagens.* Stuttgart, 1966.

Robertson, E. M. *Hitler's Pre-War Policy and Military Plans, 1933–1939.* London, 1963. Concludes that Hitler's policy was essentially a matter of improvisation.

——, ed. *The Origins of the Second World War: Historical Interpretations.* London, 1971. A valuable collection of essays, primarily by British historians.

——, ed. "Zur Wiederbesetzung des Rheinlandes, 1936," *VfZ* 10 (1962): 178–205.

Rusinow, Dennison I. *Italy's Austrian Heritage, 1919–46.* Oxford, 1969. An excellent treatment of an important problem.

Scott, William E. *Alliance against Hitler: The Origins of the Franco-Soviet Pact.* Durham, N.C., 1962.

Seabury, Paul. "Ribbentrop and the German Foreign Office." *Political Science Quarterly* 66 (1951):532 ff.

——. *The Wilhelmstrasse: A Study of German Diplomats under the Nazi Regime.* Berkeley, Calif., 1954. An analysis of the machinery of government in operation, "the behavior and moral responsibility of the bureaucratic technician in modern society."

Siebert, Ferdinand. *Italiens Weg in den zweiten Weltkrieg.* Frankfurt am Main, 1962.

Sontag, Raymond J. "The Last Months of Peace." *Foreign Affairs* 35 (1957):507–24.

——. "The Origins of the Second World War." *Review of Politics* 25 (1963):497–508. Intelligent, balanced analyses.

Taylor, A. J. P. *The Origins of the Second World War.* London, 1961. Brilliant and perverse work which has led to much rethinking of the problem on the part of all serious historians, but has also given aid and comfort to German ultranationalists and Nazis, old and new.

Thorne, Christopher. *The Approach of War, 1938–1939.* London, 1968. Excellent brief synthesis.

Toscano, Mario. "Eden's Mission to Rome on the Eve of the Italo-Ethiopian Conflict. "In *Studies in Diplomatic History and Historiography in Honour of G. P. Gooch,* pp. 126–52, edited by A. O. Sarkissian. London, 1961.

——. *The Origins of the Pact of Steel.* Baltimore, 1968.

Watt, D. C. "The Anglo-German Naval Agreement of 1935: An Interim Judgment." *Journal of Modern History* 28 (1956):155–75.

——. "The Rome-Berlin Axis, 1936–1940: Myth and Reality." *Review of Politics* 22 (1960):519–43.

——. "The Secret Laval-Mussolini Agreement of 1935 on Ethiopia." *Middle East Journal* 15 (1961):69–78. Excellent articles, drawing on much original research.

Weinberg, Gerhard L. *The Foreign Policy of Hitler's Germany: Diplomatic Revolution in Europe, 1933–1936.* Chicago, 1970. A brilliant and authoritative work.

———. *Germany and the Soviet Union, 1939–1941.* Leiden, 1954. Detailed analysis based on documents available at that time.

Wiskemann, Elizabeth. *The Rome-Berlin Axis: A History of the Relations between Hitler and Mussolini.* London, 1949.

13. AUSTRIA AND THE ANSCHLUSS

Beiträge zur Vorgeschichte und Geschichte der Julirevolte. Vienna, 1934. An official publication of the Austrian government on the abortive Nazi Putsch of July 25, 1934.

Brook-Shepherd, Gordon. *The Anschluss: The Rape of Austria.* London, 1963. A useful account by a British journalist.

———. *Dollfuss.* London, 1961.

Conway, John S. "The Organization of the Anschluss: Hitler's Strategy for the Seizure of Austria." *World Affairs Quarterly* 30 (1959):122–33.

Eichstädt, Ulrich. *Von Dollfuss zu Hitler. Geschichte des Anschlusses Österreichs, 1933–1938,* Wiesbaden, 1955. Detailed and well documented.

Die Erhebung der österreichischen Nationalsozialisten im Juli 1934. Bericht der historischen Kommission des Reichsführers SS. Edited by H. Steiner and L. Jedlicka. Vienna, 1965. A document collection.

Gehl, Jürgen. *Austria, Germany, and the Anschluss, 1931–1938.* London, 1963. Emphasizes the importance of the Austrian problem for German-Italian relations.

Gulick, Charles A. *Austria: From Habsburg to Hitler.* 2 vols. Berkeley, Calif., 1948.

Jedlicka, Ludwig. *Ein Heer im Schatten der Parteien. Die militärpolitische Lage Österreichs, 1919–1938* Graz, 1955.

Koerner, R. R. *So haben sie es damals gemacht. Die Propagandavorbereitungen zum österreichanschluss durch das Hitlerregime, 1933–1938.* Vienna, 1958.

Ross, Dieter. *Hitler und Dollfuss. Die deutsche österreich-Politik, 1933–1934.* Hamburg, 1966.

Schuschnigg, Kurt von. *Austrian Requiem.* New York, 1946.

———. *Farewell Austria.* London, 1939. American title, *My Austria.* Translated from the German, *Dreimal Österreich.*

———. *Im Kampf gegen Hitler.* Vienna, 1969. A blending of recollections and documentary evidence. Reveals much about the attitudes of the author.

Sweet, Paul R. "Mussolini and Dollfuss: An Episode in Fascist Diplomacy." In *The Tragedy of Austria,* edited by J. Braunthal. London, 1948.

Sündermann, Helmut. *Die Grenzen fallen. Von der Ostmark zum Sudentenland.* Munich, 1939. A rapturous Nazi chronicle.

Whiteside, Andrew G. *Austrian National Socialism before 1918.* The Hague, 1962.

14. CZECHOSLOVAKIA AND THE SUDENTENLAND

Das Abkommen von München 1938. Tschechoslowakische diplomatische Dokumente, 1937–1939. Prague, 1968. A Czechoslovak publication of their own government documents.

Beneš, E. *Memoirs of Dr. Edward Beneš: From Munich to New War and New Victory,* London, 1954.

Berber, Fritz, ed. *Europäische Politik 1933–1938 im Spiegel der Prager Akten.* Essen, 1941. A Nazi publication of captured Czechoslovak documents.

Brügel, J. W. "German Diplomacy in the Sudeten Question before 1938." *International Affairs* 37 (1961):323–31.

———. *Tschechen und Deutsche, 1918–1938.* Munich, 1967.

Celovsky, Boris. *Das Münchener Abkommen von 1938.* Stuttgart, 1958.

Czechoslovakia Past and Present. Edited by M. Recheigl. The Hague, 1969. Contains important essays.

Ďurica, Milan Stanislao. *La Slovacchia e le sue Relazioni Politiche con la Ger-*

mania 1938–1945. Vol. 1, *Dagli Accordi di Monaco all'inizio della seconda Guerra Mondiale (Ottobre 1938–Settembre 1939)*. Padua, 1964.

Eubank, Keith. *Munich*. Norman, Okla., 1963.

Hoensch, Jörg K. *Geschichte der Tschechoslowakischen Republik, 1918–1965*. Stuttgart, 1966.

———. *Die Slowakei und Hitlers Ostpolitik. Hlinkas Slowakische Volkspartei zwischen Autonomie und Separation, 1938/39*. Cologne, 1965.

———. *Der ungarische Revisionismus und die Zerschlagung der Tschechoslowakei*. Tübingen, 1967.

Lettrich, Jozef, *History of Modern Slovakia*. New York, 1955. Pro-Czech and bitterly anti-Tiso. Valuable appendix of documents.

Luža, Radomír. *The Transfer of the Sudeten Germans: A Study of Czech-German Relations, 1933–1962*. London, 1964. Contains a brief, accurate, summary of German policy before 1945. Valuable notes and bibliography.

Mastny, Vojtěch. *The Czechs under Nazi Rule: The Failure of National Resistance, 1939–1942*. New York, 1971. An excellent work, but dealing primarily with the period after the German occupation.

Oddo, Gilbert L. *Slovakia and Its People*. New York, 1960. Pro-Slovak. Somewhat uncritical use of materials.

Perman, Dagmar H. *The Shaping of the Czechoslovak State*. Leyden, 1962.

Ripka, Hubert, *Munich: Before and after*. London, 1939. An important work particularly for Czechoslovak domestic politics.

Rönnefarth, Helmuth. *Die Sudetenkrise in der internationalen Politik. Entstehung-Verlauf-Auswirkung*. 2 vols. Wiesbaden, 1961. Massively detailed study.

Vital, David. "Czechoslovakia and the Powers." *Journal of Contemporary History* 1 (1966):37–67. On the comparative strength of the Czechoslovak forces in 1938.

Vnuk, F. "Munich and the Soviet Union." *Journal of Central European Affairs* 21 (1961):285–304.

Wheeler-Bennett, John W. *Munich: Prologue to Tragedy*. New York, 1948. Still valuable.

Wiskemann, Elizabeth. *Czechs and Germans: A Study of the Struggles in the Historic Provinces of Bohemia and Moravia*. London, 1938.

15. POLAND, DANZIG, AND MEMEL

Beck, Józef. *Final Report*. New York, 1957. By the Polish foreign minister at the outbreak of the war.

Broszat, Martin. "Die Memeldeutschen Organisationen und der Nationalsozialismus." *VfZ* 5 (1957):273–78.

———. *Nationalsozialistische Polenpolitik, 1939–1945*. Stuttgart, 1961. An excellent work.

Burckhardt, Carl J. *Meine Danziger Mission, 1937–1939*. Munich, 1960. By the high commissioner of the League of Nations in the Free City of Danzig.

Denne, Ludwig. *Das Danzig-Problem in der deutschen Aussenpolitik, 1934–1939*. Bonn, 1959.

Debicki, Roman. *The Foreign Policy of Poland, 1919–1939. From the Rebirth of the Polish Republic to World War II*, New York, 1962.

Kimmich, C. M. *The Free City: Danzig and German Foreign Policy, 1919–1934*. New Haven, Conn. 1968.

Leonhardt, Hans Leo. *The Nazi Conquest of Danzig*. Chicago, 1942.

Lipski, Józef. *Diplomat in Berlin, 1933–1939: Papers and Memoirs of Józef Lipski, Ambassador of Poland*. Edited by W. Jedrzejewicz. New York, 1968.

Plieg, Ernst-Albrecht. *Das Memelland, 1920–1939*. Würzburg, 1939. A nationalistic tract.

Roos, Hans. *A History of Modern Poland from the Foundation of the State in the First World War to the present Day*. New York, 1966.

———. *Polen und Europa. Studien zur polnischen Aussenpolitik, 1931–1939*. Tübingen, 1957.

BIBLIOGRAPHY

16. SCANDINAVIA

Assmann, Kurt. *The German Campaign in Norway: Origin of the Plan, Execution of the Operation, and Measures against Allied Counter-attack.* London, 1949. By a German admiral involved in the operations.

Brandt, Willy. "Das englisch-norwegische Handelsabkommen und die allierten Interventionspläne im russisch-finnischen Krieg." *VfZ* 4 (1956):345 ff.

Derry, T. K. *The Campaign in Norway.* London, 1952. Part of the British government's military history of the war, with admirable maps.

Finland Reveals Her Secret Documents on Soviet Policy, March, 1940–June 1941: The Attitude of the USSR to Finland after the Peace of Moscow. New York, 1941. Official Finnish publication.

The Finnish Blue Book: The Development of Finnish-Soviet Relations during the Autumn of 1939, Including the Official Documents and the Peace Treaty of March 12, 1940. Philadelphia, 1940.

Gemzell, Carl-Axel. *Raeder, Hitler und Skandinavien. Der Kampf für einen maritimen Operationsplan.* Lund, 1965. An important book on German naval strategy.

Hayes, Paul M. "Quislings politsche Ideen." In *Internationaler Faschismus, 1920–1945.* Munich, 1966.

Hewins, Ralph. *Quisling: Prophet without Honour.* London, 1965. An apologia, but full of important information.

Hubatsch, Walther. "Diplomatische Beziehungen Deutschlands zu Skandinavien unter dem Schatten des zweiten Weltkrieges." *Zeitschrift für Ostforschung* 9 (1960):161–84.

———. *Unruhe des Nordens. Studien zur deutschskandinavischen Geschichte.* Göttingen, 1956.

———. *"Weserübung." Die deutsche Besetzung von Dänemark und Norwegen, 1940.* Göttingen, 1960. Includes the most important documents.

Jakobson, Max. *The Diplomacy of the Winter War: An Account of the Russo-Finnish War, 1939–1940.* Cambridge, Mass., 1961.

Jalanti, Heikki. *La Finlande dans l'Étau Germano-Soviétique, 1940–1941.* Neuchâtel, 1966.

Karlbom, Rolf. "Sweden's Iron Ore Exports to Germany, 1933–1944." *Scandinavian Economic History Review* 13 (1965):65–93.

Krosby, H. Peter. "The Development of the Petsamo Question and Finnish-German Relations, March–December 1940." *Scandia* 31 (1965):291–330.

Loock, Hans-Dietrich. *Quisling, Rosenberg und Terboven. Zur Vorgeschichte und Geschichte der nationalsozialistischen Revolution in Norwegen.* Stuttgart, 1970. A thorough, scholarly study which downgrades the importance of Allied plans in Scandinavia as an influence on Hitler's strategy.

Lundin, C. Leonard. *Finland in the Second World War.* Bloomington, Ind., 1956.

Mazour, Anatole G. *Finland between East and West.* Princeton, N.J., 1956.

Moulton, J. L. *The Norwegian Campaign of 1940.* London, 1966.

Norway and the War, September 1939–December 1940. Edited by Monica Curtis. London, 1941. Useful collection of contemporary documents.

Richman, A. F. *Swedish Iron Ore.* London, 1939.

Riste, Olaf. "War Comes to Norway." In *Norway and the Second World War,* edited by O. Riste, Oslo, 1966. An excellent brief summary of Allied and German military plans and actions.

Tanner, V. *The Winter War: Finland against Russia, 1939–1940.* Stanford, Calif., 1957. By Finland's foreign minister, 1939–40.

Upton, Anthony F. *Finland in Crisis, 1940–1941.* Ithaca, N.Y., 1965. Concentrates on events leading to Finland's participation in the war on the side of Germany.

Ziemke, Earl F. *The German Northern Theater of Operations, 1940–1945.* Washington, D.C., 1959. A Department of the Army book, based on German military and diplomatic documents.

BIBLIOGRAPHY

17. THE WEST: THE LOW COUNTRIES, FRANCE, AND BRITAIN

Ansel, Walter. *Hitler Confronts England.* Durham, N.C., 1960. Stresses the importance of German public opinion in desiring invasion of Britain in the belief that only the defeat of Britain would end the war.

Avon, Earl of (Anthony Eden). *The Eden Memoirs.* Vol. 1, *Facing the Dictators.* London, 1962; vol. 2, *The Reckoning.* London, 1965.

Bogdatsch, R. "Politische und militärische Probleme nach dem Frankreichfeldzug." *Das Parlament,* 14 (1962), pp. 149–87.

Chamberlain, Neville. *In Search of Peace.* New York, 1939. Speeches and other documents of the British prime minister.

Chapman, Guy. *Why France Fell.* New York, 1969. Emphasis on factors involved in military defeat rather than on relationship between military and political problems.

Churchill, Winston S. *The Second World War.* 6 vols. Boston, 1948–53. The magnificent memoirs of Britain's wartime prime minister.

——. *The Gathering Storm.* Boston, 1948. Vol. 1 of *The Second World War.*

——. *Step by Step, 1936–1939.* New York, 1939.

——. *While England Slept: A Survey of World Affairs, 1932–1938.* New York, 1938.

Coulondre, Robert. *De Staline à Hitler: Souvenirs de deux ambassades, 1936–1939.* Paris, 1950. By the French ambassador to Berlin in 1939.

Eden, Anthony. *See* Avon, Earl of.

Ellis, L. F. *The War in France and Flanders, 1939–1940.* London, 1953.

Feiling, Keith. *Life of Neville Chamberlain.* London, 1946. Based on Chamberlain's diaries and private letters. Full of important material.

Fleming, Peter. *Operation Sea Lion.* London, 1956. A lively account, giving both the British and German sides of the story.

François-Poncet, André. *Souvenirs d'une ambassade à Berlin, Septembre 1931–Octobre 1938.* Paris, 1946. Translated as *The Fateful Years.* New York, 1949.

Gamelin, M. *Servir.* 3 vols. Paris, 1946–47. By the commander in chief of the Allied armies in 1939.

Halifax, Earl of. *Fulness of Days.* London, 1957. By the British foreign secretary, 1938–40.

Hartog, L. J. *Und morgen die ganze Welt. Der deutsche Angriff im Westen, 1940.* Gütersloh, 1960.

Henderson, Neville. *Failure of a Mission: Berlin, 1937–1939.* London, 1939. By the British ambassador to Germany.

Hillgruber, Andreas. *Hitlers Strategie. Politik und Kriegsführung, 1940–1941.* Frankfurt am Main, 1965. A masterful work dealing with Hitler's policy during the most critical period of the war, with full appreciation for the difficulties and subtleties of the situation.

History of the Times. Vol. 4. London, 1952.

Jacobsen, Hans-Adolf. *Dünkirchen.* Neckargemünd, 1958.

——. *Fall "Gelb." Der Kampf um den deutschen Operationsplan zur Westoffensive, 1940.* Wiesbaden, 1957.

——, ed. *Dokumente zur Vorgeschichte des Westfeldzuges, 1939–1940.* Göttingen, 1956.

——, ed. *Dokumente zum Westfeldzug, 1940.* Göttingen, 1960. All excellent works by one of Germany's most gifted military historians.

Joll, James, ed. *The Decline of the Third Republic.* London, 1959.

Klee, Karl, ed. *Dokumente zum Unternehmen "Seelöwe." Die geplante deutsche Landung in England 1940.* Göttingen, 1959. An excellent and comprehensive collection.

——. *Das Unternehmen "Seelöwe." Die geplante deutsche Landung in England, 1940.* Göttingen, 1958. A sound monograph.

Kwiet, Konrad. *Reichskommissariat Niederlande. Versuch und Scheitern nationalsozialistischer Neuordnung.* Stuttgart, 1968.

BIBLIOGRAPHY

Mason, Henry L. "War Comes to the Netherlands, September 1939–May 1940." *Political Science Quarterly* 78 (1963):548–80.

Meier-Welcker, Hans, "Der Entschluss zum Anhalten der deutschen Panzertruppen in Flandern, 1940." *VfZ* 2 (1954):274–90.

Shirer, William L. *The Collapse of the Third Republic: An Inquiry into the Fall of France in 1940.* New York, 1969.

Taylor, Telford. *The Breaking Wave: The Second World War in the Summer of 1940.* New York, 1967.

Wheatley, Ronald. *Operation Sea Lion: German Plans for the Invasion of England, 1939–1942.* Oxford, 1958. Excellent brief, scholarly account.

Williams, John. *The Ides of May: The Defeat of France, May–June, 1940.* New York, 1968.

18. ITALY, SPAIN, AND NORTH AFRICA

Belot, Raymond de. *The Struggle for the Mediterranean, 1939–1945.* Princeton, N.J., 1951.

Burdick, Charles B. *Germany's Military Strategy and Spain in World War II.* Syracuse, N.Y., 1968.

Carr, Raymond. *Spain, 1808–1939.* New York, 1966. A fine survey.

Ciano, Count Galeazzo. *Ciano's Hidden Diary, 1937–1938.* New York, 1953.

———. *The Ciano Diaries, 1939–1943.* New York, 1946.

———. *Ciano's Diplomatic Papers.* Edited by Malcolm Muggeridge. London, 1948. Abridged translation of *L'Europa verso la catastrofe* (Milan, 1948). All are sources of great importance.

Deakin, F. W. *The Brutal Friendship: Mussolini, Hitler, and the Fall of Italian Fascism.* New York, 1966. Important work.

Detwiler, Donald S. *Hitler, Franco und Gibraltar. Die Frage des spanischen Eintritts in den zweiten Weltkrieg.* Wiesbaden, 1962. A competent monograph.

Einhorn, Marion. *Die ökonomischen Hintergründe der faschistischen deutschen Intervention in Spanien, 1936–1939.* East Berlin, 1962. Simplistic Marxist interpretation.

Feis, Herbert. *The Spanish Story: Franco and the Nations at War.* New York, 1948. An excellent work based on the author's personal experience in negotiations with Spain and stressing the Allied economic pressure to keep Franco out of the war.

Harper, Glenn T. *German Economic Policy in Spain during the Spanish Civil War, 1938–1939.* The Hague, 1967. Adds little.

Hoare, Sir Samuel. *Complacent Dictator.* New York, 1947. By the British ambassador to Spain, with many documents.

Joll, James. "Germany and the Spanish Civil War." In *On the Track of Tyranny: Essays Presented by the Wiener Library to Leonard G. Montefiore,* pp. 125–38. London, 1960.

Kirkpatrick, Ivone. *Mussolini: A Study in Power.* New York, 1964.

Lanz, H. "Gibraltar und die Gebirgstruppe. Die deutsche Planung zum beabsichtigten Angriff auf Gibraltar." *Die Gebirgstruppe* 3 (1961):22–38.

Merkes, Manfred. *Die deutsche Politik gegenüber dem spanischen Bürgerkrieg, 1936–1939.* Bonn, 1961.

Puzzo, Dante A. *Spain and the Great Powers, 1936–1941.* New York, 1962.

Rusinow, Dennison I., *Italy's Austrian Heritage, 1919–46* (Oxford, 1969). An excellent treatment of an important problem.

Seraphim, Hans-Günther. " 'Felix' und 'Isabella': Dokumente zu Hitlers Planungen betr. Spanien und Portugal aus den Jahren 1940–41." *Die Welt als Geschichte* (1955), pp. 45–86.

Serrano Suñer, R. *Entre Hendaye y Gibraltar.* Madrid, 1947. By Franco's brother-in-law and foreign minister.

Wiskemann, Elizabeth. *The Rome-Berlin Axis: A History of the Relations between Hitler and Mussolini.* London, 1949.

BIBLIOGRAPHY

19. HUNGARY AND THE BALKANS

Allianz Hitler-Horthy-Mussolini. Dokumente zur ungarischen Aussenpolitik (1933–1944). Edited by Lajos Kerekes. Budapest, 1966.

Basch, Antonin. *Conquest by Planned Trade: Foreign Trade between Free Countries vs. Controlled Economy.* New York, 1941.

———. *The Danube Basin and the German Economic Sphere.* New York, 1943. An excellent discussion of German economic penetration.

Blau, George E. *The German Campaign in the Balkans, Spring 1941.* Washington, D.C., 1953.

Broszat, Martin. "Deutschland-Ungarn-Rumänien. Entwicklung und Grundfaktoren nationalsozialistischer Hegemonial-und Bündnispolitik, 1938–1941." *Historische Zeitschrift* 206 (1968):45–96.

Cohen, David B. "Le Pillage de l'Économie Bulgare par les Allemands," *RHDGM* 72 (1968):43–65.

Dinčić, K. M. "La politique étrangère de la Yugoslavie, 1934–1941." *RHDGM* 58 (1965):57–66.

Einzig, Paul. *Bloodless Invasion: German Economic Penetration into the Danubian States and the Balkans.* London, 1939.

Ellis, Howard. *Exchange Control in Central Europe.* Cambridge, Mass., 1941. Technical study covering previous decade in Germany, Austria, Hungary.

Fabry, P. W. *Balkan-Wirren, 1940–1941. Diplomatische und militärische Vorbereitung des deutschen Donauüberganges.* Darmstadt, 1966.

Gafencu, Grigoire. *Last Days of Europe: A Diplomatic Journey in 1939.* New Haven, 1948.

———. *Prelude to the Russian Campaign: From the Moscow Pact (August 21st 1939) to the Opening of Hostilities in Russia (June 22nd 1941).* London, 1945. By the former Rumanian foreign minister and minister to Russia.

Gornenski, N. and Kamenov, E. "Sur la Bulgarie en Guerre. La Politique Intérieure," *RHDGM* 72 (1968):23–41.

Hillgruber, Andreas. "Deutschland und Ungarn, 1933–1944. Ein Überblick über die politischen und militärischen Beziehungen im Rahmen der europäischen Politik." *Wehrwissenschaftliche Rundschau* (1959), pp. 651–76.

———. *Hitler, König Carol und Marschall Antonescu. Die deutsch-rumänischen Beziehungen, 1938–1944.* Wiesbaden, 1954. Excellent monograph, based largely on German sources.

Hoptner, J. B. *Yugoslavia in Crisis, 1934–1941.* New York, 1962. Excellent.

Horthy, Nicholas. *Memoirs.* New York, 1957. By the regent of Hungary, 1920–44. A valuable and often moving account of his hopeless situation between the Nazis and the Bolsheviks.

Juhász, Gyula. "La politique extérieure de la Hongrie de 1939 à 1943." *RHDGM* 62 (1966):19–36.

Kerner, R. J. and Howard, H. N. *Balkan Conferences and Balkan Entente, 1930–1935.* Berkeley, Calif., 1936.

Kertesz, S. D. *Diplomacy in a Whirlpool: Hungary between Nazi Germany and Soviet Russia.* South Bend, Ind., 1953.

Macartney, C. A. *October Fifteenth: A History of Modern Hungary, 1929–1945.* 2 vols. Edinburgh, 1956–57. Full of important information, but so cluttered with detail that the major problems and events are often obscured.

Presseisen, E. L. "Prelude to 'Barbarossa': Germany and the Balkans, 1940–1941." *Journal of Modern History* 22 (1960):358–70.

Ránki, G. "Der Eintritt Ungarns in den zweiten Weltkrieg." In *Der deutsche Imperialismus und der zweite Weltkrieg.* Vol. 3, pp. 415–37. East Berlin, 1962.

Schacher, Gerhard. *Germany Pushes Southeast.* London, 1937.

Schramm-von Thadden, Ehrengard. *Griechenland und die Grossmächte im zweiten Weltkrieg.* Wiesbaden, 1955. Essentially the story of German-Italian relations with regard to Greece.

Seton-Watson, R. W. *Eastern Europe between the Wars, 1918–1941.* Hamden, Conn., 1962.
——. *Treaty Revision and the Hungarian Frontiers.* London, 1934.
Southeastern Europe: A Brief Survey. London, 1940.
Southeastern Europe: A Political and Economic Survey. London, 1939. Publications of the Royal Institute of International Affairs.
Stefanov, G. "Sur la Bulgarie en Guerre. La Politique Extérieure," *RHDGM* 72 (1968): 1–21.
Sweet-Escott, Bickham. *Greece: A Political and Economic Survey, 1939–1953.* London, 1954.
Vambery, Rustem. "The Tragedy of the Magyars: Revisionism and Nazism." *Foreign Affairs* 20 (1942): 477–88.
Vogel, Georg. "Mussolinis Überall auf Griechenland im Oktober 1940." *Europa-Archiv* 5 (1950).
Wuescht, Johann. *Jugoslawien und das dritte Reich. Eine dokumentierte Geschichte der deutsch-jugoslawischen Beziehungen von 1933 bis 1945.* Stuttgart, 1969.
Zsigmond, L. "La politique extérieure de la Hongrie de 1933 à 1939." *RHDGM* 62 (1966):7–17.

20. RUSSIA AND THE BALTIC STATES

Allen, W. E. D. *The Ukraine: A History.* Cambridge, Eng., 1940.
Assmann, Kurt. "The Battle for Moscow: The Turning Point in the War." *Foreign Affairs* 28 (1950):309–26.
[The] *Baltic States: A Survey of the Political and Economic Structure and Foreign Relations of Estonia, Latvia, and Lithuania.* London, 1938. A publication of the Royal Institute of International Affairs.
Bilmanis, Alfred. *The Baltic States and the Problems of the Freedom of the Baltic Sea.* Washington, D.C., 1943.
——. *A History of Latvia.* Princeton, N.J., 1951.
Blau, George E. *The German Campaign in Russia: Planning and Operations, 1940–1942.* Washington, D.C., 1955.
Bräutigam, Otto. *Überblick über die besetzten Ostgebiete während des 2. Weltkrieges.* Tübingen, 1954. By an official of the Rosenberg ministry.
Carr, E. H. *German-Soviet Relations between the two World Wars, 1919–1939.* Baltimore, Md., 1951.
Clark, W. *Barbarossa and the German Campaign in the East, 1941–1945.* London, 1965.
Dallin, Alexander. *German Rule in Russia, 1941–1945: A Study in Occupation Policies.* London, 1957. Excellent and important.
Dallin, David. *Soviet Russia's Foreign Policy, 1939–1942.* New Haven, 1942.
Erickson, John. *The Soviet High Command: A Military-Political History, 1918–1941.* London, 1962. An important work.
Fischer, George. *Soviet Opposition to Stalin: A Case Study of World War II.* Cambridge, Mass., 1952.
Ilnytzkyj, Roman. *Deutschland und die Ukraine, 1939–1945. Tatsachen europäischer Ostpolitik.* 2 vols. Munich, 1955–56.
Lacquer, Walter. *Russia and Germany: A Century of Conflict.* London, 1965.
Latvian-Russian Relations: Documents. Edited by A. Bilmanis. Washington, D.C., 1944.
Lundin, C. Leonard. "Nazification of Baltic German Minorities: A Contribution to the Study of the Diplomacy of 1939." *Journal of Central European Affairs* 7 (1947):1–28. Makes case that the Baltic Germans were thoroughly Nazified and organized, and that they represented a real threat to Russian security.
The Nazi-Soviet Conspiracy and the Baltic States: Diplomatic Documents and Other Evidence. Edited by August Rei. London, 1948.
Pusta, K. R. *The Soviet Union and the Baltic States.* New York, 1942.

Reddaway, W. F. *Problems of the Baltic.* Cambridge, Eng., 1940. Excellent background summary.
Reitlinger, Gerald. *The House Built on Sand: The Conflicts of German Policy in Russia, 1939–1945.* New York, 1960. Readable although not always entirely accurate.
Ulam, Adam B. *Expansion and Coexistence: The History of Soviet Foreign Policy, 1917–1967.* New York, 1968. Authoritative treatment.
Weinberg, Gerhard L. "Der deutsche Entschluss zum Angriff auf die Sowjetunion." *VfZ* 1 (1953):301–18.
——. *Germany and the Soviet Union, 1939–1941.* Leyden, 1954.

21. JAPAN

Butow, Robert J. C. *Tojo and the Coming of the War.* Princeton, N.J., 1961.
Drechsler, K. *Deutschland-China-Japan, 1933–1939. Das Dilemma der deutschen Fernostpolitik.* East Berlin, 1964.
Fox, John P. "Japan's Reaction to Nazi Germany's Racial Legislation." *Wiener Library Bulletin* 23 (1969): 46–50.
Gollwitzer, Heinz. *Die gelbe Gefahr. Geschichte eines Schlagwortes.* Göttingen, 1962.
Ike, Nobutaka, ed. *Japan's Decision for War: Records of the 1941 Policy Conferences.* Stanford, Calif., 1967. A valuable source.
Iklé, F. W. *German-Japanese Relations, 1936–1940.* New York, 1956.
Hillgruber, Andreas. "Japan und der Fall 'Barbarossa.' " *Wehrwissenschaftliche Rundschau* 18 (1968).
Jones, F. C. *Japan's New Order in East Asia: Its Rise and Fall, 1937–1945.* London, 1954. A readable and authoritative analysis.
Lupke, Hubertus. *Japans Russlandpolitik von 1939 bis 1941.* Frankfurt am Main, 1962.
Martin, Bernd. *Deutschland und Japan im Zweiten Weltkrieg. Von Pearl Harbor bis zur deutschen Kapitulation.* Göttingen, 1969.
Menzel, Johanna M. "Der geheime deutsch-japanische Notenaustausch zum Dreimächtepakt." *VfZ* 5 (1957):182–93.
Meskill, Johanna Menzel. *Hitler and Japan: The Hollow Alliance.* New York, 1967.
Presseisen, Ernst L. *Germany and Japan: A Study in Totalitarian Diplomacy, 1933–1941.* The Hague, 1958.
Schroeder, Paul W. *The Axis Alliance and Japanese-American Relations, 1941.* Ithaca, N.Y., 1958.
Sommer, Theo. *Deutschland und Japan zwischen den Mächten, 1935–1940. Vom Antikominternpakt zum Dreimächtepakt.* Tübingen, 1962. With an excellent bibliography.
Weinberg, Gerhard L. "Die geheimen Abkommen zum Antikominternpakt." *VfZ* 2 (1954):193–201.

22. THE UNITED STATES

Cole, Wayne S. "American Entry into World War II: A Historiographical Appraisal." *Mississippi Valley Historical Review* 43 (1957):595–617.
Compton, James V. *The Swastika and the Eagle: Hitler, the United States, and the Origins of World War II.* Boston, 1967.
Divine, Robert A. *The Reluctant Belligerent: America's Entry into World War II.* New York, 1965.
Dodd, William and Martha, eds. *Ambassador Dodd's Diary, 1933–1938.* New York, 1941.
Drummond, Donald F. *The Passing of American Neutrality, 1933–1941.* Ann Arbor, Mich., 1955.
Feis, Herbert. *The Road to Pearl Harbor: The Coming of the War between the United States and Japan.* Princeton, N.J., 1950; paperback, New York, 1964.
Friedländer, Saul. *Prelude to Downfall: Hitler and the United States, 1939–1941.*

New York, 1967. An excellent study, translated from the French, *Hitler et les États-Unis, 1939–1941*. Geneva, 1963.

Frye, Alton. *Nazi Germany and the American Hemisphere, 1933–1941*. New Haven, 1967.

Grew, Joseph. *Ten Years in Japan: A Contemporary Record Drawn from the Diaries and Private and Official Papers of Joseph C. Grew, United States Ambassador to Japan, 1932–1942*. New York, 1944.

Hass, Gerhart. "Die USA in der Kriegs-und Grossraumplanung des deutschen Faschismus im Jahre 1940." In *Der deutsche Imperialismus und der Zweite Weltkrieg*. Vol. 3, pp. 153–62. Berlin, 1962.

——. *Von München bis Pearl Harbor. Zur Geschichte der deutsch-amerikanischen Beziehungen, 1938–1941*. Berlin, 1965. A Marxist interpretation with heavy emphasis on economic motivation.

Hull, Cordell. *The Memoirs of Cordell Hull*. 2 vols. New York, 1948.

Iriye, Akira. *Across the Pacific: An Inner History of American–East Asian Relations*. New York, 1967.

Kolko, Gabriel. "American Business and Germany, 1930–1941." *Western Political Quarterly* 15 (1962):713–28.

Langer, William L. and Gleason, S. Everett. *The Challenge to Isolation: The World Crisis of 1937–1940 and American Foreign Policy*. 2 vols. New York, 1952.

——. *The Undeclared War, 1940–1941*. New York, 1953.

Leahy, William D. *I Was There*. New York, 1950.

May, Ernest R. *American Intervention, 1917 and 1941*. Washington, D.C., 1960.

Moltmann, Günter. *Amerikas Deutschlandpolitik im Zweiten Weltkrieg. Kriegs-und Friedensziele, 1941–1945*. Heidelberg, 1958.

Murdock, Eugene C. "Zum Eintritt der Vereinigten Staaten in den zweiten Weltkrieg." *VfZ* 4 (1956):93–114.

Murphy, Robert. *Diplomat among Warriors*. New York, 1964.

Nixon, Edgar B., ed. *Franklin D. Roosevelt and Foreign Affairs*. 2 vols. Cambridge, Mass., 1969.

Pratt, J. W. *Cordell Hull, 1933–1944*. New York, 1964.

Rauch, Basil. *Roosevelt: From Munich to Pearl Harbor*. New York, 1950.

Remak, Joachim. " 'Friends of the New Germany:' the Bund and German-American Relations." *Journal of Modern History* 24 (1957):38–41.

——. "Hitlers Amerikapolitik." *Aussenpolitik* 6 (1955): 706–14.

Rosenman, Samuel I., ed. *The Public Papers and Addresses of Franklin D. Roosevelt, 1928–1936*. 5 vols. New York, 1938.

Sherwood, Robert E. *Roosevelt and Hopkins*. 2 vols. New York, 1950.

Shirer, William. *Berlin Diary*. New York, 1941.

Smith, Gaddis. *American Diplomacy during the Second World War*. New York, 1965.

Trefousse, Hans L. *Germany and American Neutrality, 1939–1941*. New York, 1951.

Watson, Mark S. *Chief of Staff: Prewar Plans and Preparations*. Washington, D.C., 1950.

Weinberg, Gerhard L. "Hitler's Image of the United States." *American Historical Review* 49 (1964): 1006–21.

Wilson, Hugh R. *A Career Diplomat: The Third Chapter: The Third Reich*. New York, 1961. Correspondence and diary of the American ambassador to Germany, 1938–39.

Index

343

NAZI GERMANY AT ITS GREATEST EXTENT

Maximum extent of Axis control
— ·· — ·· — 1938 boundaries

NORWAY

Oslo

SWE

Invasion of Norway
and Denmark Apr 9, 1940

NORTH
SEA

DENMARK

Copenhag

BALT

IRELAND

Hamburg

Berlin

Oder

ENGLAND

Elbe R.

Amsterdam

London

NETH.

GERMANY

Invasion of Czecho
March 10-16, 1

ATLANTIC

CHANNEL
ISLANDS

Brussels

BELG.

Rhine R.

Invasion of Sudetenland
Oct 1-10, 1938

OCEAN

Paris

LUX.

Invasion of France
and the Low Countries
May 10, 1940

Prague

CZ

Saar to Germany
by plebiscite
Jan 13, 1935

Invasion and annexation
of Austria
Mar 12, 13, 1938

FRANCE

Vichy

Munich

Vienna

AUSTRIA

Bordeaux

Rhone R.

Invasion of Yugoslavia
April 6- 17, 1941

Milan

Po R.

PORTUGAL

Ebro R.

Marseilles

ITALY

Lisbon

Tagus R.

Barcelona

CORSICA

SPAIN

Rome

Invasion of Alb
April 7, 193

SARDINIA

Naples

TANGIER

Strait of Gibraltar

MEDITERRANEAN

Casablanca

SPAN. MOROCCO

Oran

Algiers

SICILY

Tunis

MOROCCO
(Vichy)

ALGERIA
(Vichy)

TUNISIA
(Vichy)

0   500 miles

LIBYA

FINLAND

Russo-Finnish War
Nov 30, 1939-Mar 12, 1940

Helsinki   Leningrad

ESTONIA

Volga R.

LATVIA

Moscow

LITHUANIA

EAST
RUSSIA   SOVIET   UNION   Ural R.

Invasion of Russia
June 22, 1941

R.
aw   POLAND

and invaded and divided
by Germany and Russia   Kiev
Sept 1-Sept 29, 1939   Don R.   Stalingrad

                                  Dnieper R.   Volga R.

rst   Rostov

RUMANIA   CASPIAN SEA

R.   Bucharest
                                                                              Baku
of Greece   BULGARIA   BLACK   SEA
23, 1941   Sofia

                        Bosporus
                Istanbul

                        Ankara

                Dardanelles

GREECE   TURKEY   IRAN

    Athens

                                              SYRIA   Euphrates R.   Tigris R.

EA   CRETE   CYPRUS

                                                      IRAQ

                                  PALESTINE

                                          TRANS-
                                          JORDAN

gasi   Tobruk   Alexandria   SAUDI ARABIA

            EGYPT   Nile R.